SCREENING AMERICA

Reflections on Five Classic Films

BY RICHARD A. BLAKE, S.J.

PAULIST PRESS
New York/Mahwah

Book design by Margaret Antonini.

All photos are used with permission of The Museum of Modern Art/Film Stills Archive, New York.

Library of Congress Cataloging-in-Publication Data

Blake, Richard Aloysius.
    Screening America: reflections on five classic films/by Richard A. Blake.
      p. cm.
    ISBN 0-8091-3193-5 (pbk.)
    1. Film criticism.   2. Motion pictures—United
States—Reviews.   I. Title.
    PN1995.B49735   1991   90-44706
    791.43′015—dc20   CIP

Published by Paulist Press
997 Macarthur Boulevard
Mahwah, New Jersey 07430

Printed and bound in the
United States of America

CONTENTS

CONTENTS

PART III

FOREWORD

by Andrew Greeley

I write this foreword on Shrove Tuesday after dinner with a community of Jesuits—as the Irish would say, none of the drink having been taken! The Jesuits are from the Vatican Observatory and colleagues of mine at the University of Arizona. As I drove over to their residence I thought of an attack on them in a liberal Catholic paper last year: What reason is there, the paper sneered, for the church to be interested in astronomy? Why should there be Jesuit astronomers? As Father Blake observes in the final section of this fascinating and important book, he often hears the parallel question: What is the purpose of a Jesuit film critic?

As far as that goes, what indeed is the reason for a diocesan priest to be a sociologist?

Why should a priest be anything but a priest?

What is the point in a priest being anything but a eucharistic presider, a gospel preacher and a political revolutionary?

Such questions, to be candid, are ignorant questions—they ignore history and the traditions of the church, the priesthood, and the Society of Jesus. If the questioner is determined to be unaware of history and tradition or to dismiss them as irrelevant, there can be no answer to the question. If one wishes to take a rigidly romantic and anti-intellectual position, then one should be permitted to stew in the juices of one's own ignorance.

If one cannot imagine why it is utterly appropriate for a Jesuit to be a film critic and indeed why it is essential that at least one Jesuit actually be a film critic, then there is very little that someone else can do to change one's mind.

A Latin poet summed up the only answer that can be given: *Homo sum: humani nihil a me alienum puto.* I am a human being and I don't believe that anything human is alien to me. The church is interested in the whole range of human behavior and nothing which humans do is beyond the church's range of interest. While Catholic laity who are trained in the various disciplines and professions do indeed mediate between the church and these professions, a priest trained in one of the professions, in a very special way, *ex officio* one might say, speaks of the problems and the insights of that profession to the church and offers to the profession those insights and perspectives which, if they are not specifically Catholic and priestly, are especially likely to be available to the priest.

This is not a particularly new idea, especially not in the community of men who constitute the Society of Jesus. The Jesuit contribution to art, literature, science and scholarship in the four hundred and fifty year history of the Society is so evident as not to require documentation. The Jesuit superiors who strongly supported Father Blake's professional training in film criticism had no doubt about the theory and the tradition which approved of training in that discipline. They would have thought it absurd to question either the professional training or the importance of cinematic art to the human condition.

However in the late 1960s both the Society and the American Catholic Church entered into an era of romantic radicalism which swept away virtually all of the traditions of the past. It became fashionable to raise such simplistic and pietistic statements as, "What does film criticism do to help the poor? What does astronomy do for the third world? How does sociology contribute to the cause of justice and peace?"

The Catholic (or, to use David Tracy's term, the analogical) imagination would respond, if it were given a chance, that the Catholic tradition has always believed that you should say "both . . . and" instead of "either . . . or." One must be concerned about the poor and the oppressed, but one must also be concerned about the whole range of human activities and interest because God lurks in all of them, and one must be concerned especially about the arts because the artist is at least potentially a sacrament maker, one who reveals the presence of God lurking in creation.

If one were looking for a fight, one could have asked whether the pious romantic was doing anything more for the poor than claiming to identify with them and whether all the talk about helping the poor was nothing more than talk.

The vocation of art and scholarship which had always been prized by the Jesuit Order was, however, dealt a severe blow by this kind of simple-minded criticism. Many Jesuits seemed to feel guilty about their academic training and abandoned the work of doing the things they were trained to do and could do well for other tasks for which they were not trained and which they did not do well.

One of my students, a skilled analyst of survey data, became a leader in radical "concern" and harangued other priests about the immorality of playing golf on their days off when there were still poor people in the world—as if the selling of clerical golf clubs would solve any of the complex economic problems.

The reader of this book will, I think, be happy that Father Blake did not succumb to the fashion of the times, but rather stuck to his beliefs and continued his study of film. In the three sections of this book, he displays three different kinds of skills. In the first he acts as an historian of the relationship (often a sorry one) between Catholicism and the motion picture. In the second he reexamines with skill and insight five classic American films which tell us much about American culture and also much about the human condition. In the third he engages in what I would call theological reflection on the role of the priest scholar/critic. Each of the sections is important, each in its own way.

If Father Blake didn't exist, I would like to suggest, the church and the Society would soon have to invent someone like him. As an institution which has championed the visual arts since the beginning of its history, the church certainly knows in its collective pre-conscious that it must have a special interest in such a powerful and pervasive artistic medium as the film. It will surely realize in the not too distant future that only historical accident is responsible for the negative and moralistic attitude toward film which Father Blake chronicles in the first part of this book. When the curtain went up in Hollywood, American Catholics were, or more precisely were thought to be, simple and beleaguered immigrants whose faith and morality were under attack in a hostile society. At the same time the film industry was dominated by men who were, to put the matter most charitably, insensitive to religion. The story of these two communities interacting with each other does not make pretty reading.

Moreover, despite the Second Vatican Council and despite the

changing social and economic condition of American Catholics, it is
not clear that the unhappy history is finished. Church leaders still feel
compelled to condemn. The film industry still stumbles and bumbles
when the subject is religion.[1]

This conflict relationship between film-maker and church explains, I think, the reason why Catholic film-makers are so little appreciated by the institutional church in this country and why the
United States has yet to produce a Catholic film-maker of the skill of,
let us say, Eric Rohmer in France. There is not yet in this country a
cultural context of appreciation of film in the church and appreciation
of the Catholic imagination in the film industry which would make it
possible for someone like Rohmer to work with ease. There may be
Catholic imaginations (particularly Italian Catholic) at work in American film but such imaginations do not yet work easily and confidently,
secure (relatively) in both their religion and their art.

Here is where the Jesuits, I submit, should move in. It is part of
the genius of their tradition to occupy the middle ground between
the church and art. Jesuit film critics like Father Blake, I would argue,
must patiently and doggedly ply their trade before the historical accident which has alienated the Catholic institution in this country from
film-making can be undone.

In his third section Father Blake seems to be pointing in this
direction. The Catholic critic interprets the film and American culture which is reflected (in part) in the film in a constructive and yet
critical fashion to Catholics and to church leadership. In a parallel
fashion his Jesuit colleagues from the Vatican Observatory interpret
the dazzling new discoveries of cosmology to church leaders and
theologians (to those few of both who want to listen).

There is another issue I must raise. In addition to speaking to the
church, do Catholics bring to the scholarly and artistic and critical
disciplines a special contribution which if not uniquely their own is
nonetheless most likely to be found among Catholics and much less
likely to be found by others?

I set my Jesuit hosts arguing with each other at dinner tonight on
this subject: Do they approach the study of the galaxies with a (somewhat) unique point of view which is much less likely to exist among
astronomers who do not have the same background? I'm inclined to
think they do, but I will leave that debate to them. I know that I bring
a special perspective to sociology—a Catholic imagination which is
both more sympathetic to intimate community structures and more
likely to take their existence into account precisely because my imagi-

nation from the earliest years of my life has been shaped by Catholic imagery of sacramentality. I have no monopoly on such a perspective, but few sociologists who are not Catholic are as insistent as I am about these dimensions of human social structure. Indeed it is precisely this perspective which has shaped an ongoing debate between me and my good friend Professor James Coleman—a debate which neither of us will ever win.

The question in the present context is whether Father Blake's five excellent critical essays in the middle section of this volume, never explicitly Catholic, display the kind of perspectives and insights that one would be much less likely to find in a film critic who was not a Catholic and a Jesuit.

Can one exercise secular critical tools in a totally secular fashion and not be influenced by one's own pre-conscious imaginative picture of the nature of the world and the nature of the relationship between the world and the Ultimate?

I rather think not.

Thus I conclude that, while Father Blake's criticism is not explicitly Catholic, it is nonetheless shaped by a Catholic imaginative perspective and thus offers an important contribution (though not an absolutely unique one) to the literature of film criticism. His is a Catholic (and Jesuit) voice which has something important to say, and not merely because he has the same training in film criticism as any other skilled critic, although the training is essential because in its absence the specific Catholic and Jesuit voice will never be heard.

The issue then is not how Catholics are and can remain different from anyone else, but rather what special contribution they can make precisely because of their own special imaginative tradition.

While there is nothing explicitly Catholic, then, about Father Blake's five essays, I think it most unlikely that they could have been written by someone who did not have his special Catholic perspective.

To illustrate with another example: rarely does my colleague from the Chicago *Sun Times* Roger Ebert note his Catholic background and affiliation. Yet if one reads all his reviews (as I do religiously, you should excuse the expression), one knows that one is in touch with a Catholic critical sensibility—especially in such disparate matters as Woody Allen's theological films or *The Last Temptation of Christ* or *Hail Mary*.

What Roger Ebert is to movie reviews, I submit, Richard Blake is to film criticism (and they both trespass often on each other's turf).

Both are trained, confident, and highly effective Catholic voices which do not have to insist explicitly on their Catholic orientation to have a profound Catholic effect.

We are lucky to have both of them.

Tucson   Andrew Greeley
Shrove Tuesday 1990

NOTE

1. One of the few disagreements I have ever had with Father Blake is about Martin Scorsese's *The Last Temptation of Christ.* I have a much higher opinion of the film than he does. As I read this manuscript I finally began to understand the reason. As a film critic he sees the many weaknesses of the film as an exercise in cinematic art. As a sociologist of the religious imagination I was swept away by the incredible power of the religious imagery and was not concerned about anything else. I have great admiration for Father Blake's defense of the Godard film *Hail Mary* despite the condemnation by the Vatican. While not a great film, it was not blasphemous either in intent or in content. In the case of both films, the directors were not religiously insensitive, but church authorities, it seems to me, were artistically insensitive—and patronizing to their people.

INTRODUCTION

"This Is Where I Came In"

Miles Monroe (Woody Allen), harried antihero of *Sleeper* (1973), wakes up two centuries in the future. He is horrified by the brave new world he discovers, and because he is unable to fit in to this new version of humanity, he is considered subversive, an enemy of the state. With his new-age girlfriend, Luna (Diane Keaton), he is pursued by his enemies. At one point in the chase, he discovers a dust covered Volkswagen Beetle in a cave. At the first touch of the ignition, the two hundred year old car roars back to life and enables Miles to escape. The moral of the story: Well-made things age well.

Miles' adventures provided a preview of my own awakening in the world of film scholarship. A few years ago I had the opportunity to share Miles' experience. Nearly fifteen years after finishing formal studies in film and after twelve years of doing film reviews while on the editorial staff of *America* magazine, I traded my editor's blue pencil for a faculty library card through a scholar-in-residence program at Georgetown University. In the years I had been away in the distant galaxy of journalism doing editorial work for *America*, visitors from another planet had taken over the film journals. Linguistic analysts and deconstructionists had staged an academic coup and held the field hostage. Syntagmatics, semiotics and kinesics scampered over the occupied territories like ants at a picnic. In a few swift seasons, it seemed that film scholars had given up on watching movies in order to imitate the most arcane of the methodologies of the more traditional disciplines.

For months I felt like Miles Monroe: an alien in his own country. It took a while to reach the conclusion that these newer styles of analytic criticism have undoubtedly yielded rich rewards to professional scholars with the patience to pursue them. At the same time I recognized that they offered very little for my own interests. For many years I had been reviewing films for the highly educated but nonprofessional readership of *America,* and I had gone back to the books because I wanted to teach film to undergraduates in liberal art programs. Although my curiosity was piqued by the novelty and exotic vocabulary of the new style, each time I viewed a film my critique invariably grew out of the classical methods I learned in graduate school and had been using for review writing. As film-goers used to say as they left the theater, "This is where I came in," and this is where I will stay.

My negative reaction to analytic criticism is not altogether Neanderthal or mindless. My work in film criticism has been exclusively a work of mediation. I write and teach for audiences of nonspecialists. Many of the readers of my reviews do not see many films themselves, and most, I am willing to bet, have never in their lives read a scholarly article in a professional film journal. Nor do they intend to. They do, however, recognize film as an important contemporary art form, and they read reviews because they want to become more knowledgeable about the cultural scene. Among my students it is rare that anyone voices an interest in becoming a film scholar. With my encouragement they are more intent on learning to "read" films as part of the humanistic background indispensable for educated people in this century. This series of essays is directed toward readers like the people who read my reviews and take my courses.

Like Miles Monroe, I was fortunate enough to find a sturdy, dependable Volkswagen for my journey. The classic methods of criticism I had been trained in, like classic automobiles, age well. They are accessible to a wide variety of readers. Furthermore, in addition to using a somewhat dated methodology, I have decided to discuss only five very familiar American films, even though the professional journals seem to favor citations of obscure Bulgarian animators from the 1920s. My belief is that a journey across familiar territory, like the five benchmark films selected for this study, makes for an enjoyable trip, and reading about films should, above all, be enjoyable. Neither the methodology nor the subject matter should be intimidating. A few thoughts on the projected itinerary may make the excursion even more relaxing and rewarding.

Although this study avoids a great deal of the recondite language and methodologies used by today's film scholars, it is still intended as a serious study of film criticism, and film criticism differs hugely from film reviewing. The point may be obvious, but it is still worth making.

As one who does both, I do not intend to glorify criticism at the expense of reviewing. Both are valuable, but they are different.

When one writes as a film reviewer, the work is necessarily subjective. Reviewers tell their readers enough about the film to enable them to decide whether they should go out and spend seven dollars for a ticket. The best reviewers explain their reasons for liking or disliking the particular work with painstaking clarity, but their reaction is still largely subjective. Even reviewers like Gene Siskel and Roger Ebert who have worked together as a team on television for many years frequently disagree, and the most they can say is that their tastes differ. Serious readers of reviews gradually learn whose taste coincides with their own and which reviewers they should simply ignore.

Reviewers try to answer the question "Is it any good?" and only after they have settled that question may they move on. Most periodicals dedicate so little space to reviews that rarely can their reviewers move on very far. Critics seldom worry about enjoying a film. For them the work is an object to analyze. They ask what makes it work, and how effective it is. As a parallel instance, it is conceivable that a scholar could write the definitive commentary on *The Fairie Queene* while giving no hint whether he or she finds Spenser's work fascinating or a colossal bore.

Reviewers in newspapers or on the local television news deal with the films that have reached the public that day, or, in the case of weekly magazines, that came out last week. They rush from the screening room of the local distributor to their word processors and rarely have the luxury to do much by way of research. They see the film once and make their judgments instantaneously. A bout of indigestion or a spat with the spouse may contribute to a scathing review of a respectable film. A pay raise at the office or a chilled martini from the producer may lead to a rave review for a clinker. (There is a reverse logic that can work on a reviewer. When I regularly reviewed miniseries at television network headquarters in New York, I was fairly certain that if the producer was content to serve warm white wine in plastic glasses to the press, the series was probably good enough to stand on its own. On the other hand, a fully stocked bar, shrimp salad and uniformed servers almost always meant that the series would be dreadful, and the producers were hoping that the reviewers would either be rendered benevolent by drink or fall asleep before they realized how horrible the show was. Given enough experience, a perceptive journalist could write the review on the basis of the hors d'oeuvres.)

Unlike reviewers, critics cannot dream of using shrimp salad as a criterion of excellence, nor can they assume the luxury of forming an opinion after one screening. Where the reviewer is necessarily subjective, the critic tries to be systematically objective. Critics write for peers—if not for scholars, at least for people as interested in films as they are. Their feelings, as such, are immaterial unless they can demonstrate from the text the roots of their pleasure or displeasure. Generally, critics write about films and directors that have achieved something of a "classic" status, like two hundred year old Volkswagens. While reviewers are essentially reporters telling readers whether they think the new film is any good, critics are scholars. They try to articulate their reaction to a particular film by situating it in its own proper context. They know something about the studio, the director, the script writer or the social situation from which the film was created. They try to explain these contexts to their readers. The only context reviewers are interested in is next Saturday night at the Bijou and whether the readers of the column will find the film entertaining.

Critics and reviewers alike can be tinged with ideology. For example, they can be Marxists, feminists or fundamentalist Christians. The difference between the two, however, demands that critics defend their statements by citing the text of the film, while reviewers can justifiably mention their own feelings of revulsion or elation at what they saw on the screen without giving much by way of explanation. Having one foot in the academic world, critics often profess allegiance to a particular school of criticism and a favorite theoretician. The most erudite of the critics frequently scorn the work of those with other ideological or academic styles.

Although the roles and work of critics and reviewers are quite different, at the same time it must be noted that the division between the two is not always clear. Many of the best reviewers are also competent critics. Some few weekly and monthly periodicals actually encourage their reviewers to provide a critical context for the work under review. Pauline Kael in *The New Yorker* and Stanley Kauffmann in *The New Republic* are two examples of reviewers who are competent critics.

This present study is a work of criticism. Part I provides a quick history of the development of film criticism in the United States. It starts with the criticism that emerged from religious communities, because they were especially important in the early years. In fact, it would not be much of an exaggeration to claim that the churches actually invented film criticism, as opposed to the reviewing carried by the daily papers, in the first years of the century. The churches, and other social institutions, were terribly concerned about the effects of film-going on the public, especially on youth, and from voicing their concerns about various individual films they devised the first primitive forms of film criticism. Film historians generally gather film writers from these early days together under the heading of social-impact critics. This style of criticism still appears today in several guises. Sex-and-violence issues remain important matters for critics, and specialized groups have their own particular agenda. Feminist critics, for example, try to uncover the impact that films have had on the image of women in America.

Not all church activity in film stemmed from a concern for public morality. Before World War I, the churches began to see film as a valuable catechetical tool, and shortly after World War II a form of sophisticated film criticism entered into the intellectual life of the churches. From there it was but a short step to the curricula of the religious and secular universities, where it combined with several nonreligious disciplines. In the classrooms the overtly "religious" style of church-originated film criticism of the 1950s developed a more catholic style.

This study will trace origins of the two most important critical schools: auteur criticism and genre criticism, both of which will be used extensively in Part II. Auteur criticism, coming out of Paris immediately after World War II, became the dominant critical method for over thirty years. Its practitioners center their reflections on the contributions of the directors, and even today the shelves of film sections in book stores are still dominated by studies of individual directors. Genre criticism developed in the late 1970s in the United States, where the critics tended to regard the director as only one member of the production team. They argued that placing such weight on one artist from among a team of dozens was a romantic notion that worked well for poets but had very little applicability to film production. What they found a more fruitful basis of their study was an analysis of the formulas that Hollywood developed for its mass audiences. Why, for example, did the Western achieve the dominance it did, what are its components and why did it disappear so quickly? Does such a life cycle reveal something about America as well as about the films?

In the last several years, critics have begun looking at the studios and the people who ran them. Their method is historical and biographical, since they maintain that the studio executives made ultimate decisions. These "moguls" assembled their own creative teams, determined a studio style to fit their own tastes, and shaped the product that appeared under their names. Any director, writer or actor who defied them was summarily fired.

Part II is an attempt to put these various methods into practice by looking closely at five extraordinary classics. The earliest is *Frankenstein* (James Whale, 1931) and the latest is *The Maltese Falcon* (John Huston, 1941). It was a decade of extraordinary creativity in Hollywood, and the effects of the period linger to the present. Every horrifying creature must be compared to Boris Karloff's Monster, and every detective is a descendant of Humphrey Bogart's Sam Spade.

The five films can truly be called benchmark films, but their selection still may raise questions. Other individual films are undoubtedly more important—*Gone With the Wind* (Victor Fleming, 1939) and *Casablanca* (Michael Curtiz, 1942), to mention two obvious examples. Other directors surely deserve mention, like Charlie Chaplin, Orson Welles, and D.W. Griffith. Several important genres are ignored: Why no musicals, documentaries or science fiction? Why nothing from this half of the century? Why no foreign films? Why no television? Good questions those, and they deserve an answer.

This is intended as a study of film criticism. The films invite the reader to investigate the different critical methods as they apply to particular individual samples. Each of the films represents a particular identifiable genre, and at the same time each is the product of a significant auteur. Each was chosen because it is a fertile subject for both auteur criticism and genre criticism. All, moreover, are products of one decade in American history. In Hollywood those ten years saw the development of the sound film from its primitive era to one of extraordinary subtlety. The 1930s then contain the discovery of a new art form, and the five films chosen are milestones in that formative period. On a wider horizon the 1930s saw enormous change in American society as it staggered from the Depression toward World War II. The five films show five different reflections on that calamitous period in the nation's history.

Each of the chapters in Part II contains four sections. The first provides an example of auteur criticism by supplying biographical and artistic information about the director. The second explores the genre of which the film is a sample. These are followed by a plot summary and commentary of the film under discussion.

The plot summaries are detailed, and purposefully so. In most film books, readers and students are baffled by the criticism because they have never seen the film in question, or, if they have, do not recall a particular scene. The summaries, it is hoped, make the book self-contained. Reading a summary, however, is a poor substitute for seeing the film, yet, realistically, how can a reader be expected to have immediate awareness of each film while reading the commentary? In the commentaries I try to apply the methods of auteur criticism and genre criticism explicitly to each of the films. I would hope that the summaries not only make the commentary intelligible but encourage the reader to track down the film in the nearest video store.

Other devious motives underlie this work. If it were to be used as a textbook, I would hope that it would provide students and teachers with a method for using popular films as a means to study American culture during one decade, the 1930s. As such, it could provide a methodology for understanding other periods in the twentieth century: the war years, the cold war, the 1960s, the me-decade, etc. Films, after all, are wonderful artifacts that lead directly to an appreciation of the culture that made them. Furthermore, although I treat only five films, I mention a great many others as examples of the genre or of the director's work. With a methodology in place, these ancillary titles could provide the material for an entire semester or year.

General readers, too, should regard this collection of essays more a beginning than an end. Since videotape versions of the classic films have reached into every drugstore and supermarket, a book like this could provide the incentive for a new generation of viewers to enjoy the classic films of the Hollywood studio era.

Finally, one dilemma plagues this book from the outset. Since it was written with both the academic reader and the general reader in mind, the level of documentation became problematic. Certainly, I want to cite sources where such documentation is appropriate, but I am determined not to scare away casual readers who merely want to explore a few beloved classic films.

Endnotes provide a reasonable compromise for the appearance of the page, but they do not solve the problem altogether. These films are old friends. I have studied them and taught them for several years. If there is a just God, someone has kept track of the number of term papers and essay questions I have read about them. I am afraid that I simply do not recall where many of the observations expressed in these pages come from. They may be original, and I hope many of them are. Where they are borrowed, I fully intend to give full accreditation to the author, but admit to fallibility in carrying out this resolve. In instances where I could readily locate the source of an idea, I document the statements scrupulously, perhaps to a fault. My most important criterion for documentation is my desire to assist the reader eager to track down further reading on a given topic. If the work is successful, readers will quickly turn from these brief essays to additional reading and viewing.

PART I

Chapter One

MEDIUM AND METAPHOR

In *Understanding Media,* a book that became a fad in the 1960s, quaint in the 1970s, and may one day be recovered as a seminal classic, Marshall McLuhan wrote: "All media are active metaphors in their power to translate experience into new forms."[1] Most students of any discipline, if they take their work seriously, soon learn this.

My own first experience with active metaphors came in the first weeks of high school when, true to the methods and syllabus of the day, teachers assaulted us poor bewildered freshmen with the intricacies of Latin and Greek grammar. The strange language was a medium that soon became an active metaphor for classical culture. The beauty of the structures hinted at the orderly universe the ancients inhabited, or at least believed they did.

Later, as the semesters passed and the languages became more manageable as media, we eager young scholars marched through their histories and poetry, their drama and philosophy, each of which became another avenue into the mind and heart of a culture long past: Caesar and Cicero first, then majestic Virgil and beloved Homer, Sophocles with his passion and Plato with his wisdom, Livy and Thucydides each telling the story of his people. An occasional photograph of a vase from Crete or a wall painting from Pompeii put visible flesh on the skeleton of literature and philosophy. The architecture hinted at aspirations of a time when the human spirit soared. As the years passed, we not only learned about the artifacts and achievements of these inventors of western civilization, but gradually we learned about the peoples themselves. Most of us learned at least to admire them, and a fortunate few even learned to love them.

As we tramped along through our classical studies, these linguis-

11

tic, literary, and philosophical monuments of the ancient world served then both as media and as metaphors, in the McLuhan sense. These early writers and artists translated their lived experience into artifacts, which in turn serve us, centuries later, as metaphors that enable us to reconstruct the original experience. Their words and images function as media of communication between past and present, spanning the centuries and transmitting civilizations long vanished to yet one more generation of students. And the very reason these media remain so powerful through the years is that they serve as effective metaphors for the experience of the ancient world. The Greek and Latin authors working at their scrolls provide metaphors that enable us to understand their world. Finally, as embodiments of the depth of experience of past civilizations, these literary monuments can offer an understanding of the human condition as it is repeated and relived in countless civilizations throughout history. Odysseus and Oedipus, pure expressions of Greek culture, tell us a great deal about our own, for in a sense they are Everyone.

Is there any similar set of media and metaphors a thoughtful person can study in an attempt to appreciate the culture of the United States in the twentieth century? The answer is yes, but with some cautions. The movies are a resolutely American metaphor. They are more often glitzy than profound. Hollywood, the Rome and Athens of the new world, is a town of high finance and low culture. Money dominates art. The studios were founded by poor immigrants of little refinement, mostly poor Jews from eastern Europe. The artifacts are relentlessly egalitarian and democratic: whoever sells the most tickets is the greatest artist; whoever owns the studio and pays the salary makes the final artistic judgment. Intellectuals traditionally despise American movies, yet for all their limitations the rest of the world is captivated by them. Everyone tries to imitate them, but nobody can. In describing the American film industry, a picture of the wider American culture begins to emerge with embarrassing clarity. The movies are the art we love to despise, just like the country.

Trying to understand contemporary American culture by studying its media leads to a set of problems far different from those confronting the scholar of the classic world. The classicist faces intimidating gaps in information. The evidence is fragmentary, and much surely has been lost through the centuries. The literature and art that remain may or may not provide a completely accurate picture of the culture, and the possibility of misinterpretation is always present. In addition, the study of poetry and art surely reflects more the concerns of sophisticated elites than of the impoverished masses. Archaeologists and anthropologists are still trying to fit missing pieces into the puzzles of ancient civilizations.

By contrast, contemporary American scholars live with an overwhelming abundance of information. The twentieth century American landscape teems with media and metaphors of experience as it is lived by every social class, in every region and at every moment since the landing of the earliest settlers. Not only do they have mountains of printed pages now made more accessible than ever through the wonders of computerized retrieval systems, but they have photographs, recordings, documentary film, videotapes and, of course, motion pictures.

Over a decade ago, Arthur M. Schlesinger Jr. noted the privileged role of the Hollywood film in understanding American culture. He observed that film carries "a deep but enigmatic truth," because it is a collective art form.[2] A novel, for example, might be the expression of a quirky vision of one individual artist, but a film, by contrast, represents the collaboration of dozens, possibly hundreds of artists. For a particular film to be made, many people, from writers, directors and movie stars to producers, publicists and bankers, must make their own contribution to the finished product. If a critic, like an archaeologist, can dig down into the finished product, different layers of artistic expression can be distinguished, but, taken as a whole, the work represents a broad cross-section of American artistic expression.

Furthermore, films are not created in an aesthetic vacuum to satisfy the creative impulse of a solitary artist. When Hollywood undertakes to make a film, it is because the producers expect it to make money. Professionals stake millions of dollars on their ability to guess what will appeal strongly enough to audiences to make them buy tickets, presumably several millions of dollars worth of tickets. The accuracy of their guess-work can be measured easily enough through box office results. Some films, for one reason or another, do not gain a following; other minor low-budget films become extremely popular. In the last analysis, the public has final dictatorial power over Hollywood production. It votes with its ticket purchases on what artistic expression is acceptable, entertaining, illuminating or inspiring. One successful film will often spawn a generation of sequels and imitations, from "The Return of . . ." so popular in the 1930s to the far more blatant and less imaginative ". . . : Part VII."[3]

Until recently serious critics of the cultural scene tended to dismiss the Hollywood film as vulgar and commercial rather than artistic. It is not difficult to see why. Without doubt Hollywood does produce a tremendous quantity of very expensive junk each year, and some of the most spectacularly bad films are often among the most successful at the box office.[4] Yet, to be fair, movies at their trashiest cannot compare with the awfulness of the novels that top best seller lists. And as for artistic quality, even the worst-made Hollywood film has a degree of professionalism that unpublished poets and short story writers, and basement painters, playwrights, composers and sculptors could not aspire to on their best days. Quite simply, most allegedly artistic output in all media is quite dreadful. The Hollywood product is just more expensive trash than anyone else's, except, of course, television, which has the dubious honor of being both more expensive and trashier. Despite all this, some Hollywood films are extraordinary achievements and these deserve careful, respectful, and even loving attention.

The awful films, studied collectively, can provide a rich field of inquiry for anthropologists and sociologists, or even for historians of the popular arts. For present purposes, the occasional excellent films are far more important, and all but the most biased cultural critics admit that the motion picture industry, particularly in the United States, is capable of producing more than an occasional film of excellence. These benchmark films are a particularly useful avenue into American culture on two counts. First, from the point of view of the producer: American artists working in concert with other artists have found the medium of film and the particular film of excellence an effective way to express their own experience and vision. Second, from the point of view of the consumer: vast American audiences have found in certain classical films a meaningful interpretation of their own personal experience.[5] They like going to the movies, and when a film is especially well done, they resonate with its meaning. Such films never age, really. Each generation of American audiences can come back to them with fresh eyes and fresh appreciation.

Film then is a uniquely American medium and metaphor. It plays a significant role in our cultural expression in a way it does not in other societies. It is undeniable that Americans have made more excellent films consistently and over a longer period than has any other national group, a fact noted with some regret by the French critic and film-maker Eric Rohmer: "The finest American films it has been my lot to see have more than anything else made me fiercely envious and sorry that France should have abandoned the pursuit of a claim to universality that it once—not long ago—affirmed so strongly, and that we should have let the flame of a certain idea of man be extinguished in order to be re-lit across the ocean; in short we must admit defeat on ground to which we have a rightful claim."[6]

Furthermore, throughout its history Hollywood has consistently attracted the finest talents from around the world, and its product has dominated world markets to such an extent that American films are the mainstay of the industry in every corner of the world.[7] While it is true that American films have been a dominant force in world popular culture, Schlesinger perhaps overstates the case to some extent when he argues that "film is the only art where the United States has made a real difference."[8]

The point at issue in considering the importance of film in American culture might best be stated through analogy. If one wants to understand Greek culture, study the epics and tragedies, the architecture and the philosophy. For Quattrocento Florence, look at the paintings. For medieval France, trace the development of the cathedrals. For Elizabethan England, become familiar with the theater, but, for Victorian England, with the novels. These are the art forms that flourished, dominated and best embodied a particular historical moment. Similarly, if one wants to gather some sensitivity to the United States in the twentieth century, then go to the movies.[9] Film, I maintain, provides one important, and often neglected, field of inquiry for some comprehension of American culture.

American "culture" is a vast territory to try to conquer and occupy with any one incursion. A look at some of the most important films Hollywood produced does little more than provide one more cluster of tiles in a vast mosaic.[10] It is, however, one additional way to view a familiar landscape. A close look at five classic films may help uncover some of the metaphors that the artists have tried to fashion in order to mediate their lived American experience through the decades to the present day.

A pointed contrast may further clarify the relationship between film and culture that is under discussion at present. The single most ambitious work of this type is Siegfried Kracauer's *From Caligari to Hitler: A Psychological Study of the German Film*, first published in 1947. In this exhaustive huge study of the German film beginning with the first great international success, *The Cabinet of Dr. Caligari*, directed by Robert Weine in 1916, the author describes economic and political structures of the film industry in Germany, analyzes the styles and imagery common to the nationalized production center at Ufa studios, summarizes content and themes common to all sorts of individual films, and concludes that the films show that the rise and nightmare of the Hitler years were obvious consequents of the German mind in the post-World War I era. He is using the films like a psychiatrist using dreams as avenues into the subconscious. He

writes: "What films reflect are not so much explicit credos as psychological dispositions—those deep layers of collective mentality which
extend more or less below the dimension of consciousness."[11] The
study is fascinating, even though its conclusions remain questionable,
since it was written with the unfailing wisdom of hindsight. He wrote
after the tragedy of war, and of course the pieces fit neatly into the
pattern he uses to support his thesis.

Where Kracauer included everything about German films, from
the economic structure of the studios to the lighting of individual
scenes, this study will be highly selective. Where he was psychoanalytic, this is more the realm of the journalist-observer. Where his
focus of attention is primarily pre-war German society and second-
arily how the films reflect some of the inner dynamisms leading to
war, in this present study the films themselves remain at the center of
attention in the hope that they can provide some slight shaft of light
into American society. Kracauer is a social psychologist fitting films
into the patterns of German history as they subsequently unfolded; I
am a film critic reflecting on films as they embody their American
social context. My primary interest remains focused on the films
themselves rather than the social commentary.

In particular, looking at several key films can provide a rather
unorthodox look at several religious elements in American society,
surely not from the point of view of the theologian or historian of
religion, nor that of the sociologist or anthropologist, but rather from
the perspective of a film critic's asking what kinds of values and relationships seemed to find expression in some examples of this characteristically American art form. To avoid any possible misunderstand-
ing of the method, some historical background on the relationship of
religion and the film industry is essential.

By way of "coming attraction," this historical survey will trace
the development of film criticism from the specialized interests of the
religious communities through its entry into the university environment, where the critical concerns shift abruptly. Even more striking,
in this academic setting, is the shift that takes place in the critical
approach to the popular American film. Serious film criticism started
with the churches as a concern with moral issues in popular entertainment and gradually, with the help of the academic community,
evolved into a concern with artistic expression. As a still later development, critics began to look at the classic American films and discover
levels of artistry they never expected. But this is only a "coming
attraction." To reveal any more of the plot at this time would spoil
the story.

Almost from the beginning of the commercial film industry, religious personalities and organizations have taken it very seriously, and the relationship has often been adversarial. It is important to gain some historical perspective on this relationship to set the present discussion in its proper historical context. The mixture of cinema and religion provides a volatile chemistry, and it is important to have some idea of how the elements have combined in the past.

In the history of culture, film is an extremely new art form, and naturally it caught the traditional guardians of public morality quite by surprise when it first flickered into public consciousness. Although projected films and peep shows were popular enough novelties before the turn of the century, in the first decade of the twentieth century they were well on their way to becoming a big business. Mass entertainment had become a new form of heavy industry, and no one knew how it should be regulated, if indeed it should be regulated at all.

In his *Film: A Democratic Art,* Garth Jowett, a film scholar working out of the University of Houston and the University of Windsor, Ontario, has chronicled in detail the rise of the film industry and its reception by the traditional custodians of the public taste. By 1908, he relates, more than eight thousand nickelodeons dotted the urban landscape.[12] What caused uneasiness among some community leaders was the fact that these new motion pictures were the first authentic "mass" medium. It was an unprecedented phenomenon. The movies reached masses—as groups rather than one-at-a-time, like newspapers, for example—indiscriminately without the intervention of the customary and reliable gatekeepers, like the family, the churches, the libraries, or the schools. Any child with a few pennies could skip school for an afternoon and sit in a makeshift theater, to watch slapstick comedians or action adventure thrillers.

The churches were not alone in early attempts to monitor the film industry, nor were the concerns at issue the traditional questions of sex, violence and the corruption of public morality.[13] The issues were much broader. For example, the progressive social reformer and founder of Hull House in Chicago, Jane Addams, felt that motion pictures running in the five hundred nickelodeons in the city filled the minds of impressionable children with dangerous illusions.[14] Similarly, John Dewey, whose educational philosophy stressed activity on the part of students, saw film as an invitation to a dangerous passivity, and, of course, young people were receiving messages and values outside of the school environment where they could be carefully monitored.[15]

Many critics were not concerned about the content of the films at all, but rather with the unhealthy atmosphere in which they were shown. Many believed that these dark, crowded theaters, often infested with vermin and filled with the poorest and most unwashed segments of the population with their attendant livestock, were breeding grounds for disease.[16] Since many screening rooms were set up behind saloons and attracted their own casts of unsavory characters, many expressed fears of an unhealthy moral climate as well.

The early film critics who roared from the pulpits of the churches were as much concerned with the competition as with the morality of film content. Sunday was the most popular day for going to the movies, and even if a trip to the nickelodeon did not cut directly into church attendance, it certainly did compromise the spirit of the sabbath observance.[17] In 1908, after listening to testimony from clergymen of several denominations, led by Canon William Shaefe Chase of the Interdenominational Committee for the Suppression of Sunday Vaudeville and Mr. Frank Moss of the Society for the Suppression of Vice, Mayor George B. McClellan created a suppression of his own. He ordered all the movie houses in the city of New York closed until further notice. His Christmas Eve manifesto included the provision that they could be reopened only after the owners promised to remain closed on Sundays.[18]

The theater owners quickly got the courts to allow them to reopen their businesses, but they had received a salutary scare. By early 1909 the owners and producers were collaborating with the National Board of Review, an agency formed in cooperation with the People's Institute, a progressive agency founded by Charles Sprague Smith, formerly a professor at Columbia University, in order to further relationships between the city's poor immigrants and cultural elites.[19] One of the early projects of the institute was a campaign to clean up the moral environment of the poor by elevating the quality of entertainment provided in movie houses and cheaper theaters.

The producers and theater owners found Smith an eager ally in their program for self-censorship, even though their motives may have been incompatible. Smith wanted to sanitize the movies, and with them the lower classes; the owners wanted to avoid any form of censorship from outside the industry and protect their investment by keeping the theaters open. The executive committee was made up of prominent Jews like Samuel Gompers, wealthy Protestants like Andrew Carnegie, university presidents, representatives from the Federal Council of Churches, the YMCA, and the New York School Board, and professional moral watchdogs like the Rev. Charles Parkhurst of the Society for the Prevention of Crime and Anthony Comstock, the notorious postal inspector.

Curiously, this all-male board held the power to pass or withhold approval on any film shown in New York, but the reviewers were one hundred and thirteen women volunteers, who presumably had a more highly developed sensitivity than the men who passed judgment. Curiously, too, the Catholic Church was not represented.

Mayor William Gaynor, the Democratic reform mayor who succeeded McClellan in 1912, was an enthusiastic supporter of the Progressive agenda, and the entertainment industry was an obvious target for his reformist rage. (His rage might have been further inflamed by his family's experience with the theater: two of his daughters eloped with men they met in cabarets.)[20] He increased police manpower assigned to the theaters, and by the Motion Picture Ordinance of 1912 he raised the licensing fee for theaters from twenty-five dollars to five hundred dollars in the hope of attracting a more affluent, and thus more responsible, type of businessman into the industry. The combination worked. Fear of an impromptu inspection from the vice squad, who might find on the premises films without the board's seal of approval, and thus obscene, might lead to closings, fines, and the loss of the five hundred dollar license. This pattern worked so successfully in New York that it became the standard for enforcing the board's authority throughout the country.

After reviewing the history of these early days, Jowett reaches several rather illuminating conclusions. The questions and protests from different parts of the country, from clergy, politicians and educators, were rather uniform. "Each group," he writes, "in every part of the country attacked the same problems—crime and delinquency, sexual license, false information, physical dangers and antisocial behavior."[21] Movies were questioned and attacked on all sides, even though at the time very little scientific data was available. No one group had a monopoly on vilifying the movies, nor did any group feel the need for any hard data to substantiate its instinctive distrust, dislike and disdain of the movies.

This conclusion is important, since in the popular imagination the Catholic Church has often been portrayed as taking the role of chief censor and imposing its sectarian moral principles on a pluralistic American society. That was a role that was to develop much later on, and in a much more moderate and constructive fashion than is often currently believed. In fact, Catholics were generally rather restrained in their reactions to movies in the early days of the industry. As a church of fairly recent immigrants, the Catholic Church was more tolerant of the foreign ways that Nativist American Protestants found suspect if not positively decadent. As a rule, these Catholic newcomers from Ireland, Germany and Italy were less likely to find the "sophisticated" European customs presented in early films threatening than were the sons and daughters of the Puritan immigration that came from England and Scotland nearly three centuries earlier.

Catholics of the time also had a happy schizophrenia about the sabbath observance. They were dreadfully rigid about church attendance on Sunday, but were perfectly comfortable with harmless entertainment throughout the rest of the day. As long as their flocks went to Mass on Sunday morning, the Catholic clergy did not seem terribly concerned about keeping them out of the movies on Sunday afternoon. As an interesting parallel, while Protestants preached prohibition, Catholics encouraged temperance.[22]

To keep a balanced picture, it must be noted that in the early days of motion pictures, regulating public morality was not the only interest the churches had in this new invention. There was a positive side as well. From the very beginnings of the film industry, religion was a big seller. As early as 1907 the American *Passion Play* was being shown. The Italians were first to move the religious spectacle into the marketplace with Enrico Guazzoni's *Quo Vadis?* (1912) and Giovanni Pastrone's *Cabiria* (1913). America's D.W. Griffith was quick to join the procession with *Judith of Bethulia* (1913) and the Babylonian segment of his tetralogy *Intolerance* (1916). George Loane Tucker's *Miracle Man* starring Lon Chaney was popular in 1919. By 1923 Cecil B. DeMille became the supreme pontiff of spectacle and piety with *The Ten Commandments*. In 1926 Fred Niblo challenged DeMille's pontificate with *Ben Hur*, but the next year DeMille reasserted his claim to primacy with *King of Kings* and later with *The Sign of the Cross* (1932). The film historian Gerald Mast has pinpointed the success of DeMille, and implicitly his many imitators: "His religious films flirt with righteousness and sell conventionality. In both versions of *The Ten Commandments*, DeMille was far more interested in the splashy sinful doings around the golden calf than in the righteous thunder and lightning on the mountain."[23]

For good or ill, film was a splendid medium for presenting traditional Bible stories, even despite Hollywood's fascination with pagan orgies and somewhat sentimentalized versions of some of the stronger messages of scripture. Nonetheless the churches welcomed these popularizations as effective auxiliaries for their own evangelistic mission. The Bible as rewritten by Hollywood may not have been the most accurate translation of the word of God, but people watching Bible epics on the screen did pay attention to it, and were occasionally moved by it. What more could a homilist hope for? Prompted by the success of these edifying—or at least palatable— commercial films, several of the churches began to make their own movies and use them for instruction on "the effects of wickedness and righteousness."[24]

By 1921 wickedness had clearly taken the ascendancy in Hollywood, and thus began a series of events that over the next fifteen years would bring the churches, especially the Catholic Church, seriously into the business of monitoring moral content of the movies.

To begin with, in a very few years after its founding, the National Board began to lose its authority. D.W. Griffith's *The Birth of a Nation* (1915) had established film as an artistic medium that cut across American caste barriers. A more sophisticated audience wanted a more sophisticated product, and it was very profitable to provide it for them. If the board did roar on occasion, the lion had lost its teeth. It was recognized as a creature of the film industry, and the function of the industry was to make money. The board had been a useful tool to provide the illusion of serious self-regulation and thus avert the possibility of censorship imposed from without.

Then, too, America was changing. The war had opened the mind of America to the exotic and wicked ways of Europe, and film audiences could not get enough sultry vamps like Theda Bara or Latin lovers like Rudolph Valentino. In many instances the rise of the publicity agent and the fan magazine made the off-screen antics of the stars as fascinating as their exploits in the movies, and just as wicked.

Fans and ordinary moviegoers have always been fascinated by the lives of the stars, looking upon their foibles with a DeMillian ambiguity. They adored their idols of the silver screen with near veneration, while feigning repugnance at their excesses recounted in all their gaudy detail in the popular press. By the end of 1921, the repugnance was no longer feigned but quite real; in the following two years it became obsessive.[25]

The most notorious cause of this turnabout was the death of Virginia Rappe after a sordid party hosted in San Francisco by Roscoe "Fatty" Arbuckle, one of the most popular comic actors of the day. The 320-pound actor was accused of a sadistic rape that led directly to her death. Twice the Arbuckle trial ended with a hung jury, and finally, in 1923, he was acquitted after the jury deliberated for six minutes, but it was too late. The press had kept the story alive for three years, and the star's career was destroyed forever. With the help of friends he directed a few films under the name William B. Goodrich, but he never appeared on the screen again.

In 1922, during the period of the Arbuckle trials, Wallace Reid, a classic "matinee idol," was admitted to a sanitorium for drug addiction complicated by alcoholism. He died there the following year, at the age of thirty-two.

Also in 1922, William Desmond Taylor, a successful actor and director and president of the Screen Directors Guild, was murdered in his Hollywood home. No convictions ever came from the case, but Mabel Normand, one of Charlie Chaplin's leading ladies, and Mary Miles Minter, also one of Hollywood's brightest stars, were both seen in his company on the night of the murder. Neither was charged with the crime, but their flourishing careers withered immediately. Mabel Normand, who was rumored to be romantically involved with Taylor and whose vigorous social life had led to rumors of drug addiction, became a natural target of speculation in the tabloids. Since drugs were believed implicated in the murder and Taylor had recently become involved with Minter, the gossip mongers were ready to conclude that Normand had committed the crime in a jealous rage.[26] She was officially exonerated, but she never regained her former star stature, since at the peak of the publicity her chauffeur was discovered over the murdered body of Cortland S. Dines, a Hollywood millionaire. It was guilt by association, but nonetheless the public handed down the death sentence on her career.

These sensational crimes aroused a moral consciousness that had already become uneasy with the private lives of their favorite stars. The beloved Charlie Chaplin, for example, at the age of twenty-nine, married a sixteen year old girl in 1918, when he was already being challenged as a "shirker" for not fighting in the war. Two years later the couple obtained a divorce, and in 1924, at the age of thirty-five, he married another sixteen year old.

Ironically, gossip columns wallowed in a long-standing romance between the newspaper magnate William Randolph Hearst, the man who built his empire on sensationalist journalism, and his protegée Marion Davies. The couple met in 1917, and by 1919 he had formed Cosmopolitan Pictures to produce her films. Mrs. Hearst refused to grant a divorce to allow them to marry, but his extraordinary wealth allowed them to flout conventional social and moral standards. Despite the publicity he was able to generate for her through his newspapers, the films all lost money, largely because of the lavish production he demanded as a backdrop for her talent. They shared a

110-room, 55-bath beach house at Santa Monica, and their luxurious castle San Simeon formed the backdrop of Orson Welles' *Citizen Kane* (1941), a story based loosely on the Hearst-Davies romance. As the scandals multiplied, the public became less willing to wink and forgive. Hollywood had become the new Sodom.

The industry's reputation had become so tainted that some individuals and communities began to suspect that any product coming from this moral wasteland must, in fact, be tainted with the corruption of its origins. Even more telling than the threat of censorship was the financial crisis: so sordid had Hollywood's reputation become that by 1922 only one New York banker, Otto H. Kahn, would do business with the industry at all.[27]

Tinseltown clearly had an image problem, and the image stemmed more from fact than from illusion. As public outrage grew, on March 14, 1922 the studios joined forces to form the Motion Picture Producers and Distributors of America (MPPDA), later to be renamed the Motion Picture Association of America (MPAA), an organization that would function as the public relations arm of the industry. Chosen to captain this frigate through the storms of controversy was the redoubtable Will H. Hays, elder in the Presbyterian Church, former chairman of the Republican National Committee, and current Postmaster General in the Harding Administration. In addition to providing some positive publicity for Hollywood, the Hays Office, as MPPDA was known, tried to convince the public that it was channeling the industry's efforts to regulate the moral content of its own films.

This pretense of self-censorship was orchestrated to diffuse pressure from the state and city governments that threatened to impose their own form of censorship with local boards of review.[28] The threat of federal censorship remained, and both federal and local boards seemed to have legal authority since the Supreme Court ruled in Mutual Film Corporation v. Ohio (1915) that movies are a purely commercial enterprise and thus not subject to the free speech provisions of the First Amendment.[29] This legal precedent was not effectively reversed until *The Miracle* case (Burstyn v. Wilson) in 1952, when Justice Tom C. Clarke of the U.S. Supreme Court, writing for the majority, ruled: "It cannot be doubted that motion pictures are a significant medium for the communication of ideas."[30]

In 1924 the Hays Office issued "The Formula," a brief document of stupefying vagueness that promised untiring efforts "to establish and maintain the highest possible moral and artistic standards of motion picture production."[31] Norms of that type threatened no one in the industry, nor did it convince the public that Hollywood was serious about regulating its own product. In 1927 the office responded to its critics by publishing a list of "Don'ts and Be Carefuls." The eleven "Don'ts" that were not to be put on the screen at all included the obvious topics from "sex perversion" to "ridicule of the clergy." The twenty-five "Be Carefuls" that were to merit "special care" included topics ranging from "the use of the flag" to "the sale of women" and "surgery."

The year 1927 does not stand out in film history for the publication of the "Don'ts and Be Carefuls," however. On October 6 *The Jazz Singer* opened in New York, and with it the age of sound arrived, creating a whole new set of problems for the Hays Office. The belief was current in Hollywood that dialogue too sophisticated or even vulgar to be received by radio in the nation's living rooms would be an effective attraction to lure audiences away from "Amos 'n' Andy" and back to the Bijou. The Hays Office responded to the challenge of the talkies by issuing a comprehensive and detailed "Motion Picture Production Code" in 1930. Contrary to current belief, the document was far less negative than the "Don'ts and Be Carefuls," and contained a philosophy of morally responsible film-making that in many respects and with some adjustments for the changes in public mores could serve well today.

The anonymous authors of the Code were reputed to be the Rev. Daniel Lord, a Jesuit priest, and Martin Quigley, a Catholic layman and editor of the *Motion Picture Herald*, a respected trade paper.[32] From this point on, for good or ill, fairly or not, efforts to pressure Hollywood into responding to demands for sensitivity to the moral standards of large segments of the public have been associated with the Catholic Church.

A short parenthesis is important at this point. Some few film historians appear all too eager to castigate the Catholic Church for trying to articulate objective, measurable standards of moral acceptability. It is all to easy to look back to a sixty year old statement and find in its quaint expressions sinister undertones of a scrupulous, sex-obsessed Catholic Church willfully imposing its moral standards on a pluralistic society. Gerald Gardner, for example, in *The Censorship Papers*, writes of the Production Code: "If George Bernard Shaw and Eugene O'Neill had written the code, it might have been a defensible document; but, alas, it was written by a Jesuit priest, Father Daniel Lord, and a prominent publisher and Catholic layman, Martin Quigley."[33] The bigotry revealed in such remarks is regrettable, but even more regrettable is the historian's failure to recognize that the "Don'ts and

Be Carefuls" were published three years earlier, but do not merit an "alas," presumably because they were composed by persons who did not happen to be Catholic.

Writing about morals and movies without appearing prudish is a difficult task. The secular academic community was just as frustrated as Jesuit priests and Catholic laymen in trying to propose objective standards for its psychological research on the effects of movies on behavior patterns of viewers. Of particular interest in this regard is the twelve volume set of studies commissioned by the Payne Foundation and published in 1933.[34] For example, in one of the studies Charles C. Peters, professor of education at Pennsylvania State University, tries to assign numerical values to the reactions of various classes of viewers to common movie situations, like "aggressiveness of a girl in love-making." He places these numbers along a spectrum ranging from "invites man to companionship" to "resorts to physical manipulation."[35] After nearly six decades, this scientific prose seems just as quaint as the Code, but it was the only language available at the time. End of parenthesis.

Despite its warm reception in the film community, the Code was more admired than observed. At first, producers were invited to submit scripts for a reading by the Studio Relations Committee, and one year later the submissions were made compulsory. The committee could make its recommendations for changes, but it had no power to enforce them, and as a result the tone and content of motion pictures changed very little in the years immediately following the publication of the Code.[36]

In October 1933, Catholic impatience with the quality of films was channeled toward action when Archbishop (later Cardinal) Amleto Cicognani, recently appointed apostolic delegate from Pope Pius XI to the United States, decried "immoral motion pictures" in his address to a convention of Catholic Charities in New York. Several American Catholics quickly seconded the comments of the pope's official representative.

Later that year, the Episcopal Committee on Motion Pictures drafted a strategy to pressure the industry into a more effective form of self-regulation by holding out the possibility of nationwide boycotts. The committee did not propose legislation for censorship, nor did it want to act as censor itself, policies that other churches had endorsed. Rather, having found dialogue fruitless, it simply proposed alternate means to encourage Hollywood to take its own Code more seriously. The bishops were clear that their objective was not control over the industry, but the pastoral care of their flocks.

On April 11, 1934 the recommendations of the committee went out privately to each of the dioceses, and each bishop was entrusted with the task of implementation on a local level. The usual strategy adopted by the bishops involved pastoral letters published in the diocesan press, occasional organized demonstrations directed against offensive films or offending theaters, and a series of mandated sermons by the priests of the diocese on the moral dangers of the movies. Cardinal Dennis Dougherty of Philadelphia was more direct: he ordered the Catholics of his diocese to boycott all motion picture theaters.

In heavily Catholic neighborhoods, especially in the big cities, box office receipts tumbled, and the message went out to both Hollywood and to the bishops that the rules of the game had changed.[37] The Catholic bishops discovered quite by accident that they had a nuclear strike force at their disposal, and the industry began digging air-raid shelters. By June 9, the "Legion of Decency" had reached the pages of *The New York Times,* a sure sign that it had come of age.

If the American bishops had been swift in responding to Archbishop Cicognani's call to arms, the film industry was even swifter in its counterattack—or capitulation, as some would have it. By July the Production Code Administration was formed under the direction of Joseph Breen, a journalist with suitable Irish Catholic credentials and a readily recognizable Irish name. His office would review a film at each stage of production, pass on recommendations to the studio, and if the film passed all the criteria of the Code, it would receive a seal of approval. Release of a film without the seal would bring a fine of twenty-five thousand dollars a day on a defiant studio.

Catholics accomplished in a few months what educators and other religious groups had been attempting for years. The reasons for this success are not difficult to explain. The Catholic Church then, even more than now, was monolithic and hierarchical. While other churches were fragmented into different denominations and sects, each speaking through its own leaders, the Catholic Church spoke with a unified voice, and dissent, though not unknown, was even less welcome then than it is today. In those days when a bishop spoke about any topic at all, it would be an unusual Catholic who would question his authority publicly. Catholics also had the numbers, about twenty million of the sixty million self-acknowledged church-goers in 1930. In addition, the Catholics had a remarkably efficient communications system in place. Every single Catholic was expected to attend services and listen to a sermon every single week, thus forming a ready-made audience for a bishop's statement. A network of diocesan newspapers and national magazines debated the question at length for the education of Catholic opinion leaders. Finally, the Catholic population was concentrated in the cities, where a boycott could have maximum effect.

Success does exact a cost, however. As a result of the church's effectiveness in forcing the motion picture industry to put teeth into its Code, the relationship between the Catholic Church and Hollywood is invariably caricatured as one of antagonism, censorship and pressure tactics. This certainly contains an element of truth, but the fact is that the dialogue has advanced considerably from the early 1930s, and both participants have changed their postures.

In "Freedom of the Movies," a study organized out of the University of Chicago and published in 1947, researcher Ruth Inglis states that the charge of Catholic domination of the PCA was "unfounded."[38] It is, however, undeniable that the PCA kept in mind the criteria formulated and publicized by the Legion. In the thirty years the two organizations functioned together, only five times did the Legion condemn a film passed by the PCA.[39] This is one instance of the secular and religious realms thinking as one. It must further be acknowledged that although the Legion did not directly act as censor, its indirect influence was considerable. Since many exhibitors found it unwise to offer objectionable films to their patrons, the Legion's "condemned" rating would, in fact, limit a film's distribution and thus its profits. With one eye on the balance sheet, the producers preferred to regulate their own films, avoid conflict with the Legion, and thus maximize distribution and profits.

As the American film-going public and the membership of the Catholic Church became more diversified in the post-war years, it became obvious that the old Code had to change. The Code of the PCA and the criteria of the Legion of Decency underwent continual revision. In 1958 the Legion revised its ratings to give greater account to the sensitivities of different age groups, and in 1960, after many revisions, the Code was rewritten entirely. In response to the influx of popular foreign films, changing social sensibilities in the 1960s, and more venturesome films from American independent producers, many "exceptions" were granted, and, in fact, the Code was dead. On November 1, 1968, the Motion Picture Association of America replaced PCA with its own classification system, whose categories were quite similar to those used by the Legion. The appropriate rating was to be displayed prominently in advertising and during the opening titles at each screening. The philosophy of both groups evolved into an attempt to achieve that delicate balance between the maximum possible freedom for artistic expression and legitimate protection from adult themes for young people.

In 1966 the Legion of Decency, recognizing the anachronism of its militant title, changed its name to the National Catholic Office of Motion Pictures. Its new policy would be one of encouraging the production of films of quality, rather than criticizing what it perceived as lapses of taste and threats to morality. The oaths that continued to be recited in some churches in some dioceses revealed this shift in emphasis. The original oath read, in part: "I wish to join the Legion of Decency, which condemns vile and unwholesome moving pictures, and I unite with all who protest against them as a grave menace to youth, to home life, to country and to religion." As early as 1957, the revised oath revealed a change in direction: "I promise to promote by word and deed what is morally and artistically good in motion picture entertainment. I promise to discourage indecent, immoral and unwholesome motion pictures especially by my good example and always in a responsible and civic-minded manner." This positive approach, as it slowly developed, signaled an entirely different relationship between the churches, especially the Catholic Church, and the motion picture industry.

NOTES

1. Marshall McLuhan, *Understanding Media* (New York: McGraw-Hill, 1964), p. 57.

2. Arthur M. Schlesinger Jr., in the foreword to *American History/American Film*, ed. John O'Connor and Martin A. Jackson (New York: Unger, 1979), pp. ix–x.

3. Thomas Schatz, in *Hollywood Genres* (New York: Random House, 1981), pp. 15 and 16, explains the mutually influential relationship between audiences, directors, and the studios. By buying tickets, audiences tell the studios what kind of movies they want to see. Studios interpret the signals and commission more of the types of films that proved successful in the past. Thus is created a film genre. Directors, in turn, educate their audiences by providing variations and modifications in these preestablished genres. As a result some film types remain popular, with variations, for years until the market simply wearies of the genre, as happened to Westerns and musical comedies.

4. Critics, in film as in any other art form, must be careful in

dismissing any work, since later generations may have reason to revise original opinions. The Western films of John Ford are an interesting example. Not one of the Ford's six Academy Awards came for a Western, but these have become the most respected works of the director often considered to be America's finest. This question is addressed by Andrew Sarris in *John Ford: Movie Mystery* (Bloomington, Ind.: Indiana Univ. Press, 1975), pp. 14–18.

5. The English critic Robin Wood, in *Howard Hawks* (London: BFI Publishing, 1983), p. 8, observes: "The Hollywood cinema represents a kind of art that has largely disappeared; to find anything comparable we have to go back to Elizabethan drama. No other contemporary art form has been able to speak to all social and intellectual levels simultaneously and show a comparable achievement."

6. Eric Rohmer, "Rediscovering America," *Cahiers du Cinéma* 54, Christmas 1955, translated and published in *Cahiers du Cinéma: The 1950's: Neo-Realism, Hollywood, New Wave*, ed. Jim Hillier (Cambridge, Mass.: Harvard Univ. Press, 1985), p. 88.

7. William K. Everson, in *American Silent Film* (New York: Oxford, 1978), pp. 317–333, describes the huge influx of Europeans and adds the interesting observation that after 1924 Hollywood believed adding European "sophistication" to its films would help counteract the inroads made on its audiences by the new medium of radio. Arthur Knight, *The Liveliest Art: A Panoramic History of the Movies* (New York: Macmillan, 1978), pp. 99–102, covers similar territory in outlining Hollywood's predilection for exotic "artists" from Europe in the era of the silent film. Gerald Mast, *A Short History of the Movies* (New York: Macmillan, 1986), p. 152, provides a partial list of the major directors from Germany who fled the Nazi regime. He does not mention the dozens if not hundreds of technicians who also fled to Hollywood during those years. Many artists from other countries came to Hollywood for economic reasons rather than political: the American studios paid more for their services. Martin Dworkin, in "General Editor's Foreword" to Lewis Jacobs' *The Rise of the American Film: A Critical History* (New York: Teachers College Press, 1967), pp. vii–xvii, discusses the internationalization of Hollywood after World War II, since many film centers throughout the world have been producing films with distinctly American themes.

8. Schlesinger, p. x. While I would agree with the author on the preeminence of film as an American art form, I would be slow to offer the impression of exclusivity he implies in the next sentence: "Strike the American contribution from drama, painting, music, sculpture, dance and even possibly from poetry and the novel, and the world's

30   SCREENING AMERICA

achievement is only marginally diminished." For one example, if Americans have dominated cinema, they have nearly monopolized jazz.

9. The premier French film critic André Bazin, in "On the politique des auteurs," *Cahiers du Cinéma 70,* April 1957, trans. and reprinted in Hillier, p. 258, calls American film a classical art: "The American cinema is a classical art, but why not then admire in it what is most admirable, i.e. not only the talent of this or that film maker, but the genius of the system, the richness of its ever vigorous tradition, and its fertility when it comes into contact with new elements. . . ."

10. Marshall McLuhan, *The Gutenberg Galaxy* (Toronto: Univ. of Toronto Press, 1962), p. i. Throughout his work McLuhan rejected the demand for closure generated by the literate mind and thus he continually refrained from drawing air-tight conclusions to his reflections, a habit that made his writing as infuriating as it was stimulating.

11. Siegfried Kracauer, *From Caligari to Hitler: A Psychological History of the German Film* (Princeton, N.J.: Princeton Univ. Press), p. 6.

12. Lewis Jacobs, *The Rise of the American Film* (New York: Teachers College Press, 1968), p. 54. This edition is a reprint of this important history of film first published in 1939.

13. Garth Jowett, *Film: The Democratic Art* (Boston: The Focal Press, 1976), through his introduction and first four chapters, pp. 1–107, documents the early development of the motion picture, the social forces that made it possible, and the various attempts to regulate it and its audiences. Dr. Jowett's exhaustive research in these chapters provides the basis of this highly compressed history of the controversies generated by the early films.

14. Jane Addams' book, *The Spirit of Youth and City Streets* (1909), is cited by Jowett, p. 78. A more complete history of the relationship between social reformers and the film industry is found in "Rescuing the Family, Urban Progressivism and Modern Leisure," in Lary May, *Screening Out the Past: The Birth of Mass Culture and the Motion Picture Industry* (Chicago: Univ. of Chicago Press, 1980), pp. 43–59.

15. Jowett, p. 92. Dewey visited the Edison studio, then known as the factory, in 1912. While he was enthusiastic about movies as a learning device in general, in an essay he published the following year, "The Effect on Education and Morals of the Motion Picture," he

cautioned that the use of films "will, for a time at least, strengthen the idea, already much too strong, that the end of instruction is the giving of information and the end of learning is absorption."

16. Jowett, pp. 82–84.

17. Jowett, p. 94.

18. Jowett, pp. 111–112.

19. May, pp. 54–55, provides the basis for this story of the founding of the National Board of Review.

20. May, p. 56.

21. Jowett, p. 94.

22. Jowett, p. 246.

23. Mast, p. 112.

24. Jowett, p. 93. These early films produced by church groups are the forerunner of the classroom short films that have become commonplace in catechetical programs today.

25. The Arbuckle, Reid and Taylor scandals are listed in Everson, p. 296. Fuller information is supplied among the alphabetical references in Ephraim Katz, *The Film Encyclopedia* (New York: Perigee/G.P. Putnam's Sons, 1982).

26. Robert Sklar, *Movie-Made America: A Cultural History of the American Movies* (New York: Vintage, 1975), pp. 78 79.

27. Jowett, p. 166.

28. Several states actually succeeded in forming boards of review: Pennsylvania in 1911, Ohio in 1913, Kansas in 1914, Maryland in 1916, Florida and Massachusetts in 1921, New York and Virginia in 1922. Massachusetts lost its board through a referendum, and other states debated the issue and failed either in the legislature or through gubernatorial veto: Iowa, Maine, Nebraska, South Dakota and Wisconsin. Cf. Jowett, p. 119.

29. Jowett, pp. 166ff.

30. Randall, pp. 25–30, describes the issues of the case.

31. The complete document, as well as subsequent documents, can be found in Jowett, pp. 466–472.

32. Jowett, p. 240.

33. Gerald Gardner, *The Censorship Papers: Movie Censorship Letters from the Hays Office, 1934–1968* (New York: Dodd, Mead & Company: 1987), xvi.

34. The studies were undertaken by the Committee on Educational Research of the Payne Foundation at the request of the National Committee for the Study of Social Values in Motion Pictures.

Each of the studies was conducted independently, and they were published collectively under the title *Motion Pictures and Youth,* general editor W.W. Charters (New York: Macmillan, 1933).

35. Charles C. Peters, *Motion Pictures and Standards of Morality,* in *Motion Pictures and Youth* series (New York: Macmillan, 1933), pp. 15–16.

36. Jowett, p. 242n, points out that the failure of the Hays Office during these years made the creation of the Legion of Decency inevitable.

37. Jowett, p. 248, offers a more detailed chronology of the events that led to the creation of the Legion of Decency, a mere summary of which is provided here.

38. Jowett, p. 400.

39. Randall, p. 206, lists the five discrepancies, when the PCA issued a seal and the Legion gave out its condemned rating: *Son of Sinbad* (1955), *Baby Doll* (1956), *Kiss Me, Stupid* (1964), *The Pawnbroker* (1965), and *Hurry Sundown* (1967).

Chapter Two

FROM CENSOR TO TEACHER

The active partnership between the American film industry and the religious communities continues to advance unevenly, but there is progress, a great deal of it. Every few years a controversy like that surrounding Martin Scorsese's *The Last Temptation of Christ* (1988) will come along and remind both sides just how far they have come in the last thirty years and how far they have to go.[1] In fact, noisy debates of this kind break out so rarely these days that when they do come along they tend to take everyone by surprise. Not too many years ago, however, a picture like *The Last Temptation of Christ* that was thought likely to arouse such passion would never have gotten through the Production Code Administration in the first place, and if by some miracle it had, the descendants of Cardinal Dougherty would have been noisily threatening excommunication for anyone who dared to see it. In 1988 nothing of the kind happened at all. By comparison, conflicts today are mild affairs indeed.

After several sneak previews in New York and Los Angeles in August, The Department of Communication of the U.S. Catholic Conference finally did give *The Last Temptation of Christ* a "C" rating, as a warning that some Catholics could find it tasteless, but few representatives of the mainstream churches were stoking the furnaces of hell for the curious who wanted to see either what all the fuss was about, or how Martin Scorsese could possibly turn the ponderous five hundred page 1955 novel of Nikos Kazantzakis into a movie. The more virulent protests were left to Fundamentalist Christians (both Protestant and Catholic), and by late September even their constituencies dwindled as audiences had a chance to see the film and judge for themselves if the criticisms were overblown. Most people were

33

more bored than outraged by what they saw on the screen, and the controversy died out in a few short weeks. By the time the new films were released for the Christmas season, *The Last Temptation of Christ* was all but forgotten, a fate it richly deserved.

The path that led to this change to a more moderate response to films by the mainstream churches can be marked with a few milestones that reflect a more tolerant attitude in society as a whole. The return of the veterans from World War II, the baby boom, the move of the middle class from ethnic urban enclaves to the more homogenized suburbs, the advent of television, and perhaps a dozen other social factors surely contributed more to the change in attitude than any books from the universities or documents from the Vatican. At the same time, however, it is fair to select a few statements by church people to show how the changes in secular society at large were influencing mainstream religious thinking in the United States on the question of the movie industry. The relationship that had once been seen as somewhat adversarial, with church leaders trying to protect their members from immoral films, had become more collaborative, with religious writers and organizations stressing the positive artistic values of quality films. Concerns shifted from the moralistic to the artistic.

Preeminent among American religious writers calling for a new approach to film was William F. Lynch, S.J. (1916–1987), a professor at Georgetown University in Washington, D.C., long concerned with the relationship of theology to the creative imagination. In *The Image Industries*, a brief essay its publisher notes as having been "cited by the Thomas More Association as 'the most distinguished contribution to Catholic publishing in 1959,' " Father Lynch explores the popular arts—film, television and advertising—from the viewpoint not of morals but of imagination.[2]

The first moral issue he raises, and the most important, is freedom of the imagination, and he assigns specialized tasks to artists, theologians, critics and the universities in the ongoing struggle to keep the imagination free.[3] Lawyers, politicians and pressure groups do not enter into his consideration. Several chapters later he augments this notion of morality by adding the notion of "workmanship": "There is nothing more basically immoral than a contempt for workmanship and that contempt for human beings and audiences which goes with it."[4] His enemy throughout his study is the mass production of culture, which leads a small cadre of men and women in the communications industries to mass-produce and reproduce shoddy, predictable products in the belief that they are giving the public what it wants. He fears then that the few practitioners who control the media will use their low-quality products to manipulate the imagination and thus deprive it of its freedom. Through these reflections he has shifted the "moral" critique of the media away from the standard sex-and-violence or corruption-of-youth arguments to concerns about the systematic and indiscriminate anesthesia of the public imagination.

Ever the philosopher, Father Lynch grounds his line of reasoning in the writings of Jacques Maritain, whom he cites: "Art is concerned with the good of the work, not the good of man."[5] Continuing beyond the quotation Father Lynch provides in his text, one can see that Maritain backtracks a bit by insisting that the distinction is not perfectly neat. For the purposes of arguing his point to his own imagined audience, Father Lynch concludes the citation with Maritain's quote from Oscar Wilde: "The fact of a man's being a poisoner is nothing against his prose." In the rest of the paragraph, which Father Lynch does not quote, Maritain jousts with Wilde by saying that being a poisoner may not destroy his prose, but being a drug addict may. For the final riposte, he adds an observation from Baudelaire that an "exclusive passion for art . . . progressively destroys the human subject and finally . . . destroys art itself."[6]

With appropriate cautions for reading too much into texts by looking for what is omitted as well as what is present, it is fascinating that Father Lynch ended the citation where he did, faulting Maritain for presenting only a partial view. As is clear from the complete paragraph, Maritain did not believe in a complete separation between art and morality, as one might erroneously conclude from reading the half of Maritain's observation that Father Lynch presents. The reason for Father Lynch's truncated text may well be that both Maritain and Baudelaire retain vestiges of the kind of moral categories (drug addiction and self-destructive behavior) that are too close to the traditional concerns of moralistic critics and theologians. He omits Maritain's attempt to show that the distinction between art and morality is not absolute in order to present his own analysis in his own terms. Consequently, he opens the question of morality on a different level of discourse: for him, honesty and sensitivity on the part of the artist are more important moral issues than a presentation of tasteless sex or gratuitous violence. Showing contempt for the public imagination by dishonesty and insensitivity or by turning art into a for-profit image industry is the pervasive evil he wishes to confront.[7] Referring to drug addiction, as Maritain does, to clarify his distinction between art and morality seems to return the discussion to the older moral questions of personal behavior.

Since *The Image Industries* was a study that reflected the change of attitude among American Catholics and other mainstream religious communities, it may seem a bit churlish to cite its shortcomings, but they are significant.[8] The very limitations of the book, as they are recognized today, point out the direction that the dialogue has followed in America in the thirty years since the essay first appeared. Father Lynch redefined the issues and set the direction of the dialogue for years to come. His contribution was enormous. By way of comparison, the fact that the Wright Brothers never thought of using jet engines in no way detracts from their work, but aviation has soared a long way since Wilbur and Orville sputtered over the dunes at Kitty Hawk in 1903.

The inevitable limitation in his work is simply that Father Lynch, despite his keen awareness of the importance of the new image culture, was then and remained predominantly a man of letters, an admirable product of print culture. Trained as a philosopher with his doctoral work at Fordham University on the metaphysics of Plato, he approached film and television almost as though they were strange new forms of literature. He mentions individual films, directors and critics rarely, and when he does, he is quite uncomfortable with them and unsympathetic to them.

Father Lynch is, for example, worried about the montage theories of the Soviet director and theoretician Sergei Eisenstein (1898–1948). The political climate of the 1950s, with its near-hysterical fear of communism, may well have been a factor in his discomfort. It certainly did not help matters that Eisenstein's theory of montage is often described in the Hegelian terminology that provides the basis of Marx's dialectical materialism: thesis, antithesis, and synthesis. That is, shot A (thesis) plus shot B (antithesis) results in a new entity that is neither A nor B, nor A plus B, but a combination of both that is a new reality (synthesis).[9]

In fact, Eisenstein himself borrowed most of his theory and terminology not from Hegel, Engel, Feuerbach or Marx but from the famous film-and-psychology experiments of Lev Kuleshov (1899–1970). While working at the School of Art, Architecture and Sculpture in Moscow, Kuleshov spliced a close-up of an expressionless actor, Ivan Mozhukin, onto a shot of various objects. If he used a bloodstained knife, for example, he drew the response from viewers that the actor's face was that of a killer. Through the processes of perception, the viewers transformed the two realities shown them into something new that did, in fact, not exist either in reality or on the screen. Shot A (the expressionless face), the thesis, was transformed by being juxtaposed to shot B (the knife), the antithesis, in such a way that the two shots together created a new reality, a synthesis, which could be interpreted as the face of a killer. The art of the director or editor manipulated the imagination of the viewer to allow it to create the face of a killer from the neutral face of an expressionless actor. These experiments are widely accepted as providing the theoretical basis for montage, which is the essence of film art.[10]

Father Lynch understands quite well what Eisenstein means, but he reads the Soviet communist with no little suspicion: "He [Eisenstein] now declares that the original actual and free process has been all wrong, that the point of imaginative unity for a film must be determined in advance—there seems little doubt that he is referring to a state ideology commanded from above—and that every image and rhythm used by the director must *use* (I would say fixate or seduce) the audience. In a word, the artist must know what he wants to *do to* the souls in front of him" [italics his].[11]

What Father Lynch fears as a form of totalitarian mind control, to be expected of convinced communists, is little more than the fundamental premise of editing. In the process of shooting and cutting a film, a director must determine in advance what effect he or she is striving for. Naturally, then, in the hands of a skillful artist the selection of shots and their juxtaposition (montage is Eisenstein's word) will accomplish that preplanned effect in an audience.

In *Film Form*, Eisenstein describes the individual shot as a "brick" or "building block" which the director and editor must use to fashion a building of their choice.[12] Like many critics from a literary background, Father Lynch seemed to believe that in the making of a film, dramatic action merely unfolds in front of a camera, which is situated to get the best view. He seems little aware, at least on any practical level, of the purpose of shooting scripts, sets, lighting, and especially of editing, the factors that form the essence of film art.

This literary bias becomes blatant when Father Lynch devotes a section of his chapter "The Magnificent Imagination" to the praise of the original print version of *The Diary of Anne Frank*, which he cites with extensive quotations. Ever the classicist, Father Lynch derives his meaning of magnificent from its Latin roots: "to make great." His implication is that the original material is not great in itself, but the imagination can be manipulated into making it great. A "magnificent" imagination then is one that is bloated and makes the trivial into something ponderous, another form of the manipulation of the imagination that Father Lynch finds so troublesome.

His quotations from the book are impressive, but his introductory remarks show a lack of concern for the film as a film: "*The Diary* is now in production as a movie, and I do not wish to prejudge the film. . . . Certain of the production details make one fear that the film may deal heavy-handedly with the gentle art of Anne Frank."[13] He does not mention the director George Stevens or his earlier work, nor does he feel that it is necessary to see the film (rather than reading about its prerelease reports) in order to evaluate its emotional impact and artistic integrity.

In a parody Father Lynch invites his readers to recall the images Hollywood has characteristically used to recreate fear: "great war clouds and a violent storm, waves of marching men with steel-piked helmets, bursts of machine-gun fire, the falling bodies of slaughtered women and children, drum beats and screams."[14] He continues with several pages of additional quotations from *The Diary of Anne Frank* to establish his point that Hollywood and its masters of the image industries, "men of a new Roman Empire, the new masters of our imagination," could never rival the simple elegance of Anne Frank's prose.

The prose is certainly, as Father Lynch maintains, quite powerful, and the greatest film in the world could not rival or even reproduce it. Thus his argument is irrefutable, but at the same time the conclusion is meaningless. Prose is not film, nor is it music, painting, sculpture or ballet. Each of the media is different, and each medium has its own strengths and proper techniques. They cannot be compared without accounting for the differences, and no serious critic would attempt such a simple unqualified comparison today.

If Eisenstein's manipulation of the emotions of his audiences raises suspicions because of its echoes of communist ideology, then Alfred Hitchcock (1899–1980) found himself in trouble because of his reliance on fantasy. Father Lynch is particularly incensed by "A Voice in the Night," a science-fiction parable made for television.[15] Again, he expresses little interest in Hitchcock's other works, especially the extraordinary variety and quality of his films. The offending television story, as it is summarized, involves a man and a woman clinging to a log in the midst of a stormy sea. They reach land, enter a castle of peacefulness, gradually find the peace invading their bodies and eventually are transformed into sponges. The problem for Father Lynch is that the viewer is mesmerized by the power of the story and cannot "think of a ring, or of a sauce for a salad, or of a first meeting in a schoolhouse. You can neither think nor feel; the lines of nature, external and internal, have been obliterated."[16]

At first it may be surprising that a critic with such a strong classical background would object to the power of this type of fantasy. The great myths of Greece and Rome and their literature are filled with the most marvelous supernatural furniture, like monsters and conjurers, voyages to strange worlds of gods and magicians, visits to the dead and visions of the future. Why criticize Hitchcock for being like Homer or Virgil?

Father Lynch, as a man of the printed word, seems somewhat uncomfortable with the power of images to concentrate and direct the attention. For him, fantasy is acceptable only on the printed page, where the imagination transforms those endless combinations of lifeless printed letters into its own extremely lively mental pictures.[17] This bias is understandable, since, after all, the central moral issue of the essay is the freedom of the imagination. But simply because of the nature of the medium, an artist in film or television cannot allow the same degree of freedom to the audience as the literary artist.

Father Lynch, at least at this point in his thinking, does not seem to appreciate that the artist in film or television must go several steps further than the novelist or poet. The director must select and present actual concrete, visible objects to an audience; the writer merely suggests and turns the creative process over to the reader.[18] To return to the example of the ancient epics, Homer can suggest the beauty of Helen of Troy in ways as indirect as having old men on the walls comment as they see her that she is worth fighting this terrible war.[19] By contrast, if Hitchcock were to try to film the *Iliad*, he would have to select a living actress of a particular size, shape, personality and appearance to play Helen. He would have to dress her in a costume, hire someone for make-up and hair styling, put her in a setting, light her, select the camera angle and distance that would best reveal what he wants to say about her, and finally edit the shot into a sequence of other shots that may comment on her role in the story. The viewer is powerless to contest any of these decisions or to alter the final effect. It is then because of the nature of the medium rather than any sinister intent to manipulate the minds of the audience that the film artist must dominate the material and thus the audience to a far greater degree than the poet or novelist.

Thus as the film artist is more domineering, the audience for a visual presentation must necessarily become more passive and even submissive. For Father Lynch this factor constitutes a regrettable loss of freedom. This could be a debatable point, because, in fact, intelligent film viewing can be an extremely demanding and exhausting experience. In reality, however, so few people watch movies this way that in large part Father Lynch's regret is justifiable.

Despite the temptation to quibble on the point, it is important to note that to his credit Father Lynch finds this loss of freedom of imagination and manipulation the key problem with the Hitchcock television play. It is amazing that a cleric completely ignores the apparent "morally-uplifting" point of the parable. During the 1950s, many writers were concerned with "conformism," the Levittown culture of uniformity, lonely crowds and men in gray flannel suits. Hitchcock's story, as Father Lynch synopsizes it, certainly comments powerfully on the dangers of the cult of comfort. These elements of the content do not seem to interest him at all. He is more concerned with the dangerous impact of the medium on the imagination than of the benefits of edifying content on the soul.

As much as Father Lynch betrays understandable limitations in his perception of film and television as media and art forms, it is clear that he has moved far beyond the traditional interests of the religious communities, who would have praised the Hitchcock program for its elevating message.

Other transitional works followed *The Image Industries* and continued along the path that Father Lynch had opened. In 1961 *Movies, Morals and Art* paired Frank Getlein (1921–   ), then art critic for *The New Republic*, a resolutely secular journal of politics and the arts, with Harold C. Gardiner, S.J. (1904–1969), then literary editor of *America*, the national Jesuit weekly magazine of commentary. That same year with Dorothy Getlein, Mr. Getlein published *Christianity in Modern Art,* and Father Gardiner was known beyond the readership of the magazine for his books *Norms for the Novel* (1953) and *Catholic Viewpoint on Censorship* (1959).

Like Father Lynch, both the lay art critic and the clerical literary critic approached film as something analogous to their own area of specialization. This had two results. First, both authors treated film as a serious art form, something akin to their own traditional arts, namely literature and painting. But second, by doing that, they had to rely on the terminology and methods of a largely borrowed critical analysis, as though film were a kind of painting or literature. Also like Father Lynch, both critics showed some familiarity with cinema concepts, such as montage, for example, but the terms did not seem terribly important in their subsequent presentations.

In the second essay in the volume, which for present purposes will be treated first here, Father Gardiner begins his reflections in the traditional clerical fashion by demanding a "status quaestionis." The point of the inquiry, he avers, is to determine when and how movies can be considered moral or immoral. Since he is contributing the second essay, he presumes that the reader is already familiar with the artistic analysis presented by Mr. Getlein. He sees his contribution as a return to the moral questions, with a difference however. He insists on a holistic approach to morality, rather than a catalogue of offending scenes and themes. He writes: "The *total* artistic judgment, the *complete* critical evaluation of a piece of art, includes a moral dimension" [italics his].[20] By the end of his initial chapter he proposes an agenda for reflection that looks very much like a return to the traditional one posed by religious communities from the earliest days of the nickelodeon: "What is an immoral film? How much of it can be immoral without making the entire film subject to condemnation? Does any subject matter, of itself, make a film immoral or does it all depend on the mode of treatment? Can a film be immoral for some viewers and morally acceptable to others?"[21]

As a man of letters, Father Gardiner argues that film artists deserve as much latitude as writers in dealing with sordid subject matter. The question then is not one of content but of style of presentation, both for fiction and for films: "It is not so much the subject matter as such, but the mode and tone of the presentation, which will largely determine the moral climate of a film."[22] Further, citing Pope Pius XI's encyclical *Vigilanti Cura* of 1936 as his inspiration, he affirms that any universal code or rating system is virtually impossible. Cultural, personal, and educational factors allow for a wide variety of responses to any individual film. Father Gardiner echoes the mentality of the Hays Office with his concern that if sin is presented, it must be presented as sin, but he opens up the concept of sinfulness to include topics such as materialism and moral indifferentism rather than the usual questions of sex and violence.

For the greater part of his essay, then, Father Gardiner provides a sophisticated reworking of traditional questions. In the final chapter, however, he turns to the positive value of films and argues that they, like any other art form, have the power to provide moral benefits for their audiences. In this context, his notion of morality is a distinct change from the traditional proposition that the viewing of "good" films, that is, those in which virtue is rewarded and sin is punished, can provide inspiration and motivation for people to "do good and avoid evil," or, in Catholic terminology consecrated by generations of use in the Baltimore Catechism, "to avoid the near occasions of sin." He is interested in films that "foster spiritual growth by expanding the horizons of our charity."[23] By seeing films of excellence, Father Gardiner argues that viewers can experience the moral struggles of movie heroes and grow in understanding of problems as they exist in distant regions of the globe.

Father Gardiner concludes his reflections on a homiletic note: "All art is but a dim reflection of the primal creative act, and as God could not create except from and with love, so the artist pours his love into what springs from his mind, and his small creation will generate love in those who rejoice in it."[24] To dust off the jargon of psychology, he rejects "behavior modification" as the spiritual value of quality films and looks instead to a deepening of insight and breadth of vision, which tilts his understanding of the moral values toward the aesthetic. He has, as it were, entered through the front door of the old, militant Legion of Decency, examined the traditional furniture, and quietly redecorated the place with bright modern designs without raising a fuss.

Mr. Getlein is equally quiet in designing and proposing his own new decor. For example, he devotes a chapter of his essay to "Art in General and in Particular," in which he tries to find a functional understanding, if not definition, of art. Quite expeditiously, in his second of six chapters he reaches a conclusion quite similar to the one Father Gardiner reached at the end of his reflection. "Art," he writes, "has the power to catch us up in a vision of itself which mysteriously often turns out to be a vision also of ourselves and reality at large, including the reality of God."[25] Mr. Getlein rounds up the usual suspects for this kind of discussion from Aristotle to Maritain, but then continues his argumentation by explaining that the cinema has its own proper techniques and characteristics that qualify it to be called an art form in its own right.

As he continues the discussion, Mr. Getlein devotes a section of a chapter to D.W. Griffith (1875–1948), whom he calls the "creator of the art of the film," and he explains why he justifies that extravagant but perfectly accurate statement. Then he moves on to other "artists," like the great comedians of the silent film, Harold Lloyd, Harry Langdon, Buster Keaton, and, of course, Charlie Chaplin. In the final chapter, he lambastes *South Pacific* (Joshua Logan, 1958) for distorting sex and most pious films from Cecil B. DeMille's Bible spectaculars to *Going My Way* (Leo McCarey, 1944) for distorting religion.[26] In both topics he moves a bit beyond the predictable. On the question of sex he is more concerned with the plausibility of the relationships of the characters than with the propriety of lyrics, costumes, and dances. When he discusses religion, he is more irate about easy sentimentality that poses as piety than about respectful treatment of churches, doctrines, and clerics.

The concluding, summary statement deserves quoting as an important signpost of the shift in direction in Catholic criticism: "When Catholics allow the irritations of the industry to make Catholic interest in the motion picture exclusively a matter of holding a sexual Geiger counter against *décolletage* and *double entendre*, they write off art, demean sex and betray religion."[27]

Several points are important in Mr. Getlein's presentation. His idea of a religious critique of films passes far beyond the censorship model that even at the time of his writing is rapidly passing out of vogue. He recognizes film as an art form, and one with its own methods. Among these he mentions editing, lighting and music, even though these factors are not terribly important in his own analysis. He acknowledges the central role of the director, and he mentions several by name. He seems aware that this field he is exploring is something with a content of its own that should be recognized if one is to write about its theory with any authority, just as a critic can be expected to have seen, studied and read about many paintings and painters before formulating a theory of the aesthetics of form, mass and color in the world of the impressionists.

Finally, and perhaps most importantly, in his positive approach to film, Mr. Getlein sees as at least one of its goals "a vision also of ourselves and reality at large, including the reality of God." Although he wrote independently without the collaboration of his co-contributor, his conclusions are quite similar to Father Gardiner's. Films and film criticism do then continue to have a moral impact, not in the morally uplifting sense of Jane Addams and the progressives, nor in the negative sense of the Hays Office and the early Legion of Decency, but rather the critics believe that a good film, like a good specimen of any other art form, provides a vision or insight into the world that may eventually lead to a clearer vision of the role of the creator. The two essays, starting from a different set of questions, eventually show a remarkable convergence.

The thinking reflected in the works of Father Lynch, Mr. Getlein and Father Gardiner shows that by the early 1960s film was in a position to be taken seriously as an art form by the religious communities. In addition, film, like the other arts, provides a valuable tool for insight into the world and, ultimately, to its creator. As such, it would not be long until film study moved into the world of academe.

Used skillfully, cinema could become a useful handmaid to the queen of the sciences, theology. In other contexts, this young maiden, an art form born in this century, could be enlisted, cajoled or wooed into the service of other traditional academic disciplines as well. As will become evident, the usefulness and flexibility of films would be enormous assets in getting the study of film moved into the universities, both secular and religious, as Father Lynch forcefully proposed even while expressing reservations about the power of the media over the imagination.[28] On the other hand, using film as an adjunct to something else will temporarily slow down the development and presentation of film as a suitable field for its own academic discipline with its own proper methodology.

In the 1960s, then, film entered the curriculum often as a dependent satrapy in academic departments whose main interests lay far from cinema or television. An enterprising student could take a film course as an elective for English requirements, for fine arts, for speech and theater, for psychology or philosophy. Film, then, even if it had its own course listing in the official catalogue, would become an auxiliary for something else, like an elaborate audiovisual aid for the main business of the department.

In English departments, for example, film could provide a painless way to present the plot outlines of classic novels to slow students. A more sophisticated approach was provided by George Bluestone's *Novels into Film: The Metamorphosis of Fiction into Cinema*, which first appeared in 1957.[29] After offering a sixty-four page theoretical introduction to the differences between literature and film, Professor Bluestone leads his readers through a cross-media analysis of six novels commonly offered to college undergraduates: Liam O'Flaherty's *The Informer*, Emily Bronte's *Wuthering Heights*, Jane Austen's *Pride and Prejudice*, John Steinbeck's *The Grapes of Wrath*, Walter Van Tilburg Clark's *The Ox-Bow Incident*, and Gustave Flaubert's *Madame Bovary*. By showing students how a story is transformed as it is adapted into a screenplay and then photographed and edited, he attempts to explain not only the original work but the nature and techniques of the two art forms: the novel and the film.

Although the use of film in various departments within a college or university was far from an ideal arrangement for the development of film study as part of a liberal arts program, at least the field had begun to reach the campuses, and some faculty and some students were beginning to discuss films as something important. The sole portable 16mm. projector with speakers built into the carrying case and wheeled into a classroom on an ad hoc basis from the audiovisual department in the library—if the chemistry department wasn't using it that day to show one of those promotional films from DuPont on the wonders of the polymer—began to be replaced with stationary equipment, screening rooms designed and equipped for the showing of films, good sound systems, window shades that actually shut out sunlight and chairs that permitted the three-hour version of *The Birth of a Nation* to be shown as a somewhat more pleasurable experience than a three hour visit to an orthodontist. Film had at least arrived in the academic world, and throughout the 1960s it began to move out of the guest room and build a home of its own.

Another transitional phase during this period was the advent of the film society, which became a fixture on many campuses and in other settings as well. One widely circulated book about film societies was *The Filmviewer's Handbook*, written by Emile G. McAnany, S.J. and Robert Williams, S.J., and published in paperback by Deus Books in 1965.[30] In the days long before videotape, forming film societies was an efficient way for pre-Panasonic film buffs to see and share 16mm. prints of their favorite classic films. These informal organizations would often prepare a complete film series lasting through the semester or the entire year, complete with printed program notes, an introduction by a speaker, and a panel or open discussion after the screening. As the authors offer suggestions for designing a program of films for a society, they explain that these series could either be a cross-section of films to appeal to varied tastes or be organized around a theme: genres (like Westerns, musicals or documentaries), directors, nations or even stars.[31]

Long before videotape blossomed on the shelves of every public library, drugstore and supermarket in the land, foreign and classic American film distribution was limited to "art houses," those few small theaters located in affluent neighborhoods in only a few large cities. Even they generally specialized in foreign-language films rather than American classics, and to keep the international ambience they offered their clientele espresso rather than popcorn. John Wayne would have been stopped at the door.

In their introduction the authors direct their suggestions about forming film societies to a wide variety of constituencies: "college and university film societies who want to be more than 16mm. 'art theaters,' independent film societies, church groups, women's clubs and business and professional organizations who, by means of some kind of organized viewing of movies, desire to add to their knowledge and appreciation of the motion pictures. Further, it is possible that this handbook can be used by secondary and college teachers who are trying to add movie appreciation classes to their schools either as regular classroom material or as an extracurricular activity."[32] It may be indicative of the involvement of the churches in this phase of film study that the two authors of this particular book, addressed as it is to many types of nonreligious educational and social groups, are members of the Society of Jesus (Jesuits), a Catholic religious order, and this Deus Book was published by The Missionary Society of St. Paul the Apostle (Paulists).

The intent of the work, as well as the readership these authors envision, clearly extends beyond narrowly religious concerns. They hope to help interested parties of all sorts to collaborate more effectively in furthering the appreciation of film as film. The theory is admirable, and no doubt many film societies functioned exactly that way. On the other hand, it is not difficult to imagine sponsoring organizations selecting films and preparing presentations to further their own particular goals. Would it be altogether unreasonable, for example, for a Catholic chaplain of a Newman Center at a secular university to sponsor a series of films to raise questions of faith for his membership? Discussions of films have always been recognized as excellent devices to allow people to explore controversial or personal issues under the illusion of objectivity. It is, for example, much safer for the young people at the Newman Club center to discuss the loss of faith of the Knight in *The Seventh Seal* (Ingmar Bergman, 1956) than to articulate and share their own personal religious struggles.

Little wonder then that so many of the films featured by film societies were theme movies that could lead a group into a serious discussion of some social, psychological or theological issue. American films, thought at the time to contain little more than mindless entertainment in comparison to the weighty questions explored by European and even Asian directors like Akira Kurosawa and Satyajit Ray, received surprisingly little attention. Of the seventy-seven films shown most frequently in American film societies from 1961–1964, only two of the top ten features were American: *Citizen Kane* (Orson Welles, 1941) and *The General* (Buster Keaton, 1926), although an evening of Charlie Chaplin shorts must be included as well. Only seven American features appear among the remaining sixty-seven films on the list, but as a monument of good sense two of those star the Marx Brothers.[33] Neither John Ford nor Frank Capra gets a mention.

As a fairly safe speculation, one suspects that the programs in film appreciation in the colleges reflected this same perspective, and certainly departments of theology or philosophy in the colleges would have found classic foreign-language films more readily suited to their own purposes than the American product. Even more than the weighing and worrying about major theological themes, the great hunt for religious symbols became a more popular campus sport than tossing a frisbee. Every broken loaf of bread out of an Italian lunchbox could be identified as a eucharistic symbol, and every soul-tormented Swede who stretched out his arms to lean against a door frame became a crucified Christ figure. This was a period when subtitles were a sure sign of respectability, and in the patois of the faculty clubs Fellini-and-Bergman seemed to have become one word, meaning the opposite of everything that was wrong with American films.

At the close of the decade, a refreshing change from the American inferiority complex can be perceived in *Theology Through Film,* written by Neil P. Hurley, S.J. in 1970. As its title states plainly, the purpose of this book is to put films at the service of theology. Young people, according to Father Hurley writing at the close of the terrible 1960s, are exploring questions of "Vietnam, racial integration, the democratization of educational and economic opportunity, a greater participation of society and politics, more latitude in forms of life style (hair, sex, dress and even drugs) and even an acceptance of youth as sexually endowed human beings. No one will deny that motion pictures face these issues—*now.*"[34] The strategy, then, is to raise questions for young people through films and lead them toward a theological reflection on the questions that may or may not proceed toward more traditional theological discourse, like scripture and the ordinary teachings of the churches.

As he develops his "cinematic theology," Father Hurley invites his readers and their students to investigate through the use of key films questions as diverse as Freedom, Conscience, Sex, Death, Evil, Grace and Sacrificial Love. In the penultimate chapter, entitled "A Cinematic Theology of the Future," he not only suggests a study of science/future fiction films as a form of secular prophecy, but he invites his readers to look at the values operative in recent films to gather hints of the values operative today that will shape the future.[35]

In the final chapter, Father Hurley presents an alphabetical list of films that could be profitably used in the theology classroom along with a brief notation offering suggestions of some topics that these films could introduce.[36] Here, two refreshing changes appear in the college "use" and religious treatment of films. First, the book is still clearly an effort to make films a form of visual aid to the teaching of another field, and thus much of the methodology, like the types of questions raised and the conclusions targeted, comes from theology, not film. Still, despite his assigning film a subsidiary function, Father

Hurley does show a certain sophistication in dealing with film as a medium and with individual films that is lacking in many of the earlier studies coming from church professionals. He is aware of treating films as entities with their own individual qualities that can be criticized in their own right before they yield center stage to the theological questions. He cites Marshall McLuhan often and frequently with uncritical enthusiasm, as would be expected in any book published on this topic in 1970.

To his credit, Father Hurley wants those who read the book and follow his suggestions to be knowledgeable of the particular genius of both the medium and the particular film they are using. *Wild Strawberries* (Ingmar Bergman, 1957), for example, is not merely a facile springboard to get an au courant professor and his class into a discussion of a Christian theology of death; it is a work of art in its own right. Theology is still Father Hurley's major interest, but he shows an understanding of the medium that was not present in Father Lynch's earlier seminal work.[37]

The second refreshing change is the striking rehabilitation of the American film that Father Hurley's selection of model films reflects. The list contains sixty-six major entries, with other films mentioned for purposes of additional study or comparison. Of these, thirty-seven are American films, and several others are English language films. No doubt many of the titles and this American tilt were part of a deliberate strategy to make the material more accessible to American college students, but nonetheless it is significant that more than half the movies selected are American. At this point in time, people in the churches and in the academy are beginning to overcome their addiction to subtitles. They are no longer apologetic about recommending *Rosemary's Baby* (Roman Polanski, 1968) or *2001: A Space Odyssey* (Stanley Kubrick, 1968). Even if they are not yet ready to admit that these works have value in themselves, at least they can be identified as the films that young people see, address the questions that interest them, and thus are worthy of serious attention.

If popularity and accessibility by young people are important criteria in selecting films for use on campus, why include foreign-language titles at all? After all, children of the television generation are notoriously impatient with subtitles, as they are with silent film, even, surprisingly, with the madly energetic early comedies of Chaplin and Keaton. As part of his notion of "cinematic theology," Father Hurley, who once served an overseas ministry in Chile, places great value in expanding the horizons of students to include sympathy with foreign countries. He writes: "It is my belief that motion pictures stimulate a new kind of awareness whereby moviegoers are allowed to be present at the total unfolding of the human spirit in all the varying conditions in which it strives for transcendence. In other words, film helps a global audience to see itself for the first time as a part of a transcendental community."[38] In this idea can be found echoes of Marshall McLuhan's once fashionable notion of the world's becoming a "global village" through the power of worldwide mass communications systems.[39]

Foreign films then are important for opening the horizons of students and raising questions in different cultural contexts. For this reason they should be included in a theology program for American students. Yet in no way does Father Hurley imply that foreign language films are qualitatively better than American films, nor does he suggest that they propose more profound theological theses than American films. This represents a remarkable change from the Fellini-and-Bergman snobbery of the previous decade.

Why did American films suddenly reach such a new level of respect among Americans, in the universities, and among church professionals, who a few years earlier were willing to canonize Fellini and Bergman as latter-day incarnations of Aquinas and Luther and excoriate Hollywood as Sodom with palm trees?

NOTES

1. Richard A. Blake, "The Universal Christ," and Richard H. Hirsch, "The Film and Its Implications," *America* 159, 5 (August 20–27, 1988) 99–102, and Richard A. Blake, "An Autopsy on 'Temptation,'" *America* 160, 8 (March 4, 1989) 199–201. Mr. Hirsch writes as the secretary for communications of the U.S. Catholic Conference, whose office now has assumed many of the roles of the Legion of Decency and the National Catholic Office for Motion Pictures. His reasoned tone in putting forth his own position (and one may infer that of his office) and his impatience with some of the more outspoken critics are a fine example of the evolution of the official Catholic attitude toward the motion picture industry.

2. William F. Lynch, S.J., *The Image Industries* (New York: Sheed and Ward, 1959). The citation appears on the dust jacket of Father Lynch's next book, *Christ and Apollo: The Dimensions of the Literary Imagination* (New York: Sheed and Ward, 1960).

3. *Image Industries*, pp. 9–18.

4. *Image Industries,* p. 114.

5. Jacques Maritain, *Creative Intuition in Art and Poetry,* Bollin-
gen Series XXXV 1 (New York: Pantheon, 1955), p. 50, quoted in
Image Industries, pp. 136–137.

6. Maritain, p. 51.

7. The level of abstraction at this point makes the argument difficult to follow. After maintaining that the theologian and the artist
really have separate tasks, he offers several points of convergence in
their concerns that would invite collaboration: "For what the artist is
essentially interested in is the expression, involving judgments but in
the most concrete terms, of the total life and movement of the soul as
it engages with the reality outside of itself, especially with the reality
of each current moment of history. I do not think it too much to say
that indeed the artist wishes to 'save' that soul in the sense that he
wishes to keep its various acts of sensibility straight and real and even
moving with a freedom that really belongs to the children of God"—
Image Industries, p. 140.

8. Since the American scene is under discussion in these pages,
the developments in other countries and documents from Rome are
somewhat beyond present concerns. It should be mentioned at this
point, however, that writers like Father Lynch, the board of the Legion of Decency (National Catholic Office for Motion Pictures) and
reviewers in Catholic periodicals like *America* and *Commonweal*
found ample support in their work from *Vigilanti Cura* of Pope Pius
XI (1936) and *Miranda Prorsus* of Pope Pius XII (1957). In October
1955 Pope Pius XII gave an address to theater owners on "the ideal
film": "An ideal film, then, can also represent evil, sin and corruption. But let it do so with serious intent and in a becoming manner, in
such a way that its vision may help deepen knowledge of life and of
man, and improve and elevate the soul." Quoted in Frank Getlein and
Harold C. Gardiner, S.J., *Movies, Morals and Art* (New York: Sheed
and Ward, 1961), p. 166.

9. David A. Cooke's *A History of the Narrative Film* (New York:
Norton, 1981), pp. 171–177, is a recent restatement of the dialectical
understanding of montage in film editing.

10. A succinct summary of the Kuleshov experiments and their
relationship to the theories of Eisenstein can be found in Ephraim
Katz, *The Film Encyclopedia* (New York: Perigee, 1979), pp. 672–
673. Peter Wollen, in *Signs and Meaning in the Cinema* (Bloomington,
Ind.: Univ. of Indiana Press, 1969), devotes a chapter to the develop-

ment of Eisenstein's theories and especially his relationship to Kuleshov, Marx and Engels—pp. 39–50.

11. *Image Industries,* p. 79.

12. Sergei Eisenstein, *Film Form: Essays in Film Theory,* ed. and trans. by Jay Leyda (Cleveland: Meridian, 1964), pp. 36–37. Eisenstein, world famous for his films *Strike* (1924), *Potemkin* (1925), *Ten Days That Shook the World,* also known as *October* (1928), *Alexander Nevsky* (1938) and *Ivan the Terrible* (1942–46), became a faculty member on the State Cinema Technicum in 1928 and later was appointed professor of cinema research at the All Union State Cinema Institute. In 1947 he became head of the Cinema Research Center. The first draft of *Film Sense,* a collection of his essays, was compiled in 1946. Soon after the revolution, the Soviets organized film schools to train the directors who would unify their own people into a new nation and carry the message of the revolution to the outside world. Although the purpose of these institutes was obviously propagandistic, the Soviet achievement both in film-making and in theoretical writing was remarkable. Nothing like them existed in the United States, where the movies were considered little more than commercial entertainment, created, as it turned out, by a tiny band of geniuses who grasped the possibilities of these money-making gadgets and created an art form out of them. Unlike the Russians and the French, the Americans never showed much interest in writing books about cinematic theory, nor, it might be safely said, in reading them. They were too busy making films and money.

13. *Image Industries,* p. 103.

14. *Image Industries,* p. 105.

15. *Image Industries,* pp. 100–101.

16. *Image Industries,* p. 102.

17. To be fair to Father Lynch, it must be remembered that the important studies on the impact of different media on the senses were not yet in circulation: Marshall McLuhan's *Explorations in Communication* (Boston: Beacon, 1958), *The Gutenberg Galaxy* (Toronto: Univ. of Toronto Press, 1962) and *Understanding Media* (New York: McGraw-Hill, 1964). Much of McLuhan's inspiration can be traced to his colleague Harold A. Innis' *The Bias of Communication* (Toronto: Univ. of Toronto Press, 1951), a book that gained little attention until it was reissued in 1964 with an introduction by McLuhan. Although he deals little with images and concentrates on the rise of print civilization, Walter Ong's *Ramus, Method and the Decay of Dialogue*

(Cambridge: Harvard Univ. Press, 1960) presents a useful paradigm for understanding the different effects and methods for perception through different media.

18. Siegfried Kracauer in *Theory of Film: The Redemption of Physical Reality* (New York: Oxford Univ. Press, 1965) presents a book-length treatment of the question of the concrete in the aesthetics of film. Of particular interest is his chapter "Basic Concepts," pp. 27–40.

19. Homer, *The Iliad*, Book III, lines 156–160. The prose translation of E.V. Rieu, *The Iliad* (Baltimore: Penguin, 1950), p. 68, reads: " 'Who on earth,' they asked one another, 'could blame the Trojan and Achaean men at arms for suffering so long for such a woman's sake? Indeed, she is the very image of an immortal goddess. All the same, and lovely as she is, let her sail home and not stay here to vex us and our children after us.' "

20. *Movies, Morals and Art*, pp. 103ff.

21. *Movies, Morals and Art*, p. 114.

22. *Movies, Morals and Art*, p. 110.

23. *Movies, Morals and Art*, p. 177.

24. *Movies, Morals and Art*, p. 179.

25. *Movies, Morals and Art*, p. 23.

26. *Movies, Morals and Art*, pp. 85–99.

27. *Movies, Morals and Art*, p. 99.

28. In *Image Industries*, pp. 18–19, Father Lynch urges the universities to develop programs to train critics of popular culture. His complaint that many such programs are directed toward the training of technicians rather than humanists was at the time of his writing and remains today quite justifiable. Again, he is perfectly justified in maintaining that "these industries or professions [the media] can do a much better job of technical education than the universities can." Yes, on-the-job training with professionals is almost always more effective than classroom projects in teaching the technical side of media production. Although one can readily agree with much of Father Lynch's critique of technical training, still he does not express in these paragraphs any awareness that even the most humanistic critic needs some familiarity with the technical side of media production and distribution in order to make informed judgments on the quality of the artifact. In his thinking as expressed in this chapter, the interested philosopher or literary critic seems to have all the tools needed to become a media critic. This age of enlightened amateurs was a necessary and valuable transitional phase to serious media study in the universities.

29. George Bluestone, *Novels Into Film: The Metamorphosis of Fiction into Film* (Baltimore: The Johns Hopkins University Press, 1957).

30. Emile G. McAnany, S.J., and Robert Williams, S.J., in *The Filmviewer's Handbook* (Glen Rock, N.J.: Paulist, 1965), pp. 71–152, provide a popular handbook for establishing and running a successful film society. Although the intent of the authors is nonsectarian, the comments of these Jesuit collaborators are especially suited to the context of a church affiliated school or church film society.

31. McAnany and Williams, pp. 160–185.

32. McAnany and Williams, p. 9.

33. McAnany and Williams, p. 157. The films are *The Birth of a Nation* (D.W. Griffith, 1915), *Intolerance* (D.W. Griffith, 1916), *Grand Hotel* (Edmund Goulding, 1932), *The Night of the Hunter* (Charles Laughton, 1955), *The Magnificent Ambersons* (Orson Welles, 1942), and two Marx Brothers' films, *Duck Soup* (Leo McCarey, 1933), and *A Night at the Opera* (Sam Wood, 1935). Robert Flaherty's long classic documentaries, *Nanook of the North* (1922) and *Louisiana Story* (1948) also made the list.

34. Neil F. Hurley, *Theology Through Film* (New York: Harper & Row, 1970), pp. ix–x.

35. Hurley, pp. 166–170.

36. Hurley, pp. 177–190.

37. While Father Lynch criticized *The Diary of Anne Frank*, a film he had not seen, from a literary point of view, Father Hurley calls it "George Stevens's film of one of the great humanistic documents of this century. The atmosphere of brooding evil in Nazi-occupied Holland does not dampen the ardor of youth. As the Jewish adolescent in hiding with her family, Millie Perkins embodies the courage of her race. The workings of grace—faith, hope and charity—are artistically insinuated in this touching movie about one of the less anonymous religious martyrs of the Third Reich"—Hurley, p. 180. Mention of the director, the atmosphere and the leading actress was not important to Father Lynch's analysis a decade earlier.

38. Hurley, p. 171.

39. *The Gutenberg Galaxy*, pp. 31–32, is the most direct expression of the concept of the "global village," and in this brief passage McLuhan acknowledges a debt to Pierre Teilhard deChardin, citing at length *The Phenomenon of Man* (New York: Harper & Brothers, 1959), p. 240. As the transistor miniaturized communications equipment, in the 1980s the experience of receiving signals became more privatized in a way that neither Teilhard nor McLuhan could have

anticipated. Listeners and viewers now use the media to create their own private worlds and shut out external reality. For a fuller explanation of questions that have arisen about the validity of the global village concept, see Richard A. Blake, S.J., "Condominiums in the Global Village," *America* 146, 22 (June 6, 1982), 433–436.

Chapter Three

FROM TEACHER TO LEARNER

As might be expected, American films rose to new levels of respectability not from American efforts but as the result of several unrelated developments in Europe and through the devotion of a small coterie of tireless French film critics who sharpened their critical vision in the Cinémathèque Française and honed their polemic skills in the pages of *Cahiers du Cinéma*.

The phrase "as might be expected" is not intended ironically. It is a statement of fact. As film studies moved into the universities, foreign films attracted the most attention simply because they were more suited to the academic demands of the various departments that "used" films than were the American products. In the early days, "Fellini and Bergman" were respectable. John Ford was not. Outside the country, the burden of snobbery was not quite as overwhelming, and French critics could view the American film with much more openness than their American counterparts.

There are good reasons for the delayed entry of American films into the American academic world. American film-makers have traditionally been reticent about their personal philosophy, techniques or theories behind their work, and when they do wade into waters of critical theory through interviews, they are very quickly in over their heads and often become muddled, pompous or coy. D.W. Griffith, Charlie Chaplin, Orson Welles, Frank Capra, John Ford and Woody Allen, all generally recognized as great film-makers, composed no great theoretical essays. Frank Capra's fine autobiography, *The Name Above the Title,* is revealing of both the artist and his methods, but its method is anecdotal rather than systematic.[1] In the academic world, a field without a respectable printed literature is not a respectable field of serious academic inquiry.

Perhaps the most illuminating statement by an American film-maker on his theory of film was made by Mack Sennett (1880–1960), the comic genius behind the Keystone Kops, Fatty Arbuckle, Mabel Normand, Charlie Chaplin and a dozen other stars of the silent come-dies, when he said: "We made funny pictures as fast as we could for money."[2] The statement has a refreshing honesty about it, and should be taken very, very seriously. The American film industry, from its beginnings to the age of the *Rambo* and *Rocky* assembly-line produc-tions, is a commercial enterprise.

Producers are investors who in other circumstances may just as easily have invested in car washes or fast-food franchises. They look for a return on their investment, and they hire professionals to secure that return for them. In the American ethos, directors have tradition-ally been considered merely technicians, people who get an idea from the writers and move it from script to screen as quickly and cheaply as possible. In Hollywood, by far the most important members of the producers' teams have been and remain the movie stars, those few personalities, some of whom are competent actors, who guarantee that people will go out and buy tickets. Here's a simple test: How many people know who directed any of the *Rambo* series? Or care? But everybody knows that the series stars Sylvester Stallone. Quite simply, people pay to see John Wayne, not John Ford.

This was not always the case. In the earliest days actors were just as anonymous as directors. Their names rarely appeared on the screen or in the ads. But as early as 1910 the notion of marketing personalities was developed by Carl Laemmle, founder of Indepen-dent Motion Pictures, when he lured the actress Florence Lawrence, then known only as "The Biograph Girl," into his own Independent Motion Picture Company. At that time Biograph was a member of the Motion Picture Patents Company, which was really a trade associa-tion masterminded by Thomas Alva Edison to exercise complete con-trol over the new industry.[3] He and his associates foolishly believed that the heart of the motion picture industry was technology rather than fantasy, and they thought that by controlling patents on the equipment, they could build a monopoly. Thus in plain language the Patents Company was a trust, and it was identified as such by the U.S. government in 1913. Four years later it was ordered to dissolve.[4] In recognizing that he was dealing in dreams rather than hardware, Carl Laemmle had a much better intuitive sense of the industry than Edison's business and legal advisors.

The Patents Company steadfastly refused to use the real names of its performers. It was afraid, with good reason, that once these actors became known as individual personalities, they would demand higher salaries and would even shop around for other companies to meet their salary requirements. This, of course, would have been a form of competition that ran counter to the whole idea of establishing a trust in the first place.

Carl Laemmle's Independent Motion Pictures (IMP), a mite in comparison to Patents, gambled on being able to meet the competition by first creating celebrities through publicity, and then marketing their names as well as the movies they appeared in. Shortly after he hired Florence Lawrence from Biograph, he leaked the story to the press that she had been killed in a trolley car accident in St. Louis. The news might have gone unnoticed, but the next day he took full-page ads in the trade press to deny the report. He claimed that the whole story was a hoax, invented by Patents to hide the fact that the actress, known to the public only as "The Biograph Girl," had been lured away from her old studio to work for Independent.

Laemmle's double invention (really a double outright lie) worked perfectly. Crowds gathered to see for themselves that "The Biograph Girl" was indeed alive and had been reborn as "The Imp Girl." Naturally, films featuring the now famous Florence Lawrence attracted audiences, and Laemmle found it to his advantage to attract other actors, transform them into movie stars and keep them in the public eye with slickly orchestrated publicity stunts. By 1912, with the introduction of *Photoplay,* the age of the fan magazine had begun —with the generous cooperation of the studios and a new occupational group, the personal publicity agents.[5]

Two years after the death and resurrection of Florence Lawrence, Carl Laemmle raided Biograph again. This time he proudly announced that "Little Mary is an Imp now," soon to be known by her own name, Mary Pickford. Her fame would last longer than Florence Lawrence's, and Carl Laemmle was well on his way to creating his Universal Pictures empire, which for its part would last longer than Biograph or any other of the Patents Company members. While all these stars were being launched into the Hollywood heavens, few film-goers paid any attention to who was directing them, unless perhaps Cecil B. DeMille or D.W. Griffith was involved.

Critics and reviewers were not in much of a position to change the situation. Film criticism, as we know it today, had not yet been invented. The fan magazines generated puffery, and the trade papers counted the receipts. Journalists, assigned to the motion picture beat, simply told their readers whether or not they would enjoy seeing the film, and thus the craft of reviewing, as distinct from criticizing, came to be. Moralists and other social impact critics looked at films' influence on society, and literary critics, with their borrowed methodology, focused on the narrative and psychological qualities of the screenplays. Naturally, these favored adaptations of lofty literary and dramatic works. And so the status of the American film, with its audience's fascination with stars and general disregard of directors, remained in an artistic and critical limbo for nearly forty years.

In Europe, and in particular in Italy, in the closing days of World War II, a dramatic refocusing on the art of the film began with European output and would soon lead to a massive revaluation of Hollywood. The neorealist school of Italian directors presented a different type of motion picture to the world's screens. Some few stars, like Anna Magnani and Silvana Mangano, emerged from this movement, but more often than not the lead actors were nonprofessionals. Reviewers did not recognize them, nor could they pronounce or spell their names. The script writers fared no better. By default, then, critics were forced to discuss directors and cinematic styles. And what material for discussion they had: Luchino Visconti's *Ossessione* (1942), Roberto Rossellini's *Open City* (1945) and *Paisan* (1946), Vittorio DeSica's *Shoeshine* (1946) and *Bicycle Thief* (1948), Giuseppe DeSantis' *Bitter Rice* (1949), and perhaps a dozen other near greats. This seemed to be much stronger stuff than the "parade of stars" style of MGM musicals coming out of Hollywood during the same period.

This neorealist school of directors put in place the foundation of a national cinema that would, a few years later, produce Federico Fellini and Michelangelo Antonioni, both dominant voices in the 1960s. These were two of the names that reached celebrity status during the years of American fascination with foreign-language films, and they were joined by Ingmar Bergman of Sweden, Luis Buñuel of Spain, Jean Renoir, Alain Resnais and the nouvelle vague directors of France, François Truffaut and Jean-Luc Godard, Satyajit Ray from India, and Akira Kurosawa and Kenji Mizoguchi from Japan. Little wonder that American film critics, looking at Hollywood movies, suffered a massive inferiority complex during those years. Among thoughtful Americans, American film certainly seemed to suffer by comparison. It was, according to the common dialect of the tribe, commercial, superficial and inane. This judgment was partially right and, at the same time, very, very wrong.

This low estimation of American films, now seen by most critics to be a terrible misperception, raises an interesting chicken-and-egg question. Did American intellectuals actually find foreign-language films superior, and thus give foreign directors the recognition that they withheld from American directors, or did the process flow in the opposite direction? Is it possible that American reviewers and film-goers recognized the names of foreign directors—a handy way to identify the films, since few foreign actors were well known here—and thus elevated the director and his role to a superior status and assumed that their films were of a higher quality? Simply because serious film-goers at the time referred to "a Bergman film" or "a Buñuel film," but rarely to "a Hawks film" or "a Ford film," did they invest the foreign directors and films with a seriousness denied, for example, to a John Ford film which would have been referred to in the United States as *"The Searchers,* a cowboy movie starring John Wayne," even though it may be one of the finest films ever made in the United States or anywhere else? Did this linguistic quirk in American reviewing lead to the assumption that foreign-language directors were superior to their American counterparts?

In France, however, as early as the start of the 1950s, several years before directors, foreign or domestic, became hot topics among brie-and-chablis critics on campuses and in coffee houses across the United States, a serious revaluation of the American film and its directors had already begun to gain credibility. If the postwar creative outburst primarily in Italy but in other countries as well forced critics to turn their attention to directors, then the students who gathered around the Cinémathèque Française in Paris were ready to accept the challenge of reassessing the role of the director in the history of films from the earliest days of film-making, not only in Italy but in Hollywood as well. Their studies were to lead to several startling conclusions.

The gathering of this extraordinary circle of critics and their fascination with the Hollywood film is a fascinating story. It begins on September 2, 1936 when Henri Langlois (1914–1977) founded the Cinémathèque as a resource for film students, directors and ordinary enthusiasts. The original collection contained but two films, one American, *The Birth of a Nation* (Griffith, 1915), and one French, *The Fall of the House of Usher* (Epstein and Buñuel, 1928). Thus, the French-American pattern was set from the very first day.[6] By the end of the German occupation of Paris in 1944, the collection had risen to twenty-seven hundred films, thanks to the collaboration of a German officer and cinéphile, Major Frank Hensel. By official Nazi policy, British and American films were understandably considered subversive and should have been confiscated.

Soon after the war, the weekly screenings resumed, and Langlois and his associates were eager that the new generation of French film-makers and critics have the opportunity to see the American masters whose films had been unavailable during the Occupation. The Cinémathèque was the elementary and secondary school for a brilliant class of critics, many of whom would graduate into directing their own films: among them Truffaut and Godard, Jacques Rivette, Eric Rohmer and Alain Resnais. Their daily lessons were drawn from these newly imported American films, and as a result all of them either majored or minored in the American film. If Langlois was their principal, supervising curriculum, faculty and admissions, André Bazin (1918–1958), the premier film historian and critic in the country, if not the world, was their beloved mentor. It was a rare gathering of talent.

Annette Insdorf, biographer of François Truffaut, describes this interest in American films among the young French cinéphiles who gathered around Langlois and Bazin:

> Here they learned to love directors like Howard Hawks and John Ford. . . . The Cinémathèque made them aware and enamored of genres: Westerns, musicals, gangster films, 'film noir'—and of the Hollywood studio system. The genre conventions and production methods were seen as necessarily limitations that defined the possibilities of personal expression for American directors. Paradoxically enough, their limited knowledge of English made them uniquely equipped to appreciate individual cinematic style.[7]

The films from Hollywood, denied these young students during their entire adult lives, burst upon the scene like a firecracker at high Mass. It was different and more intriguing than anything they had ever seen, including the Italian films that had already entered the mainstream of critical thinking among serious American and British as well as French reviewers at the time.

By way of parenthesis, with uncanny irony, cultural history was repeating itself. A century earlier, the works of Edgar Allan Poe appeared in French in translation. The French immediately recognized him as a writer of genius in the Romantic tradition. In the United States, however, where his stories appeared piecemeal in the popular press of the time, no one paid much attention. He was considered a hack. French enthusiasts, among them Baudelaire, Mallarmé and Valéry, forced a serious reconsideration of Poe's stories and poetry among American readers.[8] Similarly, American critics, having viewed Hollywood films one at a time as they were released, became overly familiar with them, and the familiarity bred its predictable quotient of contempt. In contrast, the French, seeing them with fresh eyes, began plotting a revolution in the world of film criticism.

Oddly enough, the French critics forged their tools for revaluating Hollywood not on the American films they were viewing, but on the neorealist films from Italy. The postwar fascination with neorealism films had given the young critics the beginnings of a methodology that they would gradually transfer to the study of world cinema and push to its limits in their analyses of the American directors. These Italian films had enough in common that they could be discussed as a unit, yet each director placed his own individual stamp on the work. In studying the Italians, the French learned how to look at the Americans, who similarly made films that looked alike, but bore the undeniable mark of their creator.

What appealed to the Cinémathèque critics was the gritty, semi-documentary style through which the Italians were able to capture the pathos of the closing months of the war and of the peoples caught in this unforgiving movement of history.[9] Much of the Italian style was a fortuitous accident, since the evacuation of the Nazis and the invasion of the Allies left little quality film and few studio resources. Much of the filming was done literally with war surplus equipment and film stock, begged from the Allies, stolen from the Fascists or abandoned by the retreating Nazis.

These new Italian film-makers, then, went into the streets and villages, using the equipment, film stock and techniques of the documentary photographers who were recording the battle scenes for the warring armies and the press services. Without sound stages and professional actors, the films portrayed a stark black-and-white portrait of human suffering and endurance that captivated critics around the world. The unadorned natural look of the films was a startling change from the perfectly lit studio product that audiences throughout the world had come to expect.

Surely, reasoned the critics, since these films lacked the usual teams of studio professionals, their power must be the product of a single controlling artistic vision, and that artist, they concluded, must be the director. As the neorealist films reached Western screens, critics in Paris and elsewhere centered their attention on the films' creators, Rossellini, DeSica and Visconti, with an intensity offered to few earlier directors. The critics at *Cahiers du Cinéma*, a journal that Bazin founded in 1951 as a successor to the *Revue du Cinéma* which he started in 1947, tirelessly interviewed directors with the reverence accorded to genius and at the same time with a most irreverent probing of their methods and ideas.[10]

These Italian directors, the French critics breathlessly concluded, had returned cinema to the people and to the realities of the workaday world they inhabit. The rough-hewn look of their films was prized for its own artistic power, and anything bearing the taint of studio illusion was scorned for making the world too pretty. For example, in a thoughtful and illuminating essay, André Bazin, the most moderate and least polemical of the *Cahiers* critics, predicted in 1957 that Federico Fellini's *The Nights of Cabiria* would be severely criticized by his colleagues for being "too well made."[11] He entitled his article " 'Cabiria': A Voyage to the End of Neorealism."

Bazin rejects this criticism, arguing that Fellini had successfully incorporated the qualities of a more traditional kind of studio filmmaking while preserving the qualities of neorealism that his colleagues in the critical establishment found so powerful. What Bazin perceived in the infatuation of the *Cahiers* critics with the Italian neorealists is more than a grainy visual style approximating the newsreel. It was rather a clear appreciation that the quality of the film rests in the images it presents, the actuality it captures, rather than the narrative line or in studio artifice, like literary scripts, elaborate costuming, decorative sets and professional "acting" by movie stars.

The skillful director does not create meaning from studio artifice but rather extracts meanings from these surfaces of reality, whether they be found in a littered alley in Rome or on a soundstage of a studio.[12] The director, then, rather than the screenwriter is the true *auteur* or author of the film. As the auteur method of criticism developed, Bazin's more open-minded treatment of studio films would clear the way for the reassessment of Hollywood directors who somehow managed to extract truth from images even in the midst of the most elaborate studio equipment in the world. Critics around the world would be shocked to discover that the *Cahiers* circle considered Hollywood directors equal to or surpassing all but a few of the European auteurs.

The proverbial shot heard around the world was an essay entitled "A Certain Tendency of the French Cinema," written by François Truffaut, then twenty-two years old, in *Cahiers du Cinéma*, No. 31 (January 1954).[13] In this article he attacks the "tradition of quality" that the French cinema had long taken pride in. Citing a list of films and directors scarcely known outside of France, he accuses them of dishonesty. The French, he claims, have fallen into a dangerous pattern of having scriptwriters provide the quality, while directors merely put their literary concepts on the screen. The result of this division of responsibility is fragmentation and superficiality; the result of the essay was to question everything orthodox critics had determined admirable in the French cinema. If the old criteria for excellence, which made the European films seem superior, could be challenged, then perhaps a new set of criteria could evolve, and this would place the American film in a new position in world cinema.

Truffaut was strong in attacking the old traditions of film-making, but he was much less sure in this essay about the direction he wanted film criticism to take. He wanted a unified cinematic expression in every aspect of production through the personality of an auteur, but the meaning of the word auteur, which would become central to French criticism in the 1950s, is by no means clear. This fuzziness has led to many abuses and misunderstandings of the method on both sides of the Atlantic.[14] Ironically, none of the French critics, who by American standards seem overly given to theoretical, abstract analysis, ever produced a systematic explanation of what the term really means. As late as 1957, Bazin pointed out: "Our finest writers on 'Cahiers' have been practicing [auteur criticism] for three or four years now, and have yet to produce the main corpus of its theory."[15] "Auteur" is rather one of those maddeningly fluid concepts that evolved gradually through a series of reviews of individual films, and as such it is used by different critics with slightly different meanings to suit different polemical and critical purposes. The *Cahiers* critics argued for years among themselves about the word and about the application of its meaning to individual films and directors. Their controversies were stimulating and provocative, but were often confusing as well.

At the risk of oversimplification, the idea of the auteur could be characterized as a neoromantic literary concept, since it begins with the talent or person behind the work rather than the work itself.[16] Immediately, the use of the term "literary" causes problems, since the auteur critics self-consciously reject any association with literature. For them films are vehicles through which artists express themselves. Thus one looks at Orson Welles as his personality shows through *Citizen Kane*, rather than *Citizen Kane*, a film by Orson Welles. In deliberately provocative criticism, this distinction is taken literally, but for more moderate practitioners of the auteur method it is a question of emphasis: the director is almost always the most important factor to be examined in evaluating a film, although occasionally a producer (like Sam Goldwyn) or stars (like the irrepressible Marx Brothers) may be the dominant personalities in determining the character of a given film.

Among the *Cahiers* critics, a director becomes an auteur once he or she becomes the controlling force in the development of a motion picture, but they never quite agreed about what this control means or how exactly it takes place. Two major senses of the word gained acceptance. First, according to some critics, directors become auteurs if they actually write the screenplay, or at least strongly influence it. In this technical sense, such a person is an auteur because he or she influences each phase of the production, from concept to the actual filming. Second, other critics offer a more elusive meaning of auteur. For them, the director's personality must be present in each scene of the film, in such a way that the visual appearance of the frame and the themes present in the film are but reflections of the auteur's personality. A perceptive auteur critic then could never mistake a frame or a still from Orson Welles for one from John Ford. This second notion is sufficiently vague to have provoked endless debate, but it will be invaluable in reassessing the Hollywood studio film.[17]

Despite the endless intellectual kamikaze raids these young polemicists staged against one another's point of view, when they began to examine the American film with the same seriousness they gave to the Italians, they were agreed on several basic points. What the French critics recognized was, first, that Hollywood as a system had created and dominated an art form, and, second, that several individuals, working within that system, deserve to be recognized as masters of their art form, or, simply, auteurs.

In December 1955, nearly two years after Truffaut's famous manifesto, Eric Rohmer (1920–   ) followed Truffaut's criticism of the French cinema with an unflattering contrast to American films. He recounts his discovery in 1939, after seeing *It Happened One Night* (Frank Capra, 1934), that American film had a quality of universality that the French film had lost. France was speaking to its own respectable middle class; Hollywood was speaking to the world. With enthusiasm bordering on extravagance and syntax bordering on hysteria, he extols the virtues of Hollywood as a system of excellence:

> In the midst of an output that, like any other, numbers both masterpieces and disasters, to see a film by Griffith, Hawks, Cukor, Hitchcock, Mankiewicz, or even a comedy, a thriller or a Western by a lesser-known signatory, has always been enough to reassure me and convince me that for the talented and dedicated film maker the California coast is not that den of iniquity that some would have us believe. It is rather that chosen land, that haven which Florence was for painters of the Quattrocento or Vienna for musicians in the nineteenth century.[18]

In part, Rohmer suggests what everybody knew. Hollywood attracts the best talent because it has the money. He defies the common wisdom, however, when he refuses to accept the belief that Hollywood corrupts its talent and forces the newcomers to produce meretricious films to cater to the lowbrow tastes of a mass audience. Rohmer dares to suggest that Hollywood dominates the world market because it produces better films than any other country, an opinion certainly heretical and possibly blasphemous according to the critical canonists of the day. Rohmer was not alone in his beliefs. The reassessment of the American film became a kind of crusade among his colleagues as well. According to Jim Hillier, the indefatigable editor of the first two of the projected four-volume English-language collection of *Cahiers* essays, one of the principal achievements of the *Cahiers* critics as a whole was "the systematic elevation of Hollywood movies to the ranks of great art."[19]

One clarification is necessary at this point. Although the *Cahiers* critics are most associated with the American film, a perusal of the pages of the magazine, the editors' lists of "best films of the year," and the films they label masterpieces reveals that the American film was not an overwhelming preoccupation of theirs.[20] At least they did not fix their attention and adulation exclusively on California when selecting articles for publication or titles to include on their "best of the year" lists. Hollywood did, however, provide the perfect battleground for testing their theories, and as the theory of auteur criticism gained notoriety, the studies they did on the American film were read and discussed throughout the world. As a result, they are invariably associated with the American film, and in turn the reinstatement of Hollywood's artistic reputation is traced almost exclusively to their efforts.

The reasons for this radical revaluation of the American film by these critics at this time are complex. The *Cahiers* critics began their revolution with quite a noisy fusillade in their own country when they simply rejected the "French cinema" and its "tradition of quality." By rejecting the films of one country, they needed another for purposes of comparison. The Italians had been done to death by this time, and even the most staid French critics realized and admitted their unique quality. But if one wanted to be outrageous, compare the French to the despised cinema of Hollywood. Since American films were traditionally treated with contempt by intellectuals, comparing them favorably to the French "tradition of quality" had its own peculiar shock value.

This selection was not gratuitous. The critics who learned their trade around Bazin and Langlois at the Cinémathèque knew and appreciated the American film. At this perfect polemic moment, they brought their respect for Hollywood to the forefront of the assault. The vitality and technical excellence of the Americans stood as a reproach to everything they found reprehensible at home. They would use the Americans to attack and revitalize the French.

While arguing about the relative merits of national cinemas, they were able to think of Hollywood not only in terms of individual films but also as a system. While they retained their admiration for individual classics of the European directors, they were awed by the consistent quality that the American studio system was able to produce.

André Bazin underlines this notion of the excellence of the Hollywood tradition when he cites the "American cinematic genius" for presenting "American society just as it wanted to see itself."[21] It does not attempt to cover over the contradictions present in this capitalist society by presenting pure escapist entertainment, but it offers a realistic portrait of the people. He finds in the Hollywood film, taken as a class, the same kind of realism that the Italians had in their neorealistic movement. Bazin suggests that the penetrating insight and honesty that the Italians accomplished through limited resources and by turning their lenses on the poverty and corruption in the streets and villages of a war ravaged country, the Americans had been achieving for years. Oddly enough, the Americans developed their artistic vision of the real world in superbly artificial studios and through a magnificent variety of films whose main intent is to create fantasy: Westerns, musicals, screwball comedies, hard-boiled detectives and science fiction.

Once the Hollywood studio system is identified precisely as a system, and a commercial one at that, as Rohmer had insisted, then it follows that individual American directors can be called auteurs of excellence precisely because of their ability to express their own personalities within the constraints that the American studio system imposes on them.[22]

This Hollywood version of personal expression, though found in a context different from that of the great European auteurs, can meet either or both of the two criteria that the French critics set up for their auteurs: it can take place first on the level of script and content, like recurring themes and interests repeated over a variety of films, or, second, on the level of visual style, identifiable throughout the auteur's work. The fact that the stories are often selected by semiliterate producers, the budget set by corporate headquarters a continent away, and the cast chosen by talent agencies does not weaken an auteur's opportunity for self-expression or even control over the materials of the film; it intensifies it, but within established limits. For example, once the producer selects the story, the auteur may alter it to fit his or her own personal interests. Or, even if they do not have control over the script, the directors are generally left free to design, light and shoot the scenes. Thus an auteur is able to create a personal visual style.

One might compare a poet's learning to write within the constraints of the sonnet format; the success of the effort within the fourteen-line structure increases admiration of the talent. Another poet may compose a long inspirational epic, but be a failure as an artist. It takes an informed and perceptive critic to understand both the format and the way the poet has used it. Similarly, according to the *Cahiers* critics, an artist expressing himself through a low-budget "B" detective story while making money for the studio can be a true auteur if he is able to use the format with skill. Another director, working on a classic novel, a big-budget musical or a morally uplifting costume drama, may be little more than a technician, since the work bears none of the personal expression of an auteur.

Appreciation of this kind of artistry does not come easily to critics educated in a literary tradition. They start with the film, not the filmmaker. If a critic begins with the director, and understands, say, John Ford's romantic concept of America's Westward expansion as part of a never-ending quest for an ever-receding promised land, then his less successful cowboy movies and social statements, even when naively expressed on individual occasion, take on a significance as part of the larger context of the artist making the statement. The fact that he can come back to themes of interest in many contexts and create an identifiable visual style in films dealing with diverse subjects only increases admiration for his talent.

By way of illustration, in May 1953 Jacques Rivette wrote an article on Howard Hawks that demonstrates both the weakness and the strength of the auteur style of criticism.[23] He shows the arrogance and overstatement of many of the *Cahiers* essays in his opening paragraph: "The evidence on the screen is the proof of Hawks's genius: You only have to watch 'Monkey Business' to know that it is a brilliant film. Some people refuse to admit this, however; they refuse to be satisfied by proof. There can't be any other reason why they don't recognize it." So much for reasoned, persuasive discourse. Either the reader sees in the film what the author does, or is hopelessly benighted. After this abrasive rhetorical onslaught, Rivette discusses several of the themes that run through Hawks' films, from Westerns to comedies to melodramas, and at the end a reader might well be ready to take a second hard look at *Monkey Business* (1952) and admit there may be more to it than appeared at first screening. Rivette skillfully uses Hawks the auteur as a means to enter the films.

This apodictic and inflexible approach to directors soon led to the "politique des auteurs" (a policy for directors). At its worst it meant that the *Cahiers* reviewers set a policy ahead of time to determine which directors would receive raves and which would be panned. Only reviewers who were favorable toward a director would be given space to review the film. The assumption was that a good auteur–that is, one approved by the staff–would always provide a good film or at least an interesting one, while a poor director would always produce a poor film.[24] The method, according to its strongest advocates, admits no exceptions. Hitchcock can do no wrong; Huston can do no right.

Bazin, once again the moderate, stresses the value of auteur criticism, but refuses to follow the parade to its illogical conclusion. In his opinion, mediocre directors can provide an occasional excellent film almost despite themselves, and great directors can produce clinkers.[25] If Homer nods, Welles can snore. He warns against a cinematic personality cult that blinds reviewers to the actual value of a particular film.

Before tracing the movement of auteur criticism to the United States, one further observation about the French critics will be useful for subsequent reflections. Although they wrote about the auteur's personal stamp and about unique visual styles and said little explicitly about content, the "politique" did contain a preference for a certain kind of theme. John Hess, an American critic, pointed out this unarticulated criterion in 1974 when he wrote:

> The most important determinant of an auteur was not so much the director's ability to express his personality, as usually has been claimed, but rather his desire and ability to express a certain world view. An auteur was a film director who expressed an optimistic image of human potentialities within an utterly corrupt society. By reaching out emotionally and spiritually to other human beings and/or God, one could transcend the isolation imposed on one by a corrupt world.[26]

Their concern for human dignity and moral values in the auteurs they scrutinize is remarkably consistent.

This concern should not be surprising since, strange as it may seem, many of the *Cahiers* critics had a strong Catholic bent. Amédée Ayfre was a priest who wrote regularly for *Esprit,* a Catholic journal of theology and culture. Rohmer and Bazin were active Catholics, and Truffaut similarly had a Catholic background. As a group they reacted against the leftist hegemony in the arts after the war and tried to encourage the reassertion of traditional values. The directors they praised as auteurs frequently expressed interest in those same moral values.

Jacques Rivette, for example, writes that Howard Hawks "is the only American director who is able to draw a *moral*. His marvelous blend of action and morality is probably the secret of his genius."[27] "Morality" as Rivette uses the term is not merely an adherence to some external code of conduct, since Hawks' heroes can often be quite immoral in the conventional use of the word. What Rivette finds "moral" in Hawks' films is the consistency with which the auteur presents a world in which his characters are caught in confining circumstances and yet are able to take command of their lives. Their actions have consequences, which they accept. Life is not a game of chance, but a struggle, and through the contest comes dignity.

As Hawks relates his characteristic theme of human triumph, he relies not on contrivance but on the surfaces of the physical realities that he photographs. His universe supplies a demanding test for the spirit of his characters, but it also presents the possibility of victory, which one might dare to call "redemption." In selecting his own visual style for presenting this world he endows it with meaning. Rivette unites his notions of moral struggle and reverence for the material world when he writes: "Hawks first of all concentrates on the smell and feel of reality, giving reality an unusual and indeed long-hidden grandeur and nobility."[28]

This is a theme echoed by Eric Rohmer in his ecstatic "rediscovery" of the American film in 1955. He laments the fact that film-makers around the world reduce destiny to fetishism and theology. In contrast he observes: "In some of the finest American films it is instead posed, as in the fifth-century tragedians, in terms of *morality:* or by reference to religion, which, be it a Protestant sect or Irish Catholicism, is sparing of both external ceremony and flights of mysticism, and is above all the promulgation of a moral code of living."[29] The French, he maintains, present too much analysis. The Americans do not impose a meaning on reality; they are able to present the real world as it exists in its mixture of good and evil.

Although he is writing of the Italian neorealist films, rather than Hollywood, Père Ayfre praises this kind of ambiguity as a "phenomenology of grace." "The ambiguity is the mode of existence of the Mystery which is the safeguard of freedom. Whatever the appearances to the contrary, a Christian will have no difficulty in recognizing, from a mystical point of view, a level and a quality which is at least equal if not superior to the worlds created by Bresson."[30] (Bresson tried to interpret religious experience in overtly religious films such as *The Diary of a Country Priest* [1950]. Père Ayfre's criticism did not deter Bresson from making *The Trial of Joan of Arc* in 1962.) Bresson, according to this criticism, dictated his moral or religious interpretation of the world in his films, where Ayfre preferred to see the phenomena of good and evil coexisting.

In a relentlessly honest presentation of the human condition, a believer can perceive the movements of grace in a world tainted with evil. He summarizes the argument: "It is the very nature of grace to be hidden and ambiguous precisely because it is the human face of the transcendent mystery of God." This absence of overt religion that Père Ayfre finds praiseworthy in the Italian neorealists will transfer quite readily to the *Cahiers* critics' rediscovery of the American film, which earlier critics had tended to see as amoral in its superficiality.

There is paradox here. Where many intellectuals in the United States found lofty theological and philosophic themes in many of the European films of the era, the *Cahiers* critics found, as Rohmer puts it, "the reverse of a sentimental holy picture." Where these same intellectuals found American films naive, commercial and inane, the *Cahiers* critics discovered a profound respect for the value of personal struggle in a very ambiguous moral universe. The Americans did not feel a need to impose a meaning on the world from without, but they could invite their audiences to look at their world and see the meaning in it. For the *Cahiers* critics with their concern for morality, Hollywood seemed more profound and honest than the bulk of European productions.

Up to a point, the reverence for the ambiguities of the material world and their use of morality as a criterion of excellence put the *Cahiers* critics on the side of Father Lynch, Father Gardiner and Mr. Getlein, who addressed similar questions in the United States a few years later. The major difference is that the French critics allowed meanings, even theological and ethical meanings, to emerge from the films themselves. The American religious critics, by contrast, relied on comparative analysis: they brought a fully developed theological perspective to the art form and tried to show how the two could be reconciled. The American critics are easier to read because they are essentialists, and their method is deductive. They write about film in the abstract, as a medium or as an art form. They line up their theological propositions and conclusions unflinchingly. When they cite individual films, it is for the purpose of furnishing an example to illustrate or establish the premise they have already explained.

The French on the other hand are extremely difficult to follow. Their theories emerge piecemeal through reviews of individual films, and undoubtedly through arguments with one another that readers can only imagine as they try to fathom fragments of a conversation in progress. The French are existentialist and inductive. They start with an experience of the individual films and then use them to establish their theories. They are critics who first immerse themselves in films and then let their observations of dozens, if not hundreds of individual films lead them to generalizations about "neorealism" or "Hollywood." It is a messy process.

Frequently, this theological path to Hollywood through Paris holds many maddening twists of ideology, which may or may not be intended to be taken seriously. The *Cahiers* critics do not, for example, attempt to impose a Christian vision on the work under discussion, nor do they consciously judge the morality of the characters and situations on the screen by their own personal religious standards or by any other extrinsic, predetermined norms. They view the works carefully and allow the "phenomenology of grace" to speak for itself. Deliberate attempts at edification revolt them as much as unimaginative direction. The American religious critics similarly rejected sentimental piousness, it is true, but it is quite clear that they would not at all mind a bit of sophisticated moralizing. *A Man for All Seasons*, si; *Going My Way*, no.

The Americans who approached film from a religious perspective tended to approach it from the outside—as moralists, theologians, or literary critics: Father Lynch, Father Gardiner, Mr. Getlein and Father Hurley, for example—and they invite the film to lead them to something beyond itself, like an awareness of God in the lives of the characters; well-disposed Christian viewers can then transfer this vicarious religious experience into an awareness of God in their own lives. Thus, for example, appreciating Ingrid Bergman's faith during her martyrdom in *Joan of Arc* (Fleming, 1948) might lead to a deepening of faith in the life of the viewer. This is "edification" that may or may not be sentimental or pietistic. It may not even use overtly religious imagery. In an often used example, Gelsomina's (Giulietta Masina) self-sacrificing love for Zampano (Anthony Quinn) in *La Strada* (Fellini, 1954) can be used to demonstrate Christ's love for humanity, even though the narrative involves a tiny itinerant carnival in Italy immediately after World War II.

The French approached the films from within. They did not search for religious themes, nor did they try to lead their readers to a reexamination of their own faith through films. As dedicated students of film, who incidentally as good Frenchmen were by the way scarcely ignorant of philosophy and literature, they looked at the shots and the camera, the lights and the script to discover the personal touches of their favorite directors. They did not import the methods or preconceptions of alien disciplines. When they saw the moral ambiguity of the world presented on the screen, those of Christian sensibilities were able to contemplate the presence of grace in the nobility of those engaged in the struggle of life. They did not try to move from the screen to theological reflections or even more into the lives of faith of their readers and the film's viewers.

The apparent ambivalence to morality in its conventional sense led to a strange irony. Some American religious critics concerned with public morality tended to shrink from Italian and later French "New Wave" films, many of which were directed by former *Cahiers* critics, because of the unsavory situations and characters they presented. At times, according to their tastes, good was not sufficiently rewarded nor evil adequately punished. For the French, however, exploring a conflict of good and evil and refusal to draw obvious moral conclusions was a kind of morality that they most appreciated in the Italian neorealists and in Hollywood.

The Miracle (Rossellini, 1950) provides a handy example. In the story, written by Federico Fellini, a slow-witted country girl (Anna Magnani) is seduced by a shepherd and becomes pregnant. In her confusion she tells the townspeople that she is the Virgin Mary and St. Joseph is the father of her unborn child. The film's intent is to present the different reactions of the village to the poor girl's fantasy. American critics are impatient with such dangerous reflections. They prefer to have the moral conclusions drawn with perfect clarity: either the girl must be punished for her indiscretion or the town for its cruelty. In either event, references to the Nativity outside the traditional New Testament setting must be regarded as suspect.

The film raised a storm of protest among American Catholics. The Archdiocese of New York under the leadership of Cardinal Francis Spellman, the Legion of Decency, and even the Catholic War Veterans all denounced the film as blasphemous and offensive to Christians. The police confiscated the film, and the American distributor, Joseph Burstyn, had to take the case all the way to the U.S. Supreme Court before he won the right to show the film.[31]

The French had a quite different response to Rossellini and his films, as Jacques Rivette pointed out in 1955:

What is it he [Rossellini] never tires of saying? That human beings are alone, and their solitude is irreducible; that, except by miracle or saintliness, our ignorance of others is complete; that only a life in God, in his love and his sacraments, only the communion of the saints can enable us to meet, to know, to possess another being than ourselves alone; and that one can only know and possess oneself in God. . . .

Rossellini, however, is not merely Christian, but Catholic; in other words, carnal to the point of scandal; one recalls the outrage over "The Miracle"; but Catholicism is by vocation a scandalous religion; the fact that *our body*, like Christ's, also plays its part in the divine mystery is something hardly to everyone's taste, and in this creed which makes the presence of the flesh one of its dogmas, there is a concrete meaning, weighty, almost sensual, to flesh and matter that is highly repugnant to chaste spirits.[32]

Rivette saw beauty and religious meaning in the conflict of good and evil in very concrete, human terms. He is comfortable with the messiness of the Incarnation, through which the goodness of God visits a world of sinners. He is moved by the loneliness of the girl unable to understand the wrongs that have been done to her, not only by the shepherd, but by the self-righteous who scorn her pathetic fantasy. True morality, for Rivette, is the honest portrayal of this struggle, not the limning of simplistic morals to take out of the story. In a world where good and evil co-exist, the pointed moral of a story is a lie.

The American reaction, based primarily on a misreading of the film, was undoubtedly conditioned by personal events in the life of the director, Roberto Rossellini. In 1948, during the filming of *Stromboli*, a romance developed between him and the star, Ingrid Bergman. When she left her husband of eleven years, Dr. Peter Lindstrom, to join Rossellini in Italy, both she and her earlier films were vilified. What fanned the flames even higher was the fact that *The Miracle* opened on December 10, at the peak of the Christmas season, with its understandable sensitivity to anything involving a nontraditional reference to the Nativity. The controversial film released in the wrong season so soon after Rossellini's involvement in the Bergman scandal only confirmed the low opinion many Catholics already had of the moral tone of many Italian films and their directors. To many Americans it seemed that this sleazy Italian had corrupted Joan of Arc and Sister Benedict from *The Bells of St. Mary's* (McCarey, 1945).

In contrast to these harsh judgments of the neorealist films and directors in America, the *Cahiers* critics were claiming for them a position of moral superiority, precisely because they did not shrink from examining evil in the world. On this issue, at least, the French film critics—some Catholic, some secularist—had a sounder theological appreciation of the Incarnation than many of the more irate American religious leaders who became involved in the issue.

The auteur method, developed in France and applied so fruitfully to American films, soon made its way across the Atlantic and into the mainstream of American critical writing. The American agenda, however, shied away from the more arcane theoretical considerations of the French, and the religious questions that pop up occasionally in *Cahiers* essays hold a rather low priority for the Americans, as they do for the British auteurists who clustered around the British Film Institute in London.

Shorn of its religious concerns, then, the auteur method paused briefly in London, where it acquired an English language vocabulary (while preserving the consecrated French technical terms), and then entered the mainstream of American criticism, domesticated, housebroken, and in an infinitely more intelligible form largely through the efforts of Andrew Sarris. It is not so much that Sarris simplified the method as that the method simplified itself by the time Sarris got involved. He was concerned with film in itself, as were the *Cahiers* critics, but he showed little interest in the kinds of religious and philosophic questions that swam under the surface of the French writers.

In 1961, Sarris, then a reviewer and editor for *Film Culture* in New York, spent several months in Paris in the company of André Bazin. In an infrequent autobiographical note, he describes the events of "that fateful year" as turning him into "not merely a cultist but a subversive cultist with a foreign ideology."[33] (The term "cultist," as Sarris explains, holds a deliberate religious connotation. He chose it after many conversations with Bazin, who spoke of "devotion" to films and even referred to film festivals as "religious revivals.")

By the time Sarris arrived in Paris, the young critics of the *Cahiers* circle had exhausted themselves with some of the more recondite points of their auteur criticism, and were perhaps less inclined to make outrageous statements calculated to infuriate whatever establishment they had chosen to infuriate on any given day. The method was older and wiser, and so were its practitioners, many of whom were now too busy making films themselves to bother infuriating anyone.

It did not take Sarris very long to nail his heretical theses to the pages of *Film Culture*. In the spring issue of 1963 he wrote a sixty-eight-page article entitled simply "The American Cinema."[34] In his one-page introduction he offers his own justification for a complete reconsideration of the American cinema, director by director. He does not mention that the French had already advanced quite far in this work. The bulk of the article is a systematic catalogue of each of the major directors, beginning with Sarris' "pantheon" of great auteurs like Ford, Chaplin and Welles, to lesser known practitioners of the craft. He lists the films chronologically and offers a brief evaluation of the auteur's work as a whole. The final sixteen pages provide "A Directorial Chronology, 1915–1962," in which Sarris lists the major films of each year with their respective directors. It is a monumental work of scholarship.

The article created shock waves among film critics and scholars in the United States. Mentioning the director in a review had always been standard practice, and occasionally the director's contribution to the film could be cited. A few major ones even commanded serious attention. Everyone knew of D.W. Griffith and Charlie Chaplin, for example. In this respect, Sarris' writing a lengthy catalogue of directors was not surprising. What was startling, however, was the importance he attached to their work and his insistence on taking their work as a unified whole rather than looking for little signature touches in individual films that could be interesting but scarcely of much importance in evaluating the work. To paraphrase coach Vince Lombardi, for Sarris the director "is not the most important thing; it's the only thing."

This was more than a question of emphasis. If Sarris had written about the overwhelming influence of Orson Welles or Robert Flaherty on the finished product, no one would have paid much attention, but he applied his auteurist method right across the broad spectrum of Hollywood's product. He included mass-audience, commercial directors, like Howard Hawks and Alfred Hitchcock, among the greats. (The French, of course, had been taking these directors seriously for years.) At the same time, many of the traditional "prestige" directors, like John Huston, Elia Kazan, David Lean, William Wyler and Fred Zinnemann, became in Sarris' listings merely "Fallen Idols." One quirky judgment has provided ammunition for anti-Sarris and anti-auteurist critics for years: "[Frank] Tashlin [an American comedy writer] and Jerry Lewis may become *the* American comedy directors by default."[35] In traditional circles, anyone who took Jerry Lewis seriously could not be a serious critic.

In the next few years Sarris interviewed directors, and in 1967 he published a collection of conversations with American and foreign auteurs, entitled *Interviews with Film Directors.* In the introduction, he renews his commitment to the discovery and revaluation of auteurs in the world of film.[36] He acknowledges the observation that American directors have always functioned as part of a team or a system, and thus have less independence than authors in other media, or even than film directors in Europe. Despite this fact he is unwilling to admit that they cannot be elevated to the level of auteur. He remains convinced that many American directors were and continue to be the controlling influences in the life of a film.

One historical observation is particularly pertinent today. In the past, Sarris writes in 1967, Americans and movie-goers throughout the world had little sense of film history. In the 1940s, for example, few people would have had any exposure to the films of the 1930s or 1920s. The observation is quite accurate. In the 1940s films changed at local theaters twice each week, and last week's offering was simply forgotten as stale merchandise. A very few classics might appear on occasion in some of the big cities or around major universities. A communist students' organization, for example, might drag out *Potemkin* (Eisenstein, 1925) to foster a discussion of Soviet politics. Other than in these specialized circumstances, where would audiences have any opportunity to see past films?

In the early 1950s, Sarris notes, television changed the pattern. Hollywood opened its vaults to television broadcasters and a whole new generation of viewers had free access to movies by the masters, their obscure pictures as well as their masterpieces. Despite the name, some "Million Dollar Movies" often featured two-bit clinkers, but it was precisely in these rarely shown minor works that critics could observe the personal touches of great directors. As the old films reached television audiences, not only film students but the general public as well were able to observe the themes and personalities of the auteurs for the first time. Young American film scholars were thus very much familiar with the notion of looking back at the commercial films of an earlier era with a view toward understanding the development and consistencies of a director. As film study worked its way into colleges and universities, and the "Fellini and Bergman" phenomenon accustomed people to talk about directors while they were pondering alienation and leaps of faith, auteur criticism became a natural method of criticism for the television generation to follow in its study of American films.

If Sarris were to reissue this introduction today, he would cer-

tainly mention the controversial new world of videotapes. Purists
continue to scorn taped movies, and with good reason. Color and
clarity are lost, the size and aspect ratio is distorted to fit the dimensions of the television screen (a particularly severe problem for wide-
screen releases), and the quality of sound reproduction is far below
that of a commercial theater.

Despite these negative factors, videotape has made a magnificent
contribution to film study. Over the last five years, classic American
films have become available in every supermarket and shopping mall
in the country. Even very modest school libraries house collections of
tapes, which now are often far less expensive than books. These easy-
to-use cassettes serve roles in classroom teaching, private screening
or scholarly research. Twice then in the last forty years, the technology of television, once thought to be the dread enemy of the motion
picture, has brought an explosion in the possibilities for film enjoyment, education and scholarship.

By 1968, the original article in *Film Culture* had grown into a
book: *The American Cinema: Directors and Directions 1929–1968.*
The one-page introduction of the original became an eighteen-page
statement on the values and method of auteur criticism.[37] It is probably the clearest explanation of the method in English. Sarris finally
wrote the systematic essay that the French, for all their brilliant analysis of individual films and directors, never quite got around to.

Sarris begins his study of American films by pointing out a difference between "forest" critics and "trees" critics. It has been fashionable to take Hollywood as a single entity, the forest, and lament its
crass commercialism which has sapped the talent from many fine artists. If critics look at the trees, the individual films, they get quite
another impression. Hollywood may have produced fewer masterpieces to compare with the giants of the European cinema, but Europe has produced fewer competent works. "If Hollywood yields a
bit at the very summit," Sarris writes, "it completely dominates the
middle ranges."[38] One of the reasons Americans may at first be reluctant to accept this statement is due to a process of selection: only the
best European films are distributed in the United States. American
audiences rarely see the duds, so of course Americans believe that
European films are superior to the American product. Sarris well
might have compared the situation to the American perception of
British television. Viewers of public television think all British pro-
gramming is on a par with "Masterpiece Theatre," scarcely realizing

that the wretched stuff dies somewhere between Co. Kerry and Nova Scotia and happily never makes it across the North Atlantic. A lot of it makes "Golden Girls" look like Tolstoi.

Addressing a challenge that the French astutely avoided, Sarris actually attempts to define auteur criticism:

> Ultimately, the auteur theory is not so much a theory as an attitude, a table of values that converts film history into directorial autobiography. The auteur critic is obsessed with the wholeness of art and the artist. He looks at a film as a whole, a director as a whole. The parts, however entertaining individually, must cohere meaningfully.[39]

The auteurists then will be more interested in seeing Howard Hawks as he expresses himself in *Scarface* (1932) than in the individual film itself. Their criticism will begin with the auteur and include his other works as important parts of their analysis of the film in question. *Scarface* is merely a chapter in Hawks' "directorial autobiography."

Sarris admits some weaknesses in the method. The worst of the auteur critics simply look at the director's name and state that the film of a favorite director is obviously better than a film by another less favored director, simply because it is. Here Sarris echoes the reservations of Bazin. The judgment may be true, but it must be made only after intensive analysis of both directors in question. Sarris rejects rigid, inflexible judgments altogether: "The auteur theory is merely a system of tentative priorities, a pattern theory in constant flux. . . . Auteur criticism implies a faith in film history as a continuing cultural activity."[40]

In the closing paragraphs of the essay, Sarris raises a difficulty that dedicated auteur critics, including Sarris himself, have never seemed to address comfortably, that is, the relationship between the American auteurs and the constraints of the system in which they function. American critics, Sarris points out, have often assumed that European directors approach more perfectly the ideal of complete control. One reason for this is simply because although American critics do know something about the problems of working within the Hollywood system, they are usually quite unfamiliar with foreign production methods, which can be just as irksome to a director as those of the American studios. In many countries, he points out, the director must contend not only with the studio but with government bureaucracies as well.[41]

As a confirmed auteurist, however, he must explain the possibility of a director's becoming an auteur in a studio system that distributes responsibilities among many individuals. He maintains simply that personal creativity can exist in Hollywood because it has. In trying to explain the fact, he places priority on the second criterion of the French critics, that is, the importance of visual style. American directors often do not have much to say about the script (the first criterion) or the stars, but at the same time they are generally left alone in creating the "look" of the film. In most cases the director routinely supervises the work of the camera crew, lighting engineers and, to some extent, the actors and editors.

The appearance of the film is all-important for Sarris. He finds that most critics look at content of a film, and judge in terms of "what." An auteur critic is more interested in a style, the "how," and that is the auteur achievement. If the auteur puts a personal touch on a film, even one with a second-rate script, then the artist has added another chapter to the directorial autobiography and produced a film worthy of attention and respect.

Not long after Sarris and his followers made auteur criticism the dominant critical school in the United States, another group of critics turned its attention to those very story lines that had been all too easily dismissed as "second-rate." The newer approach became known simply as "genre criticism." In part it was a healthy reaction against the cults of personality that had grown up among some practitioners of the *politique des auteurs*. The genre critics took one step back from the creative personalities and turned their attention first to the various formula stories that formed the framework within which Hollywood auteurs were able to express themselves. Although these two critical viewpoints could be antagonistic, in the age that followed the early political frenzy of the *Cahiers* critics the two methods complement each other quite neatly. Used together by pragmatic and eclectic critics more dedicated to films than to ideology, the twin "methods" enable a viewer to approach both the "form" of a work of art (the visual style and personal expression so beloved of the auteur school) and the "content" (the story types and visual conventions imposed by Hollywood's commercial imperatives).

Genre criticism in itself is scarcely new, but its importance has increased dramatically since the auteur critics raised the study of the American film to a new level of seriousness. From the earliest days of the backroom nickelodeon, film-goers were aware that they were watching "slapstick comedy," "cowboys and Indians," "romances," or "cops and robbers." Individual viewers no doubt soon discovered their own personal preferences and eagerly awaited each new recycling of the same familiar type of material. Reviewers, and those few writers who began the practice of criticism, routinely used the notion of genre in a negative sense. The term of the day was the "formula film," a stock story that Hollywood mechanically ground out in its customary assembly-line style of production.[42] (Those who were around at the very start of the industry might well have recalled that the first East Coast "studios" were called "factories." Even to this day, Hollywood refers to itself as "the industry," and its output as "product." The assembly line analogy is then quite appropriate.)

The style of genre analysis reached a new pre-auteurist plateau when Robert Warshow, a critic of popular culture writing for *Partisan Review*, was able to distill certain elements common to large classes of films. His two most famous essays of this type are "The Gangster as Tragic Hero" (February 1948) and "Movie Chronicle: The Westerner" (March–April 1954). In these highly literate essays he describes the characteristics of both the heroes of this modern cultural expression and the society that created them.[43]

A very large question remains, however. Once a film can be classed as a "formula film," does the classification say anything about the quality of the film or the talent of its makers? For the genre critics, the answer is a resounding no, but they had to take several steps to make their response convincing. The genre critics believe that an individual artist can produce a work of excellence within the confines of the genre. The fact that it is a formula work cannot preclude quality. After the auteurists convinced the world that Hollywood films, even of the formula variety, could be considered works of art and their makers artists, the genre critics began to think of the formula films as though they were dealing with classical literature.[44] In a classical or preromantic tradition, innovation and originality are not values. The sculptor, for example, strives to create a Venus more beautiful than any of the hundreds of Venuses that earlier sculptors had been making for centuries. Original subject matter is not important. The work and the artist are judged not by innovation but by execution. The auteur critics, it must be recalled, had already begun evaluating works by looking at the modes of execution, which they named personal vision and visual style. Since the auteurists became widely read, originality and innovation were less important than consistency.

Similarly, the classical playwright does not keep an audience in suspense at the outcome of the drama, because it knows what happens to Oedipus or Medea before it takes its hard stone seats in the amphitheater. Nor is it looking for some unusual sequence of dialogue and chorus; it knows when and how the chorus must appear to comment on the action. If anything, tampering with the audience's expectations would spoil the enjoyment of the piece. The classical play-goer derives pleasure from seeing how the artist retells the old, familiar story. How convincing are the motivations, how poignant the emotion, how lovely the poetry?

The comparison serves well for the formula film. Film-makers, for commercial motives probably not much different from Sophocles' or Shakespeare's, routinely fashion their works to satisfy the expectations of the audience, and thus of the producers who raise the money for the work in the first place. Yet, even in the process of making a product to sell tickets, they are still capable of producing works of art. Commercial viability does not preclude art. After all, most of the world's finest painting and music were done with one eye on artistic immortality and the other on pleasing the whims of wealthy patrons and securing another commission.

The genre approach to films not only recognizes these facts of life in film production, but it considers them essential elements in any realistic form of film criticism. It starts not with the director but with the formulas themselves. It tries first to uncover their dynamics and weigh the individual film in the context of the family of films it happens to be born into. Almost inevitably, the next step involves perceiving the personal stamp that the director puts upon the material that is inherited from the studio. It reverses the priorities of the auteurist.

This hybrid critical method has been extremely fruitful, for it corrects the auteurists' excessive concern with the individual artist and moves the Hollywood system, precisely as a system, to the center of the act of creation. The irony is that the *Cahiers* critics deeply appreciated Hollywood as a system, but only inasmuch as it provided an arena for the function of solitary artists, who use the materials of their industry and overcome its constraints. Genre critics go further. They see the system, studio, director, and mass audience as each playing a positive role in the act of artistic creation. They do not attempt to isolate the contribution of a single auteur, but rather acknowledge the complex financial and artistic world in which a film is made. In this they are closer to the reality of American film-making than the auteur critics.

In the excellent introduction to his book *Hollywood Genres,*

Thomas Schatz points out a circular and mutually interactive relationship between audience, director and studios.[45] The audience influences film production by buying tickets. It tells the producers what kind of film it wants and the director how it wants it done. It is a force that must be weighed very carefully, and as such it is an integral part of the artistic process of creating a film. (In recent years the creative role of the studio has frequently been supplied by the independent producer, who, if anything, is even more sensitive to audience demand than the large studios. The independent puts all the financial eggs in one basket by trying to make one blockbuster every few years. One serious miscalculation brings bankruptcy, whereas a studio can spread out its losses over several films produced in the course of a year.)

Since the studios provide the funding for the next film, the director has no choice but to follow instructions. The studios tell the directors what they expect and impose limits on their artistic freedom by supplying story, script, actors, production facilities, and creative teams. By responding to the demands of the market and exercising the power of the purse, they, no less than the audience, exercise extraordinary influence on the finished product and must be considered part of the artistic process. Samuel Goldwyn, for example, considered himself the film-maker and the director merely a production supervisor hired for the job. When someone mentioned William Wyler's direction of *Wuthering Heights*, Goldwyn responded: "*I* made 'Withering [sic] Heights'; Wyler only directed it."[46]

Finally, directors as the third members of the troika not only respond to the demands of the markets and the studios, but they educate them. They teach audiences first to recognize significant images within a genre. For example, a white hat signifies the classic Western hero, and the man in the pin-striped suit and fedora, carrying a violin case, should not be hired as a baby sitter. In a domestic comedy or a musical, these images would have no meaning at all. Once the conventional language of the genre is established, directors can push back the meaning of the images and extend the complexity and range of the genre. Maybe the white hat represents cowardice and the violin case holds not a tommy gun but a real violin—which may or may not explode when a certain note is played. The studios abet the director by financing and releasing the "innovative" genre film to the public and monitoring its response. If the public will not accept the innovations, the variations will be dropped and replaced with others. If no variation is successful, the genre will become stagnant and die.

The process then is extremely conservative, as is appropriate for such an expensive investment. Few entrepreneurs are going to risk millions on a product that has not been tested, at least by comparison to other similar products. For this reason, the careful analysis of the genre film, as the formula film is now called, leads a critic to note and evaluate tiny shifts in emphasis and style that signal both the personal stamp of the director and the evolution of the genre itself. The generalizations about a genre are only the context for a rigorous analysis of the individual film within the genre.

Defining a genre is no simple task. It involves a critic in a maddening philosophic dilemma. To define a genre, one must necessarily view a number of films within the genre and then extract from them the characteristics that should be found in all films within the genre. However, what films fit into the category in the first place? The selection of individual samples depends on a prior, vague and unarticulated notion of what the genre is, and in turn the samples will undoubtedly determine the formal definition of the genre.[47]

An extreme example may illustrate this conundrum. Everyone knows what a Western is. It takes place on the frontier and usually centers around a conflict with Indians or bandits, but would New York State in *Drums Along the Mohawk* (Ford, 1939) count? If a Western must be located further west, then would *Oklahoma!* (Zinnemann, 1955) satisfy the criterion? If not, then how about that generation of singing cowboys, like Gene Autry and Roy Rogers? If music disqualifies, how about comedy, say *Blazing Saddles* (Brooks, 1974)? If the answer is "yes," why would most viewers accept *Ride the High Country* (Peckinpah, 1962) as a Western without question, even though the aging gunfighters, Randolph Scott and Joel McCrea, are frequently played for laughs. Outdoors? *Rio Bravo* (Hawks, 1959) seldom moves away from a hotel and a jailhouse. Genre critics are by no means agreed on their definitions, a factor that makes their writing thought-provoking, and at times infuriating.

Rather than become lost in these fascinating but unresolvable theoretical questions, most critics and reviewers are content to look for a congeries of "inner and outer forms," not all of which may be present in any particular film, but enough of them will indicate that the film fits into a particular genre and can be discussed as a member of that class.[48]

The outer forms would be visual materials: Stetsons, six-guns, horses, the town on the edge of the desert. Often these visual conventions or icons achieve a precise meaning because audiences have been educated through the genre to assign precise meanings to them: a man in a black suit and string tie is clearly a gambler; the derby marks a man as citified, either the town's editor or a salesman from the East; a man riding in a buckboard is weak, unless, of course, he is escorting a lady, but he will have to return to the saddle to rescue her or avenge her honor.

The inner forms are more difficult to define. These are the basic themes that are appropriate to the genre. For example, a Western will deal with the establishment of order through conflict or the Westward expansion of America.[49] Gangster films portray the evil results of rebelling against social conventions, and the musical presents the reconciliation of imagination and reality on a stage. Thematic criteria become especially slippery concepts, since rarely do they appear in a film in a pure and easily recognizable form. Each film within the genre and each director and scriptwriter present an individual interpretation of the theme.

To complicate matters even further, the genre is not a static concept. It develops through a primitive stage, ripens into a classic period, and eventually deteriorates. For example, Westerns and musicals, immensely popular in the 1950s, have all but vanished from the screen.[50] Audiences have tired of them, it is true, but, more to the point, they have tired of themselves. Once the conventions have become established, invariably they become rigid. Directors must rebel against them, and thus make the conventions laughable or revolting. The first path leads to parody, like *Ride the High Country* and *Blazing Saddles* or *Butch Cassidy and the Sundance Kid* (George Roy Hill, 1969). Through the second path, the film-makers hope to keep the genre on a life-support system after it is brain-dead by upsetting the conventions: the heroes may be psychopathic killers, like *The Wild Bunch* (Peckinpah, 1969), or the hero who cleans up the town may be an amoral killer himself, motivated by a personal grudge rather than community spirit, like the Clint Eastwood character in several of his Westerns between 1964 and 1978. Eastwood later turned to parody with *Bronco Billy* (Eastwood, 1980), which seems to have ended his career in the saddle.

Since genres routinely develop and reach a peak and then begin to deteriorate, the genre critic must possess a keen sense of history, both of films and of their social context.[51] It is possible to describe the changes within a genre or the popularity of one type of film at a particular time as a reflection of the audience that wanted them and of American society as a whole. For example, the musical flourished during the peak years of the Cold War, when audiences dearly wished that all conflicts could be resolved with a lively production number. Fantasy was obviously more attractive than the reality of the day. Again, the Depression created an audience for the screwball comedy in which class differences could be laughed at and overcome by each side's recognizing the basic goodness of individuals of the other class. Poverty is easier to bear when it is supported by a light-hearted belief that the poor are more human and possibly morally superior to the rich.

Another comparison to the literary criticism of the classics is helpful on this point. In his essay "Leopards and History: The Problem of Film Genre," Frank D. McConnell recalls Jacques Maritain's "Dante's Innocence and Luck."[52] Maritain believes that certain classic works, like *The Canterbury Tales* or *The Divine Comedy*, are products of an age as well as an author. The genius of the poet consists in receptivity to the age in which he lives, and thus the poems can be read as monuments of an era as well as products of an individual author. The point is illuminating for any reflection on the Hollywood genre films. They grow out of a certain moment in history, show an audience of a particular time what it wants to see, spawn sequels and develop conventions of such clarity that eventually a group of related films can be called a genre. When the times change and the genre no longer has anything of importance to say to its audience, it dies. The genre critic is especially sensitive to the changing social context of film-making.

Styles of film criticism develop as well. The 1960s marked the arrival and dominance of the auteur method and the rediscovery of the excellence of the American popular film. The 1970s saw the revitalization of genre criticism, but what has happened in the 1980s?

It is clear that once film studies established a beachhead on university campuses and spawned their own generation of professional journals, the development would not stop. It has, however, become more specialized, and, true to the style of academic disciplines, it has become more fragmented and more arcane. Now the professional journals feature specialists writing for their peers in a way that as yet has little bearing on an everyday understanding of films by the educated lay person.

A few of these contemporary methods will be mentioned only briefly, but not because they are unimportant. On the contrary, they are the cutting edge of the field, but like many cutting edges they remain a bit too delicate at their present stage for use in this contemplated series of reflections on the American screen.

One group can be linked together by its psychological interests. Much of the methodology began in linguistic analysis and has led to a study of codes and signs and their ability to communicate information. These critics try to deconstruct the meaning of a given film by reducing it to its signs.[53] Someday perhaps the psychoanalytic methods will enable critics, reviewers and movie-goers to understand more clearly what happens during the viewing of a motion picture. At present it is the realm of scholars and researchers.

A more accessible branch of historical scholarship has shifted the focus from both the directors and the genres to the studios themselves.[54] The logic here is unassailable. If the genre critics have introduced the studios and their markets into the artistic process, then it follows that the more one understands about the influence of the studios and the market forces on the industry, the better one can grasp the films and the work of the artists who make them. Perhaps, then, it is justifiable to begin the evaluation of a film precisely at the point where all these creative energies converge, that is, with the studio. This branch of critical scholarship has much to offer, but at the same time histories of studios and moguls, mergers and bankruptcies often seem more congenial to readers of *Forbes* than to subscribers to *Film Quarterly*.

Finally, feminist critics have raised public awareness of the role of women in the American film.[55] It is a topic that cries out for serious exploration, but again, for present purposes, it is more useful to consider issues as they arise in individual films rather than separate the method into a specialized form of criticism in itself.

NOTES

1. Frank Capra, *The Name Above the Title: An Autobiography* (New York: Macmillan, 1971).

2. Mack Sennett, epigraph to "Cloud Cuckoo Country," in Richard Dyer MacCann, ed., *Film: A Montage of Theories* (New York: Dutton, 1966), p. 160, a selection from Mack Sennett, as told to Cameron Shipp, *King of Comedy* (Garden City, N.Y.: Doubleday, 1954), pp. 86–90.

3. Recounted in David A. Cook, *A History of the Narrative Film* (New York: Norton, 1981), pp. 39–40.

4. Gerald Mast, *A Short History of the Movies* (New York: Macmillan, 1986), p. 46.

5. Mast, p. 96.

6. For a full-length treatment of the founding of the Cinémathèque, see Richard Roud, *A Passion for Film: Henri Langlois and the Cinémathèque Française* (New York: Viking, 1983) pp. 13–28.

7. Annette Insdorf, *François Truffaut* (Boston: Twayne, 1979), cited in Roud, p. 65.

8. Patrick F. Quinn, *The French Face of Edgar Poe* (Carbondale, Ill.: Southern Illinois Univ. Press, 1957), pp. 9–27, traces the impact of Poe on the French literary world.

9. André Bazin, *What Is Cinema?* Volume II, ed. and trans. by Hugh Gray (Berkeley: Univ. of California Press, 1971), p. 20.

10. Jim Hillier, *Cahiers du Cinéma*, ed. Jim Hillier (Cambridge, Mass.: Harvard, 1985), p. 178. This paradoxical observation is drawn from Jacques Rivette's interviews with Roberto Rossellini, printed in this collection of *Cahiers* articles.

11. *What Is Cinema?* II, p. 83.

12. Siegfried Kracauer, *Theory of Film: The Redemption of Physical Reality* (New York: Oxford, 1965) is a book-length treatment of the communicating power of the surfaces of objects.

13. Reprinted in Bill Nichols, ed., *Movies and Methods: An Anthology* (Berkeley, Cal.: Univ. of California, 1976, pp. 225–237.

14. Peter Wollen, *Sign and Meaning in the Cinema* (Bloomington, Ind.: Univ. of Indiana Press, 1969), p. 80.

15. Hillier, p. 75.

16. Hillier, quoting Malraux, p. 6.

17. Hillier, p. 75. Agreeing with Hillier that two meanings of the term exist among the *Cahiers* critics, Peter Wollen offers a more precise distinction. One group, he maintains, argued from a literary point of view: the director who writes the script injects his own interests and preoccupations into the film, and thus is the true auteur. The other group is more concerned with the painterly or photographic point of view: it looks at the visual style, regardless of who wrote the script or whose ideas are presented, and sees the work of an auteur in the visual appearance of the images on the screen—Wollen, p. 78.

18. Eric Rohmer, "Rediscovering America," *Cahiers du Cinéma* 54 (Christmas 1955), in Hillier, p. 89.

19. Jim Hillier, in "Introduction," Hillier, p. 1.

20. Jim Hillier, "Introduction" to *American Cinema*, Hillier, p. 73. The yearly lists of best films selected by the *Cahiers* critics include several American releases each year, but the lists in no way reflect the

adulation of "the American film" that appears in many of the most quoted articles and reviews of *Cahiers:* Hillier, p. 278.

21. André Bazin, "On the *politique des auteurs*," *Cahiers du Cinéma* 70 (April 1957), in Hillier, pp. 251–52.

22. André Bazin, "On the *politique des auteurs*," *Cahiers du Cinéma* 70 (April 1957), in Hillier, p. 258.

23. Jacques Rivette, "The Genius of Howard Hawks," *Cahiers du Cinéma* 23 (May 1953), in Hillier, pp. 126ff.

24. André Bazin, "On the *politique des auteurs*," *Cahiers du Cinéma* 70 (April 1957), in Hillier, p. 248.

25. André Bazin, "On the *politique des auteurs*," *Cahiers du Cinéma* 70 (April 1957), in Hillier, p. 256.

26. Jim Hillier, in "Introduction," cites the American critic John Hess, *La Politique des Auteurs*, in *Jump-Cut*, May-June 1974 and July-August 1974, in Hillier, p. 6.

27. Jacques Rivette, "The Genius of Howard Hawks," *Cahiers du Cinéma* 23, (May 1953), in Hillier, p. 128.

28. Jacques Rivette, "The Genius of Howard Hawks," *Cahiers du Cinéma* 23 (May 1953), in Hillier, p. 130.

29. Eric Rohmer, "Rediscovering America," *Cahiers du Cinéma* 54 (Christmas 1955), in Hillier, p. 90.

30. Amédée Ayfree, "Neorealism and Phenomenology," in *Cahiers du Cinéma* 17 (November 1952), in Hillier, p. 190.

31. *The Miracle* case, properly *Burstyn* v. *Wilson* (1951), settled the dispute that began in 1950 with the licensing of *The Ways of Love*, a trilogy of European films distributed in the United States by Joseph Burstyn. *The Miracle* was later released separately and opened at the Paris Theater in New York on December 10, 1950. Mr. Burstyn argued that his First Amendment right of free speech had been violated when the police seized the print. The following year the case reached the U.S. Supreme Court, which affirmed Mr. Burstyn's right to show the film in the United States. Ironically, this ruling made illegal subsequent attempts to ban films through government authority, thus overturning the principle set forth in *Mutual* v. *Ohio* (1915) that films are purely commercial enterprises and not covered by the free speech provisions of the Constitution. Edward de Grazia and Roger K. Newman, *Banned Films: Movies, Censors and the First Amendment* (New York: Bowker, 1982), pp. 232–233.

32. Jacques Rivette, "Letter on Rossellini," *Cahiers du Cinéma* 46 (April 1955), in Hillier, p. 201.

33. Andrew Sarris, *Confessions of a Cultist: On the Cinema, 1955/69* (New York: Touchstone, 1971), p. 13.

34. Andrew Sarris, "The American Cinema," *Film Culture* No. 28 (Spring 1963), pp. 1–68.

35. *Film Culture*, p. 46.

36. Andrew Sarris, *Interviews with Film Directors* (New York: Avon, 1967), pp. 11–12.

37. Andrew Sarris, "Toward a Theory of Film History," in *The American Cinema: Directors and Directions 1929–1968* (New York: Dutton, 1968), pp. 19–37.

38. *The American Cinema* (1968), p. 23.

39. *The American Cinema* (1968), p. 30.

40. *The American Cinema* (1968), p. 34.

41. *The American Cinema* (1968), p. 36.

42. Tim Bywater and Thomas Sobchack, *An Introduction to Film Criticism: Major Approaches to Narrative Film* (New York: Longman, 1989), pp. 84–86.

43. Both are reprinted in Robert Warshow, *The Immediate Experience: Movies, Comics, Theatre and Other Aspects of Popular Culture* (New York: Doubleday Anchor, 1964), pp. 83–106.

44 Thomas Sobchack, "Genre Film: A Classical Experience," in *Film Genre*, ed. Barry K. Grant (Metuchen, N.J.: Scarecrow, 1977), pp. 39–43.

45. Thomas Schatz, *Hollywood Genres: Formulas, Filmmaking and the Studio System* (New York: Random House, 1981), pp. 3–13.

46. Related in A. Scott Berg, *Goldwyn: A Biography* (New York: Alfred A. Knopf, 1989), p. 333.

47. Edward Buscombe, "The Idea of Genre in the American Cinema," in Grant, pp. 25–38.

48. Buscombe, in Grant, pp. 31–32.

49. Kitses, pp. 9–10.

50. Schatz, p. 38.

51. Bywater and Sobchack, pp. 99–100.

52. Frank D. McConnell, in "Leopards and History: The Problem of Film Genre," in Grant, p. 13.

53. Wollen, pp. 116–155, gives a summary of the sources of semiology as it was then, in 1969, being adapted to cinema. He mentions prior work in France and Italy by Umberto Eco, Roland Barthes, Christian Metz and Pier Paolo Pasolini. A milestone marking the entry of semiotics into mainstream, if specialized, criticism in the

United States was the publication of Christian Metz's *The Imaginary Signifier, Psychoanalysis and the Cinema,* tr. Celia Britton, Annwyl Williams, Ben Brewster and Alfred Guzzetti (Bloomington, Ind.: Univ. of Indiana, 1982), a collection of essays originally copyrighted in France in 1977.

54. Among the more prominent examples of this type of research might be listed an anthology *The American Film Industry,* ed. Tino Balio (Madison, Wisc.: Univ. of Wisconsin, 1986), Douglas Gomery, *The Hollywood Studio System* (New York: St. Martin's, 1986) and Thomas Schatz, *The Genius of the System: Hollywood Filmmaking in the Studio Era* (New York: Pantheon, 1988).

55. Molly Haskell, *From Reverence to Rape: The Treatment of Women in Movies* (Chicago: Univ. of Chicago Press, 1987). Originally published in 1974, this remains a timely discussion of the topic.

PART II

Chapter Four

LESSONS FROM HOLLYWOOD

Analogies are pesky figures of speech, but they can be extremely useful. Their purpose is to illuminate by way of comparison. They prove nothing, nor are they intended to. With these limitations in mind, I offer an extended analogy as a summary of the historical survey presented in Part I and as an introduction to the following collection of five essays on selected American film classics.

Although the comparison may seem stretched, recalling the relationship of the churches to the physical sciences can provide a kind of workable paradigm to explain the relationship of the churches, and of the academic community, to the strange and alien but wondrous land of Hollywood.

The pairing of science and religion has been a stormy one through the centuries, and well it might be. The stakes are enormously high, but a common language was often missing at critical junctures. Their methodologies frequently seemed not only incompatible but irreconcilable, as Galileo discovered. At first glance, or second, their goals seemed mutually exclusive. Science relies on free inquiry to push forward the frontiers of knowledge; the churches rely on tradition, sacred writings and authority to preserve the purity of what has been revealed in the past. Science is concerned with the affairs of this finite world, while the churches deal with matters of eternity. Through the centuries, conflicts were inevitable.

Science, so it seemed to the religious establishments, had the power to undermine the faith, and so the alchemists with their alembics and the astronomers with their telescopes had to be watched carefully and controlled. What if they proved that the world was not made in six days of exhausting labor for the creator, or that the earth

93

was not the center of the universe, or that the sun could not have stopped dead still in the sky for Joshua? In those days of extremely literal reading of the Bible, any scientific discovery that challenged the words of scripture had to be declared heretical and dealt with promptly before it undermined the faith of simple believers.

If that line of reasoning seems quaintly medieval, we moderns cannot afford to be smug about our present-day open-mindedness. In our own century Darwin and Freud struck the same kinds of theological sparks among the churches. In these more recent controversies, however, the focus has changed from fear of destroying "the faith" to a well-founded fear of undermining personal morality. If humans are descended from monkeys, why shouldn't they behave like them? Thus Darwin threatens the Judaeo-Christian fabric of Western society. This battle still rages in the textbook controversies of California: What must children be taught about the relative merits of "creationism" and "evolutionism"?

And if the person is victimized by subconscious and therefore unknown drives and compulsions, as Freud and his followers taught, then where is personal responsibility for human behavior? Through the courts, society faces this problem every time a defendant offers a plea of impaired judgment by reason of mental incompetence. Can morality survive if such notions gain widespread acceptance, especially among ordinary people who may not be able to make the distinctions and add the nuances that great scientists do?

Religious thinkers throughout the centuries who agonized about such topics were not ignorant bigots. On the contrary, they were extraordinarily perceptive in catching on to the significance of what was happening in the laboratories and university lecture halls of their time, and they shuddered. Let us not go on record as approving the burning of books or their authors, but simply as pointing out that the fears of the churchmen were reasonable, even if some of their responses were not. To their credit they realized that something terribly important was going on and they took steps to meet the challenge to the world order as they understood it. Most of their secular contemporaries had not the slightest idea what was happening.

The response of hysteria was not the only one. Theologians and preachers could and often did use the discoveries of the scientific world for their own purposes. St. Patrick was a good botanist when he told his pagan congregations that the three leaves of the single shamrock were a model of the Trinity. (If some equally clever Druid had picked up a four-leaf clover to refute Patrick, the course of Irish history might have been quite different.) In the present day, apologists for the miracles at Lourdes and the Shroud of Turin have routinely used scientific data to explain their beliefs to the curious but skeptical, just as the skeptical use the same methods to challenge the beliefs of the faithful.

Today science enjoys a much broader role in religious thought than merely as a battleground for apologetics. Scripture scholarship, for example, underwent a revolution through the discoveries of modern archaeology and linguistics, and it is difficult to imagine what the understanding of the sacred texts would be without them. Some have even cited the "Big Bang" theory as evidence that Genesis was right after all and the universe did begin with the creation of light.

Moralists today have also grown dependent on the sciences. Not many years ago, when Freud and Darwin were regarded with such suspicion, their scientific theories were seen as a threat to personal morality. The commandments, the manuals and canon law had all the answers, if few of the questions. Current moral issues, however, are closely linked to science, and any worthwhile moralist searches for more data to illuminate the issues: When does life in the womb become human? When does a patient actually die and thus absolve family and physicians from the obligation of further medical care? What are the limits of genetic engineering? When do various cultural expressions distort the core meaning of religious truths? How must wealth be distributed among peoples? What are the dangers to the atmosphere from nuclear and chemical discharges, and when do the data compel a conclusion that some matters of public policy with regard to the environment are immoral? Good ethicians or theologians today cannot afford to distance themselves from the world of science.

The story of this outrageously abridged history of the church and science seems headed for a happy ending. With few exceptions, the theological and religious communities no longer look upon the sciences as a threat to faith and morals or as a mere catechetical tool. For the most part they no longer try to publicize useful findings and suppress the uncomfortable, under threat of excommunication, or its modern equivalent, public vilification.

In the past thirty years, many in the current generation of religious professionals and active lay people have marched off to the finest secular universities to become proficient in the scientific disciplines: sociology, medicine, psychiatry, economics, anthropology, geology, or even ichthyology. They enter their fields as competent, respected scientists. Their work can be studied by their secularist, agnostic and atheistic peers for its contribution to the field. They do

not enter the demanding worlds of the academy on a tourist visa with
the notion of taking a few snapshots to warn their friends at home
about the vile customs of the natives or to prove the superiority of
their own country. Instead they are citizens in good standing in the
scientific and academic communities and see their roles as mediators
between realms, not adversaries.

Through their work these men and women make a double contribution. First, they enrich their own disciplines by representing the
values of their respective religious traditions in a secular learning
environment. Christians, for example, by their competence and their
faith, are able to "Christianize" without proselytizing. The process
takes place in this way: as Christian scientists are respected for their
work, their beliefs gain respect as well, even from those peers who
choose not to embrace them. It may come as a surprise to some reso-
lute secularists that a person can both be a good scientist and embrace
faith in a personal God at the same time. Second, scientists with a
religious commitment can enrich enormously the more properly theological dialogues within their own communities. They elevate the
level of discourse in their own religious bodies and enable the official
leadership to make informed decisions on matters involving complex
data. Nothing helps intelligent discussion and policy decisions as
much as information. And nothing leads more directly to unfortunate
policy directives as surely as ignorance. Witness the productive relationship between moralist and physician on the question of euthana-
sia, and try to imagine how incomplete each would be without
the other.

The most noted paradigm of this style of scientific-religious dialogue is Père Pierre Teilhard de Chardin, S.J. As a professional paleontologist he collaborated in demanding research projects around
the world. As a person of great faith and breadth of imagination he
was able to synthesize his religious beliefs and his work. As a result he
created some of the most influential spiritual writing of the mid-cen-
tury. His popularity, among scientists, theologians and students, religious professionals and lay people alike, indicates that he had something terribly important to say. He addressed scientific questions as a
man of faith and questions of faith as a man of science. In this scientific
age his observations are invaluable, whereas in an earlier century his
reflections might have been regarded as a threat to religion. The fact
that he was initially misunderstood, opposed and condemned during
his lifetime and then, only a few short years after his death in 1955,
was recognized as a significant theologian proves how quickly the
churches' attitude toward science has been in the process of change.

Two points are crucial about Père Teilhard's work. First, he did not impose his faith on his research. His scientific work stands on its own merits, and was scrutinized by his peers precisely as scientific. He worked side by side with other scientists of many faiths or of no faith at all. He contributed to the journals, visited the universities and joined in the archaeological digs. He did not, for example, examine the fossils with a view toward proving or disproving some theory of creation. On this level, his work was rigorously objective. If it were anything else, he would never have been seriously regarded in the scientific community.

Second, even though today he is known to the reading public more as a religious writer than as a scientist, during his lifetime he never abandoned his scientist's commitment to objectivity. His discovering a religious aura in his scientific work was by no means a form of subjectivism. As a man of faith he was able to uncover and articulate a theological dimension in the data that was already there. He did not impose a meaning from without. What he wrote about so movingly was his own poetic response to the discovery of God already present in matter. He did not celebrate the discovery that he could successfully impose his own deep religious beliefs on his scientific work. He did violence neither to science nor to theology; he treated both with reverence.

The parallels between natural science and film study in their relationships with the churches are striking, even though the time factor is quite different. Science has had centuries to work out its productive truce with theology, but the American film has had only ninety years. A lot remains to be done, and perhaps the comparisons to the world of the sciences can put several of the still prickly issues into a proper historical context. Perhaps both film scholars and church people can profitably reflect on the history of science to discern a similar development.

By way of summary of the history developed in chapter 2, in the beginning church professionals and others recognized that film was going to be an important social force, and they regarded it with suspicion. In this they were perceptive, even though at times misguided in their response. Galileo was burned at the stake in his time, but during *The Miracle* controversy Joseph Burstyn merely had his theater padlocked by such perceptive but misguided people. From the earliest days of the nickelodeons, many believed that the film industry represented a threat to the moral fabric of American society and thus must be rigidly controlled. Their initial insight proved quite accurate. We are only now beginning to realize the immense impact that the images of film and television have had on America's moral values. At the same time we have come to realize that a policy of unrelieved confrontation based in ignorance and suspicion has had little success in changing anything. The dialogue between the film industry and the churches, like that of the sciences and the churches in an earlier age, benefited enormously by the presence of several individuals who understand both film and the churches' mission.

Well into this century, and perhaps even into the present, many Americans viewed different ideas from different cultures as suspect, and the churches aligned themselves with several secular forces to guard the American people from dangerous images and ideas. These guardians of the moral order, both lay and religious, developed a morbid, almost prurient interest in finding objective criteria for acceptability. The goal seemed to be to force the industry to create a product that would disturb or offend no one: the most sheltered, the most narrow-minded, the most pietistic, the most scrupulous, the child. For years the crusade almost worked, and it is kept alive today by a very outspoken and effective minority on the religious right.

As the pluralism in American society forced a breakdown in the consensus that films had to be tailored to fit the preadolescent sensibility to protect public morality, some religious writers began to find theological themes in some films, using them as Patrick had used the shamrock. Both St. Patrick, the botanist, and William Lynch, S.J., the film critic of the 1950s, demonstrated at least a rudimentary knowledge of their subjects, botany and film, but the primary interest for both was clearly theological. Films, like shamrocks, were a means to an end. This interest marked the beginning of a dramatic shift. Before long, in the age of "Fellini and Bergman," church institutions and church-related colleges were actually encouraging the screening of adult and foreign language films, despite the "C" rating by the Legion of Decency. Some church people even found a fruitful religious message in films that portrayed adult relationships, despair, or a frustrated search for meaning.

Over the last thirty years, film study has entered the intellectual mainstream of the universities. It has developed its own methodologies, which have advanced far beyond plot and character analysis as an offshoot of literary criticism. Indeed much of the literature in the professional journals is as inaccessible to the layman as articles in journals of physics or biology. In their work first on the Italian neorealist directors and later on the American cinema, the critics of the *Cahiers* school and their followers have opened up vast areas of interest, like visual style, directorial expression and studio influence. Each of these fields required its own language.

Through their work a new-found respect for the Hollywood film arose. The American popular film has become a worthy subject of study in itself: in the academy because of its intrinsic worth as an art form and an expression of a cultural moment; in the churches, not because of the theological questions that can be imposed on the script or the moral tensions discovered in the characters, but because it is an expression of the inspired artists who often understood the longings and achievements of their contemporaries better than the church bodies themselves. Compare a film to a homily. Which is more likely to be received and remembered? Which speaks more to the people as they are? Which commands and gets a higher price of admission?

Film, of course, has terrible limitations as a homilist. In the first place, most popular films are purely commercial enterprises and contain little of value. In addition, audiences for serious films remain distressingly small, and many even in the small select audience cannot "read" the images they see with any facility. Think of it this way. Most people spend years in school taking English courses to learn how to understand a novel or a poem. Even then, the results are not necessarily successful. Most people presume they can "read" a film without any training or systematic reflection. Literacy, in image as well as in word, rarely comes through raw intuition.

To serve this need, film education has become more professionalized. Since it has become increasingly specialized during the years, does this mean that the religious communities have to back off and admit they have nothing to offer the study of film? Must one conclude that since Americans now accept a pluralism of tastes—"permissive" and "tolerant" are words used by conservatives and liberals respectively to describe the same phenomenon, even though each reveals its own value judgment—the churches can no longer credibly address the moral issues raised by films? Or does it mean that any attempt to locate religious "content" must be viewed as a form of subjectivism, a foolhardy attempt to impose a religious sensibility upon a work that claims to be unabashedly secular? Decidedly not. It is possible to read films objectively, and at the same time from a religious perspective, without imposing meanings on the text.

An example may help. Woody Allen is Jewish, and many of the themes of his work arise from his Jewishness. This is a fact, an objective truth that any critic must consider as part of his films' creation. However, to look through his brilliant *Hannah and Her Sisters* (1986) for evidence of Old Testament or rabbinic teaching could be a foolhardy enterprise, although some scholar may be able to do it someday. The film is a perfectly secular romantic comedy, despite its profundity. Jewish theology has nothing to do with it. Similarly, in his brilliant *Crimes and Misdemeanors* (1989), where he uses Jewish religious vocabulary to probe religious issues, his audiences can read the drama in perfectly secular terms or even transfer it to a Christian setting without doing violence to the text. Any rich work of art allows for many "correct" readings.

At the same time, it is quite appropriate to cite the American Jewish experience as presented by authors like Philip Roth, Saul Bellow and Bernard Malamud or comedians like Jackie Mason and Rodney Dangerfield as enriching their work. Their heroes are talented, perhaps have some money and friends, yet they feel themselves ever the outsiders in a culture that can never accept them totally. They long for love and respect, and this is constantly misinterpreted as their being pushy, manipulative and selfish. When they withdraw, they are labeled insecure, or clannish. The plight of the Jew in American society provides these very different artists with the stuff of comedy and tragedy, and often both at the same time.

A Christian shares many of the same experiences, because they are human experiences as well as Jewish experiences. The mode of expression, however, may be very different. In looking at *Hannah and Her Sisters*, for example, the first step for a critic is to try to discover what Woody Allen is saying, and why and how he says it and shows it. This involves recognizing and naming, at least internally, the Jewish background of the auteur. The ideas and feelings expressed through the characters on the screen, however, are not necessarily exclusively Jewish experiences. As an artist, Woody Allen explores the universal human condition. A Christian sees the events on the screen through the prism of his or her own life, which is a Christian life. It is then inevitable that a Christian critic will reflect on these universal experiences precisely as a Christian. In *Hannah and Her Sisters*, Woody Allen addresses questions like death, the impermanence of relationships in urban society, a need to belong, the insecurity of the talented and not-too-talented alike, the power of family ties, destructive addiction and, most important, the redeeming quality of self-sacrificing love.

Beware! "Redeeming" is a Christian word, and it could set loose a chain reaction: the endless quest for Christ-symbols. Such a search would be unfair to Mr. Allen, who is Jewish, and to his film, which is secular. In addition, it would be as fruitless as sifting through the scenes for Talmudic references. "Redeeming," however, may be the best word that Christian critics may be able to find to express what they see in the film. Hannah (Mia Farrow), through her patience, generosity and love, is able to save several members of her family from their self-destructive behavior. This does not make Hannah a Christ-figure, as some would have it, but it does mirror a style of life that a Christian holds out as an ideal because it was embraced by Jesus the Christ.

Clearly, Christians have no monopoly on this kind of self-sacrificing love; a non-Christian can embrace the same values just as easily, or, more accurately, with the same degree of difficulty. The love Hannah displays is there in the text on the screen. A critic's calling her a Christ-figure is adding something that is not there. Using a term like "redeeming" may be as good a way as any to express admiration for the character that Woody Allen has created.

No critic or viewer approaches a film without a life history. This is inevitably part of the experience of viewing a film. Only the strictest ideologues of the deconstructionist school would deny the Marxists their right to see in films evidence of class conflict, or the feminist critics the right to discern evidence of the oppression of women. Some ideological critics are tiresome, and often they are wrong, but often too they are more sensitive to these issues than other critics, and often their insights can be most helpful. The point is that what they see in the film must be there; it cannot be imposed by a critic's wishing it were there. Observation born of ideology is inaccurate and ultimately silly.

Christian critics have the same privilege, but like their Marxist and feminist colleagues, they cannot move upstairs too quickly or carelessly. They bring their own bundle of experience and values into the screening room. Aware of their own sensitivities, they must be particularly careful to treat the film with reverence and allow it to speak for itself.

This process depends on knowing how films work. They must consider the interests of the auteur in other films that shed light on the film under discussion. They must be sensitive to the demands of the genre and the constraints of the studio. The analysis must remain respectful of the text, and it must offer some insight to those who find Christian values irrelevant or even distracting.

That is the goal of the chapters that follow. The subsequent essays on the five American classics may not appear explicitly Christian or religious at all. That is deliberate. None of the films were intended to be religious theses, and it makes little sense at this late date to baptize them against their will. If some explicitly Christian meanings appear during the discussion of the issues the film raises, then that is a bonus, not the primary intent of the criticism.

Nor is the point of the essays to draw sweeping conclusions about "American culture." The goal is far more limited. These critical essays are a modest attempt to examine in some detail some American masterworks with the help of contemporary, secular methodology, just to see what is there and how it got there. These exercises should reveal something about the society that produced them. The fact that the writer is a priest may imbue both the essays and the films with a certain complexion at times, but it is intended that any observation be supported by the text of the film itself. These chapters should be uncompromisingly nondenominational, just like Woody Allen's "Jewish" films.

At this point we stand next to Père Teilhard at a cluttered table of bones and notes and calipers, in the company of scholars, trying to understand what is there in front of us. The synthesis of *The Phenomenon of Man* or the poetry of *The Divine Milieu* lies somewhere in the future.

Chapter Five

THE SCREWBALL COMEDY
IT HAPPENED ONE NIGHT

The Auteur: Frank Capra

Frank Capra's early life gives little evidence that he would become one of America's great directors of comedy. Poverty and early failures should have given him a dark vision more suited to gangsters and tragedy, yet the opposite is true. His simple stories and naive idealization of "plain folks" mask a sophisticated technique and optimistic message. Yet for all his sometimes preachy acts of faith in the American way, he was, above all, one of Hollywood's supreme entertainers. Audiences of the 1930s and 1940s loved each new film, and today film critics, who until recently might have scorned "Capracorn," find in his work more and more to admire.

In 1897, when Frank Capra was born in Sicily, emigration was his family's only chance to escape from poverty.[1] In 1903 they moved to Los Angeles to join the oldest son, Ben, who had run away from Sicily, found work as a deckhand, and jumped ship in New Orleans, only to end up cutting sugar cane. Ben was forcibly taken from Louisiana to cut cane on an island somewhere in the Pacific, escaped by rowboat, was rescued by an Australian steamer bound for San Francisco and eventually worked his way down the coast to the orange groves around Los Angeles. Thus the Capra beachhead was established in California. When Frank, his parents, a brother and two sisters joined Ben in 1903, they were, of course, desperately poor. Frank Capra writes: "The prime challenge an ignorant peasant family faces in a foreign land is to keep alive. Never mind sending kids to school. Get the moola."[2]

In that environment, where even a trip to the nickelodeon was a

103

luxury, the arts would have to wait. Young Frank, however, was shrewd enough to realize that education promised more "moola" in the long run. He earned a degree in chemical engineering from C.I.T. (California Institute of Technology), but after a stretch of teaching ballistics to artillery officers during World War I, he found few jobs available for graduate engineers, other than building stills for the nation's great growth industry, bootlegging. Despite his near desperation, he rejected a $20,000 offer from the mob. Rather than seek a life of crime, he sank even lower by taking a job in another and even more disreputable growth industry: the movies.

At the time he did not know a lens cap from a light meter, but he lied to get a job as a director, and the rest, as the cliché has it, is history. Pocketing his money for directing his first silent film in 1922, *The Ballad of Fultah Fisher's Boarding House*, he found the studios no more interested in his talents than the legitimate chemical companies had been, but he was intrigued by the potential of the industry. As a prematurely retired engineer, he was able to find a job as a technician, developing and splicing film. He progressed from repairman to editor and finally to writing comedy routines for Hal Roach, who fired him after six months. By some miracle he was able to join the King of Comedy, Mack Sennett, as a writer and uncredited director for the rising star Harry Langdon. He later became Langdon's actual director, but was again fired, apparently because of Langdon's jealousy.

Trying the East Coast, he directed Claudette Colbert's first film, *For the Love of Mike* (1927), but it was such a disaster that the beautiful young star of the Broadway stage decided never to make another film. Humiliated, yet needing cash, Capra had to agree to a huge pay cut, and he returned to the Sennett studios to make two-reel comedy fillers.

Help soon arrived from a surprising quarter. Eager to break into the big time with his fly-by-night studio, Harry Cohn of Columbia Pictures offered him a job as a contract director in 1928. In desperation, Capra took the job. Desperation accurately describes the motivation. The studio was known as "Columbia the Germ of the Ocean," and Harry Cohn, to put it gently, was not beloved. At his death, Rabbi Leon Magnin was asked if he could find "one good thing" to say about him in the eulogy. The rabbi replied: "He's dead."[3] Years later, Capra was said to have used Harry Cohn as the model for his ruthless tycoons, played with venomous relish by Edward Arnold and Lionel Barrymore. Columbia was not a terribly attractive proposition, but

Capra did not have much of a track record to bargain with, and any job was better than the poverty he had known as a boy.

Sound was in its infancy, and everyone, even the most experienced directors, was forced to learn how to use the new medium. In a very real sense, they were all starting from scratch together. After making seven silents at Columbia, Capra used sound for the first time in *The Younger Generation* (1929). After two years and six more pictures, he made *Platinum Blonde*, starring Jean Harlow, and written by Robert Riskin who would form an enormously successful artistic partnership with Capra that would last for nineteen years and through eleven films.[4] Riskin's scripts provided Capra with the material for his most successful films: *It Happened One Night* (1934), *Mr. Deeds Goes to Town* (1936), *Lost Horizon* (1937), *You Can't Take It With You* (1938) and *Meet John Doe* (1941). Four of the Capra/Riskin films were clones: *Riding High* (1950) was a reworking of their *Broadway Bill* (1934), and after Riskin's death in 1955, Capra made *Pocketful of Miracles* (1961), his last feature film, from their earlier collaboration *Lady for a Day* (1933). Their other joint efforts include *Miracle Woman* (1931) and *American Madness* (1932).[5]

In *Platinum Blonde* the characteristic Capra themes begin to take shape. A romance develops across the barriers of social class. Anne Schyler (Jean Harlow) is beautiful (obviously), rich and spoiled, while Stew Smith (Robert Williams) is a work-a-day newspaper man. From infatuation to marriage, Stew tries to enter her world but cannot. He is eventually rescued from his intolerable marriage by Gallagher (Loretta Young), an old pal, a fellow reporter and thus a woman from the same social caste. In these days before the Production Code, Capra allows Stew to marry Anne, and then, after leaving her, share his apartment with Gallagher, whom he will eventually marry. In later films the relationships will be more delicately presented on the screen. The result will be a much lighter and funnier battle of the sexes, in which the skirmishes are purely verbal and no one really gets hurt.

In *Platinum Blonde* and *It Happened One Night* (1934) the conflict between social classes, mirrored in the battles between the lovers, will be limited to economic class: rich vs. poor, tinted, of course, by the social conventions stereotypically attributed to each class. The rich, for example, speak with vaguely British tones and the poor with a lilt of New York. (Since sound was new and speaking actors rare in the movie business, Hollywood had to import a great deal of ready-made talent from the legitimate stages of Broadway and London's West End. The phonetic contrast between the two groups of actors fit nicely with the American conception of upper- and lower-class accents.)

While Capra's bias lies with the working classes, he is no ideologue. This is surprising in light of his background. The rich are arrogant and frivolous, it is true, but the poor can be equally arrogant, and what is more they are capable of great scheming to make a few dollars or gain a bit of respect. The comedy comes from rubbing these worlds together and watching the sparks fly. In Capra's hands the combat is not one-sided. Also, the gulf between the two narrows as Capra grows more sure of his message. In *Platinum Blonde*, the classes are absolutely incompatible, and Stew must retreat into his own world to find happiness. In *It Happened One Night* the couple does cross the line of class to unite for an improbable but inevitable happy ending.

In the later comedies Capra expands the notion of class boundaries to include more than mere economic distinctions. For want of a better term, the conflict could be described as simple against sophisticated. Often this is presented as country virtues opposed to urban wiles, with the presumed moral superiority of rural people. In *Mr. Deeds Goes to Town* (1936) the slow-talking tuba player Longfellow Deeds (Gary Cooper) comes to New York to take possession of his inheritance, only to be manipulated by Babe Bennett (Jean Arthur), a slick newspaperwoman looking for a story. In *Mr. Smith Goes to Washington* (1939) Jefferson Smith (James Stewart) is set up by a corrupt political machine to come to the U.S. Senate as a walking rubber stamp. He is educated in the ways of the Capitol by Saunders (Jean Arthur), a slick political publicist. In *Meet John Doe* (1941) Long John Willoughby (Gary Cooper), an ex-baseball player, is manipulated by a conniving newspaper woman, Anne Mitchell (Barbara Stanwyck), into fronting for an ambitious businessman with political aspirations, D.B. Norton (Edward Arnold). In each of these cases the simplicity of the bumpkin-hero wins over the heart of the urban heroine.

The story takes a bit of a twist in *You Can't Take It With You* (1938). In this play by Moss Hart and George S. Kaufman, the roles are reversed. Wealth is represented by Tony Kirby (James Stewart), the son of the archetypical industrialist Anthony J. Kirby (Edward Arnold). Tony falls in love with Anne Sycamore (Jean Arthur), a poor working girl from an unconventional, rather zany, family. Tony learns to reject the artifice and the trappings of power and in his mediator's role he wins Anne and unites the families.

In the last of his great comedies, *It's a Wonderful Life* (1946), the role of mediation is even more complicated. Mary Hatch (Donna Reed) represents the values of small-town America, which are being challenged by the greedy developer, Mr. Potter (Lionel Barrymore). Caught in the middle is George Bailey (James Stewart), who contemplates suicide on Christmas Eve to escape from the financial pressure put on him by Potter's organization. Through a divine illumination, an angel named Clarence (Henry Travers), George discovers the power of the little people of the small towns. In this film the crossing of class boundaries is vaguer. Mr. Potter is simply excluded, and George, who hovered in the middleground (metaphorically by flirting with death), rejects Potter's world of wealth and power and himself crosses over to embrace Mary's hometown values.

This master theme in Capra's work casts light on many facets of his artistic vision. As a poor immigrant who eventually prospered, he has great faith in the ideals of "America," at least as a concept if not always as an actuality. For example, *Why We Fight,* the series of documentary training films he made for the War Department during World War II, has a surprisingly nasty racist tinge to it. He seemed consumed by hatred of the enemies of the American way, not as political adversaries locked in war, but as personal threats. In his fiction films he created an America of Mom, the flag and apple pie right out of Norman Rockwell's covers for *The Saturday Evening Post.*

What is bad about America is only a misguided abuse of capitalism and other forms of power, but once "the big shot" is confronted by the intrinsic goodness of "the little guy," he either repents the error of his ways, as in *You Can't Take It With You,* or is clearly beaten, as in *Mr. Smith Goes to Washington.*

The conflicts Capra presents between sparring couples who are destined to work through their difficulties and marry reflect the conflicts in American society. With patience and tolerance for "the other fellow," class differences can be resolved as well. Depression audiences, of course, loved the optimistic vision of a new classless society. They longed for the day when the greedy robber barons would be faced down by the common man, when capitalism would learn the price of its avarice and become a benevolent force in solving the world's social problems, and when all the institutions of society and government would be purged of self-seekers and serve the people.

Capra's notion of conflict resolution is, of course, utopian, but Utopia lies at the heart of Capra's vision of America. He presents an America of the imagination and then structures a conflict between it and the America of actuality.[6] In Capra films the dream comes true. The idealized America wins out over the real twentieth century America that Capra and his Depression audiences knew. In the Capra fantasy world there is no need for riot in the streets to dislodge the corrupt, but only an awareness of small town decency. When the couple from opposite sides of the tracks are finally reconciled, the fundamental goodness of the American people triumphs.

American institutions form a special problem for Capra. Often they become the agents of repression for "the little guy," and as such must be regarded with extreme suspicion. Yet the institutions are organs of a democratic society, and as American institutions they must be regarded as sacred. Capra resolves his dilemma by preserving the integrity of the institutions, while admitting that occasionally they may come under the power of corrupt individuals and forces. The people must remain vigilant. Once they reassert themselves and repossess what is truly theirs, the problem is resolved: the U.S. Senate in *Mr. Smith Goes to Washington,* the courts in *Mr. Deeds Goes to Town,* the real estate business in *You Can't Take It With You,* the banks in *It's a Wonderful Life,* the media in *Meet John Doe* and *Mr. Deeds Goes to Town.* The American churches, oddly enough, play no role for good or ill in the Capra universe.

With his idealization of the common man and working class values, Capra has often been mistakenly pegged as a New Deal Democrat. This is far from the truth. He mistrusts government intervention in human affairs and tolerates it only when the individual, representing the common man, is able to purge the institutions of professional bureaucrats and profiteers and control the structures with old-fashioned common sense. Solutions to problems in Capra's films never come from organizations; they come from individuals, even when they unite as an informal collective, the people, as in *It's a Wonderful Life* and *Meet John Doe.* When Andrew Sarris refers to John Doe as "a barefoot fascist, suspicious of all ideas and doctrines, but believing in the innate conformism of the common man," he may have had in mind the creator as well as the creature.[7]

Does Capra's Catholicism influence his world view and subsequently his films? Yes and no. He makes few references to religion in his autobiography or in his films. When he does, he seems to be drawing on popular mythology rather than theology. For example, Clarence, the angel in *It's a Wonderful Life,* is really a fairy-tale character. In the opening sequence, during the titles, prayers for George Bailey rise up to heaven. As lights pulsate to accompany their voices, Clarence discusses George's plight with St. Peter. The shots establish a world of childlike fantasy far removed from the world of big business that has driven George to despair. It is the standard conflict between imagination and reality that is so much a part of the Capra vision. The machinery of a popular, somewhat sentimental version of heaven is extremely well suited to his purposes.[8]

Clarence leads George to an appreciation of his own life and the love he has received from his family and friends, rather than the love he has received from God. Setting the action on Christmas Eve may suggest the coming of Christ into George's life, but the idea, although it is compatible with the theme, really seems difficult to substantiate from the text of the film. Christmas, in its secular sense of fellowship and peace with its sentimental overtones, seems far more in keeping with the ideas Capra develops in this film as well as in his other films. The crisis of faith his characters deal with is more faith in themselves, or faith in America. It is resolved by fantasy, by returning to the original values of the democracy and its citizens, not perhaps as they actually are, but as Capra and his audiences want to believe they are.

In the climactic scene of *Meet John Doe*, Doe is explicitly compared to Christ. He is preaching a message of love in a world of greed. The scene was an afterthought, one of five possible endings shot and test-screened. All were unsatisfactory. By Capra's own admission, he and Riskin could not figure out how to end the story. They could never allow Gary Cooper to die, nor could they wave a magic wand and create a phony happy ending. Throughout the film Doe is the hollow man, a charlatan who allows himself to be used by D.B. Norton. Only when he sees how far his actions have taken him does he try to undo the damage. Finally, to redeem himself and to make amends for the harm he has done to his followers, he contemplates suicide. After trying several versions, Capra and Riskin put on an appendage that ends with Doe's resolve to go on living, while the sound track swells with Beethoven's "Ode to Joy." By Capra's own admission, it is a disappointing ending to an otherwise extraordinary film.[9] If the reference to Christ is anything more than cultural shorthand to express an example of self-sacrifice, it is an appendix and not part of the original inspiration of the film.

Even though Capra's films resist religious interpretation, and a critic would be foolhardy indeed to try to force the issue, a kind of Christian ethos is certainly present. In the Capra world, men and

women take responsibility for their actions and live with the consequences. The prelapsarian world of the imagination is spoiled by human evil, which may come from either malice, like D.B. Norton's, or a
temporary loss of direction, like Babe Bennett's. Good, simple people
find themselves caught up in this world of evil and must choose
whether or not to oppose it. When they opt for virtue, they are triumphant. As for the sinners, the opportunity for correcting the wrong is
offered; those who accept find reconciliation in the unification of the
two worlds of fantasy and reality. Those who reject are simply excluded from the happiness of the final synthesis.

This is a profoundly Christian doctrine, although by no means
would I argue that it is exclusively Christian. In many religious traditions the human person is free to decide between sin and virtue,
between avarice and altruism. Sin ruptures community, while virtue
heals. Both coexist in the world. In Capra's films virtue is triumphant,
and even the sinners responsible for the conflict receive an opportunity for redemption. Some will reject the opportunity, and some will
accept. This does not make Doe, or Deeds, or Smith, or Bailey a
Christ-figure—not necessarily. To cast them in the role is to limit
Capra's message too narrowly. In addition, it is difficult to support the
comparisons through the internal evidence of the films. Capra offers
virtually few persuasive visual or verbal clues that he would like his
audiences to deify his heroes, or, in the case of Mary Hatch Bailey in
It's a Wonderful Life, his heroines.

The temptation is always present, however, to read the internal
evidence according to a predetermined thesis. At a moment of crisis
the heroes appear overwhelmed by the forces of evil. Their enemies,
the rich and powerful, seem to have the power to destroy them. Doe
and Bailey actually contemplate accepting death, since their respective suicides may overwhelm the forces of evil. Smith faces a metaphorical death by his political suicide on the floor of the Senate, and
Deeds surrenders his wealth and then faces annihilation as a person
through his violent outburst in the courtroom. All these are freely
chosen forms of death, demonstrating "Greater love has no man than
this, that a man lay down his life for his friends" (Jn 15:13).

But is this search for explicit parallels ultimately productive? The
story of sin and the redemption of the sinner through the love and
courage of another is a human story as well as a Christian story. In
trying to understand the films, using the concepts and vocabulary of
the Christian tradition may be helpful tools as long as it does not twist
the films to its own purposes. It is sufficient to say that Frank Capra's

vision of his world and of America is both human and Christian, and to say that is to say quite a bit.

The Genre: The Screwball Comedy

Near the end of *It Happened One Night*, Alexander Andrews (Walter Connolly), father of the spoiled heiress Ellie (Claudette Colbert), insists on getting his prospective son-in-law Peter Warne (Clark Gable) to admit his love for Ellie: "Do you love her?" An exasperated Peter barks back: "Yes, but don't hold that against me. I'm a little screwy myself." This line is suspected of creating the name of one of the most popular genres of the 1930s and 1940s, the Screwball Comedy. Moreover, the film set the style of the genre along with Howard Hawks' *The Twentieth Century*, released a few months earlier. Hawks' innovation had been to have the glamorous stars (John Barrymore and Carole Lombard) of the screwball world of the theater involved in the zaniness themselves. Conventional theatrical and film practice left the comedy to lower-rank "sidekicks" and character actors, while preserving the romance for the leads. Capra went a step further, a giant step in the development of the genre: he mixed the social classes and showed that, from the perspective of the outsider, everyone is a little screwy.

Screwball comedies do not have a precise definition, and they embrace a wide field of romantic comedy types.[10] They do not have a regular list of stars, as, for example, the presence of Buster Keaton or Laurel and Hardy would automatically place a film in the category of Slapstick Comedy. Some of the most well-known Screwball personalities were versatile actors equally identified with other genres: Gary Cooper and James Stewart with Westerns or Katharine Hepburn and Barbara Stanwyck with melodrama. At any rate, while Slapstick is an actors' medium and everyone identifies films by the stars and their style, like Chaplin, Lloyd, or the Marx Brothers, Screwball is more the directors' medium: Capra, Sturges, Hawks, Cukor, and the best of the Screwball directors were not confined to the genre but directed all sorts of films.

Furthermore, the characteristics of the genre change appreciably as it develops. Depression themes of class conflict dominate the early stages, but as the world edged toward war, domestic struggles became less important and provided only a remote background for a romantic comedy. The romance between lively young lovers became

far more important than social commentary for most directors. Frank
Capra will be a notable exception to this trend. He uses the romance
to illustrate his social issue, and some critics feel that this was the
surest sign that he was losing contact with his audience in the later
stages of his career.[11]

Since no definition will be completely satisfactory, it may be
more productive to describe a few traits ordinarily found in most
examples of the genre. If this statement seems overly cautious, it is
with good reason. In this genre to a greater extent than any other,
critics continually find themselves caught in the chicken-and-egg dilemma. The selection of criteria determines what films fit into the
category, yet the selection of films determines the criteria that appear. Since this is not an exercise in the polemics of critical theory, a
tentative description of several commonly accepted characteristics of
the genre will be more useful than a set of iron-bound criteria.

The Screwball world is generally populated by wealthy, attractive socialites, whose lunacy becomes apparent only when they are
thrust into contact with more down-to-earth types, again usually from
the working classes. Later on, ostentatious wealth will become less
important, and the Screwball arena will become merely a sophisticated, urban professional world of journalists, politicians and
bankers. At times the Screwball roles are reversed: in *You Can't Take
It With You* the poorer Sycamore clan is zany, and its antics provide
most of the fun, while the wealthy Kirbys conform to all the rubrics of
civilized behavior. As the film progresses, however, the audience is
asked to reexamine its notion of sanity: Who is really sane after all?

Romance blossoms between a Romeo and his unapproachable
Juliet. In the Screwball Comedy it is not the Capulet-Montague blood
feud that keeps them apart and leads to tragedy, but rather because of
background, family status, wealth, or possibly only personal style, the
two squabble and move from caper to caper until the differences are
resolved and the couple is united, or reunited, since a divorced
married couple often provides the comedy and romance in the later
Screwball Comedies, notably *His Girl Friday* (Howard Hawks, 1940)
and *The Philadelphia Story* (George Cukor, 1940).[12]

The humor is verbal rather than visual. Rarely do the lovers get a
pie in the face or a kick in the pants, but they skewer each other with
rapid-fire put-downs. Radio had prepared audiences for lightning-
quick oral humor. This type of film comedy that developed with the
coming of sound is thus clearly distinct from the visual Slapstick style
that dominated the silent era. Howard Hawks even developed the
technique of overlapping dialogue in which one character begins a

rejoinder before the provoking gag line was finished. The need for articulate, wise-cracking characters led many writers to set their Screwball Comedies in newspaper offices, where the heroes or heroines look over their typewriters to zing their colleagues, or rush out of the press room to cover the latest follies of the rich. The rich, of course, do not have to cultivate the verbal skills at work. They have been to the best schools and sharpen their fangs in witty society every day. They seem to do absolutely nothing but sit around cultivating their screwiness.

The plots are true formula stories, in the sense that from the opening sequence no one in the audience has any doubt about the outcome of the film. Even more, as the stars of the genre became well known, audiences knew the outcome as soon as they saw the cast list in newspaper ads. If the billboard outside said "Tracy and Hepburn," for example, could there be any doubt about who would be engaged or reconciled in the final scene? The fun comes from the collection of odd characters—the stuffed shirt, the scatterbrained aunt and the zany uncle—and the impossible predicaments the couple finds itself in on its way to discovering true love.

Invariably the character development is propelled by erotic tension. From the start the characters are destined to fall in love. The audience realizes this, even though one or both of the lovers may not. While they are drawn together, they reject the notion of a union because they are aware of the differences that separate them. For a later version of this kind of tension, recall the early days of the television series "Moonlighting" and "Cheers." In both the wise-cracking street-wise man pursues the reluctant woman who is beautiful and more refined. His coarseness and her fussiness block their romance, even though everyone in the viewing audiences realizes that they are in love with each other. The lovers, of course, cannot admit the fact, even to themselves. In each episode they squabble and torment each other, only to be reconciled in time for the final commercial. They renew their warfare in the next episode. A casual relationship, as both series tried for a short time, would kill the tension and destroy a great deal of the comedy.

The tension was more effective in the age of the Screwball movies. Sexual mores were different. The contrast is obvious. Both David Addison (Bruce Willis) in "Moonlighting" and Sam Malone (Ted Danson) in "Cheers" boast openly of their many relationships with women. To them a momentary fling with the co-star is just another conquest to brag about. Unlike most of their maternal predecessors in the Screwball films, the romantic heroines of the television age have had their own relationships, to be sure, but they are not gross enough to brag about them. The vulgarity of the men and the propriety of the women are merely morally neutral characteristics of their opposing worlds, like preferring beer over wine, or rock over Bach.

Nowadays, in popular entertainment the morality of the sexual relationship and the issue of sexual exploitation are not in question at all. The assumption of the script is that recreational sex is the accepted norm for attractive young adults today. In these recent television Screwballs, then, the erotic tension has little to do with sex. The dilemma for the woman is whether she will lower her somewhat stuffy social standards by crossing into his more realistic world or whether she will maintain her posture as socially superior. For their part, the men have to decide whether to compromise their standing as amoral sexual athletes and accept a veneer of civilized conduct long enough to woo the woman.

By use of sexual relationships as a model for social class conflict, these television series are really reverting to the earliest phases of the Screwball Comedy films. The technique is less effective, because if casual sexual relationships are the expected norm, then very little is at stake. The conquest is made or not made; it makes little difference. No one is hurt and no commitments are made. The morning after is the same as the afternoon before. In sharp contrast, when the films ended with a final embrace, it meant marriage and commitment. The social classes were fused forever, and a great deal of tension was generated before each of the parties would make that leap into commitment.

This is not to maintain that people were any less active sexually in the 1930s than they are now. That remains a question for sociologists, not film critics. At least this much is true: American social conventions at the time, strictly enforced in Hollywood through the Production Code, acted as though the only natural result of romance was marriage. The union at the end of a romantic comedy was not a casual relationship but a lasting bond. This is part of the fantasy. The lovers are so disparate and their worlds so incompatible that in the real world their marriage would not last through the honeymoon. In the Screwball world, however, the final embrace seals them for life. Lifted to the realm of social commentary, the fantasy holds out the impossible expectation that the competing social classes will be unified permanently. The real world does not work that way. The differences remain, as a moment of reflection shows. The Screwball social fantasy then is dishonest, but so is all fantasy. That is why Depression audiences kept coming back for more. The happy endings of the

Screwball world offered more hope than their own world, even with
the New Deal.

The Plot: *It Happened One Night*

Ellie Andrews (Claudette Colbert) is confined to the family yacht
by her father, Alexander Andrews (Walter Connolly), to keep her
from consummating her hasty civil marriage to King Westley (Jame-
son Thomas). In a rage she dives overboard and escapes, planning to
rendezvous with King in New York. She boards a bus in Florida, while
her father sends out detectives to find her before she reaches King.

In the bus station Peter Warne (Clark Gable), a reporter, drunk-
enly argues with his editor, is fired, and boards the bus with Ellie.
They argue about a seat, and finally are forced to share it. At the first
stop her suitcase is stolen, and her refusal to report the theft raises
Peter's suspicions. As the trip continues, she chooses a seat apart from
Peter, but a huge sleeping man continuously rolls over on her. She
retreats to Peter's seat and wakes up wearing his sweater and having
slept on his shoulder.

At the next stop, Jacksonville, Ellie's long lunch makes her miss
the bus. Peter by this time has seen the picture of the fugitive heiress
in the newspaper and waits with her for the next bus, nearly twelve
hours later. He promises not to turn her over to her father if she will
let him write her story, which he believes will enable him to regain his
job with the paper. She reluctantly agrees. He telegraphs the editor
with the proposed story.

During the next part of the journey, Ellie is again forced to sit
next to Peter when an obnoxious passenger, Oscar Shapeley (Roscoe
Karns), tries to flirt with her. A bridge is washed out, and the bus
cannot continue on its way. Their meager resources will not permit
separate accommodations for the night. They are forced to share a
cabin, pretending to be married. She is furious. He lends her a pair of
his pajamas, and between their beds he stretches a clothesline and
blanket, which he calls "the walls of Jericho." The next morning, as
he prepares breakfast, she stands on line for a turn in a shower cabin.
She is ebullient with her adventure. Peter berates her for not knowing
how to dunk a doughnut properly. After breakfast two detectives
arrive looking for Ellie Andrews. Peter and Ellie feign an argument as
a married couple. When the befuddled detectives leave, Peter con-
gratulates his partner.

On the bus once more, the passengers entertain themselves by singing "The Daring Young Man on the Flying Trapeze." The bus driver is distracted by the song and drives into a ditch. A woman faints from hunger and Ellie gives her little boy Peter's last ten dollar bill. Shapeley has seen the papers, too, and he also recognizes Ellie. He tries to claim a share of the reward money from Peter, but Peter pretends to be a dangerous kidnapper and scares him off. Realizing that Ellie could be recognized again, Peter leads her off through the woods. As he carries her across a stream over his shoulder, she says she has not had a piggyback ride in years, and he scorns her for not knowing what a real piggyback ride is. They sleep in a hayfield. She is frightened when Peter wanders off to look for food. As he covers her in his raincoat, they almost kiss. The next morning they hitch a ride after Ellie literally stops traffic by flashing her leg after Peter has been unsuccessful with the more conventional thumb. The driver tries to run off with Peter's suitcase, but he chases the thief and takes the car to continue the journey north.

Frantic about his missing daughter, Alexander Andrews decides to relent and allow his daughter to marry King. He hopes that by publicizing his change of mind, she will return. Instead, when Ellie reads the story in the newspaper, she urges Peter to spend one more night in a cabin, even though they are only three hours from New York. She asks about his plans for marriage, and when he describes his ideal woman, Ellie crosses the wall of Jericho and offers to be that woman for him. He rejects her overture, but reconsiders, sneaks away and drives to New York to deliver the story to his editor. He wants the thousand dollars in his pocket before proposing.

When the owners of the motor inn awaken her and demand their rent, Ellie believes that Peter has abandoned her. Sensing rejection, she calls her father and asks him to come for her. King joins the motorcade; they pass Peter on the road and retrieve Ellie. Plans for the wedding move forward, but Ellie still loves Peter, as she admits to her father. Mr. Andrews sees a chance to get rid of King, whom he despises. Peter is convinced that Ellie has walked out on him, and out of wounded pride he writes to Mr. Andrews demanding the $38.62 that he spent on Ellie during their cross-country caper. When she discovers that they have been discussing money, she mistakenly believes that Peter only wants the reward money and in a fury goes ahead with her marriage plans. King arrives for the wedding in an autogyro, a kind of primitive helicopter. As they walk down the aisle together, Mr. Andrews tells Ellie about the money and offers her one more chance to change her mind. With wedding veil billowing behind her, she bolts from the altar to find Peter. Mr. Andrews buys off King and has their wedding annulled. He telegraphs the couple at their motel in Glenns Falls, Michigan to give them the news, and the film ends with a blast from a toy trumpet as the blanket wall of Jericho tumbles to the floor.

COMMENTARY

Capra has consistently explored social issues in his films. *It Happened One Night* is no exception. At the outset, then, it is essential to see Peter and Ellie not only as an engaging couple in a romantic comedy, as they most certainly are, but as representatives of their respective social classes. They fulfill all the stereotypes, as Capra, from his working class perspective, would have initially perceived them. Peter is unemployed, but proud. He will not be pushed around by anyone. He is tough and resourceful, an idealized Everyman. Ellie is a spoiled brat; everything has been handed to her on a silver coal shovel. She has never worked for a living, and she has not the slightest clue about the meaning of money. She is irresponsible and unfailingly egocentric. She cares about no one's feelings, not even her father's.

The stereotypes will not last. This is a classic journey film, along the lines of a *Ship of Fools* pattern or even Chaucer's *Canterbury Tales*. During their travels the pilgrims discover and reveal quite a bit about themselves, and in the act of discovery they are transformed— within limits. For Ellie and Peter the trip begins in the South, possibly in the waters off Miami Beach where class distinctions are most pronounced and the social-class system was believed to be most rigid. Using the South as he did should not lead to the anachronistic conclusion that Capra is including race in his exploration of American class structures. He was a man of his times, not a prophet of the concerns that will receive long delayed attention twenty years in the future. Capra is not presenting a subtle comment on the American apartheid of the time, since he gives very little indication in any of his films of his concern with racial issues. In Florida the super wealthy have their yachts and their private planes, and the working classes have their Greyhound buses, their rickety jalopies, and their feet. For Capra this land of clear class distinctions provides a fine starting place for the journey, but he quickly abandons any concern with geography. The action in the center of the film could take place anywhere from Georgia to New Jersey. Only in the final stage do they refer to being only three hours from New York and somewhere near Philadelphia.

Their ultimate destination is New York, and for the Sicilian immigrant the city is the quintessential melting pot, in myth at least. By living and working together in the megalopolis, the various ethnic groups and social classes will be fused into the American nation of Capra's dream. But the journey does not end in New York. After the reconciliation, Ellie and Peter head west. The final fusion of social classes takes place in Glenns Falls, Michigan, part of that symbolic heartland where American values are believed to be found in their purest form. Like most Americans, rural or urban, Capra bought the myth of agrarian moral superiority. After sending the lovers nearly the length of the East Coast, Capra has to have them leave the land of King Westley and Ellie's socialite friends to find happiness in the new, pure America. In keeping with the theme of moral regeneration of a new classless American society at the end of the journey, and probably with the encouragement of the Hays Office, the motel owner tells his wife that he knows Peter and Ellie are legally married because he saw the marriage license, an improbable discovery unless he happened to be searching their luggage.

In the opening sequences both Ellie and Peter are tightly confined by the demands of their social station. Ellie is literally locked into her stateroom. The stewards, working men, listen to her argument with her father from the other side of the sealed hatchway. Similarly, Peter is pushed into a phone booth in the bus station, his escape shut off by his friends. They cheer him on, delighted to hear him tell off his boss and unaware that the boss has already hung up and Peter is merely acting out the script his friends have written for him. Capra presents the workers of these Depression days as downtrodden but spunky, and they have solidarity. As Peter leaves the phone booth, his friends escort him to the bus in a mock regal procession, calling out, "Make way for the King." The use of the title "King" here—and it never recurs—is an ironic reference to King Westley, whose place Peter will take, and to the nobility of the workers, even when they are a bit drunk.

As the journey continues, the burden for growth falls disproportionately on Ellie. By bolting from the stateroom and diving into the ocean, she deliberately breaks away from the confinement of her class. She "takes a plunge," and next appears in the bus station, at this time still a tourist among her inferiors. She "hires" a woman to buy a ticket for her so that she can elude the detectives. Since his sympathies lie with the working classes, Capra sees nothing much in Peter that has to be changed. He is as brash and smug at the end as at the beginning. His only change has been to look upon Ellie and her father somewhat more sympathetically. The one member of the upper classes Peter cannot accept is King, who is rejected by the Andrews family as well. Even his name puts him into a royal class, which is by nature excluded from Capra's vision of a classless society.

By her ability to be transformed, Ellie is the narrative and thematic center of the film. Her changes are crucial for Capra's belief that the wealthy are really good people, and that once the rich and poor begin to understand each other, then the rich will solve America's social problems without government interference. Ellie is the only woman in the story, aside from a few bit parts. On one extreme, she must reject Oscar Shapeley, who represents all that is grotesque and sexist in the working classes: "Shapeley's the name, and shapely's the way I like 'em." On the other side, she finally sees through King Westley, a bloodless wimp whose love can be bought off for one hundred thousand dollars. When he drops out of the sky in his autogyro for his own wedding, it is as though he had come from another planet. He certainly does not belong on this one. Both Shapeley and Westley are cartoon caricatures of their respective social stations. As a member of the upper class, Ellie is immediately repulsed by Shapeley's patter, but only gradually does she learn that in his own way King is just as obnoxious.

In Capra's vision, neither class is accurately defined by its caricatures, Shapeley and Westley, and each is redeemable. The father figures are crucial to the eventual union of the couple. Alexander Andrews originally appears to be an old tyrant, eager to thwart the romantic aspirations of his daughter. He appears to be a blustering father, intent on forcing Ellie into some prearranged marriage of financial convenience. Capra lets his audience jump to that erroneous conclusion. As the story unfolds and especially as Capra reveals more about King, Mr. Andrews becomes more the loving, doting father with a good sense of humor and shrewd practical skills. He personally reorganizes the strategy for the search for his daughter when the detectives fail. He thinks to have the car waiting in the driveway if Ellie decides to run out on King during the wedding ceremony.

Similarly, Capra misleads his audience about Henderson, the editor, who is first seen firing Peter. As he shouts into a phone in his office, he appears as one of the bosses whose capricious decisions can deny a man a livelihood in the midst of the Depression. In subsequent scenes, however, he is a harried workingman himself, shouting into two phones to bring the paper out on time. When Peter brings the story of Ellie's escapades to him, he gives out the thousand dollars as he promised, but when he is led to believe that the story is a hoax, he naturally kills it, but then reads it anyway as the statement of a friend.

Peter returns the thousand dollars, and the editor tells him to sober up and come back to talk about a job. Under the gruff exterior, he has shown compassion, and his kindness teaches Peter that his extreme form of independence is destructive. Like everyone else in the world, Peter needs friends. He cannot continue as an uncompromising loner. After the meeting, Peter is somewhat humbled and is ready to rejoin the team rather than feel he must carry on by himself. The two "father figures" make it possible for Ellie to change and for Peter finally to accept her change.

Like it or not, rich and poor are forced to make the journey of America together. From their individual spaces of confinement, Peter and Ellie find themselves confined together, and in the early stages of their journey the two are locked in tight, claustrophobic interiors: the inside of the bus, small cabins or an old convertible. Even the outdoor scenes take place in the dark and are shot in tight sound-stage sets. Only gradually, as they become more at ease with each other, does the camera open up to light and space. The closeness makes them both uncomfortable. At first they argue over a seat in the bus that Peter had just wrested from the bus driver (Ward Bond) in a shouting match. He feels he earned the seat, while Ellie feels that it, and everything else, is her inheritance. She simply takes it. It is cramped, but they endure each other's presence.

On the next stage of the ride she takes the initiative, out of self-interest, to join him. A huge, fat man keeps falling over on her, and she disengages herself to sit with Peter. Later, it is Peter's turn. As Shapeley blathers on with his insulting monologue, Peter dislodges him by saying that he wants to sit with his wife. Rich and poor then, for whatever their motives, can travel together and even be an advantage to each other. In sitting together, Ellie, it must be noted, acts from self-interest, Peter from altruism, even though he claims Shapeley's voice was getting on his nerves. Both had crossed the boundary, and for the first time the idea of "marriage" surfaces, even though only as a pretense to get rid of Shapeley.

The pretense becomes a bit more serious that night when they are forced to share a cabin. The wall of Jericho seems an acceptable solution to their dilemma. It satisfies social convention, even though it does nothing to ensure respectability. In the cabin they have ample opportunity for being "unrespectable," but at this time they still believe that they hate each other. Romance is not a possibility at this stage in their relationship. The attraction, however, is clear to Capra and the audience, even if not to Peter and Ellie. The air crackles with sexual tension. As they prepare for bed, Peter disrobes, with commentary, in front of Ellie. Only when he reaches for the buttons on his pants does she run over to her side of the wall. The tension is kept alive, however, as she finally decides to undress and tosses her lingerie on the top of the wall. Peter, who moments before took delight in her embarrassment during his undressing, becomes embarrassed himself and asks her to remove her underclothes from his sight. Capra is showing that the classes really could find each other attractive, but are forced by mere social convention to adopt the strategies that keep them apart. Custom, not necessity, keeps the classes apart.

The next morning Ellie crosses the border again when she learns she must go outside and stand in line to use the shower. Wearing his pajamas, robe and slippers, she accepts his world with a certain amount of happiness. On the bus she had worn his sweater and then his scarf, but by this time she is completely covered in his clothes. She is wearing nothing of her own which would symbolically tie her to her past. Peter has taken her clothes to have them pressed. After her shower she even accepts an awkward apology from Shapeley, where she might have been expected to retort with an arrogant insult. She is adapting gradually to Peter's world, literally standing in his shoes. At the next cabin she is even comfortable playing Peter's wife. The housekeeper refers to her as "Mrs. Warne," and when the detectives try to find out if she is the missing heiress, she enthusiastically plays the part of a fabricated Mrs. Warne, the bawling daughter of a plumber. The detectives retreat before the attack of her thunderous tantrum.

In the final motel scene, Ellie crosses the wall of Jericho completely. Recognizing that she is falling in love with Peter, she delays their return to New York, a mere three hours away, to have one more night with Peter. At her prompting he tells her about the woman he would want to marry. She bolts from the bed, embraces Peter, and proposes marriage, which he rejects because of his own pride. He realizes he has no money. In this last motel scene of their journey to New York, Capra definitively breaks down the class barriers through Ellie's initiative. The only thing still keeping them apart is the reluctance of Peter to accept her proposal. In Capra's world, the working classes are embarrassed to accept any overture of the wealthy for fear it would cast them in the role of welfare recipients.

In many other smaller episodes Ellie shows her willingness to enter his world. During their first stay in a cabin Peter buys a toothbrush for her, but later, after their night in the hayfield, she asks him to pick a seed out of her teeth with his penknife. Again during their breakfast after their first night in the cabin, Peter is outraged at her method of dunking doughnuts, proclaiming that rich people don't do it the right way. She smiles calmly at his outburst. As they cross the stream after leaving the bus, he begins another tirade. He claims that rich people don't know how to give piggyback rides. She argues openly with him, but she accepts the ride in a playful spirit. The next morning, however, Ellie proves just how practical and resourceful rich people can be. She has listened patiently to another one of his pompous lectures on the art of hitchhiking. Vaguely amused at his failure to get a ride, she takes over. Her leg proves far more effective than his thumb in stopping traffic. She is not too stuffy to get what she wants, and at this moment she wants a ride. During the scene in the haystack, he brings her raw carrots to eat. She is revolted by the idea, but later on, during their ride in the convertible, she has experienced enough hunger to try the carrot. After feeling the hunger of the poor, she can accept the diet of the poor.

The process of crossing the boundary is recapitulated in the final scene in the bus. To pass the time, the passengers organize an impromptu songfest. To the accompaniment of a makeshift band, they sing "The Daring Young Man on the Flying Trapeze," with a new singer, one a sailor in uniform, taking each verse. Everyone joins in the chorus, and several dance in the aisles—everyone except Peter and Ellie. At first they are rigid and out of place. At the second chorus Peter relents and joins in. Finally, no longer able to resist the fun, Ellie surrenders her chilly self-control and sings with them. So does the bus driver, who runs into a ditch and thus ends the first segment of their journey together.

The wreck shows another facet of Ellie's development. At first she is totally irresponsible with money. After her suitcase is stolen she loses her ticket, and then with very little money to her name she would have bought a box of chocolates from a vendor unless Peter with his working class practicality had stopped her. Rather than snack in the bus station, she insists on having lunch in a fine hotel, which makes her miss the bus. Her extravagance to this point is all selfish. After joining in the song and experiencing the wreck, she is moved when a woman faints from hunger, and she gives her young son the ten dollar bill that Peter had been saving for their expenses. He is reluctant to give the money away, but since money means so little to her, she gives it away readily. She has no awareness of the practical consequences of her generosity, but her action shows a new side to her character.

The working classes cannot afford this charming trait; in fact their concern for money can be quite disagreeable. Shapeley, once he discovers Ellie's identity, tries to extort half the supposed reward money from Peter. Only the threat of violence frightens him away. The driver who stops to pick them up is apparently interested in more than Ellie's leg. According to Peter he makes a business out of stopping for hitchhikers and then running off with their luggage. After the bus accident, none of the ordinary people who had sung and danced a hymn of solidarity offers to take up a collection for the woman who has fainted, nor does anyone offer food to her son. When Peter is desperate to get to New York, he has an agonizing bargaining session with the filling station attendant, who will not extend credit to Peter even after an offer of collateral. He rejects Peter's suitcase because he already has one, and holds out for his hat. Peter's agitation does not prompt him to generosity. Finally, when the motel owners discover that Peter's car is gone, they evict Ellie in the middle of the night and even refuse to allow her to make a phone call to her father. They show not the slightest sign of compassion, and tell her to walk to the sheriff's office and make her call from there.

This is the level of Depression-hardened America that Peter comes from, yet his attitude toward money separates him from the more disagreeable side of poverty. He is not particularly generous with his money because he wants to help Ellie in her distress. For him she is an investment. He believes that getting an exclusive on her story will win back his job. He does need the self-respect that money brings, and for this reason he feels he must have the thousand dollar royalty in his pocket before he can marry Ellie. When the editor withdraws the story from the paper, Peter returns the money, realizing that he did not earn it. One could argue that the fee came for writing the story, which he did. He could have tried to keep the money, but for him it is more honorable to return it because the story was not printed.

The key to Peter's character is revealed in his final conversation with Alexander Andrews. He wants what is his: $38.62. For him, as a relatively poor man, it is a matter of principle, and he cannot allow himself to be swindled. At the same time, he dismisses the ten thousand dollar reward. This also is a matter of principle, although he does not name it as such. He is careful with money and surely recognizes its importance, but he is unwilling to exploit people, no matter how desperate he is or how easily they can afford it. He will take advantage of Andrews no more than he will of his editor. He reveals the noble side of the working classes to the Andrews family, just as Ellie has revealed the compassionate side of the wealthy.

During the early stages of their journey, they are incapable of recognizing these virtues in each other. They are slow to deal with each other as persons. They never even call each other by name. At first Ellie uses the incredibly pompous "Young Man" and after their first night in the cabin tries the less formal "Mister." Fed up with her arrogance, Peter calls her simply "Brat."[13] They resolutely depersonalize each other and react to the cartoon caricature that each has of the other. Only through time and forced interaction with each other can they learn first accommodation, then mutual dependence, and finally love. Such is Capra's optimistic scenario for the United States during the Depression.

The Depression itself appears in the film as a form of deluge. Water imagery is crucial to the development of the theme. The storm, the Depression, forces them into a cooperative venture neither is happy about. First, it brings a change in the natural order of things that forces them to accommodate. A heavy rainstorm washes out a bridge and forces the couple to share the cabin. Initially she stands outside protected by his raincoat. When Ellie wants to leave, the downpour forces her to remain with Peter. Second, the water brings a kind of cleansing. In the line outside the shower room she becomes one of the masses, simply waiting for her turn to use the common facility. Her pretenses and illusions of superiority are washed away, to such an extent that she can retaliate in kind to the girl who sticks out her tongue and speak civilly to Shapeley. Finally, the water represents a rite of passage. When they leave the bus and strike out on foot, they ford a stream in her notion of a piggyback ride. Actually she is draped over his shoulder like a sack of potatoes. During the ride she playfully pokes him in the back with his shoes, which she is carrying, and he responds with a good-natured but energetic slap on the bottom. The exchange of blows during this crossing signifies the change in relationship that has been taking place. The formality that has divided them has gone and they can be comfortable, even playful with each other. In all three instances, the use of water to indicate fertility hovers in the background, as though hinting that this relationship will be ultimately fruitful.

Linking the water imagery to the Depression seems more congruent to Capra's economic and social themes than tying it to baptismal symbolism, but both have their value. Baptism, too, upsets the "natural" order of sin and brings the new order of grace; it is a cleansing and represents a passage into a new life. It is a form of fertility; in the life of grace, good works bear fruit. Without denying this kind of interpretation, Capra is dealing not with personal salvation but with the economic redemption of the American people. The Depression, in his optimistic view, may in the long term bring the kind of restoration of primitive American values needed to create the utopian society he envisioned.

The story seems to end happily ever after. The drama of social integration is completed.[14] The classes are joined, having discovered there is more uniting them than separating them. Individuals from different classes even share the same vices. Peter drinks when he believes he has lost Ellie, and in a remarkably similar shot Alexander Andrews drinks to celebrate getting rid of King Westley. The foreground is dominated by bottles and the telephone.

The story ends as it began. Peter and Ellie are in the confined space of the cabin together, while the audience stands with the motel owners outside. The real world remains sealed out by the closed doors, while the couple inside enjoy the happiness of the world of the imagination. Peter and Ellie have torn down the wall of Jericho, and are prepared, rich and poor, to live as one. Outside the cabin, in the real world, a marriage between two such different and headstrong people could not be expected to last a month, but of course Capra was not interested in reality. He created a myth that he will rework several times and his colleagues will develop through the next two decades. The Screwball formula leads its audiences into a world of illusion that happy endings are inevitable, a welcome thought for a world plunging from the Depression into world war.

It Happened One Night struck the right chords in Hollywood as well as with the movie-going public. It scored a sweep during the Academy Awards presentation, taking Oscars for best picture, direction (Capra), script (Riskin), actor (Gable) and actress (Colbert).[15] Still furious with Capra and the film itself, Claudette Colbert attended the ceremonies wearing a brown business suit rather than the customary formal gown, explaining that she had to catch a train later that night.[16] When she received her Oscar, she stopped for a moment at the microphone and said "I owe Frank Capra for this." All of Hollywood owed Frank Capra for this, and its usual way of paying a debt is imitation. The Screwball Comedy was firmly established as the most durable genre of the coming decade.

Frank Capra was the total auteur who created and packaged the myth for a tired world. He was involved in the conception and writing of the scripts, and on the sound stage supervised every aspect of the creative process. The artistic vision was his; now it is ours.

NOTES

1. The biographical data included here is taken largely from Frank Capra, *The Name Above the Title: An Autobiography* (New York: Vintage, 1971). Much of the material, in summary form, can be found in entries in *Leslie Halliwell's Filmgoer's Companion*, eighth ed. (New York: Charles Scribner's Sons, 1984), and Ephraim Katz, *The Film Encyclopedia* (New York: Perigee, 1981).

2. Capra, p. 6.

3. Recounted in A. Scott Berg, *Goldwyn, A Biography* (New York: Alfred A. Knopf, 1989), p. 484. This characterization of Columbia might have been unfair. Under Cohn's stewardship it made money consistently, but at the cost of ruthless economizing on salaries and low-budget production. Cf. Douglas Gomery, *The Hollywood Studio System* (New York: St. Martin's, 1986), pp. 161–167. As for Harry Cohn, no one seems to have come forward to offer suggestions for Rabbi Magnin's eulogy.

4. Thomas Schatz, *Hollywood Genres: Formulas, Film Making and the Studio System* (New York: Random House, 1981), p. 185. *Platinum Blonde* was not their first collaboration. Riskin wrote the play, *Bless You, Sister* with John Meehan upon which the film *The Miracle Woman* (also 1931) was based. Jo Swerling and Dorothy Howell, however, received credit for the screenplay. For *Platinum Blonde*, he joined the other two writers in the credits.

5. Schatz, p. 185.

6. For my appreciation of Capra's struggle between the worlds of imagination and actuality, I am especially indebted to Raymond Carney, *American Vision: The Films of Frank Capra* (London: Cambridge Univ., 1986), especially his essay on *Meet John Doe* pp. 347–376, and *It's a Wonderful Life*, pp. 377–435. Many of the author's suggestions on the reading of the films have been so assimilated into my own appreciation of the films that citation of each point of convergence would be impossible. Professor Carney's work has been extremely helpful in my rereading old favorites with new eyes.

7. Andrew Sarris, *The American Cinema: Directors and Directions 1929–1968* (New York: Dutton, 1968), p. 87.

8. Carney, p. 425.

9. Capra, pp. 303–304.

10. Jim Leach, "The Screwball Comedy," in Barry K. Grant, ed., *Film Genre: Theory and Criticism* (Metuchen, N.J.: Scarecrow, 1977), pp. 75–77, points out that the difficulty of settling on a definition is one of the reasons so little serious study of the genre has been produced.

11. Leach, p. 82.

12. Schatz, pp. 162–165.

13. The title "Brat" had a background. Capra recounts that both stars were on loan to Columbia. Harry Cohn did not like to keep contract actors on salary and preferred to save a few dollars by working deals with other studios for particular films. Neither Gable nor Colbert was happy with the arrangement. Gable drank heavily, and Colbert became so demanding on the set that the crew called her either "Froggie" or "Brat." Part of the chemistry between the two actors developed because they really could not stand each other, and the name "Brat" went into the film naturally. Capra, pp. 164–170.

14. Schatz, pp. 32–34.

15. Until *Patton* almost repeated the sweep in 1970, *It Happened One Night* stood alone with that achievement. *Patton* won for best picture, direction (Franklin Schaffner), script (Francis Ford Coppola and Edmund H. North) and best actor (George C. Scott). There were no major parts in *Patton* for an actress, and that award went to Glenda Jackson for *Women in Love* (Ken Russell).

16. Capra, pp. 171–172.

Chapter Six

THE GANGSTER FILM
SCARFACE

The Auteur: Howard Hawks

Frank Capra's early days as a poor Sicilian immigrant did not seem a likely preparation for the optimistic view of America and the resolutely happy endings always associated with his name. The paradox is reversed with Howard Hawks, a man from a comfortable, established American family, who Andrew Sarris maintains "has stamped his distinctively bitter view of life on adventure, gangster and private-eye melodramas, musicals, westerns and screwball comedies, the genres Americans do best and appreciate least."[1] While Capra helped Depression audiences escape from their troubles and assured them that everything would turn out well in time, Hawks turned toward the interior landscape and found there a nest of problems that ordinary people could understand. One helped America laugh its way through the Depression; the other held up a mirror to its dark side.

Capra was beloved by audiences and the industry. Hawks was not—at least not warmly. Hawks made forty-two pictures in his career. Few lost money, but none of them was a box-office "smash." None stands out as a masterpiece, and none won a major Academy Award, except for Gary Cooper as best actor in *Sergeant York* (1941). The growing war fever certainly influenced the voting, since the film itself does not hold up well through the years. Finally recognizing its oversight, in 1975 Hollywood presented Howard Hawks with an Academy Award for cumulative artistic contribution to the motion picture industry.

Growing up, Howard Hawks was everything that the young

Frank Capra might have wanted to be. He was resolutely Middle American, born in 1896 into a wealthy family in the lumber and paper business in Goshen, Indiana. He did not like to describe his father as a "lumber baron" with its sinister connotations, possibly because it cut too close to the truth.[2] The family moved to Neenah, Wisconsin in 1898, and when Mrs. Hawks became ill, the family settled in Pasadena, California in 1906. As could have been predicted, the young Howard went back East for his education, high school at Phillips Exeter Academy and college at Cornell University, where he graduated with a degree in mechanical engineering in 1917. He was tall and slender, an amateur tennis champion with a passion for racing cars.

Immediately after college Hawks joined the Army Air Corps as a pilot, and after the war he found a suitable place as a designer and pilot for an aircraft factory. Being financially secure, he felt no urgency to get on with a money-making career. He decided to explore possibilities in the movies, and signed on as a prop man at Famous Players-Lasky studios. In 1922 he financed two short films, which he directed himself, but even then he was not permitted to become a studio director.

Hawks' education and lifelong habit of reading made him a bit different from the other members of the prop team, and soon he moved into the story department which he headed in 1924. In this capacity he was responsible for acquiring the rights to the properties from which he developed film concepts. He stayed with the project by working on the scripts and organizing the staff to produce the finished product. During this time he wrote his own scripts and sold them to other studios, but his real ambition was directing. Jesse Lasky would not let his talented young writer out of his niche in the story department, so when Hawks brought a promising script over to Fox he offered it to them only on the condition that he be allowed to direct it. Fox bought the package, and in 1926 Howard Hawks directed his first film, *The Road to Glory.*

Already in these early years the Hawks style for making films was in place. First, while the other pioneers in Hollywood were trying to master the techniques of film-making by building on the legacy of D.W. Griffith, Hawks remained a literary man. Throughout most of his career, he claimed to be more interested in stories and characters than in the mechanics of film-making which he was content in the early days to leave to others. This was not altogether true. Even before Hawks became recognized as one of the masters of the American cinema, he was acknowledged as a consummate craftsman. In the Hollywood tradition, he rejected the term "artist."

Both professionally and personally he remained close to some of the finest literary talent in Hollywood: Ben Hecht, Charles MacArthur, Dudley Nichols, John Huston, and, most notably, William Faulkner. One author he could not lure to Hollywood was Ernest Hemingway, who almost dared him to try to make a film of what he considered his worst story: *To Have and Have Not*, which Hawks did make in 1944, with a script written by Jules Furthman and William Faulkner. He was successful in getting Faulkner to come to California, but when it became clear that Faulkner had other interests, Hawks was shrewd enough to let him pursue his own writing in Mississippi while retaining him as a story consultant and scriptwriter for special projects. Even after his Nobel Prize for Literature in 1950, Faulkner remained close to Hawks and continued to advise him on difficult story ideas. Hawks also continued to write scripts, but he claimed to be nothing other than a storyteller, certainly not a Nobelist.

Secondly, even as a young director, Hawks started a project from the selection of material and stayed with it through the various steps of writing to the shooting and final cutting. Put negatively, at no stage of the process was Howard Hawks far away from the film he was making. Much of his actual writing is uncredited, since the Screenwriters Guild required that a director of a particular film have written at least fifty percent of the script to qualify for a credit.[3] As director and often as producer as well, he was not eager to see his name on the screen one more time during the titles, so he rarely kept track of how much he contributed. Many of his most inspired additions to the text were penciled in during the actual shooting.

Hawks preferred to produce his own films, and he moved from studio to studio rather than attach himself to any one studio where he could then fall under the rule of the moguls of the executive suite. As the producer he could select the talent himself and organize his own crew. He was a tyrant on the set. Louis Giannetti relates how he ended a display of temperament from Humphrey Bogart by picking the legendary tough guy up by the lapels.[4] Lee Marvin, another tough guy, never even made it to the studio. He told Hawks he did not want him to direct the film *Monte Walsh* as though he (Marvin) were John Wayne. At seventy years of age and rapidly gaining the recognition that had long eluded him, Hawks did not appreciate an actor's advice on how to direct. Hawks told Marvin he should have no fear of being as good as John Wayne, and that exchange ended the project. William Fraker directed the film in 1970.[5]

By his involvement in writing and his total control of every subsequent phase of production, Hawks certainly met one of the two major criteria of the *Cahiers* critics to qualify as an authentic auteur. As they learned about his creative style they were attracted to him, and as they watched his films they became aware of a unique visual style as well, which is the second criterion. Only in the final decade of his life did Hawks enjoy the recognition in America that the French critics offered him.

For the greater part of his career, Hawks was ignored by critics and film historians. The conventional opinion was that he was a competent craftsman who brought pictures in on schedule and within budget, but that he was clearly no artist. He was a journeyman director who brought no innovation to the art form and a writer who lacked originality. Furthermore, he worked almost exclusively on Hollywood formula films, after the genre had been defined by other, more creative talents.[6] For example, it was commonly believed that *Scarface* (1932), released a few months after William Wellman's *Public Enemy* and Mervyn LeRoy's *Little Caesar*, merely followed the trend established by the two Warner Brothers classics. History flatly contradicts this perception of *Scarface*. The film was shot in 1930 around the same time as the other two gangster classics, but the material was considered too controversial for public consumption. Howard Hughes, the producer and a personal friend of Hawks, refused to yield to all the demands of the Hays Office and withheld the print for two years while negotiations dragged on.[7] Hughes, who had no pressing need to recoup his investment, was in no hurry to release it. Had he held out another two years, when Hollywood got serious about its production code, *Scarface* might never have been released at all. Those who resist the notion of genre and still believe that genre films are a form of legal plagiarism might find in Bryan Foy's *The Lights of New York* (1928) the model for all three classics. Since innovation is not a preeminent value in film-making, it is perfectly understandable that the original has all but disappeared, while the three imitations are as powerful today as they were when they first appeared.

Notwithstanding this one misperception about *Scarface*, the judgment is fundamentally accurate. Hawks did not create new genres, nor did he relish innovation. He exploited the genres that others had developed, and even before his rediscovery he was recognized for handling the possibilities of the formulas quite well. He liked action-adventure and comedies, and he resolutely avoided offering messages or morals in his work. Through the 1940s and early

1950s, while "the movies" were becoming "films" and moving into the art houses and campuses, Hawks seemed destined to be left behind by the critics.

All of that changed once the *Cahiers* critics and their British and American colleagues began their second look at the Hollywood film. Clearly, when the French undertook their massive reassessment of the American film, they saw something in the works of Howard Hawks that the rest of the world had been missing for a quarter of a century. In the years that followed, as the genre critics began to understand the dynamics of the formula film and appreciate the fact that a genre film is not a "constraint" on auteurs but a form that actually liberates their personal vision, then Hawks' stature grew as quickly as cost overruns on *Heaven's Gate* (Cimino, 1980). By his death, the day after Christmas 1977, he was commonly regarded among the finest of American directors, on a level with John Ford, D.W. Griffith, and Charlie Chaplin who died the previous day.[8]

Just what did the French see to begin this revaluation of Howard Hawks? In their reaction against the literary tradition in the French film industry, the *Cahiers* critics prized the straight direct style of Hawks' storytelling technique. He never used flashbacks to complicate the narrative line, which hurtles forward at a breathless pace without distraction. He avoided moralism and let the actions themselves reveal their own consequences in the moral order. His camera rested at an objective eye level, and when he moved it up or down, a character or relationship could be defined with extraordinary economy. He used the Hollywood genres, all of them, and seldom moved beyond the genre, but, according to the French, he simply used them more effectively than anyone else. He was able to use the materials of the American genre film to present his personal vision and visual style; he did not have to move outside the established forms of the industry to express himself. For the French, Howard Hawks represented all that was excellent in the Hollywood studio system.

In his remarkable article in *Cahiers* in 1953, Jacques Rivette invites his readers to look at Hawks with a new sense of appreciation.[9] He finds in Hawks a unique mingling of comedy and tragedy which act reciprocally to uncover what he and Sarris after him both call "a bitter view of life." Angelo (Vince Barnett), a comic character in *Scarface*, has funny lines in a tragic story, but his comedy does not keep him from being drawn into tragedy along with Tony Camonte (Paul Muni). When the two are surrounded by the police, Angelo locks two doors behind him, but his most professional action cannot protect him from being killed. Fate simply overtakes him and his comedy. Conversely, in *Twentieth Century* (1934) Lily Garland (Carole Lombard) is tragically coerced into having her life ruled once more by a psychopathic stage director, Oscar Jaffee (John Barrymore), but her metaphorical death is comic when in the final scene the camera fixes on the maze of chalk lines Jaffee is forcing her to follow.

Professionalism ranks high in Hawks' value system, and even during the Depression none of his characters was unemployed or indigent.[10] They try to take possession of their world by their actions, but the brute reality that surrounds them will not yield to their drive for mastery. In the Screwball Comedy *Bringing Up Baby* (1938), Professor David Huxley (Cary Grant)—no relation to Aldous, but the idea probably crossed Hawks' mind—is a brilliant paleontologist trying to organize the animal kingdom by reconstructing the skeletons of prehistoric animals, but he is thwarted by a tame leopard and a pesky little dog. In the Western *Red River* (1948) Tom Dunson (John Wayne), the toughest cattle baron in Texas, wants to control the entire range, the drive to the railroad, and the lives of the people around him, but he is stopped by the rebellion of Matthew Garth (Montgomery Clift) against his father figure. In the Hardboiled Detective *The Big Sleep* (1946), Philip Marlowe (Humphrey Bogart) is kept from solving a routine case by the appearance of Vivian Rutledge (Lauren Bacall) and the disappearance of a corpse. In the Science Fiction *The Thing (From Another World)* (1951), which Hawks produced and co-directed with Christian Nyby, Captain Hendry (Kenneth Tobey) is an effective leader of his men on a dangerous assignment to the Arctic, but he cannot control a vegetable that comes from outer space. In trying to organize and control their world, Hawks' heroes are stretched to the limits of their professional abilities. In the action pictures they face the danger of death; in the comedies they are merely embarrassed by the struggle.[11]

In discussing Hawks' use of straight narrative movement, Rivette expresses his admiration for the inevitability of the actions and their effects upon one another.[12] As he describes his reaction to the sequence of events in a Hawks film, one gathers a sense of fatalism. Once the action is set in motion, it rolls on to an inevitable conclusion. In *Rio Bravo* (1959), Chance (John Wayne) will eventually save the town from the Burdetts and will win the love of Feathers (Angie Dickinson). That is clear from the outset. Hawks, however, takes the story to its conclusion with a relentless unfolding of one event leading directly to the next, until it reaches the end which has been determined in the opening minutes of the film. In *His Girl Friday* (1940),

Hildy Johnson (Rosalind Russell) will have to get her story, dump her drippy fiancé Bruce Baldwin (Ralph Bellamy), and rejoin her estranged husband Walter Burns (Cary Grant). The inevitability of these outcomes winds out through each scene. Rivette sees this internal logic, even in the most improbable comic plots, as evidence of honesty and even moralism in Hawks' works.

The importance of work, professionalism and action places almost all of Hawks' films in a male-oriented universe. He is intrigued by the dynamics of a small, confined group of men facing a challenge from outside. His heroes and heroic bands revel in a kind of naive machismo, which Hawks is capable of subjecting to parody on occasion. In *Bringing Up Baby* Cary Grant, his durable romantic lead—today reviewers might call him a sex symbol—appears in a fussy bathrobe he is forced to borrow from Susan Vance (Katharine Hepburn), and in *I Was a Male War Bride* Grant is often disguised as a woman.[13] The passing of cigarettes is an expression of communion within the tight-knit band of male comrades.

Hawks gravitated to these masculine themes quite naturally, since he enjoyed the company of men and their activities together. His early passions for flying and auto racing gave way to more sedate activities, but he remained an athlete into his final years. He had race horses and a yacht. He was a fine marksman, and enjoyed hunting, fishing and skiing. Faulkner admired the way he drank, which was praise from an expert, and in more private moments Hawks enjoyed carpentry and silversmithing.[14] His marriages were not durable. His first, to Athole Shearer, sister of the actress Norma Shearer, lasted from 1928 to 1941. Then he married twice more, one marriage lasting seven years and the other six. During this time he had four children and adopted a son.

Hawks' personal life and psychological makeup is matter for biographers rather than critics. At the same time this brief sketch of his family life can provide a useful context for his handling of women in his films. Most of his women are superwomen. They set a standard that few flesh-and-blood women in the real world could ever match. They break into the tight male circle by their own professional competence and force of personality. In the process they become romantically linked to the hero, yet by contributing to the group they are "one of the boys." Although he may have had problems with his marriages and enjoyed the company of men, he was no misogynist. On the contrary, he made his women extremely interesting by giving them the best gender traits of both sexes. They are attractive and very feminine, but they are professional peers with the men. They are quick with the verbal repartee and often they take the initiative in the romance because the man is too involved in his project with his companions to realize that he is in love.

Nikki (Margaret Sheridan) in *The Thing* has a variant of a man's name and wears slacks during her stay with the crew at the Arctic ice station. She embarrasses Hendry by joking about their former romantic escapades with outrageous double-entendres. Despite her costume and locker room humor, it is quite clear to the audience, and eventually to Hendry, that she is a most attractive woman. When the team is baffled about destroying the thing, another woman comes up with the solution: "Boil it." Feathers in *Rio Bravo* is named after her very feminine clothing, and Hawks gives Angie Dickinson several opportunities to show off her exquisite and very feminine figure, but Feathers is also a professional gambler on the run from the federal marshals. She shaves Dude (Dean Martin) and, in a perfect role reversal, she stays up all night to protect the sleeping Chance (John Wayne) from a gunman. She does not fire a gun herself, but in the key gunfight she distracts the outlaws by throwing a vase through a window, thus allowing Chance to recover his rifle and finish the job. Joey Macdonald (Michele Carey) in *El Dorado* (1967) is not quite as attractive as Feathers, but she is quite good with a gun; she shoots Cole Thornton (John Wayne) and then saves his life with her rifle. By contrast, Cole's young sidekick Mississippi (James Caan) is such a terrible shot that he carries a shotgun in an oversized holster. Joey (another man's name) wears pants; Mississippi (suggestion of Miss?) wears a fancy hat that draws comment.

Hildy in *His Girl Friday* is simply the best reporter on the paper. She wears a woman's variation of a man's fedora when she is at work, and busier, more feminine clothes when she is with her wimpy fiancé Bruce. In the triangle, Walter recognizes her "masculine" talent but seems blind to her "feminine" attractiveness. With Bruce just the opposite is true, and since he cannot realize how important her work is to her, he is destined to lose her. Lily in *Twentieth Century* gets involved in the comic but destructive relationship with Jaffee simply because she has become such a talented actress.

Gentlemen Prefer Blondes (1953) stands out as an exception to Hawks' preference for placing strong women in the middle of an all-male world. Lorelei Lee (Marilyn Monroe) and Dorothy Shaw (Jane Russell) are sometime entertainers, but what they excel at is golddigging. By casting these two actresses in the leads, dressing them in fashionable and sophisticated costumes, and giving them several lavish song-and-dance numbers, Hawks leaves no doubt at all about their feminine appeal—none whatever. At the same time, the women are buddies and clearly do not need the men for survival. They continually outwit their would-be suitors, and invariably get what they want from them. In one highly symbolic scene they pull the trousers off a detective who they believe may be hiding a roll of incriminating film in his pants pocket. They clearly put him at a disadvantage. In the final scene both marry at a double ceremony, but only because it is to their advantage to end their capers and settle down, at least long enough to count their money.

In these simple genre films Hawks was articulating his own "bitter vision" of life. He saw comedy in tragedy and tragedy in the comic. His films march forward at an irresistible pace, one footstep after the next, to their fated, inevitable conclusion. With his objective camera he cast himself, and his audiences, in the role of a disinterested spectator watching the predetermined chain of events unwind. He was cool toward his subject matter. He redefined the battle of the sexes by examining gender roles long before the feminist critics had begun their work of revisionism. It was an extraordinary achievement that might have gone unnoticed, simply because he found that the Hollywood genre film gave him all the forms he needed to express his own intensely personal vision of his world.

His direction, like his ideas, rarely called attention to itself, simply because he was intent to let the action on the screen do his work for him. Making himself invisible so that his characters would dominate the film is no small achievement, and it was thoroughly deliberate. He defined a good director as "somebody who doesn't annoy you."[15] If it had not been for the *Cahiers* critics with their limited grasp of English and their tireless fascination with the American film, Howard Hawks might never have had the opportunity to "annoy" a whole new generation of American critics and movie-goers. It is the kind of annoyance that has made us all quite a bit richer.

The Genre: The Gangster Film

In 1948, the extremely perceptive essayist Robert Warshow wrote: "The real city, one might say, produces criminals; the imaginary city produces the gangster: he is what we want to be and what we are afraid we may become."[16] The distinction is crucial. The gangster films came not out of pulp fiction, like the Westerns or the Hardboiled Detectives, but out of the newspaper headlines. With their gritty urban settings and tough-talking characters, they give the impression of reality, as though they are an early form of docudrama. Gangsters, however, have little to do with reality. Although the heroes are based upon real people, the film characters are mythic figures that probe the American dream and find it wanting. As such, they pose a crisis of value and identity for their audiences, especially in the United States during the Depression. They are figures to admire for their success in following the American cult of self-reliance and opportunity; they are to be pitied for taking the myth at face value and thus being destroyed by it. The gangster, then, is a truly American tragic hero.

The criminal of fact became the gangster of legend in the 1920s, the "Roaring Twenties." His immediate rise to fame was Prohibition when he stood alone as a solitary figure against the hypocrisy of the nation, which was willing to ban the sale of alcoholic beverages and yet was ready to pay a great deal of money to get them. The bootlegger was at least consistent: he exploited the national sickness for profit. He defied the institutions of government to get what he wanted: money and power. Al Capone, Bugsy Moran and Baby Face Nelson became urban folk heroes, successors to the tradition of Billy the Kid and the James Brothers. Prohibition came into effect through the Volstead Act in 1920 and was repealed in 1933. By 1928 the historical fact had provided the raw material of legend. The gangster of fact had entered popular literature and the movies and had become the gangster of myth.

During the years of the Depression, the country was continuing its long shift from a rural to an urban society, and it was not altogether comfortable with the change. The immigrant dream of boundless wealth somewhere out West had by this time yielded to the nightmare of urban poverty. According to the U.S. Census Bureau, the frontier had been officially closed in 1900, and the hope of moving on toward the West to tracts of free land and vast wealth was no longer a part of the American experience. Tenements, factories and sweatshops were the new American reality. Ignorance and disease were as much a part of the urban environment here as they were in the old country. On top of this disillusionment came the Depression, when even the most menial jobs were no longer available.

The mythical gangster struck many resonances with his Depression audiences. He is a creature of the city, born into poverty and cultural deprivation. He cannot move to a new world, and in fact he does not want to move. The gangster, however, is a fighter. He is supremely confident that he can survive and prosper within the world as he finds it. He will accept any challenge, fight any battle, use any

means, but he will endure and prosper. Audiences had to admire his
success, since he inevitably rises to the top of his field. Cars, clothes,
beautiful women, fine restaurants and nightclubs are his, but he is
marked by tragedy. His very success isolates him from his friends,
and, left alone, he oversteps the limits of his powers and is killed. Like
the classic figures of Greek tragedy, his tragic flaw is hubris, an overwhelming and destructive pride.

The gangster's ambition in his constrained circumstances puts
him on a collision course with reality. American society and social
institutions have created the cities which make the gangster possible,
but they have also created a suffocating world for him by imposing an
order on the wilderness. The order limits his opportunities. Rather
than rebel against the social order and attempt to destroy it, the gangster tries to replace society's norms and values with his own. He wants
to impose his own order on the city by expanding his territory and
driving out rival gangs. He is not, as some have claimed, rebelling
against order by trying to revert to an earlier form of chaos, where
possibilities were unfettered by social convention. On the contrary,
the gangster is not an atavist but a postmodern. He accepts the premise that social order is needed in an urban environment and even for
his own prosperity; he simply wants the order to be his order, not
society's, one that tolerates his methods and works to his best
interests.[17]

Audiences then get a double pleasure from watching his rise and
fall. His ascent reinforces the American dream that hard work brings
success; his fated demise shows that society is too powerful even for
the strongest. He is admired for making his own rules, living by them
and forcing others to do the same. For example, he makes the police
as violent as he is. He is a parody of American machismo, and as such
he exposes the dark side of the American intoxication with success at
any price. At the same time, his pride makes him despised, and there
is satisfaction in seeing his bullet-riddled body in the last scene. It
reinforces the notion of fatalism. Like people in other countries,
Americans too can destroy themselves by reaching too far and placing
themselves outside their social level. Watching the ending, an audience can become reconciled to the facts of the Depression. Some
people are fated to be poor and unemployed, and to want too much is
to invite destruction.

The message, then, would seem to be extremely conservative and
moralistic, and indeed the studios did all they could to make it appear
that they were presenting a morality play to inspire young people to
avoid a life of crime. It was difficult to take that claim seriously. As

they appeared in the films, the gangsters were the most attractive, interesting people. In contrast, the police, politicians and journalists were traditionally smug, self-righteous and unforgivably dull. For all but the last ten minutes, audiences watch a fascinating, dynamic young man rise to the top, making all his fantasies come true, and sinister, corrupt and equally brutal guardians of public order stopping at nothing to get him. After the final stutter of gunfire, audiences cannot possibly leave the theater with the conclusion that crime does not pay, when for the last hour and a half they have seen that it does pay quite well indeed. Under the pretense of moralism, the films were actually subversive. They elevated individual self-interest over the interests of society.

Violence is a necessary part of the drive toward success, and the films are filled with violence, but choosing violent means to his end is not the cause of the tragic hero's downfall. With characteristic insight, the critic Robert Warshow bases the tragedy on an unfair dilemma.[18] The hero is driven to success, and failure to succeed is a form of death by American standards. Success, however, is evil. In an egalitarian society, standing out from the pack is suspect and the ostentatiously successful man must be brought down. The conflict, then, is not between good and evil, or between criminals and the police, or between acceptable and unacceptable means to achieve desired ends. The principal conflict exists within the protagonist himself. He is torn between his individualist drive to excel and his social need to fit in with his environment. The tragedy is both his, because he cannot use his considerable energies to become a constructive citizen, and society's, because its rigid patterns cannot make room for him. His frustration mirrors the dilemma of the Depression. Citizens cannot find productive work in society, and society cannot provide jobs for them.

Although almost always physically small, the gangster stands out above his peers naturally. He is tougher, more driven and perhaps smarter, like Tommy Powers (James Cagney) in William Wellman's *The Public Enemy* (1931), more calculating like Rico Bandello (Edward G. Robinson) in *Little Caesar* (1930), or simply more brutal like Tony Camonte (Paul Muni) in *Scarface* (1932). He is ruthless in overtaking his superiors, and he demeans his inferiors, even while paying them generously. His partner either deserts him, as Joe Massara (Douglas Fairbanks Jr.) does to Rico in *Little Caesar*, or is killed by a rival gang, as is Matt Doyle (Edward Woods) in *The Public Enemy*, or is murdered by his boss, as is Guino Rinaldi (George Raft) by Tony in *Scarface*. When left alone, completely alone, the gangster dies. His drive to self-interest, which is one of the elements that separates him from his friends, robs him of companionship and leads to his death.

Women have little role to play in such a world. They are orna- ments to be collected, like cars and custom-made clothes. In the myth, which the Gangster Films parody beautifully, the women are quite content to function as sexual playthings as long as they get what they want: jewelry, clothes, luxury apartments and evenings at fan- tasy-land nightclubs. They fail to domesticate their lovers, as do many of the strong women in the Westerns. Quite the opposite is true. The successful women break into the male society of the mob and as story- book gun molls adopt the antisocial behavior of the gangster/lover. Cesca (Ann Dvorak), Tony's sister, joins him for the final shoot-out and both she and Tony's girlfriend, Poppy (Karen Morley) in an ear- lier scene, join in the violence by loading magazines for Tony's tommy guns. When they cease to amuse the gangster, they are dis- carded. Kitty (Mae Clarke) tries to domesticate Tommy Powers by objecting to his whisky-drinking at breakfast. She is answered with a grapefruit in the face and vanishes from the picture, the perfect image of expendable women in a gangster's world.

Family relationships form a special problem in the gangster's need to stand out as a loner while keeping social roots in some kind of community. Tommy Powers' brother Mike (Donald Cook) is a dull, hard-working nerd. He tries to improve life for the family the hard way: by going to night school while working as a streetcar conductor by day. "Learning how to be poor" is Tommy's assessment of Mike's education. The sibling rivalry is no contest. In a primitive sociological statement, Mike is supposed to prove that neither genetic nor envi- ronmental conditioning necessarily determines a life of crime. Mike may be boring and pompous, but at least he is a good citizen in the urban jungle. Ma Powers (Beryl Mercer) tries to be a mediator be- tween her sons, but eventually Tommy rejects his family completely. Standing alone, he is gunned down; he tries a deathbed reconcilia- tion, but by then it is too late. Fate has already caught up with him.

Tony and Cesca prove the opposite theory. He is obsessed with her "purity," and becomes violent whenever he sees her with a man. He finally kills her husband, and thus separates himself from her, but when she comes to kill him in revenge, they embrace and die together in the final gunfight with the police. She has been as determined as he to break out of the constraints of society, even the ones Tony has imposed upon her. Together they discover the foreordained conclusion to their impossible aspirations, as though genes, environment or both determined their fate. As a true tragic hero, however, Tony leaves his dead sister and, now completely alone, faces his own death.

This fascination with the death of the solitary gangster came into the world of film somewhat suddenly. Several silent films did deal with the sordid side of city life, and many of the themes of the gangster film were already starting to evolve.[19] One of the more notable examples was *Underworld* (Josef von Sternberg, 1927). In 1927 Warner Brothers introduced an effective sound system with *The Jazz Singer* (Alan Crosland) and the public developed an instant mania for sound. Eager to satisfy the market, the studio pushed into sound, and the next year it brought out the first sound gangster film, *The Lights of New York*. Sound added immeasurably to the intensity of the drama. The dark interiors used in silent films to suggest shady dealings and danger could be a bit dull. But when huge black cars came squealing down a darkened street and machine gun fire rent the night air, the film gained excitement and intensity. The snarling voices of actors like Cagney, Robinson and Muni created memorable characters and taught generations of small boys how to talk tough in their games of cops and robbers. Gangsters and sound seemed a perfect combination, and the antiheroes of crime were monopolizing the headlines to provide ready-made publicity for the films. The race to make gangster films was on, and Warner Bros., eventually known as the Depression studio for the gritty look and tough themes it favored, took the lead.

For several reasons, the genre, like its tragic heroes, was destined not to last. A good part of the problem was external. Crime was serious business, and, for all their disclaimers to the contrary, enough watchdogs of the industry were convinced, and rightly so, that these films really did glorify criminals. The studios used elaborate ruses, but the front offices and the Hays office put more and more restrictions on the portrayal of violence. When the Code began to be seriously enforced in 1934, that effectively ended the Gangster genre in its classic form. When Prohibition ended in 1933, most of the real gangsters were either dead or in jail, and thus much of the fascination was gone. A visit to the neighborhood speakeasy for a glass of beer was no longer needed, and it cut another line of romantic identification between the public and the bootlegger.

Part of the problem was internal as well. The characters and icons of the Gangster film slid easily into other forms, and as a result the impact was diluted. Paul Muni, as an extremely versatile actor, went off to create different personalities for himself in other films. James Cagney and Edward G. Robinson also did so, but somehow the gangster aura still shone around them. Even when Cagney won an Academy Award for playing George M. Cohan in *Yankee Doodle Dandy* (Michael Curtiz, 1942), he still sounded as tough and street-smart as Tommy Powers. In the middle of the 1930s, the movie tough guys gave up the rackets and went into prison and became private detectives.[20] Cagney even became a cop in *G-Men* (William Keighley, 1935) to show that tough guys exist on both sides of the law. The gangsters left the cities and went on the lam to the country where they became bandits in chase movies, like James Cagney in *White Heat* (Raoul Walsh, 1949) and Edward G. Robinson in *Key Largo* (John Huston, 1948).

The saga of *The Godfather* (Francis Ford Coppola, 1972) and *The Godfather, Part II* (Coppola, 1974) begins as a Gangster film while Vito Corleone (Marlon Brando) consolidates his power, but it overturns the genre when he retires and dies at his family estate while playing with a grandchild. Michael Corleone (Al Pacino in both films) also begins his career in crime in the pattern of a classic gangster, but he is a survivor in changing times. He does not try to impose his criminal order on an oppressive outside social order (Michael was born into a very rich family), but rather he learns to adapt, change with the times, and fight off challenges from within and from outside the organization in order to survive. At the end he has become thoroughly corrupt and alone, but his drive for power, which isolates him from his family, leads to solitude, a psychological death rather than actual death. The rich color and Nino Rota's bouncy Italian music undercut the gritty atmosphere of the classics. The films are excellent in their own right, but simply too far removed in theme and style from the classics to fit into the category of Gangster film.

The classic Gangster film fits an era, and once removed from the Depression, it loses much of its appeal. It is difficult to imagine an ambitious crack dealer of the 1990s gaining as much sympathy as the bootleggers of the 1930s. Still, even though they are necessarily set in a particular era, even today the films of the Depression era provide a valid analysis of the contemporary American dream, with its drive toward achievement, to become somebody, and its fear of success, of becoming lonely at the top. It points to an emptiness of human accomplishment without companionship, a question that is timeless in a prosperous, materialistic society like America.

The Plot: **Scarface**

After the opening credits the camera follows a waiter dressed in an apron sweeping up after a stag party in the First Ward Social Club. Voices of Big Louie Costillo (Harry J. Vehar) and others speaking in English, but with Italian accents, are heard in the background. The waiter finds a brassiere on the floor. Big Louie expresses worries about Johnny Lovo, who wants to make trouble. Costillo claims he has enough money and other bootleggers should be allowed their share of the business. He flips a coin as he walks out to make a phone call. As he stands by himself a figure whistling an aria from Donizetti's *Lucia di Lammermoor* appears in silhouette behind a pane of frosted glass. Three shots are fired. The shadow figure drops the gun and walks away. The waiter sees the body, takes off his apron and leaves.

In a newspaper office an editor is shouting that he wants the headline to show the significance of the story: "Costillo Murder Starts Gang War." He wants to emphasize the notion of war.

Detective Ben Guarino (C. Henry Gordon) enters a barber shop where Tony Camonte (Paul Muni) is under a towel. Guino Rinaldo, known as Little Boy (George Raft), tries to distract Guarino, but Camonte stands up and identifies himself. Camonte strikes a match on Guarino's badge, and, after a scuffle, Guarino takes Camonte and Rinaldo to the station for questioning about the murder. Epstein, the lawyer, arrives with a writ of habeas corpus from a corrupt judge, and Camonte and Rinaldo are immediately released.

Camonte heads straight for a meeting with Johnny Lovo (Osgood Perkins), who is staying at the apartment of his girlfriend Poppy (Karen Morley). Camonte receives payment for murdering Costillo. He makes crude advances to Poppy in front of Lovo, but she rebuffs him. Lovo is planning a meeting of all the bootleggers on the South Side. He intends to organize the industry. He appoints Camonte as his lieutenant, but warns him about going into O'Hara's territory on the North Side. Camonte offers him a cheap cigar, which Lovo accepts, but he offers Camonte a more expensive one. They prepare to smoke, but Poppy tells them she doesn't want cigar smoke in her apartment.

In a cab, Camonte gives Rinaldo a share of his fee for having been lookout. He offers Rinaldo his formula for success: "Do it first, do it yourself, and keep doing it."

At dinner in the Camonte home, Tony asks about his sister Cesca (Ann Dvorak). Suspecting something, he finds her in the hall kissing a man, who flees in terror. Camonte tells Cesca: "No more men!" She is furious, but he calms her with a share of his money, which her mother tells her not to accept. She keeps the money and returns to her bedroom. She is cheered up by the sound of an organ grinder on the street below. She is amused by the monkey and throws a coin down for the man. Rinaldo is leaning on the instrument, flipping a coin. He catches Cesca's coin and puts it in his pocket, while tossing another one to the organ grinder. Cesca climbs up on her bed.

Lovo and Camonte enter the First Ward Social Club for the meeting with the bootleggers. It is Costillo's old headquarters. Camonte throws a spittoon through the glass with Costillo's name on it. Lovo announces his plans. One man objects and Camonte punches him. Lovo tells them that Camonte will get the business for them. Camonte wants Angelo (Vince Barnett) to be his secretary, but he can't write. They leave together.

In a rapid-fire sequence, Camonte and Angelo strongarm two bars into buying their beer, and more than they need. Another owner has ties to a rival gang and is not expected to cooperate. They bomb his establishment. They shoot their last rivals, but Lovo tells Camonte that the job is not complete because one survived. They enter the hospital and shoot him in his bed. To the background of machine gun fire, pages fly off a calendar to indicate the passage of time.

Camonte appears in a finely tailored gray suit with garish accessories. He meets Poppy on the stairs of her apartment. She is more amused than hostile at his posturing. He shows off his rings, she refers to them as "effeminate" but he does not seem to know what the word means and takes it as a compliment. He boasts of his new car with bulletproof glass. He invites her to see his new apartment, and her response is ambiguous.

Camonte enters Lovo's headquarters expecting trouble. Lovo is furious at him for moving in on the North Side. Lovo believes they are not strong enough to take on O'Hara, and Camonte quips that he is not afraid of a guy who hangs out in a florist shop. They are leaving to visit O'Hara to make a truce when a speeding car dumps off the body of one of Lovo's soldiers.

Angelo is working at his desk in Camonte's apartment. He tries on a new hat which appears several sizes too small. The phone rings but Angelo cannot get names straight or take any messages. In frustration he pulls a gun on the phone, but Camonte restrains him. Rinaldo comes in wearing a flower in his lapel, and it becomes clear that he has murdered O'Hara in his florist shop. The intercom buzzes, and Camonte takes the call himself. Poppy is coming up to visit. She finds the apartment "gaudy," and he takes it as another compliment. He shows off his shirts and "inside spring" mattress. He demonstrates the steel shutter he has on his windows and points to a sign outside: "The World Is Yours: Cook's Tours." When Angelo tells them the police are downstairs, she exits by a back stairway. As the police lead him away, Camonte tells Rinaldo to call Epstein for a rite of hocus pocus.

Gaffney (Boris Karloff), who has taken over the North Side gang after O'Hara's death, is opening crates of tommy guns. He will use these to crush Lovo's gang.

Poppy meets Camonte in a restaurant. Angelo tries to take a phone call, when the place is sprayed with machine gun fire. Rinaldo hits one of the gunmen and retrieves a tommy gun. Camonte, with Poppy and Rinaldo, takes the gun to Lovo's headquarters and shoots up the pool hall to enjoy its power. Lovo has been wounded in one of Gaffney's earlier attacks. As the gunmen leave for the raid, Poppy, who has been loading a magazine, tosses a pistol to Camonte in case his new "bean shooter" doesn't work.

Camonte's men bring seven of Gaffney's to a warehouse and mow them down with tommy guns. It is the St. Valentine's Day Massacre. Detective Guarino brings in Gaffney to show him the result of the gang war on his henchmen. Gaffney goes into hiding. A reporter finds him, explaining that the press has its ways to track him down. Another reporter enters the office of the chief of detectives (Edwin Maxwell) asking for a story on gangsters because they are colorful. The chief berates him for publicizing them.

In a publisher's office, a group of concerned citizens reproaches Mr. Garston (Purnell Pratt) for allowing his reporters to glamorize the gangsters. He responds that his papers publicize their criminal activity, which is better than ignoring them. As he continues his speech, he maintains that local police are powerless against organized crime. Citizens must exert pressure on the federal government to regulate the import of automatic weapons and to pass laws to deport undesirable aliens. The army and the American Legion should be mobilized to counter gangsters.

Dressed in tuxedos, Camonte, Angelo and Rinaldo attend a presentation of Somerset Maugham's *Rain*. When they leave the theater between acts, they receive word that Gaffney is in a bowling alley. Camonte commissions Angelo to stay to see how the play ends, while he brings his tommy gun and murders Gaffney.

After the murder, Camonte enters the Paradise, a nightclub. He moves in on a table with Poppy and Johnny Lovo, and Poppy's affection moves from Lovo to Camonte. Both men try to light her cigarette, and she chooses Camonte's match over Lovo's lighter. She dances with Camonte, after telling Lovo she did not want to dance. Alone at the table, Lovo seethes and plays with a salt shaker, holding it as though it were a pistol. In the vestibule of the Paradise, Cesca meets Rinaldo and invites him to dance. He refuses, even after she does a jazzy solo turn in front of him, and she moves off with another partner. An unknown intruder fires a pistol and the staff throws him out. Camonte is unmoved. Lovo realizes that he has lost Poppy to Camonte and is furious. As Camonte and Poppy dance, he sees Cesca dancing cheek-to-cheek with an unknown man, punches her partner and takes her home. He slaps Cesca and tears the gown off her shoulder, and their mother brings her to her room as Cesca weeps.

As Camonte leaves his home to return for Poppy, he runs into a volley of machine gun fire. He reaches his armor-plated car and chases his attackers, running them off the road. Slightly injured from the collision, he reaches Rinaldo by telephone and they design a plan to prove that Lovo had commissioned the attack on Camonte. They return to Lovo's headquarters and spring the trap. In a rage Camonte puts his fist through the door with Lovo's name on it. Camonte walks away whistling the aria from *Lucia di Lammermoor* while Rinaldo assassinates Lovo.

The door which once had the name of Costillo and then Lovo now says Antonio Camonte. Cesca enters, finds Rinaldo tearing a row of paper dolls, and flirts with him. They mention that Camonte is away for a month in Florida.

The newspapers reveal that new people at city hall are more aggressive about fighting organized crime. When Camonte returns from Florida, he learns that Cesca has moved out of the family apartment, and his mother, who has followed Cesca, gives him her new address. Cesca is playing the piano. Camonte enters the apartment and kills Rinaldo, who is there with Cesca. As she bends over the body, Cesca tells Camonte that they have been legally married.

The tickertape message to the police calls for Camonte's arrest for the murder. The police surround Camonte's fortress apartment, and as he and Angelo enter by the rear passageway the police open fire and Angelo is mortally wounded. When the phone rings, Angelo answers and it is Poppy. This is the first time he has been able to get a name. Camonte, stricken with remorse, tells her that he did not know Cesca and Rinaldo were married. As the police orchestrate their attack, Cesca enters the apartment with a gun. She cannot shoot her brother. They form an alliance for the final shoot-out with the police. She is wounded and dies in his arms. He leaves the apartment and is wounded by the police. He surrenders and the police comment that he is a coward without his gun. As they try to put him in handcuffs, he lunges toward freedom and is killed in another volley of fire from the police. "The World Is Yours" sign reappears.

COMMENTARY

The film as it was released in 1932 and as it appears today is missing several scenes from the original script prepared by Howard Hawks and Ben Hecht in 1930 in their rather loose adaptation of the novel *The Shame of a Nation* by Armitage Trail. The evolution of the film passes through many generations, each one a reworking of the same material. The story is based in fact, since its ultimate source is the life of the Chicago criminal Al Capone. The actual history was, of course, altered when the tabloid press presented its own version of Capone's life in headline prose with such force that it made him a national figure. Trail's book then transformed the popular phenomenon of Capone that had been fashioned by the press into the material of a novel. By this time fact had become fiction, and conversely in the public imagination the fiction had become fact, since the media version was far more exciting and thus more believable than the reality. Hecht and Hawks stood at the end of the line, four removals from the reality of Al Capone, the flesh and blood Chicago criminal. In their film they offer an interpretation not of the fact but of the fiction. They tried to explain the meaning of Al Capone: Why the fascination with him? What did the Capone myth say about America?

Theirs was not a happy conclusion. With their "bitter vision," they saw the Capone figure, now reincarnated as Tony Camonte, as standing for the dark side of the American dream. Getting ahead often involved corruption and violence, and Tony Camonte, by being an overt example of the evil side of success, exposed a truth about America that few wanted to acknowledge.

The eminent film historian Gerald Mast lists several scenes, omitted from the finished product, that point out Camonte as a sinister presence in the wider spectrum of American life.[21] From his study of the manuscripts, Mast discovered that Hawks had originally written a part for a character called Benson, an attorney general of the state of Illinois, who promises in his campaign speeches to rid the state of gangsters and bootleggers, while taking payoffs from both Lovo and Camonte. The legal institutions are just as corrupt as the criminal, only Camonte is more honest about it.

Before her part was sanitized, Mrs. Camonte, the materfamilias, was not merely the solicitous mediator between Cesca and Tony that she is in the present film. Rather than merely complain about Tony's work and discourage Cesca from taking his tainted money, Mama Camonte lives quite handsomely herself on her son's rackets. When she perceives Rinaldo's entrance into the family as a threat to her financial security, she sends a telegram to Tony to bring him back from Florida. She is fully aware of what he will do, but the murder will keep the money in the family. Literally, this characterization is an attack on the American myth of motherhood, as it is generally coupled with the flag and apple pie.

Finally, Mast describes a scene on Camonte's yacht in Florida, where he and Poppy, now openly living together, entertain a cross-section of wealthy guests, including "a lady novelist who writes dirty books." These respectable people find Camonte an amusing host, and they are perfectly comfortable with him, surely because he is not much different from themselves. Since it was considered an indictment of the upper levels of American society, classes that included movie executives and theater owners, this material was judged to be un-American and the scene had to be cut.

Ironically, while Hawks and Hecht were intent on pointing out the hypocrisy of the wealthy and powerful, hypocrisy was making inroads on their text. Three title cards try to preserve the moral integrity of mainstream America, while placing the burden of evil on a few individuals. The first: "This picture is an indictment of gang rule in America and of the callous indifference of the government to this constantly increasing menace to the safety of our liberty." This is followed by: "Every incident in this picture is the reproduction of an actual occurrence, and the purpose of this picture is to demand of the government: 'What are you going to do about it?' " Finally, the logic is completed: "The government is your government: What are *You* going to do about it?" The message the final version strains to present is that a few criminals have created a crisis for the nation, but that the crisis can be resolved if we, as a government and as a people, stand up and purge the few rotten apples from the barrel before Mom tries to make her apple pie while Old Glory waves in the back yard. This is far different from the Hawks-Hecht portrait of pervasive evil in American society.

Hawks' theme is undercut once again in a startlingly inept interpolation in the middle of the film. The scene was not directed by Hawks; it was added after the film was finished and obviously does not belong in the film. Immediately after the St. Valentine's Day Massacre, a committee of earnest citizens appeals to a newspaper publisher to stop publicizing the exploits of gangsters. In puffing indignation, Mr. Garston, the publisher, rants on that he is only trying to wake up the public. His newspaper will not allow America to ignore the problem of crime. It will urge the voters to demand that their legislators ban automatic weapons and tighten immigration laws. Call out the army and the American Legion, he proposes.

The primary purpose of the scene is, of course, an apologia for the film itself, which many viewers could with good reason read as glorifying Tony Camonte and his exploits. The moguls at United Artists wanted to allay any suspicion that they were releasing a sensationally violent film merely to make money. Like Mr. Garston, who (heavens forfend!) should never be suspected of merely wanting to sell newspapers, studio executives want to present themselves as crusaders for the commonweal. Selling tickets has nothing to do with their decision to release the film. Even though it appears to be violent entertainment, they want the public and the critics to accept *Scarface* as a serious "message" film that would bring about the legal reform needed to end the rule of gangsters. So the opening titles would have the gullible believe.

The note of hypocrisy is introduced in an early scene when an editor demands a more sensational headline for the story of Costillo's murder. With an equal lack of sincerity, he claims he wants to wake up the public to the fact that the murder will mean gang war. Again, no one is supposed to imagine that William Randolph Hearst or later Rupert Murdoch ever encouraged sensational headlines because they sell newspapers and boost advertising revenues.

Unwittingly, Mr. Garston's self-serving apologia not only provided an example of the kind of hypocrisy Hawks and Hecht were trying to expose, but it also undercut Hawks' main point. The publisher's xenophobic speech presumes the moral integrity of America, which is being tarnished by a few deviants, most of them foreigners. He believes that the problem will disappear if only weak-willed politicians had the courage to reassert the old-fashioned values by calling out the American Legion and the army. Hawks' viewpoint is just the opposite. The American dream of wealth, power and success has a dark side. It created a people who tamed a continent, but it also spawned robber barons, slavery, exploitation of workers, and genocide of native Americans. In addition, it created gangsters like Tony Camonte, who embodies the nightmare side of the dream. According to Hawks and Hecht, evil is deeply ingrained in the American experience, and not even the imposition of a Fascist police state, as Mr. Garston proposes, can make it go away, any more than the stocks and the dunking stool of the Puritans could eliminate sin from Salem.

Hawks does not cry out in despair over the situation. With cool detachment he simply points to the facts. It is hard to hate Tony Camonte. He is not a person who sins; he is evil incarnate, a mythic force in American society, an objective fact to observe, not a person to judge. He is more brute than human, and one cannot hate an animal, even a predator, for doing what its nature commands. That is what makes Camonte a tragic figure. He is evil from his first appearance as a shadow, not a person, when he murders Costillo. He does not descend into sin, he faces no moral dilemmas; he merely does what he is supposed to do. By refusing to condemn Camonte, Hawks has been misinterpreted as glorifying him. In fact, Hawks is letting Tony's actions condemn themselves, while allowing the audience to concentrate on the actions rather than the moral values of the man.

Tony's prominent cross-shaped scar is his mark of Cain. When Poppy first meets him and tries to insult him, she asks if he used to work for a razor company. Realizing she is needling him about the scar, he claims that he got it in the war. Lovo corrects him by telling Poppy that he got it from a blonde in a Brooklyn speakeasy. No one ever explains where it came from. That is Hawks' point. It makes no difference whether the scar came from a noble enterprise or a sordid one. It is simply there, signing Tony as one under a curse. In each of the murder scenes the X is present in some form, and its regular appearance even provokes a comic effect. Murder, the metaphor Hawks has chosen to embody evil, is just a fact of life in America.

Cruciform images in films can be misleading. They often invite a Christian interpretation, which may be congruent with the themes of the script. One could, for example, see the cross at the scene of each murder as a promise that each act of unalloyed evil will eventually fall under the sign of Christ. The evil will finally be washed away in blood when Camonte dies. This is not an entirely foolish reading of the film, but it does make Camonte a kind of Christ figure, when he is obviously more Satanic. Even this could be justified, through the theological notion that Jesus took the sins of the world upon himself in order to atone for them. The reading could be defended, but at the cost of a great deal of theological fancy footwork. Camonte as a Christ figure is aesthetically repugnant, but defensible, with difficulty. More to the point, however, is Hawks' consistent aversion to religious themes.[22] He himself claims that the cross was inspired by the X that newspa-

It Happened One Night

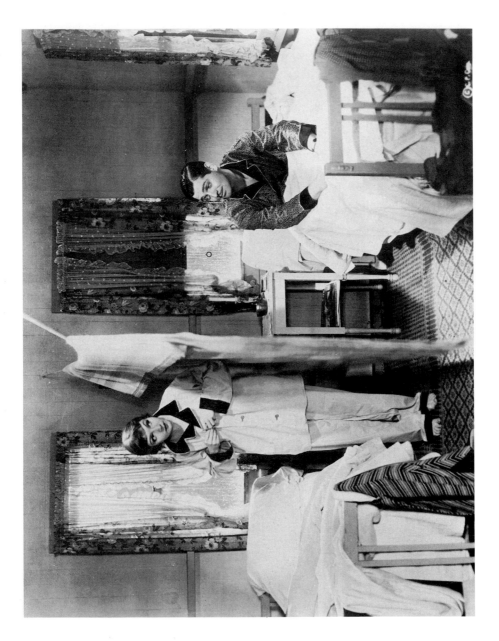

It Happened One Night

Scarface

Scarface

Stagecoach

The Maltese Falcon

The Maltese Falcon

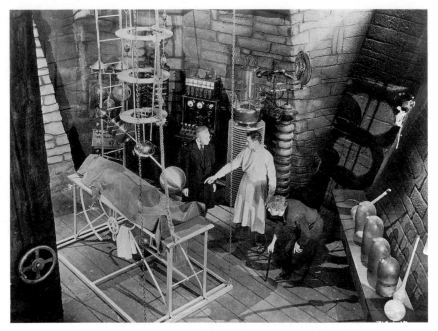

Frankenstein

pers superimposed on photographs of crime scenes to show where the bodies of the victims were found.[23]

In the film it is much simpler to interpret the X as the sign of death that is an inescapable mark carved by fate into Camonte's body. Death has no moral or even human import for Camonte; it is simply what he does. In Hawks' original ending, Tony and Cesca fight it out with the police until the building is blazing. When Cesca is killed, Camonte staggers down the back stairs riddled with bullets. His nemesis Ben Guarino awaits him. A dying man, Camonte raises his pistol, aims at the detective and fires, but the gun is empty. Guarino points his pistol at Camonte and shoots him in the face. As Camonte falls, he keeps pulling the trigger of his empty gun. To the very end Camonte plays out his fated role as an agent of death. Even as he dies, he "keeps doing it," pointlessly. In the end he is destroyed by a force as violent and ruthless in its death-dealing as himself. Despite the badge, Guarino also does what he is supposed to do.

In the final version, Camonte staggers down the back stairs, apparently wanting to surrender after the death of Cesca. Anonymous, uniformed police see him as they break down the door and open fire, wounding him slightly. Guarino reinforces the official "message" of the film by calling him a coward without his gun. When Guarino tries to put him in handcuffs, Camonte makes a suicidal lunge toward freedom, but he is killed instantly in a hailstorm of bullets.

The revised version gives him an opportunity to make a moral decision. He is, if one finds Guarino's speech convincing, a coward who chooses death rather than chains. Through the police bullets, order is reestablished in the city and the criminal meets his deserved end. Crime does not pay. The original version makes a far different statement. Camonte makes no moral decision at all. He is merely playing out his fated role to the end. He is the tragic hero, marked from the beginning with the sign of death, and by continuing to pull the trigger on an empty gun he shows no sign of remorse or change. Camonte cannot change; he is Camonte. He dies trying to kill, since that is what this engine of evil does. At the same time, when Guarino murders an unarmed man, it is clear that violence is neither confined to Camonte, nor will it end with his death.

Even though his profession is crime, Camonte, in Hawks' presentation of him, compels admiration for being the complete professional in his work. He allows no loyalty to stand in his way. As Hawks reveals more about the murder of Costillo, it becomes clear not only that Camonte did it, but that he was Costillo's bodyguard. Since his work was done so well, Lovo chooses him as his own lieutenant, the second in command. The actor who plays Lovo (Osgood Perkins) has a bland expression and lacks the animal drive of Camonte. The contrast is sharp in Poppy's apartment during their first scene together. Even though Camonte is crude in comparison to Lovo, he is obviously more suited to be a gangster. He has no embarrassment in what he does. Like a child, he imitates Poppy as she plucks her eyebrows. Like a child, too, he takes delight in firing his new tommy gun in Lovo's headquarters. Poppy refers to the gun as a toy, a "bean shooter." His early advances toward Poppy are adolescent in their awkwardness. When she visits his apartment, he asks her to test his "inside spring" mattress, and when they meet at a restaurant, immediately after he sits down, he begins to play "footsie," and she angrily tells him to stop because she has new stockings. The child-like recklessness is an ideal attribute for a criminal.

In some respects Tony Camonte is not only childish but simply dumb. His speech is crude and his taste in clothes and decor for the apartment is vulgar. His cartoon counterpart is Angelo, whom he calls "Dope." Angelo cannot read or write, and his clothes are more clownish than vulgar. Even though he appears harmless, he represents Tony's brutishness in its pure form. Camonte hires him as a secretary despite his manifest ineptitude for the job. Camonte, too, would be inept for any job other than crime. At least Angelo allows Camonte to feel intellectually superior to someone, and so he tolerates his presence despite his eye-catching incompetence. As a criminal, however, Angelo is quite adequate. He survives a shower of machine gun bullets in a restaurant by staying close to a niche that serves as a telephone booth, and this shields him. When the police drive Camonte into his office, Angelo knows enough to lock both doors of the back staircase, even though he is mortally wounded. He is unfailingly loyal to Camonte, and poses a threat to no one. Angelo is a survivor and makes a comfortable living from his mob connections until fate catches up with him.

Similarly, as a criminal Camonte is far from stupid. He executes Costillo without leaving a clue for the police. He murders cleanly, and he has far better judgment than Lovo on when to attack O'Hara on the North Side. Lovo is a cautious general; Camonte is Patton. At the same time, Camonte is not foolhardy; he knows enough to put bulletproof glass in his car and steel shutters on his windows. When he suspects Lovo of trying to kill him, he immediately forms an intricate plan to test his suspicions.

The source of Tony's strength is his single-minded determination to succeed. From their first meeting he knows he wants Poppy, and he gets her. As she and Lovo sit at a table in the Paradise, Camonte intrudes. When Poppy takes out a cigarette, Lovo extends a silver lighter and Camonte a wooden match. When she accepts his cruder light, Camonte has beaten Lovo. From the beginning Camonte wants to take over the North Side, while Lovo hesitates. At first he obeys Lovo's orders, later defies Lovo, and finally, after having Lovo murdered, accomplishes his goal. The progression of success in pursuit of the dream is obvious. Costillo is willing to share the business on the South Side, and he dies. Lovo wants a monopoly on the South Side, but will leave the North Side to O'Hara, and he dies. Camonte wants both the North Side and the South Side, and he, after an experience of invincibility, also dies.

When Gaffney's tommy guns stand in the way, he gets tommy guns of his own. At first the weapons are toys for a malevolent child. Then they are tools for a professional. He uses them first to murder Gaffney's gang on Valentine's Day, and then to murder Gaffney himself in the bowling alley, while Gaffney, too, is at play. Gaffney is a good bowler. He is going for the bonus to fill out his strike when he is gunned down. Camonte is better at the games.

During her visit to his apartment, Camonte shows Poppy the sign: "The World Is Yours: Cook's Tours," and eventually he makes his resolve come true. He eliminates all his enemies and has the entire world, North Side as well as South Side, under his control. He is so taken with the first part of the sign that he misses the irony of the second part of the sign. He does not realize that he is only passing through this world with a tourist visa. His schedule is predetermined by some celestial and uncompromising tour guide—God, fate, mortality. When the timetable calls for the bus to leave, he must board it. Even if he succeeds in gaining the world, he cannot keep it forever. He must take his snapshots, pack his bag and move on.

Camonte does not leave the world because of a professional error. He is the consummate professional in what he does. When he dies, his empire is undiminished. He even feels secure enough in his power to vacation in Florida. He does, however, fail to control his interior darkness. When he believes that Cesca and Rinaldo are living together unmarried, he loses control as he never had when Gaffney shot up the restaurant where he met Poppy nor when Lovo's henchmen tried to murder him in a terrifying car chase. In matters of business, he remains the consummate professional. Family matters, however, are different. Murdering Rinaldo on a mistaken assumption —Rinaldo and Cesca are in fact married—is a blunder that sets off the sequence of events that leads to his death. From the very beginning of the film he has been fated to die, but he cannot make decisions or errors of professional judgment that lead to his death. He simply acts out what he is and does and the consequences catch up with him.

Throughout the film, the police, too, are professionals. They are embodiments of social order, and as professionals they must take whatever means are necessary to accomplish the goals of their profession. While Camonte is a form of pure evil, they are forces of social order who can be tainted with the evil that Camonte personifies. They are impersonal forces. Neither Guarino nor the chief of detectives emerges as a human character. Both speak in monotones and calmly go about their jobs. When Epstein frees Camonte and Rinaldo, they accept the authority of the writ. When the chief gives his speech about the colorful criminal being a "yellow louse," he speaks in professional abstraction. From his professional position as a crime-fighter he inveighs against criminals with no particular animosity against Camonte. The police are not pure forms of social order, however. When Tony strikes a match on Guarino's badge in the barber shop, Guarino punches him, and at the police station he calmly hints that he will take Camonte downstairs for a beating. The Chief has no objection to this violent tactic. In the original ending, by shooting Camonte Guarino himself shows the extent of the stain of evil in the police, but in the final version the impersonal uniformed police simply carry out their function. In both versions the police as well as Camonte do what their profession determines for them. Unfortunately, the profession demands violence and ultimately murder.

In such a world, people become little more than objects, and in fact Hawks often uses objects as their surrogates even in the most dramatic moments. The X-shaped scar on Camonte's face is the most obvious. The person becomes irrelevant, and the sign of death appears at every murder, as though the spirit of evil, embodied in Camonte and imaged in his scar, has replaced the character. Camonte has become his scar, as Hawks realized when he replaced the name of Trail's novel with the simple one-word title of the film. The X-shaped mark, appearing at the site of each murder, shows the ubiquitous presence of Camonte, and naturally it is the dominant image throughout the entire film.

Other objects represent persons as well. When Camonte and Lovo meet in Poppy's apartment, she stays at a dressing table in the background, while a statuette of a woman dominates the foreground, separating the two men. Later on, as they compete for her affection, she becomes the object that separates the men, and they will treat her like merchandise. When Lovo realizes that Camonte knows he tried to kill him, he tries to buy him off by offering to let him have Poppy. Cesca, too, becomes identified with an object that defines her relationships. Early on she becomes the coin that Rinaldo flips. The coin, as a sign of their relationship, leads to his death. By tossing it at him, she is throwing herself at him. When Cesca goes to Camonte's office, she finds Rinaldo tearing out a row of paper dolls in the shape of women with flared skirts. She admires the chain and especially the one on the end, and as she flirts with him, reminding him that Camonte is in Florida, she offers to take the place of the paper dolls. She will be the woman at the end of Rinaldo's strand. Camonte refers to Rinaldo as a "tomcat," and when he needs him, he locates him by calling the apartments of his girlfriends in a series until he finds him. Cesca is the last in a series of relationships for Rinaldo.

Costillo flips a coin on his way to the telephone and death. The coin in midair becomes then a sign for the transitory nature of life and the caprice of death. Rinaldo flips the coin as a signature gesture, and each time he approaches more closely his predetermined end: in the barber shop, when Guarino and Camonte join in combat; on the street next to the organ grinder, when he first becomes attracted to Cesca (keeping her coin is not only a sign of his romantic interest, it also associates her with his death); in Lovo's office, before he murders him. Finally, when Camonte finds him in the apartment with Cesca and shoots him, Rinaldo flips the coin, probably Cesca's, one last time and collapses before he can catch it. Fate, or God, flips a human life like a coin and at any moment can allow it to fall.

Gaffney is murdered in a bowling alley, immediately after he releases the ball. The camera follows the ball, while gunfire comes from the sound track. The ball strikes the pins, knocking down all but one, which teeters wildly. With another burst of fire, the pin falls.

Since the forces of evil and social order are depersonalized to the extent they are, even becoming identified with objects at times, Hawks can afford to step back and look at them with ironic detachment. This distance gives him an opportunity to find humor in his characters' activities and their fates. Hawks does not find comedy in dying people but he does find that the human condition, with its mixture of good and evil, is a source of bemusement. Hawks' "bitter vision" enables him to find humor, where lesser talents would see only horror. Camonte's inept use of the language, crass tastes, and mugging make him a comic figure in his own right. His childish delight in firing the tommy gun in the pool room outside Lovo's office is a caricature of the violence that he intends to create with the weapon once he reaches the North Side. His apparent failure to appreciate that he is firing a deadly weapon is frightening, but funny. Even his violence has a comic side. When he throws the spittoon through the window of Costillo's office, his needless brutality has a self-parodying quality to it, as though he has delighted in finding a great way to get the attention of the bootleggers inside. When he repeats the gesture by putting his fist through the window in the same door before he orders Lovo's death, his facial intensity removes all the humor. This is the step that will make him the top man and begin the final stages of the process that will lead to his own death.

Again, the cartoon image of Camonte is Angelo. As the bullets fly all around him, he is engaged in one of his many fruitless attempts to get a name on the pay phone in the restaurant. One bullet pierces a hot-water urn, and a stream of scalding water pours all over his jacket. As he turns around, the stream lands on the seat of his pants, creating a form of burlesque low comedy, but despite his discomfort he continues his frantic conversation in fractured English. This business is also reprised, stripped of comedy, in the final sequence in Camonte's apartment. As Angelo slumps over the desk mortally wounded, he answers the phone once more and repeats his comedy routine as the noose of tragedy tightens around him. He is no longer a clown, but a tragic figure who is destroyed for his loyalty to Camonte. In the repetition of the initial comic scenes, death and comedy come very close together.

As Camonte's criminal empire spreads out through the city, his own personal world shrinks. Bulletproof glass and steel shutters close him in with his material possessions. Communication with the outside world does not become progressively more difficult, because for Camonte it never existed in the first place. He begins and ends as a man out of touch with the world outside his own criminal universe. Again, Angelo's failure to get names or messages from the phone is only a parody of Camonte's frustration at being unable to reach anyone, and of allowing anyone to reach him. At one point Angelo reaches such a point of rage that he aims his pistol at the receiver, as though showing in cartoon imagery the desperation and rage generated by Camonte's isolation. Violence is the only way men like these are able to communicate. When Camonte does complete a phone call to Rinaldo at his girlfriend's apartment, it is to plan Lovo's death. They use the telephone again by staging a bogus phone call to trick Lovo into admitting his guilt. In the final scene Angelo finally gets a message straight. The caller is Poppy, and by that time Angelo is dying and Poppy's relationship with Camonte is ended, first because she is replaced by Cesca and eventually because Camonte will die.

The pattern of isolation is a constant throughout the film. Camonte destroys everyone around him in his drive for success, and eventually he is left totally alone. He murders his two bosses in his own mob so that he can become kingpin himself. He had been bodyguard to Costillo and lieutenant to Lovo, but these positions of trust did not deter him. Then he eliminates his rivals in the North Side so that he can be alone at the top. In killing Rinaldo he loses his best friend and with him, at least for a while, his sister Cesca. Finally, as he closes the steel shutters on himself and Cesca, he shuts Poppy out of his life. In both the original and the revised endings, he goes down the stairs to his death alone.

Even though each move that Camonte makes isolates him further from human companionship, the script begins and ends with him involved in a triangular love affair. The first triangle is simple enough. Camonte and Lovo compete for Poppy. She is just one more prize to be won in the headlong rush toward success of both men. It is a rather straightforward rivalry that takes place in the external world. Two men want the same woman. The winner will neuter the loser and take possession not only of the woman but of the criminal empire as well.

The second triangle is neither simple nor simply resolved. Once Camonte has won Poppy he still has another, far more intricate triangle to resolve. The problem is foreshadowed by the scene in which Camonte, Rinaldo and Angelo, all dressed impeccably in tuxedos, attend a performance of Somerset Maugham's *Rain*. When they receive word between the acts that Gaffney is at a bowling alley, Camonte orders Angelo to stay behind to see if Sadie Thompson goes with the clergyman or the Marines. As the gunmen gather for the assassination, Angelo reports that she "climbed into the hay with the army." Camonte notes that he thought it would end that way. Given a choice between the sordid and the ethereal, Sadie Thompson chooses "the hay" with the army. Similarly, both Cesca and Poppy choose Camonte, and, even more tellingly, Camonte chooses the illicit love of Cesca over Poppy. Camonte himself did not witness the resolution of the triangle. He is so oblivious that someone else, a man of extremely limited intelligence, has to tell him about it. Camonte has a triangle of his own to resolve, and at this point he is completely unaware of its existence, let alone its resolution.

The second triangle develops entirely within Camonte's psyche. In the final section of the film Cesca and Poppy compete for Tony's soul. Poppy is blonde and wears light colored clothing. Cesca is a dark Italian and favors ominous black colors. From the earliest scenes, Camonte has been irrationally and violently protective of Cesca. At first his attitude seems a stylized form of Italian folkways, but as the film progresses his actions become more sinister. He is dancing with Poppy when he bolts away to slug Cesca's partner in the Paradise. When they return to the family home, he rants about the way she is displaying herself for other men and rips the top off one side of her dress. The dress has straps across the back that form a perfect X. The scene has erotic overtones, and with the symbol of death clearly across her back, Hawks is hinting at a latent incestuous and destructive attraction of Camonte to his sister. After leaving her, he faces death himself. He staggers out of the house, intending to return to Poppy, but when Gaffney's men ambush him with machine gun fire and then lead him into a car chase, he never returns to her. Camonte's thoughts turn from love to revenge and murder.

After their mother tells Camonte about Cesca's new living arrangement, his immediate decision to murder Rinaldo is not punishment for violating Cesca as much as the elimination of a rival. The symmetry of the script balances the murders of Rinaldo and Lovo, who competed with Camonte for the love of Cesca and Poppy respectively. In the final scene, Poppy is at home in her own apartment calling into Camonte's besieged fortress headquarters. She offers Camonte one last chance for the love of another human being. She is trying to pull him out of his own preoccupation with himself and his success by offering her love. Despite Angelo, who could never connect Camonte with a caller or a message, Poppy's call gets through to Camonte. If he can respond, even in his own brutish way, there is some hope for him. He is, however, condemned to death by his own self-centeredness. His only response is "I didn't know," which could mean he didn't know Poppy loves him, or that he loves Cesca.

Cesca, in contrast to Poppy, is situated inside the room with Camonte. It is not clear how she enters the sealed apartment, but in fact she is there. Her presence, an image of Camonte's incestuous self-love, competes with Poppy's invitation to altruism. The image includes destructiveness for Camonte, since she enters Camonte's fortress with a gun, intending to kill him as an act of revenge for the murder of Rinaldo. Before she can pull the trigger, however, she recognizes her own love for him. She exclaims, "You're me, and I'm you," as she enthusiastically loads the tommy guns for Camonte. When they realize all escape routes are cut off, they decide to shoot it out together, in a form of suicide pact. When she is wounded by a ricocheting bullet, she asks him to hold her tight. She dies in his arms, and in the original version he kisses her on the lips before he descends to his own death. Cesca is really part of himself, and in choosing her rather than Poppy, an unnatural love that must not be fulfilled, he completes the isolation that leads to his death.

Hawks is not a preacher. In *Scarface,* however, he offers a powerful reflection on the destructive power of the American myth. Depression audiences who saw the film were already disillusioned with the notion of America as the land of opportunity. Seeing its dark side so powerfully portrayed on the screen was a striking indictment of the system that had somehow passed by many Americans. Hawks had the personal vision to debunk the myth, and in the Gangster genre he had the perfect vehicle to present that vision to a vast audience of ticket buyers.

Years later, as America's role in the world is being revaluated, the notion of "systemic evil" has gained a certain currency. By its wealth and power the United States is able to bring enormous evil into the world along with the good it tries to accomplish. The evil is not necessarily the result of sinister decisions, rationally reached. It is more the fact that America's ambition, wealth and power contain within themselves the seeds of death, for others, and, more strikingly, for America itself. This is what Hawks and the Gangster film ask their audiences to ponder.

NOTES

1. Andrew Sarris, in his introduction to "Howard Hawks," a translation of an interview of Hawks by Jacques Becker, Jacques Rivette and François Truffaut in *Cahiers du Cinéma* 56, which appears in Andrew Sarris, *Interviews with Film Directors* (New York: Avon, 1967), p. 228.

2. Gerald Mast, *Howard Hawks, Storyteller* (New York: Oxford Univ. Press, 1982), p. 3. Mast's first four chapters are a biographical and critical "overview" of the artist and his works. These chapters provide the basis of the material presented here in summary form. Also helpful are the entry "Howard Hawks" in Ephraim Katz' *The Film Encyclopedia* (New York: Perigee, 1979), p. 542 and Louis D. Giannetti's chapter "The Cult of Personality: The Cinema of Howard Hawks," in *Masters of the American Cinema* (Englewood Cliffs, N.J.: Prentice-Hall, 1981), pp. 184–204.

3. Giannetti, p. 197.

4. Mast, p. 200.

5. Mast, p. 15.

6. Robin Wood, *Howard Hawks* (London: BFI Publishing, 1983), pp. 11–12, offers a list of Hawks' apparently derivative works along with their immediate predecessors.

7. Mast, pp. 75–76.

8. Andrew Sarris, *The American Cinema: Directors and Directions, 1929–1968* (New York: Dutton, 1968), p. 9, places him in "The Pantheon," the very highest category, one niche above Frank Capra, whom he places on a second level of excellence, "The Far Side of Paradise."

9. Jacques Rivette, "The Genius of Howard Hawks," in *Cahiers du Cinéma* 23 (May 1953), in Jim Hillier, ed., *Cahiers du Cinéma: The 1950's, Neo-Realism, Hollywood, New Wave* (Cambridge: Harvard Univ. Press, 1985), pp. 126–131.

10. *American Cinema*, p. 53.

11. Sarris, *Interviews*, p. 236.

12. Rivette, p. 129.

13. Clark Branson, *Howard Hawks: A Jungian Study* (Santa Barbara: Capra, 1987), p. 279.

14. Mast, p. 11.

15. Wood, p. 11.

16. Robert Warshow, "The Gangster as Tragic Hero," in *The Immediate Experience: Movies, Comics, Theatre and Other Aspects of Popular Culture* (New York: Anchor, 1964), p. 86.

17. Thomas Schatz, *Hollywood Genre: Formulas, Filmmaking and the Studio System* (New York: Random House, 1981), p. 84, contrasts the gangster film with the Western and argues that the Western hero establishes order on the frontier, while the gangster inherits order and tries to destroy it to return to a more primitive, open society. The point of the comparison is well taken, but the gangster's drive to expand his territory and consolidate or eliminate rivals seems to call for the imposition of a new kind of order rather than a reversion to chaos.

18. Warshow, p. 88.

19. Schatz, pp. 84–85.

20. Schatz, pp. 101–110, describes many of the different paths taken by the Gangster film in its diaspora to other genres.

21. Mast, pp. 74–75.

22. Raymond Durgnat, *Films and Feelings* (Cambridge: The M.I.T. Press, 1971), p. 82, believes that Hawks' Puritan work ethic has "been cut away from any belief in God." He characterizes Hawks as a Stoic and nihilist.

23. Mast, p. 89.

Chapter Seven

THE WESTERN
STAGECOACH

The Auteur: John Ford

"My name's John Ford; I make Westerns." According to the often repeated anecdote, this was the way the director introduced himself when he rose to speak to a meeting of the Screen Directors Guild which was considering a mandatory "loyalty oath" for its members during the days of blacklisting in the early 1950s.[1]

The statement is typical of the man. It is simple and direct, but it cuts through mazes of complexity to get to a stark truth. Ford, as an artist and as a person, tried to create the impression of simplicity, but he was a man of extraordinary sensibilities. At this point in his career, John Ford had already become an icon; the name contained its own meaning. As Andrew Sarris said so well: "No other director has ranged so far across the landscape of the American past, the world of Lincoln, Lee, Twain, O'Neill, the three great wars, the Western and trans-Atlantic migrations, the horseless Indians of the Mohawk Valley and the Sioux and Comanche cavalries of the West, the Irish and Spanish incursions and the delicately balanced politics of polyglot cities and border states."[2]

When John Ford, retired Rear Admiral of the U.S. Navy, spoke about loyalty oaths, the Hollywood establishment had no choice but to listen. The statement was as crisp as his editing. He had no need to fill in background or recount his accomplishments or explain his sentiments. The name "John Ford" said it all. Similarly, in his films, he let the images "say it all," and for many years his best films were underrated because Ford resolutely refused to offer comments on what should be obvious.

Singling out his Western films was another sly strategy in the context of this discussion. At the time Westerns were still in fashion in Hollywood, more for their reliable box office performance than for their artistic merit. The reassessment of the Western film as the authentic American epic form was just beginning in France through the work of André Bazin and his colleagues at *Cahiers de Cinéma,* and it had not yet gained currency among the American critical establishments.[3] By calling himself a director of Westerns, as though he had done nothing else, Ford allied himself with the rank-and-file of the American film industry and the movie-going public. Few in the room, however, would have failed to remember that Mr. Ford had also won six Academy Awards: for *The Informer* (1935), *The Grapes of Wrath* (1940), *How Green Was My Valley* (1941), and *The Quiet Man* (1952), and for two of the documentaries he made while serving in the Navy during World War II, *The Battle of Midway* and *December 7th.* Ironically, although John Ford is synonymous with the Western, no Western is included on this list of honors from the Academy.

Ford, then, was recognized by the industry as a great film artist, but not for doing the kinds of film he did best. Literary adaptations and weighty social themes were believed to be the signs of "important" films. Only after the French went to work on the Hollywood film would American critics realize what Ford knew all along. The Western is a perfect medium for exploring profound questions in a characteristically American setting. As an established and commercially dependable director, Ford could have chosen any genre he wanted to express his artistic vision, but he chose the Western as the medium most suited to his talents. He mastered his art through literally dozens of silent Westerns, from the two-reelers with Harry Carey and Tom Mix to the substantial *Iron Horse* (1924). After sound equipment had been developed to the point it could be taken out of the sound stage and used for outdoor action pictures, he returned to the Western and revolutionized the genre in *Stagecoach* (1939).

After the War, with five Academy Awards for "serious" films behind him and nothing to prove about his talent, he created a series of masterpieces set in the American West that rank with the achievement of any other American artist working in any medium. John Ford was, above all, an artist of film. He exploited the resources of his medium as no other American director ever had. He did not rely on literary prestige properties or current philosophical questions to create quality films. Ford knew what he was doing, even if his critics did not.

John Ford was an unlikely cowboy. He never lived in the West;

he created it. To this day the idea of the Western as it exists in the American imagination is less the product of history than the legacy of John Ford's artistic vision. Ford was born in 1895 on the Eastern frontier, in Port Elizabeth, Maine, where he spent the first ten years of his life on a family farm. His paternalistic and tyrannical methods on the set and his admiration for older heroes gave the impression that he was much older than he was. His bad eyesight forced him to wear heavy glasses even as a young man, and his heavy drinking and cigar smoking thickened his voice and skin at an early age. He reveled in his image as a grizzled old veteran of the Hollywood wars. By the time he reached his late thirties some actors were already beginning to call him "Pappy"—behind his back, of course.

A combination of his contempt for film historians and critics and a love of blarney covers the early years in a bit of North Atlantic fog. Ford, born Sean Aloysius O'Feeney, soon became John Martin Feeney when the family moved to Portland. Variant spellings of the family name—O'Fianna, O'Fidhne, O'Fiannaidhe—could be due to faulty Irish spelling or capricious American immigration records.[4] At times he claims to have been born in Galway, but no evidence supports this. His parents, who did come from Galway, spoke Irish at home, and so he claims to have grown up in a bilingual household. When asked about his grasp of the language, he said he simply forgot it all. At other times he maintained that his family often took steamers across the Atlantic to summer with relatives in Irish-speaking Galway, but aside from a short stay in an Irish school in Galway when he was eleven, there is no evidence that he ever visited Ireland regularly until well into his adult years.[5] As the humor was on him, Ford claimed to have been the youngest of eleven or thirteen children, but since some died in infancy the inconsistency is understandable.

John Aloysius Feeney was a farmer and saloon keeper, and although young Jack Feeney was early exposed to alcohol as a social pattern, he was kept from the family business and was sent to work driving a fish wagon. As a boy Jack was very Irish and very Catholic. He served Mass regularly in the parish church. Throughout his films he shows a rare sensitivity to the role of ritual, both religious and secular, in the life of a community. Funerals, dances and formal meals provide the settings for his explorations of American culture.

The family was clearly matriarchal, according to the traditional Irish pattern. Barbara Curran Feeney ran the house, controlled the money and disciplined the children, all eleven or thirteen of them. In his films, which by the standards of today's sensitivities appear quaintly chauvinistic, Ford naturally makes a clear distinction between gender roles. The woman is the domesticator and ruler of the household, but, as strong as she is, she has no place in the action-adventure world outside her kitchen. On the contrary, she tries to draw the male from his world of the outdoors into her own hearth-world, even though this domestication will destroy the heroic dimensions of the male. When she strays away from the home into the male world of the wilderness, she creates only added problems for the men who must take on the added responsibility of protecting her. Although she may intimidate the men in her own home, a Ford woman rarely loosens her stays, fires a gun or straddles a horse. In short, a Ford woman would be horrified at the cheeky behavior of a Hawks woman.

In 1920, when Ford was twenty-six, he married Mary McBride Smith, who was Presbyterian and divorced. At the time Jack was still active in the Knights of Columbus. The family was disappointed that the couple could not be married in the Catholic Church, but despite their Los Angeles county civil ceremony, the two remained married for fifty-three years, until Ford's death in 1973, a rare achievement in Hollywood, or anyplace else for that matter. When Mary's first husband died in 1941, they were married before a priest in Washington, D.C.[6] Although Mary fit easily into Jack's hard-drinking social life, she had no desire to become a celebrity herself, and thus reinforced Ford's notion of a clean division between the worlds of men and women.

Despite poor eyesight, young Jack Feeney was a high school athlete of more enthusiasm than skill, but at an early age he began to show real talent with his sketch pad and a passion for sailing. An indifferent student, he failed an examination for entrance into the U.S. Naval Academy, and then tried the University of Maine for a few weeks, but when a fellow student referred to his ethnic heritage—probably by calling him a "Mick"—Jack flattened his antagonist and left school forever. His impressive knowledge of military history, particularly of the U.S. Civil War, his sensitive re-creations of the paintings of the frontier artist Frederic Remington, and his uncanny grasp of the technical side of photography are all the result of private study. His contributions to the writing of scripts and his unearthing the riches of his characters seem to be a matter of instinct.[7]

With plans for further education dashed, at least for a time, in 1913 Jack Feeney followed his older brother Francis across a continent to Hollywood, where Frank had already become an established actor, director and writer. Frank by this time had changed his name to Francis Ford. The reasons for the change are lost in the Fordian blarney fog. One version has Frank naming himself after the automobile because he felt that his lowly profession would bring disgrace on the family name.[8] Another has him substituting for a drunk actor named Ford after the programs had already been printed.[9] More likely, in the social climate of the day, any ethnic name could be a disadvantage, and Francis Ford simply had a more dignified sound than Frank Feeney. Of course, neither of the Fords would give up the chance to tell a good story and admit simple expediency as the reason for changing the family name. The two Fords remained close, and as Francis' career waned, John always had a bit part for him in his films. Finding Francis Ford is for John Ford buffs the equivalent of spotting Alfred Hitchcock in his own films.

Jack adopted his brother's name and soon went to work on the sets. Francis had learned the trade from the beginnings of the industry with Edison in his New Jersey studios, and as the industry developed, he became acknowledged as a competent technician. Jack did everything on the set for twelve dollars a week. He graduated from handyman to stunts, including riding as one of the Klansmen for D.W. Griffith in *The Birth of a Nation* (1915). He shared an apartment with the cowboy star Hoot Gibson and by 1917 had graduated to directing two-reelers, many of them Westerns with Harry Carey. With the haphazard style of accreditation used in the early studios, it is difficult to know how many silent films Ford actually directed, but the number ranks easily in the dozens.[10] Most of these are lost. To add to the dignity of his new role as a director of full-length films, in 1923 he began to call himself John Ford.

During the early years, the studios were filled with real cowboys, rodeo riders and Indians searching for work as extras on the Hollywood lots. The real Wyatt Earp was retired and living in Pasadena. The life of adventure that such people represented could not but have an impact on the imagination of the young man from Maine. His most widely esteemed silent film *The Iron Horse* (1924) tells the heroic story of the building of the transcontinental railroad. His own journey from New England had already impressed him with the vastness of the continent. For the rest of his career, in one form or another, he kept returning to the achievement in moving West, conquering the wilderness and building a united nation.

Ford's heroic figures are often touched with tragedy because their conquest of the wilderness, frequently but not always the American West, leaves them without a home. They strive to find a place of rest, but it always eludes them. That is their tragic dilemma: they are men of the wilderness, and after they overcome the forces of savagery and establish civilization in the wilderness, the newly civilized area no longer has a place for them. They must move on, and thus they can never find the rest they crave. They are dedicated to the notion of building community in the ideal order, but, unfortunately for them, they remain alienated from any form of lasting community in the actual order.[11] At best they can form a temporary association of men to accomplish a particular task, and when the job is done the group disbands. For example, the heroic loner played by John Wayne often appears at a dance, a key Ford ritual of civilization, but he never joins the ladies. He may take a drink with the men at the bar, but he stands outside the group, too concerned with his task to dance—and also pathetically lonely. The community may depend on his providing the safety to allow them to dance, but he has no place with them.

The theme of frustrated homecoming finds a masterly expression in *The Informer* (1935), the first of the Ford films to win an Academy Award and establish him as a serious artist. Set in Ireland in 1922 during the time of the civil war following the establishment of the Free State, *The Informer*, based on the novel by Liam O'Flaherty, follows Gypo Nolan (Victor McLaglen) through the wilderness of Dublin's dark alleys.[12] Gypo is Joyce's Leopold Bloom without comic relief. He embodies Ireland as it has been degraded by military occupation. Gypo betrays his best friend to gain the reward money that will get him and his intended wife, the part-time prostitute Katie Madden (Margot Grahame), passage to a new home in America. Gypo drinks away his blood money, and his only homecoming is his return to the church where he seeks forgiveness from the dead man's mother. A brute of a man, in brutal surroundings, he is defeated by the very wilderness he tries to escape and dies a tragic figure, executed by his former comrades in the Irish Republican Army. From his tragedy Ford suggests that Ireland and humanity can grasp the futility of betrayal and revenge and the healing power of forgiveness. If so, Gypo's death has a purpose.

In *The Long Voyage Home* (1940), an adaptation of four short plays by Eugene O'Neill, Ole Olson (John Wayne) wants to return to his home in Sweden, but the sea, drink, and the temptations of the port cities form a wilderness that time and time again keeps him from his farm. With a much bleaker vision, O'Neill has Olson shanghaied and taken to sea once more at the end of the last play, as though the wanderer can never achieve his rest. Ford tempers the scenario. Olson is kidnaped, but before the ship can leave port he is rescued during a raid in which his redeemer, Aloysius Driscoll (Thomas Mitchell), is captured and takes his place. Driscoll then becomes the tragic figure who is buried at sea, the wilderness that has become his only home. The younger figure reaches his destination (off-camera) only because of Driscoll's heroic self-sacrifice. As was the case with Gypo, his death has meaning in Ole's liberation.

One final pre-War film shows another variation on the homecoming theme. In *The Grapes of Wrath* (1940), Ford takes the fatalistic vision of John Steinbeck and transforms it into a message of triumph. In the novel, Tom Joad, a released convict who travels with his dispossessed family from the Dust Bowl to an imagined new home in California, meets with one form of death and disaster after another in the final chapters. Badly clubbed, he must go off into hiding with no hope of finding a place of rest. As Ford reworks the material, Joad (Henry Fonda) merely escapes for a while to await a better time, while his mother (Jane Darwell) offers a populist proclamation that the "People keep a-comin'." Tom is a tragic figure in that he, and possibly his whole family, will find no home, but their efforts offer a guarantee that somehow, at some time in the future, other families like them will eventually reach their destination and find peace. Their tragedy is not nihilistic, as Steinbeck would have it, but, in the pattern of Gypo's and Driscoll's, the tragedy of Ford's characters has meaning because of what it accomplishes for others.

In making his characters search for a home, Ford thus keeps a precarious balance between the individual and the community. The individual hero longs for home but inevitably faces some form of personal tragedy. His efforts, however, can make it possible for the community to triumph. Gypo, for example, is a complete failure. His tragedy is that he cannot reach the home in America that he longs for, but he does find another home in the church and in repentance. By her act of forgiveness, Mrs. McPhillip (Una O'Connor) creates a kind of peaceful home for Gypo and reconciliation for the warring factions that have turned Dublin into a wilderness. Ole Olsen's return becomes secondary to Driscoll's heroic and tragic act that made the homecoming possible. Ole is a minor character in the film, and he slips into oblivion in the final scenes. At the end of the film the interest rests completely on Driscoll, who finds his own home in death at sea. Tom Joad never finds his home either, but his struggle alongside his family has given all the dispossessed people the courage to continue the search. In Ford's optimistic gloss on Steinbeck's text, he offers the hope of success through a mystic faith in "the people."

Not all homecomings are tragic for John Ford. Mellowing a bit from his young man's romantic sense of tragedy, his homecoming was a blissful event in *The Quiet Man* (1952). Here many of the characteristic Ford dilemmas reach resolution. Sean Thornton (John Wayne)

returns to his family cottage in Ireland to find peace after killing a
man in the ring in America. He is caught in a clash of cultures and has
to rely on his heroic skills from the wilderness by thrashing Red Will
Danaher (Victor McLaglen) in order to win the hand of his sister Mary
Kate Danaher (Maureen O'Hara). Violence and civilization, self-reliance and community, the male group and marriage are all reconciled. Mary Kate, Ford's strongest woman, leaves her kitchen and
domesticates Sean by making a wild man out of him. In a final scene, a
reprise of all the characters in the village, even Catholics and Protestants become united in the celebration.

Immediately after the War, Ford returned to his favorite theme
of individual sacrifice as the basis for community triumph with *They
Were Expendable* (1945). History was the unwitting co-author of the
script. The film is the story of the fall of the Philippines in the darkest
early days of the War. A heroic fleet of P T boats tries to hold off the
inevitable victory of the Japanese, but even after several successful
engagements the boats are destroyed and the Islands fall to the overwhelming strength of the enemy. Naturally, many fine sailors die
heroically in the battle, simply doing their jobs.

The story of their tragedy, and the tragedy of the fall of the
Philippines, is told in the film in 1945, when the country is celebrating victory, and the disastrous defeat could be put in the larger context of the Allied triumph. General Douglas MacArthur, for example,
appears in the film at the moment of his greatest humiliation, having
been ordered to abandon his troops and allow himself to be smuggled
out of the country before its fall. It surely must have been the darkest
moment of his life. As photographed, however, the actor (Robert
Barrat) assumes heroic stature, since the audience knows well the
subsequent history of the war. Like MacArthur's humiliation, the defeat of the P T boat squadron is only temporary. It prepares the way
for a far greater triumph, a resurrection from the near-dead. The
defeat of the naval unit and the Philippines is a tragedy for some
individuals, but their sacrifice makes possible the eventual triumph of
the allies, which for Ford meant America.

John Ford, the child of immigrants, sees the human quest as a
search for home, for peace, for belonging. In a complex world such a
quest is often doomed to failure for any given individual, and that is
the tragedy for modern man. He finds no resting place. The more
arduous the quest, the more tragic the failure. At the same time, Ford
is not a nihilist. Man does not struggle in isolation. If he fails tragically
as an individual, his quest may still have meaning for society. The
geographic or spiritual goal he longs for may be beyond his reach, but

THE WESTERN

the very quest is spiritually ennobling. The searcher finds redemption
in failure, and the nobility of his quest creates values in his community. Dramatically, for Ford, this is a masculine enterprise. Philosophi-
cally he is dealing with the task of all humankind, men and women
alike, to forge some meaning in life, some goal in which they can find
rest. Such a goal is often impossible to reach, but the very quest
ennobles not only the quester, but the race as well.

The Western hero provides the perfect model for Ford's vision of
the human task. His Western heroes are invariably tragic, even as
they accomplish their mission. They are men who strive to tame the
wilderness, but when the last Indian is driven off and the last outlaw
lies dead in the dust, they find that peace, a home, is as elusive as ever.
They do not understand that once they have established the rule of
law and order by their wits and their sixguns, they become obsolete
themselves. The heroes ride off alone into the sunset, to a new frontier further in the West, while the community savors the fruits of their
accomplishment. The tragedy is that the community no longer has a
role for the hero.

Ford addressed his theme directly in *Stagecoach* (1939), when
the Ringo Kid (John Wayne) rides off to Mexico with his lady Dallas
(Claire Trevor), a retired prostitute whom he has rescued from having to go back into the business. He has helped save the stagecoach
from capture by the Indians and has avenged the murder of his father
and brother by killing the three notorious Plummer brothers, but the
town has no room for an escaped convict. Doc Boone (Thomas Mitchell) comments that they have been saved from civilization. If civilization ever catches up with Ringo and Dallas, most likely they will have
to flee again, since society has no place for people like these.

After the war Ford returned to this basic Western theme. The
conflict between civilization and the individual is particularly sharp
in *My Darling Clementine* (1946). When Wyatt Earp (Henry Fonda)
comes to town, he first drives a drunken Indian and then the entire
Clanton Gang out of town. In the end he must leave Clementine
(Cathy Downs) and ride out of town, while the town, now civilized,
will probably prosper. Earp has come from the plains on a cattle
drive, and when one of his brothers is murdered he thinks of avenging
him according to the law of the wilderness. Instead he becomes marshal and establishes the rule of law and order. He even allows a barber
to put cologne on his hair, and he dances, stiffly but enthusiastically,
with Clementine on the platform of a half-built church. He wants a
place to settle down with Clementine, but he must become a killer if
the town is to survive. When violence is thrust upon him, he accepts

the challenge, but when the shooting is over, he must move on. His homecoming is thwarted, but others may raise their families in peace in Tombstone because he was better with a gun than the outlaws.

While Earp is a loner in search of a home, many of Ford's other searching heroes are members of institutions, especially the U.S. Cavalry. Ford used the cavalry to explore the conflict between the wilderness and the forces of civilization as imaged by individuals who are not loners but who are members of the civilizing institutions of society. This is the central theme of his magnificent Cavalry Trilogy. Captain Kirby York (John Wayne) in *Fort Apache* (1948) is a seasoned veteran of the Indian wars. Colonel Owen Thursday (Henry Fonda) comes from the East to take charge of the command. He longs for a command and a home in the East, but the wilderness engulfs him. Not understanding the Indians or the role of the army on the frontier, Thursday engages in a suicidal battle with the Comanches. He will not go home. He and his men are wiped out, but the army goes on, and Captain York, wearing the uniform of the commanding officer in the closing scene, leads the troops in a final parade. Thursday is the tragic hero, and yet the example of his bravery, misguided as it was, provides the strength for the army, now led by York, to continue the quest for peace. Through generations of soldiers to come, the country can build a safe dwelling place in the wilderness. For Ford, this is how the nation was built.

In *She Wore a Yellow Ribbon* (1949), Captain Nathan Brittles (John Wayne) is on the verge of retirement. As a respected senior officer, he settles a romantic squabble among his junior officers and leads a crucial rescue mission. He retires, but in an unconvincing and sentimental ending he is called back from the wilderness to take charge of civilian scouts on the frontier. His military wisdom is now passing into the mainstream of civilian society. By making retirement a central issue in the entire film, Ford stresses the obsolescence of the individual in contrast to the longevity of the army as an institution. The individual finds no resting place; he can be sacrificed, if need be. The army no longer needs Brittles, but because of him, and men like him, the army has made a civilized dwelling place of the frontier.

Finally, in *Rio Grande* (1950), Ford's vision of the army and the frontier becomes murkier. War has its dark side, since Captain Kirby York had obeyed an order to burn his wife's family estate in Virginia during the Civil War. Kathleen (Maureen O'Hara) finds that after her son failed out of West Point, he became an enlisted man and was assigned to York's command on the frontier. She comes West to buy his discharge, but both York and his son refuse. In a tense Oedipal

triangle, Mother and Father, the genteel life of the East and the
rugged life of the West, compete for the soul of the young trooper. In
a daring rescue mission, the younger York proves a hero. The film
ends with a synthesis as a parade of blue-uniformed troopers marches
to the tune of "Dixie." The older generation of Ford's soldiers may be
scarred by divisions, but their heroism makes possible the reconciliation of the future, when Yankees can march to Dixie, and Kathleen,
the Virginian, can be reunited with her Unionist husband. Because
Father and Mother have been principled and heroic, Ford would like
to suggest that their son will face no such conflict.

Ford sees heroism as the unifying bond of the country. His regi-
ments include former Confederate soldiers, the inevitable hard-
drinking Irish sergeants of whom Victor McLaglen is the archetype,
an occasional Mexican, a green recruit and a few grizzled veterans
near retirement. His army posts are America in microcosm—not perhaps as it was, but as John Ford wanted the melting pot to work.
Because of the heroism of individuals, the country can find its place in
history, its proper home. It was an idealistic, perhaps childlike vision
of the founding of America, and sadly it could not last.

Ford always had a fondness for older heroes. *Young Mr. Lincoln*
(1939) is a stark exception, but even in this instance the young hero
(Henry Fonda) is used to show the origins of Lincoln's commonsense
that stands for the best in the American people. Ostensibly about the
young lawyer from Springfield, the film is really the story of the
President whose personal tragedy enabled the Union to survive. In
the Cavalry Trilogy and in the War pictures, Ford explored the ago-
nies of command by senior officers rather than the adventures of
young enlisted men. Often facing retirement, they worry about the
legacy they leave for the younger men in their commands. His Western heroes, too, have been seasoned by the years, in contrast to the
hotheaded younger men whom they have to train for the future. They
too are concerned about passing on an heroic legacy to future generations of Americans. The Western hero, for Ford, represented what
was most admirable in the American character.

As the years went by, Ford's nostalgia for the pure heroic types of
his Western landscape started to sour. In his Western masterpiece
The Searchers (1956), Ethan Edwards (John Wayne) is a borderline
psychopath. He has the traditional credentials as a man of the wilderness. He is absolutely self-sufficient, rides and shoots better than anyone else, knows Indian lore and language, and has been tempered by
service in the Confederate army. His sense of morality, however, is

undeveloped. He fled to Mexico after the War, may have robbed a bank, and is obsessed with his hatred of the Indians, who represent the wilderness side of his own personality. The chief who slaughters the Edwards family and takes the daughters into captivity is Ethan's alter ego. Ethan is driven by a desire not only to murder Scar in revenge but also to kill the savagery within himself. He does not want to rescue his kidnaped niece but to murder her because of her presumed sexual contact with the Indians. Again, her death would be a ritual cleansing for him. Not only is Ethan unable to join in a dance, he disrupts a wedding, stops a funeral service, and desecrates a grave. A man with no respect for ritual, in Ford's world, is not human.

After a five-year search, Ethan returns to the settlement, but although he yearns to join the family celebration, everyone passes by him as they enter the house. He is left alone in the desert. Ethan clutches his chest in spiritual agony. Here, more clearly than in any earlier film, Ford begins to question the Western mystique. Edwards is a figure who commands respect, but he is also a man of uncontrolled violence who does not belong in civilized society. Being a loner compromises the heroic ideal.

A few years later, in *The Man Who Shot Liberty Valance* (1962), Tom Doniphon (John Wayne) is not sociopathic, like Ethan Edwards, but he is a man who has clearly outlived his time. An old drunk at the time of his death, he is laid to rest without his gunbelt and boots. Paying his respects is Senator Ransom Stoddard (James Stewart), who has built a political career on the myth that as a young lawyer he was the one who rid the town of Shinbone of the notorious outlaw Liberty Valance in a classic face-to-face gunfight. In fact, it was the crude but honest rancher, Tom Doniphon, who shot Valance in the back with a rifle to protect his friend. As the town prospered and the territory planned for statehood, it was clear that Stoddard, the man of books, had superseded Doniphon, the man of the gun.

When Stoddard finally tells the true story to a reporter, the editor decides to ignore the truth and "print the legend." He will not debunk the Stoddard legend, even though he knows the story is untrue. Since the film is shot completely indoors on a sound stage, even the apparent outdoor scenes, Ford is commenting that the whole Western mystique is only a legend, an artifice, no more real than the papier-mâché rocks bathed in electric moonlight beneath a canvas desert sky. In true Ford fashion, Doniphon's life ends in individual tragedy so that Stoddard and the community might prosper, but Ford is adding the comment that all this glorification of the old West is just a sham. Stoddard is just a politician protecting his image for the press. The real hero is the poor dead town drunk, whom everyone would like to forget.

Cheyenne Autumn (1964) not only questions the myth, it dashes it altogether. This melancholy and disjointed venture repeats the classic cavalry and Indian conflict from the emotional point of view of the Cheyenne. The noble tribe is displaced and longs to return to its homeland. Land speculators and government bureaucrats lie and cheat. The narrator, Captain Thomas Archer (Richard Widmark), lacks the heroic stature of the Wayne figures, but he is an honest, compassionate man torn between loyalty to his country and the revulsion with its policies. The tragic hero this time is the Cheyenne nation. Like the Joads, it suffers indignity, but it will go on. The army reaps no glory in saving the nation from the Indian scourge on the frontier; it just has the unpleasant task of moving starving women and children wherever orders from Washington tell them.

Ford cannot bring himself to impute blind obedience to unjust orders to American officers. Instead he creates Captain Wessels (Karl Malden), a former Prussian officer, to carry out the most savage tactics against the Indians under the guise of doing his duty. The traditional role of the veteran Irish sergeant played by Victor McLaglen passes over to Sergeant Stanislaw Wichowsky (Mike Mazurki), who tells stories about the Cossacks killing his family in Poland. They could be recognized by their fur hats. In Wessels' command, all the officers wear fur hats, a stark contrast to the customary buff-colored Stetsons of cavalrymen in the Ford films. The inference is obvious that in this engagement the U.S. Army had become little more than Cossacks, while the Cheyenne nation represents the forces of civilization.

When the film was released, the Vietnam protest movement was just beginning, and it is doubtful that Admiral Ford would have made such a strong anti-Vietnam policy film so early. Nonetheless, in the years after its release, anti-war protesters were quick to adopt its message as their own. More likely, for Ford, it was just one more step in a tired artist's reassessment of his earlier, simpler view of America. The assassination of John Kennedy, the Irish American President, while the film was in production may have driven Ford to an uncharacteristically gloomy view of the country and its future.

For John Ford, suffering from age, failing hearing and poor sight, and soured by alcohol, this was his sad farewell to the West. It would be a mistake to read these final films only as a cynical repudiation of his earlier works. Instead, they witness to a vigorous mind, constantly rethinking his materials. His body of work as a whole is a study of individual heroism, and if at times he painted a naive, nostalgic picture of heroes and of the country as he wanted it to be, at least he became aware of the dark side as well. In later years the dark side turned into full view, but the memory of the early years remains.

Ford's is a majestic vision of the universe. His long shots of tiny human figures lost in the immensity of Monument Valley in Arizona and Utah emphasize his belief in the triumph of the human spirit. Man occupies but a tiny spot on this earth, yet he has the spiritual resources to master his environment. He struggles to survive, yet has the breadth of heart to sacrifice himself so that some other persons or ideas might live. If the vision teeters toward naiveté, Ford should be forgiven. He was not dealing with realism, like a reporter recounting the pettiness lurking under mortal skin. No, he is a poet, describing heroic figures at their most noble, their most idealized. If he created a simplistic picture of American history, especially in his early films, he should be forgiven for that as well. He is not offering a scientific history of the country, but he is instead trying to create a portrait of the spirit of the country, not perhaps as it is, but as he wants it to be. He distills its best and eliminates its worst. For this kind of magnanimous vision, film viewers around the world can be grateful.

The Genre: The Western

Edwin S. Porter's (1870–1941) *The Great Train Robbery* (1903) was certainly not the first film to glorify the wild and woolly days of the old West. His own *Kansas City Saloon Smashers* (1901) may hold that distinction, and perhaps there were many others, now lost to contemporary audiences. The Porter classic, however, is generally considered to hold the place of honor as the first authentic "Western" movie.[13] In it all the pieces come together. Although it was shot by the Edison crew outside Paterson, New Jersey, it moved outside the closed space of his famous tar-paper studio, the Black Maria, and provided the sense of spaciousness that has ever since then been associated with the genre.

In its eleven-minute running time, Porter spliced together fourteen separate shots. Again, Porter did not invent editing. In Paris, Georges Méliès had used a primitive form of juxtaposition of shots as early as 1895, but Porter made editing an essential part of the extraordinary pacing. He jumped from one locale to another, and assumed correctly that the audience would realize that two or three actions were taking place at the same time. Because of his editing, Porter did not need title cards to lead his viewers along, but this technique, called parallel editing, as used by less talented directors did give rise to the famous cliché of the silent Westerns: "Meanwhile, back at the ranch." He allowed the imagination of the audience to fill in for the passage of time by using cutaway shots. Film historians, even those who loathe the Western film, extol *The Great Train Robbery* for its contribution to the art of editing.

The first scene is set in a telegraph office, where bandits break in, knock the operator unconscious and set a trap for the train. They board the train, enter the mail car, and, after a furious gun battle, shoot the postal clerk and blast open the safe. Meanwhile, their partners have commandeered the locomotive by killing the engineer and throwing him off the speeding train. They stop the train, rob the passengers, killing one who tries to escape, uncouple the cars from the locomotive, and make their escape in the engine. They rendez-vous with their accomplices, who are waiting with horses in the woods. In the meantime, the telegraph operator's little daughter brings lunch to her father, discovers him bound and unconscious, and frees him. The townspeople are unaware of the robbery and are en-joying a square dance when the telegraph operator breaks in and tells them about the crime. A posse rides off and surrounds the bandits as they are dividing their loot. In another gun battle the posse kills the outlaws and recovers the money. The film closes as a gunman in me-dium shot takes aim at the audience and fires directly into the camera. All this in eleven breathless minutes!

With the release of Porter's masterpiece, most of the characteris-tics of the Western film are set in place. The plot is simple, as is the morality. The traditional Western emphasizes action, violence and a black-and-white ethical code. Westerners, whether heroes, outlaws or ordinary townsfolk, do not have to wrestle with their consciences before they shoot. Violence and death by gunshot are mythic, even balletic. For this reason, many a Western hero is able to fire dozens of shots from his six-shooter, bloodshed is rare (until the 1970s, well past the classic stage of the genre), and even mortal wounds cause only a grimace and a slight stain on the shirtfront. The wounded grit their teeth and speak in shorter phrases; they do not scream out in agony. The gunplay is not supposed to be realistic; it is simply the choreography of conflict.

The plot of *The Great Train Robbery* is built on a structure that will dominate the genre for the next sixty years. Bandits from the outside disrupt the community, and the community unites to reestablish order. The townspeople show their antecedent solidarity through a ritual dance, a square dance involving all the members of the group rather than exclusive couples. The men are high-spirited and adolescent: one fires his gun into the floorboards near the feet of another man simply to perk up his comrade's solo dance. The women take no part in the violence, but their presence is essential to show that the town is a civilized space where people settle down and raise families. Similarly, children have little role in the narrative, but thematically they are extremely important. The telegraph operator's daughter, dressed in a Little Red Riding Hood cape, discovers her unconscious father, falls to her knees to pray for assistance, and unties the man, who runs to the dance not to get help for himself, but to gather a posse that will find the robbers and restore moral order to the community by punishing the malefactors. She is defenseless and vulnerable, and as such she represents the precarious future. The outlaws must be eliminated to make the town safe for little girls. This is the unspoken motivation for the posse, and it is far more convincing than a desire to risk life and limb to recover a cashbox for the railroad or the U.S. Postal System.

The iconography is in place as well. The men wear Stetsons, kerchiefs and unbuttoned vests. They carry revolvers in holsters out in the open on their hips. The horse and saddle provide the ordinary means of transportation for posse and bandits alike. The train is for women, children, and Easterners who wear suits and derbies and button their vests over their neckties. In this film the train functions not as a means of transportation but merely as a setting for the crime. It could just as well have been a bank or a trading post, but Porter judged wisely that a moving locomotive, with its huge menacing wheels and billows of smoke, is far more cinegenic than a storefront.

The Great Train Robbery provides the foundation for the Western genre, but it lacks one essential element that may even lead some purists to deny that it is a Western at all. Porter supplied no classic hero. Once warned by the wounded telegraph operator, the community coalesces of and by itself. It has no apparent leader, no mysterious stranger with a mark on his past who saves the town and rides off into the sunset in the West before anyone discovers his secret. Porter included with the print a startling medium shot of a Westerner firing his Colt directly at the camera. The shot has no relation to the action of the film. It could be spliced into the beginning or the end at the theater owner's discretion. He is the only identifiable gunman, but Porter offers no indication whether he is a member of the posse or one of the gang of robbers. Other than this single disconnected figure, no

heroic individual emerges with a personality or with a particular role
to play. The telegraph operator and the postal clerk on the train are
merely victims.

This deficiency would soon be remedied as the genre passes
through its formative stage. One of the riders in the posse in *The
Great Train Robbery* was Max Aronson (1882–1971), who achieved
notoriety of a sort by falling off his horse during the chase scene, and
the spill remained in the final print as it was released. Aronson realized the market potential of this kind of action film, changed his name
to Bronco Billy Anderson, and through his own company, Essanay, he
made over four hundred single-reel Westerns. (Aronson/Anderson
provided the "ay" and G.K. Spoor the "ess" for their contracted
version of S & A.) His films were action oriented, extolled frontier
virtues, and were often relieved by a healthy self-deprecating humor.
He was soon followed by William S. Hart (1870–1946), a successful
stage actor who switched to films and starred in his first Western role
in 1914, at the age of forty-four. A long-time student of Western lore
with ambitions to be recognized as a serious actor, Hart strove for
historic realism in the films he made for the legendary director
Thomas Ince (1882–1924). Today their films would be called "adult
Westerns."

Hart and Ince stressed character and setting, but during the years
of World War I the public wanted a lighter kind of film entertainment. Tom Mix (1880–1940) actually began making one-reelers before Hart got into the business, but rode in Hart's shadow in the early
years. As Hart's popularity declined, Mix with his wonder horse Tony
returned to pure action adventures. The character became a caricature of the frontier hero, and Mix eventually joined the Ringling
Brothers Circus. He made a few sound films, and then began a radio
program which continued for many years after his death. Hoot Gibson (1892–1962) pushed the heroics of the Mix character to extremes
and played the role for laughs. In the silent era, Westerns came in all
sizes and shapes, from one-reel and two-reel fillers for Saturday mat-
inees, serials, to a few serious full-length films like *The Covered
Wagon* (James Cruze, 1923) and, of course, *The Iron Horse*
(John Ford, 1924).

Audiences no doubt found the pace of these early silent films
breathtaking, but that alone cannot explain their instant popularity.
Other settings could have provided the same arena for intense, non-
stop action, but the Western assumed a special place in the mind of
the film-going public. In a very short time these frontier-based adventures coalesced into a recognizable genre whose self-identity was

so strong that it admitted variations in style that even crossed over into self-parody. In its many guises, the Western continued to fascinate the public not only in the United States but around the world. André Bazin, perceptive as ever of the American film, writes that the Western is "a form in need of content."[14] The genre provides a structure that can contain heroics or comedy, naive patriotism or cynical nihilism, romance or murder, outdoor action or claustrophobic drama. The reasons for the extraordinary popularity of the Western form are complex and often involve mere speculation, but it is important to try to discover why the Western held a privileged place among film-goers for over sixty years.

First, by extraordinary coincidence, the frontier as an actuality was disappearing at precisely the time the technology of the motion picture was developed to reproduce the frontier as a myth. In his famous essay of 1893, "The Significance of the Frontier in American History," the distinguished American historian Frederick Jackson Turner pointed out that according to the figures compiled by the U.S. Census Bureau in 1890, the American population had been so distributed across the continent that no region could properly be called frontier any longer.[15] This closing of the frontier led him to reflect on its historical development and even more on its formative influence on the American character.

Turner described the frontier as a shifting middle ground, separating the civilized regions, first of Europe and then of the Atlantic rim of the continent, from the wilderness of the unsettled Western regions. He pointed out the orderly progression across the wilderness, led by explorers, hunters and trappers, followed in order by traders, grazers and ranchers, then by subsistence farmers and commercial farmers, and finally by the merchants, industry and institutions that formed the towns and cities of the interior. In the 1820s the procession was heading through Kentucky and Tennessee. Fifty years later it was marching through the foothills of the Rockies. By 1890, according to Turner and his data from the Census Bureau, the procession stopped; every region was settled.

The mass migration that consumed the formative period in the nation's history left its mark on the collective American character. In order to survive on the frontier the European had to surrender his old civilized ways and learn the ways of the wilderness, like hunting, shooting, tracking, and the Indian crafts. As he strove to conquer the wilderness, in fact the wilderness conquered him. He became a new creation. Without the institutions of government to protect him, he became self-reliant, suspicious of authority and of necessity democratic. He had no stake in the land and led a restless nomadic life. The European-ness was emptied out of him and a new American-ness was born within him. When he finally succeeded in establishing civilization in the wilderness it was not a transplanted European civilization, but something new and quite different. It was called America.

Suddenly, if the census figures of 1890 were to be believed, the continent had run out of space for exploration and settlement. The frontiersman had no place to go, and this made him not only a romantic figure, as he had always been in American folklore, but a tragic one as well. By pushing the frontier Westward into the wilderness, he opened the way for civilization, which, of course, had no place for a man perceived as a relic of the old wilderness. He was caught in the currents of history. His rude ways made him an object of scorn in the towns and cities; his history of violence made him an object of fear. In either case, he became an embarrassment.

The form of the Western film is simply a dramatic expression of this fundamental American experience. The action is set on the precarious edge of civilization, where a community's stability (the town or the farm) or progress (the railroad or the wagon train) is threatened by a backlash from the wilderness (Indians or outlaws).[16] The conflict is resolved by a form of violence proper to the wilderness. The hero is experienced. He knows the terror of violence and only reluctantly embraces it to accomplish his purposes. When the task is finished and civilization prevails, he must move on toward the West where his skills may once again prove useful.[17] His journey into the sunset mirrors the ambiguity of his life: his era is in its twilight, but there is hope that the past can be relived one more time in some unspecified land further into the wilderness in the West. His homelessness is tragic, but if he stays, he must abandon the old way of life and face a metaphorical death. The promise of marriage, the traditional happy ending in other genres, would be a form of annihilation for the Western hero.

From the days of Daniel Boone, the frontier hero gripped the American imagination, and even the Europeans found him quaint and fascinating.[18] With the invention of steam presses and the advent of near-universal literacy, pulp fiction glamorizing the life on the frontier had become an extraordinarily popular form of entertainment, a kind of nineteenth century comic book. The stories of Deadwood Dick by Edward Wheeler and of Buffalo Bill by Prentiss Ingraham repeated the old formulas, and the Wild West shows of Wild Bill Cody drew crowds wherever they played.[19] The West had been glamorized in the public imagination before the movies arrived, but the movies captured the spirit magically and in a scope that could never be rivaled on the stage. The movies could bring stampedes, Indian wars and the vast American deserts to every small town and urban ghetto in America.

This explains, at least in part, the unparalleled popularity of the Western film. The classic Westerns tied together spectacle and adventure, and packaged them in the familiar wrappings of the old West. The films, like the pulp fiction and Wild West shows before them, were essentially a boy's fantasy, made believable through endless repetition, and they were treated with bemusement, if not contempt, by the critical establishments. Little matter. The public loved them.

With the release of John Ford's *Stagecoach* in 1939, the Western film entered into a new era. The emphasis shifted from action for its own entertaining sake to the psychological and dramatic elements of life in a vanishing civilization. The stories were no longer a Saturday afternoon adventure, but an epic of the frontier. The heroes were no longer rodeo riders showing off their skills, but Arthurean knights in search of an ever elusive Grail. Since, however, the epic glorifies a frontier that has passed away, and since the hero fails to gain the rewards of his quest, the stories become an authentic American tragedy. In the later Westerns, these displaced heroes either turn outlaw or cynically sell their talents to anyone who is willing to pay to have a job done.[20] They have given up any notion of making the wilderness into a civilization that rejects them. Their stories become a chronicle of a people striving for success and, having found it, discovering that success cannot bring rest.

Bazin called the new form of the Western the "Superwestern." His definition is intriguing: "The Superwestern is a Western that would be ashamed to be just itself, and looks for some additional interest to justify its existence—an aesthetic, sociological, moral, psychological, political or erotic interest, in short some quality extrinsic to the genre and which is supposed to enrich it."[21] He believes that "if the Western were about to disappear, the Superwestern would be the perfect expression of its decadence, of its final collapse." But the Western, as Bazin admits at the time of his writing, is not about to disappear. On the contrary, the postwar period saw the flowering of the genre with astonishing variety. The Superwestern had pushed back the frontiers of the genre, allowing new life to flow through it.

Jean Renoir, the noted French director, once observed: "The marvelous thing about Westerns is that they're all the same movie. This gives a director unlimited freedom."[22] As the Western reached its maturity in the 1950s, it provided a set formula for probing all sorts of questions. Audiences did not have to worry about how the story would turn out; they knew the conflict would be resolved on the side of good during a final gunfight and the hero would once again move on. The icons and characters were so firmly in place that directors and scriptwriters could resort to extraordinary shorthand in narrative exposition. Everyone in the audience knows, for example, that a solitary rider wearing black means trouble. The film does not have to stop the action to explain the fact.

Shane (George Stevens, 1953) is, for example, a classic struggle between farmers and cattlemen. The story is told from the perspective of Joey (Brandon DeWilde), a boy torn between his love of the wilderness as embodied in Shane (Alan Ladd) and his desire for civilization, which he sees in his father Joe (Van Heflin). Shane protects the family from the cattlemen, and thus tames their small section of the frontier. Joey and his mother (Jean Arthur) admire the achievement and look back on it with gratitude, but they must build the future by staying on the farm. The film is a portrait of Eisenhower-era America (which is doubly poignant in the post-Reagan era) looking back to a simpler past, like World War II, when the enemies were clear and the victories glorious, yet realizing that it must embrace the far less exciting and more demanding task of building the future.

High Noon (Fred Zinnemann, 1952) is even more explicit in its historical referents, yet critics are not agreed about its meaning.[23] Marshal Will Kane (Gary Cooper) can be interpreted as a figure of the United States standing up alone against the alien menace of Communism as represented by the Miller boys. He prevails but shows his contempt for the cowardly townspeople by throwing his tin star in the dust as a sign that America has soured in its role of international guardian of democracy for nations who will not defend themselves. Other interpreters believe that scriptwriter Carl Foreman, harassed by the House Un-American Activities Committee, developed Will Kane as an image of himself having to stand alone in defense of civil liberties while the rest of Hollywood joined in the frenzy of loyalty oaths.

In both cases, the interpretations are interesting and may increase one's appreciation of the films, but they are scarcely necessary. It is not necessary to bring in historical events extrinsic to the films to enjoy them even as Superwesterns. The mythic struggle between good and evil, the tragic hero sacrificing himself for the good of others, the taming of the frontier and the establishment of civilization —all the elements of Western genre are present even in these complex Superwesterns. Joey goes through a painful process of letting his romantic notions of the past fade away, and his growing up provides drama. Will Kane, unlike his predecessors in the classic action Westerns, has to deal with his conscience. He must decide whether to follow the rules of the old West (a man's gotta do what a man's gotta do), or whether he will follow the pragmatic ethics of the new America and simply leave town. Both Shane and Will Kane are noble anachronisms, and thus their drama becomes high tragedy.

Since critics have begun to take Westerns seriously, an astonishing variety of critical methods of interpretation have developed.[24] Critics not only have applied the ordinary canons of auteur and genre criticism, but have approached Westerns explicitly as myth, as historical record and as allegory.[25] Many are politically oriented, and writing in 1973 Philip French even divides Western films into Goldwater films and Kennedy films, depending on the hero's uncompromising adherence to an outmoded code of the frontier or his willingness to adapt to new circumstances.[26]

While any of these approaches may be illuminating for any particular film, the words of Jean Renoir remain crucial: "The marvelous thing about Westerns is that they're all the same movie. The genre, as a whole, is what makes the film appealing, and the other elements, particularly the director's personal vision, embellish and reinterpret a pattern that is already in place. The beauty of the genre is that it cuts so close to the human experience, and especially to the American experience, that one can use it like a myth, a timeless story that provides the means to interpret ephemeral events."[27] The Western myths, like the epics of Greece and Rome or the Arthurean legends, provide a simple story that can be told over and over again to help people of every generation understand more about themselves and their world.

If this is so, why did the genre collapse? One reason, of course, was that during its peak of popularity in the 1950s the Western was simply overworked and the public grew tired of horse operas. In 1958 fifty-four Western feature films were released to the theaters. Some were significant, like *The Left-Handed Gun* (Arthur Penn) and *The Big Country* (William Wyler), but most of the others were undistinguished. Too much of a good thing quickly becomes too much goods of the thing.

During this period cowboys rode in stampede numbers into television as well. The venerable movie series *Hopalong Cassidy* hopped along into television in 1948, and the show became so popular that in 1951 and 1952 William Boyd, the producer and star, made fifty-two half-hour programs. *The Cisco Kid* lasted from 1951 to 1956. Repeating in a compressed time frame the transition that Hollywood made in 1939 with the release of *Stagecoach*, television Westerns switched from pure action adventure to adult themes in 1955 with the broadcast of *Cheyenne* on *Warner Bros. Presents*. Thus began the cattle drive, with programs like *Gunsmoke* (1955–75), *Maverick* (1957–61), *Bonanza* (1959–73), and *The Virginian* (1962–70) at sixty minutes per episode. In 1959, no fewer than thirty-two Western series appeared on the living room screen.[28] Again, the volume became overwhelming.

Although overexposure through both film and television may be the single most important factor in the disappearance of the Western, it is not the only one. The stars who created the popular image of the Western hero were literally aging as their genre grew old. Only a few actors, perhaps fewer than fifty of them, became identified with the role, and as the actors aged, so did the characters they played. Younger actors lacked the heroic stature that the public found in, say, John Wayne (b. 1907) or Randolph Scott (b. 1903).

John Wayne played an old, bloated, one-eyed gunfighter for laughs in *True Grit* (Henry Hathaway, 1969), but even in a drunken stupor he was a better man than the young Texas Ranger played by Glen Campbell. In *The Cowboys* (Mark Rydell, 1972), he is shot by a psychotic Bruce Dern, and a brave but nameless team of pre-teen cow punchers continues the cattle drive without him. In his final Western, *The Shootist* (Don Siegel, 1976), he is dying of cancer. In true heroic fashion he defeats his enemies in a gunfight, but then is shot in the back by a bartender. Wayne's younger initiate avenges the death, but then throws away his gun.

Similarly, Randolph Scott in his last Western *Ride the High Country* (Sam Peckinpah, 1962) has left the range and become a make-believe Indian fighter in a carnival. He and a friend from the old days, a down-at-the-heels former lawman (Joel McCrea; b. 1905) take on one last job, but they continually complain about stiff joints. They argue about the new and the old morality of the frontier, but in a showdown these old-timers outwit and outfight their sinister, younger adversaries. Hope for future generations rests on a girl (Mariette Hartley) who is determined to stay on her family farm, even though her parents, the frontier generation, are dead. She, of course, rejects the violence of the old heroic ways, as represented by Scott and McCrea.

Natural aging was only part of the obituary. With such a torrent of Western films and television programs, writers had to stretch the boundaries of the genre to such an extent that the essential elements of the formula were compromised. Heroes became ambiguous, dialogue replaced action, and frontier morality was compromised for pragmatic reasons. Through the early 1950s variations on the basic Western themes were a sign of the vitality of the genre. Later on, the drive for originality simply overwhelmed the canons of the genre. For example, *The Misfits* (John Huston, 1961), *Hud* (Martin Ritt, 1963), and *Butch Cassidy and the Sundance Kid* (George Roy Hill, 1969), all successful in their way, borrow the materials of the Western but use them in such a way that it is not altogether clear if the films should be called Westerns or simply romantic melodramas.

Social forces outside the film industry joined with the internal factors in destroying the Western genre. President Eisenhower, elderly, a Westerner and a military man, was the embodiment of frontier virtues. When he was replaced by the young articulate Easterner John Kennedy, his homespun style suddenly seemed quaint and out of date, a relic like the old Western movie heroes. With Kennedy's death in 1963, the mild bemusement with the older generation turned to cynicism, and the terrible 1960s began in earnest. Flower power was a self-conscious reaction against the use of violence in conflict resolution. Vietnam provided a context for the questioning of American righteousness, and heroes had little place in a world of bewildering complexity and mechanized warfare. John Wayne became more noted for his benighted politics than for his superb films, and in the process of the controversies, the heroes Wayne played and the frontier values those men represented became a caricature, tainted and cheapened by the rhetoric of Vietnam.

The Westerns of the late 1960s became progressively more sour.[29] In *The Wild Bunch* (Peckinpah, 1969), a band of psychopathic killers keep alive the traditions of the old West, while the lawmen are led by a mercenary railroad detective with the moral sensitivity of a brick. The film ends with the bloodiest gunfight ever filmed, which shows the futility of violence. As early as 1964, Clint Eastwood began to appear in a series of Italian-made "spaghetti Westerns": *A Fistful of Dollars* (Sergio Leone, 1964), *For a Few Dollars More* (Leone, 1965), *The Good, the Bad and the Ugly* (Leone, 1966), *Hang 'Em High* (Ted Post, 1968), and so on.[30] These established Eastwood as the last authentic Western star, but a Western hero of a very different stamp from Wayne, Scott, James Stewart, and Henry Fonda. He knows the survival tactics of the frontier as well as any of the earlier heroes, but he lacks any moral sense. He kills without hesitation. He dresses in black like the old-time outlaws, chews soggy cigars, needs a shave, and relates to women as sex objects rather than domesticators. (By contrast, John Wayne was on the trail a full five years in *The Searchers* and never had as much as a five o'clock shadow.) In the Clint Eastwood character the lines between hero and villain are self-consciously blurred. His is a world without moral standards.

The convergence of the civil rights movement, the Vietnam War and the native American awareness led to a drastic reassessment of the Indian wars. In earlier films the Western hero fought the Indians, forces of savagery, to make the frontier safe for civilization. In the 1960s America's role in imposing order on the wilderness came under serious scrutiny. John Ford's *Cheyenne Autumn* (1964) showed how bungling, misguided policies, emanating from the East, destroyed the once great Cheyenne nation. By this time, even for John Ford, the cavalry's role on the frontier was that of unwitting accomplice in genocide rather than savior of the beleaguered wagon train.

In *Little Big Man* (Arthur Penn, 1970), the role of the army had become far more active. Throughout its episodic structure, the film debunks one Western myth after the other, as though citing instances to fill out the cynical thesis outline prepared by Ford's *The Man Who Shot Liberty Valance* (1962). It reserves its bitterest commentary, however, for the Indian wars. Since the hero, Jack Crabb (Dustin Hoffman), has lived among the Indians, the audience becomes familiar with them as individuals. During two terrible slaughters, when the cavalrymen murder women and children for sport, it watches in horror. It is an atrocity to match My Lai. On the other hand, when George Armstrong Custer (Richard Mulligan), a vain buffoon, leads his men into a trap and the Indians begin to annihilate them, Penn plays the scene for laughs. The soldiers are, after all, only getting what they deserve. The death of the soldiers, and the death of the myth that surrounded them in countless Western films, is nothing other than an ironic joke.

So the conquest of the frontier ends: with a bang, a whimper and a giggle.

The Plot: *Stagecoach*

As titles roll, a stagecoach followed by a unit of cavalrymen crosses the desert. At the end of the titles, two lone horsemen approach a dusty military outpost. They enter the commander's office and explain that the hills are filled with Apaches. They introduce a Cheyenne, who hates Apaches as much as the army does, and who confirms that the Apaches are being stirred up by Geronimo. The officer tells the telegraph operator to clear the wires to Lordsburg so that he can warn the town. An urgent message is coming in from Lordsburg, and the lines go dead after a single word: "Geronimo."

The film then cuts to the town of Tonto, as the stage arrives, driven down the street by Buck (Andy Devine), who tells station guards that he has the payroll on board. Mrs. Lucy Mallory (Louise Platt), a beautiful, pregnant young woman dressed in black and wearing a shawl, descends from the stagecoach and asks for a cup of tea. Samuel Peacock (Donald Meek), a whiskey salesman dressed in a clerical black suit and checked deerslayer hat, also leaves the stage. On the way to the hotel, Lucy meets friends, a man and a woman, and explains that she is on her way to meet her husband in Lordsburg. Hatfield (John Carradine) meets them on the sidewalk and stares at Lucy as though he knows her. Seated with her friends in the hotel dining room, she sees him again through the window and asks about the "gentleman," but is told he is no gentleman, just a notorious gambler.

In his office Sheriff Curly Wilcox (George Bancroft) tells Buck that the Ringo Kid has broken out of jail. In their conversation, they reveal that Ringo must be looking for the Plummer boys, whose testimony put him in jail. Buck says that Ringo must be heading to Lordsburg because the Plummer brothers have been seen there. Curly decides to ride shotgun on the stagecoach to Lordsburg himself in the hope of capturing Ringo.

Inside the Miner's and Cattleman's bank, Henry Gatewood (Berton Churchill), the president of the bank, takes the payroll that Buck has delivered and writes out a receipt for $50,000.

Outside, Dallas (Claire Trevor), wearing a bright plaid dress, is being escorted to the stagecoach by the ladies of the Law and Order League. She stops when she hears an uproar. Dr. Josiah Boone (Thomas Mitchell) is being evicted for not paying his rent. He pulls his sign off the wall and offers a drunken elegy to his landlady. Dallas asks him if she has to leave town. He explains that they are both victims of social prejudice, and they go off together, arm in arm. He leaves her on the porch and enters the hotel bar to try to get a free drink from Jerry, the bartender (Jack Pennick). Doc has exhausted his credit, but since he is leaving town, the bartender gives him one for the road. Doc discovers Peacock at the end of the bar and, attracted to his sample case, immediately tries to befriend him. The stage with fresh horses pulls up to the front of the hotel, and the commotion of boarding begins.

Mrs. Gatewood (Brenda Fowler) appears at the bank, shrilly de-

mands five dollars from her husband to pay the butcher, and orders
him to be home at noon for dinner with the ladies of the Law and
Order League. As she leaves, he takes the payroll from the office safe
and places it in a black valise.

Sitting on top of the stagecoach, Buck calls out the itinerary: Dry
Fork, Apache Wells, Lee's Ferry, and Lordsburg.[31] A deputy escorts
Dallas to the stage, while some men from the town leer at her. She
glances back with contempt and raises her hem to give them a good
look at her calf. Peacock and Boone board the stage, and Boone is
careful to have access to Peacock's sample case. Lucy Mallory enters,
and at the suggestion of her friends sits near the window, where she
will be separated from Dallas. Hatfield sees her through a window,
puts down his cards, and decides to join her. The cavalry arrives, and
Lieutenant Blanchard (Tim Holt) tells them that the telegraph lines
are down and Geronimo is on the warpath. His unit will accompany
them to Dry Fork, and other units will meet them at the other two
stations if they decide to go on, but the army cannot guarantee their
safety.

They have to vote about making the trip. For their own reasons,
Lucy, Curly and Hatfield decide that they must go on; Dallas and Doc
Boone feel they have no choice. Peacock and Buck want to stay at
Tonto. As the stagecoach leaves, Doc Boone offers a vulgar gesture to
the ladies of the Law and Order League. The cavalry follows them.
Before the coach leaves the town, Gatewood stops it and explains that
he just received a telegram from Lordsburg and must go there
immediately.

The stagecoach enters the desert. Buck talks about his Mexican
wife. Doc Boone laces into Peacock's sample case. Curly wonders
how Gatewood got a telegram when the lines were down. Gatewood
talks about the fine soldiers. Gatewood is shocked to find out about
Geronimo, and Doc Boone wonders why it was not part of the telegraph message he received from Lordsburg.

A single gunshot sounds, and the camera cuts to a medium shot
that tracks up to a close-up of the Ringo Kid (John Wayne) spinning a
rifle on his finger. Curly demands the rifle and says he will put Ringo
under arrest. The arrival of the cavalry escort ends the argument and
prevents a conflict. Ringo hands over the rifle, puts his saddle on the
top of the stagecoach, and enters. Ringo and Doc Boone recognize
each other. Ringo says that Doc set his brother's broken arm, but now
the brother has been murdered. Hatfield tells Boone to put out his
cigar because a gentleman does not smoke in the presence of a lady.

Boone replies that he took a bullet out of the back of a man who was shot by a gentleman.

They arrive at Dry Fork. Sergeant Billy Pickett (Francis Ford), an old drinking companion of Doc Boone's, runs the inn with his wife. He tells them that the soldiers are not there, and they must decide through a second vote whether to go on without military escort. They are confident that another troop will meet them at the next stop, Apache Wells. All but Peacock favor going ahead. They settle in for a meal around a huge table. Lucy Mallory sits at the head of the table, and Ringo holds a chair for Dallas to sit next to her, even though Dallas was walking toward the opposite end of the table. Lucy is horrified, and Hatfield tells her to come up to his end of the table where it will be more comfortable. She moves and Gatewood follows her, leaving Ringo and Dallas alone at their end of the table. Ringo tells Dallas that it is not easy to break out of jail and into society on the same day. Thinking that he is the reason for their ostracism, he begins to leave, but Dallas grasps his arm and asks him to stay with her. Ringo fills her plate and his own. Hatfield tells Lucy that he served in her father's regiment during the war. Ringo tells Dallas that he used to be a cowhand, but "things happen." She agrees. Buck breaks in to tell them that the horses have been changed and they are ready to leave for Apache Wells. The stagecoach once again enters the desert.

Inside the coach, Gatewood rambles on about the army and bank examiners, and Doc Boone once again assaults Peacock's sample case. Buck and Curly decide to take the long road over the mountains because Apaches do not like cold. Dallas offers to let Lucy put her head on her shoulder to rest, but Lucy declines. Hatfield offers Lucy a drink of water and gives her a silver folding cup. She recognizes the crest on the cup as coming from "Greenfield Manor." Rather than admit his changed name, Hatfield tells her that he won the cup on a wager. Ringo offers the canteen to Dallas, but Hatfield refuses to let her use the silver cup. She drinks directly from the canteen. As they drive on, Curly reveals that he knew Ringo's father and is convinced that prison is the safest place for Ringo, since if he did kill Luke Plummer, the two other Plummer brothers would be sure to kill him in return.

They arrive at Apache Wells and learn that the army is gone. Lucy Mallory learns that her husband has been wounded, but the Mexican innkeeper Chris (Chris Pin Martin) is not certain that the injury is serious. Dallas offers to help, but Lucy frostily refuses and enters the inn, where she faints and goes into labor. Curly carries her

into the back room with Hatfield. Dallas follows with Doc. When they
return, Dallas tells Ringo to get hot water and Doc demands black
coffee to sober up. Chris' wife Yakima (Elvira Rios) comes in to help,
and they are shocked to discover that she is Apache. Chris explains
that she is the reason the Apaches will not bother them. Doc vomits,
and he takes his bag into the delivery room, where Dallas assists him.

Hatfield, Ringo and Curly wait in the outer room, while Yakima
and the Mexicans sing around a campfire outside. She gives them a
sign and they steal away. Inside, the men think they hear a coyote, but
Dallas emerges from the back room with a baby girl wrapped in a
blanket. Doc Boone reappears and pours himself a drink at the bar.
Dallas wraps herself in a shawl and goes out through a narrow passageway. Ringo follows her. Chris stops him and confirms that the
Plummer brothers are in Lordsburg.

As Ringo and Dallas walk together in the moonlight, he tells her
that he must get to Lordsburg because the Plummers killed his father
and brother, but she tries to persuade him to escape to Mexico immediately. She tells him that she will try to find work in Lordsburg. Her
parents were killed in an Indian massacre. He tells her he was impressed with the way she handled the baby, and he wants her to go to
his piece of property in Mexico and wait for him. She says that he
doesn't know her and turns away, as Curly comes out and tells Ringo
to get back inside.

The next morning the men awaken inside the inn. Chris says
Yakima has left with his horse. She can be replaced but the horse
cannot be. Gatewood is upset because his valise is missing, but Buck
has taken it for a pillow. Doc wants a drink, which Chris supplies.
Gatewood is anxious to leave, but Hatfield reminds them of the sick
woman, and Ringo suggests that Doc look in on the patient. When
Gatewood proposes a drink, Doc shakes his head and tosses his drink
into the fire, where it flames up. As Doc enters, Dallas is fixing Lucy's
hair. She has sat up with Lucy all night. Doc asks Dallas to make some
coffee.

When Doc leaves Lucy, he finds Dallas waiting in the hall. She
tells him about Ringo's proposal, and he warns her that Ringo is
headed back to prison, and further that, once they arrive at Lordsburg, he will find out all about her past. She says with determination
that he is not going to Lordsburg. He blesses her venture. Doc passes
into the main room, where the men are once more arguing about
going on. Gatewood is insistent, while Hatfield and Peacock, whose

wife has had five children, insist on waiting a day or two to allow Lucy to recover her strength.

Doc advises waiting and sends Ringo to Dallas to help her make the coffee. Ringo tells Doc that he first went to prison when he was seventeen. He repeats his proposal to Dallas, and she says that his determination to kill the Plummers will end in destroying not only his life but hers. She persuades him to escape, cross the border and wait for her in Mexico. She says that once she has seen Lucy and the baby safely delivered to Lordsburg, she will follow him. She has hidden a rifle and saddled a horse for him.

Inside the men are deliberating again about their plans, when Curly realizes that Ringo is about to escape. Ringo mounts the horse, but he stops and Curly catches up with him and puts him in handcuffs. Ringo points to the mountains, where he sees Apache smoke signals, and says he is going nowhere.

They put Lucy and the baby into the stagecoach and take off across the desert at top speed. Gatewood calls Hatfield a tinhorn gambler and Ringo a jailbird. Peacock asks for a little Christian charity in deference to the ladies. They pull into the settlement at Lee's Ferry. The station has been burned out and the ferry has been left smoldering on the far shore. Hatfield covers the body of a dead woman with his coat, and the others prepare to float the rig across the river on logs. They see Apache reflecting signals in the mountain and realize that they have been observed. They are successful in crossing the river and head off across the desert once again.

The camera pans from the tiny stagecoach in the distance on the desert floor to a troop of mounted warriors. Several Apaches appear huge in close-up. Gatewood, believing the danger has passed, apologizes for his behavior. Doc proposes a toast, just as an arrow strikes Peacock in the chest. A ferocious running gun battle follows. Buck is wounded and drops the reins, but Ringo climbs out on the backs of the racing horses and retrieves them. The Apaches suffer heavy casualties, but the defenders of the stagecoach eventually run out of ammunition.

As capture seems imminent, Hatfield puts a pistol with its last bullet to the temple of Lucy Mallory, but he is shot before he can pull the trigger. Just then, as Lucy is praying, she hears a bugle, and the cavalry from Lordsburg drives off the remaining Apaches. When Ringo opens the door of the coach, Hatfield gasps, "If you see Judge Greenfield, tell him . . ." and he slumps over in death.

The cavalry leads the stagecoach into Lordsburg, and Lucy learns that her husband is not in danger. A nurse takes the baby from Dallas. Lucy offers an ambiguous word of thanks to Dallas, and Dallas puts her cloak over Lucy as she is carried away on a stretcher.

Some men recognize Ringo as he drives the stagecoach into town, and they run off to tell Luke Plummer (Tom Tyler), who is playing cards in a saloon. Plummer puts down his cards, and the ace of spades shows prominently. He sends a Mexican to tell his brothers, then steps to the bar and has two fast drinks, while the other men slowly back away from the bar.

Dallas takes her bonnet and purse from the stage, while Peacock is being carried away. He invites her to visit his family in Kansas City, Kansas. Curly tells Ringo that he will probably get only another year for his jailbreak, and Ringo asks him to see that Dallas gets to his place in Mexico. Gatewood wants Ringo arrested immediately, but the Lordsburg sheriff arrests Gatewood instead, because the telegraph wires have been repaired and Gatewood's theft is known in Lordsburg. Ringo says that he wants ten minutes with Dallas, and Curly agrees. Ringo shows Curly the three bullets he has saved for his errand, and he puts them in his rifle.

Ringo walks with Dallas past a row of saloons, where women ply their trade in the doorways. She tells him to leave her, but he insists on finding out where she lives. The other two Plummers arrive at the bar and drink with Luke while they wait for Ringo. Doc Boone enters and asks for a drink at the end of the bar. Luke Plummer asks the bartender for the shotgun, and as he starts to leave, one of the bar girls tries to stop him. He brushes her aside. Ringo and Dallas proceed through the red light district, and she becomes more agitated that Ringo finally knows her past profession and her plans for future employment. Dismissing this new information, he repeats his proposal of marriage and tells her to wait for him on the sidewalk before she descends to the bordello before them. Buck enters the bar and tells the Plummers that Ringo will come in a few minutes. Luke and his brothers start out, but Doc stops them and tells him to leave the shotgun behind. Luke does. As he leaves the bar, his girlfriend tosses him a rifle from a second-story balcony. A newspaper reporter rushes into the pressroom to set up a story about the death of the Ringo Kid.

Ringo and the Plummers meet in the main street. Dallas hears the gunfire and is distraught. Luke enters the bar slowly and falls dead on the floor. Dallas hears Ringo approach and they embrace. Doc and Curly bring up a wagon to take Ringo to prison, offer to let Dallas ride with him for a bit, and then spur the horses to a gallop. As the rig races away, Doc comments: "Well, they're saved from the blessings of civilization." They ride off toward Mexico into the rising sun of a new day.

COMMENTARY

In *Stagecoach* Ford's image of the advent of civilization in the wilderness is not a cheery one. His towns bring out the worst in the people who live in them. Virtue is to be found out in the wilderness, where his characters face elemental trials with courage and generosity. The pilgrimage begins in Tonto, meaning "stupid" in Spanish. Its citizens may not be stupid, but they are a most unpleasant lot, from the hypocritical ladies of the Law and Order League to equally hypocritical men who follow the town prostitute to the stagecoach and leer at her legs as she climbs aboard.

Lordsburg, their destination, is anything but the Lord's town. Its major industries are drinking, gambling and vice. The journey does not end in a promised land, as might be expected in stories with a journey motif, but in a visit to hell. Throughout the journey, the pretenses of civilization as shown in stupid Tonto are stripped away and the evils that it brings with it appear in all their garish horror in Lordsburg. Against this backdrop, Ford spotlights each of his characters, who represent different facets of civilization as they react to the ordeals they endure in the wilderness. In Lordsburg Ford shows the hell that civilization has built in the wilderness, and in this grotesque setting he reveals the worth of each of his protagonists.

By all rights, Ringo, the skilled gunman and escaped convict, and Dallas, the prostitute with a new job awaiting her, should fit most easily into the world of Lordsburg, but they clearly do not fit in. Their inner goodness belies their superficial identities, and they will find a more suitable rest in their search for a home. Through their love they are able to save each other from a life in Lordsburg and move on to a new world further out in the wilderness. They are, as Doc Boone ironically puts it, "saved from the blessings of civilization."

Most of the others do not belong in Lordsburg either. Peacock, a gentle man often mistaken for a clergyman, will recover from his wound and return to his family in Kansas City, Kansas. Lucy Mallory, possibly more humane because of her contact with Dallas, will be reunited with her husband and follow him to an army post. Curly and Buck will return to Tonto to resume their old lives.

Hatfield, the gambler and assassin, and Gatewood, the thief, belong in Lordsburg. One will be buried there, and the other will go to jail there, at least for a while. Only Doc, the participant observer of the drama, remains in a state of ambiguity. He is going nowhere. His future rests in the bottle, where he can create his own wilderness and avoid the blessings of civilization thrust upon him by his profession.

Later on, particularly in *My Darling Clementine* and the Cavalry Trilogy, Ford will refine and simplify his notion of the conflict between civilization and the wilderness. As it appears in his later works, the theme that became associated with Ford is one of triumph once the town is cleaned up and the surviving Indians are back on the reservation. That theme is the product of World War II, when the Allies were able to vanquish the forces of barbarity. *Stagecoach*, however, is a Depression Western. Civilization's "blessings" provide no more peace for Dallas and Ringo than they do for the Joads in *The Grapes of Wrath*, which Ford made the next year. In both films hope arises not from civilization and its institutions, but from the frontier virtues of a people determined to survive.

Since survival is the issue at this point in Ford's career, the primary hero of the film is, as the title suggests, the stagecoach itself. Other figures, particularly Ringo, function only as secondary heroes. The stagecoach is America itself, and Ford presents two very distinct photographic views of it. When shot from the exterior, the stagecoach is a frail, miniature toy, overpowered by the vast spaces of Monument Valley but heroically pushing forward into the wilderness. American civilization is a delicate entity, ever threatened by the hostile forces of the wilderness surrounding it but ever moving forward to insert itself into the interior wilderness of the continent. As it moved from the Atlantic to the Rockies, it faced continual danger, but it prevailed.

The interior image of the stagecoach offers precisely the opposite impression. It is maddeningly claustrophobic. The passengers are jammed in against one another in an impossibly cramped area. Ringo, the last to board, has no seat and must sit on the floor between the others where he functions as a mediator during their endless squabbles. This is another portrait of America, a canvas containing convicts, drunks, gamblers, embezzlers, snobs, crooked bankers, dumb teamsters, prostitutes, and overwhelmed lawmen, pushed together by chance and making their journey into the wilderness together. The magic of America is that this most unpromising cast of characters forms a community and builds a nation together. Something about the experience of turning the wilderness into a nation purifies the bulk of them. Only Gatewood fails the test completely, and that is because he is a man who places self-interest above community interest. Even

Hatfield finds a form of redemption by shielding Mrs. Mallory with his own body during the final moments of the Indian attack.

Ford and the scriptwriter Dudley Nichols switch back and forth brilliantly between these twin perspectives, and the changed point of view gives the film a classic dramatic structure of four acts, each of which involves character development followed by external action. The first takes place in Tonto, where in a series of brilliant vignettes Ford economically introduces all the characters, except Ringo, who as a man of the frontier must be first met in the desert. The stage leaves town and the characters begin to interact. Ringo appears. The second act takes place at Dry Fork, where the brilliant dining table sequence defines the relationships between the characters. Back in the stagecoach they act out the sociodrama around the ladies' use of the silver drinking cup. The third act is set at Apache Wells, where Lucy delivers her baby and Ringo and Dallas plan to meet in Mexico. This is followed by the trip to Lee's Ferry, the fording of the river, the Indian attack, and the rescue by the cavalry. The final act takes place in Lordsburg when Dallas finally realizes that Ringo knows about her and still wants to marry her. It is followed by the gunfight and the start of their trip to Mexico.

While the stagecoach representing America is the primary hero, Ringo is the major secondary hero. From his first appearance spinning his rifle as the camera tracks in to a close-up of his face, it is clear that he transcends realistic limitations. He is the Western hero. He possesses all the frontier virtues that have come down from popular literature about Daniel Boone, Abraham Lincoln and Buffalo Bill. The first stage of the conquest of the wilderness is the arrival of the stagecoach in Lordsburg, indicating the survival of America in its perilous crossing of the continent and concomitant conquest of the Indians. At the completion of its journey at Lordsburg, the civilization that springs up is worse than the savagery it supplanted.

The secondary conflict between true civilization and the savagery of the pseudo-civilization of Lordsburg must be resolved by Ringo, the solitary Western hero who rides into town as a stranger and performs the prescribed ritual of purification. He performs his task by asserting the values of the frontier, which he has just personified in his battle in the desert. He must cleanse the new civilization of its perversion, seen in urban wilderness created by the outlaw Plummers, and he must rescue Dallas from a life of prostitution, which again is one of the "blessings" of a perverted civilization. The rite of purification is pure myth, and it requires death: three bullets for three outlaws, and each one miraculously finds its mark.

Death is an unavoidable part of the cleansing ritual because the Plummers represent the wild side of Ringo, which he must destroy. As a hero of the frontier, Ringo is part wilderness and part civilization. The Plummers are the wilderness without any taint of the civilizing function of the frontier. They killed Ringo's father and brother, framed Ringo for a murder, hold Lordsburg in terror, and have escaped punishment. This part of the American character must be eradicated, but only according to the rules of the frontier. Doc Boone, functioning as referee, takes the shotgun away from Luke, because the fight must be as fair as it can be with three mortal men against one mythic hero. Since Ringo is carrying a rifle, the odds seem to shift in his favor, but being a favorite would compromise the heroic nature of his victory. Ringo must be the underdog if his agon is to hold mythic value. When Luke's girlfriend, a bar girl, tosses him a carbine, the odds shift back to the Plummers, and Ringo's triumph can appear truly glorious, as it must be for the frontier hero.

In a frontier town, the institutions of society are not yet firmly enough entrenched to purge the wilderness in its pure form as embodied in the Plummers. That task remains for Ringo, a man of the frontier, the Western hero. But in his act, Ringo is killing part of himself and making himself a misfit in the town. He adopts the violent methods of the Plummers and surpasses them. He has gunned down three men in the middle of town. The legal institutions of civilization can take care of its own criminals, as when the sheriff puts handcuffs on Gatewood. It is ambiguous with the frontier hero, when Curly first arrests Ringo and then lets him go, even after a triple murder of revenge. It cannot, however, deal with the unbridled savagery of the Plummers. That is the role of Ringo, and he must accomplish his task alone.

The other instrument of the law, the cavalry, similarly has only a precarious control over the frontier. Through its telegraph office, it is the center of communication for the territory, but Lieutenant Blanchard can do little more than warn the passengers about Geronimo if they insist on going on. Twice, at Dry Fork and Apache Wells, the army fails to appear, and at Lee's Ferry it could not prevent the massacre. It is truly powerless to control the wilderness in any effective way. During the siege of the stagecoach, it is the frontiersmen, especially Ringo, Curly and Buck, with help from Hatfield and Doc Boone, who fight off the forces of savagery. The cavalry arrives finally, but only after the frontiersmen have performed their heroic tasks. The individualists establish order in the wilderness; the army only consolidates what is already won.

The racial element cannot be ignored in this phase of Ford's thinking. The frontiersmen fight to the end and cavalry rides to the rescue of white womanhood.[32] The sexual element is surely present, and in *The Searchers* (1956) Ford will revise his thinking drastically when he portrays Ethan Edwards as deranged for wanting to kill his kidnaped niece because she has become squaw to a "buck." Hatfield is not deranged, but he is equally preoccupied with Lucy's virtue. He calmly slips his last cartridge into the chamber of his revolver and prepares to kill Lucy to save her from the "fate worse than death." He cares little about Dallas, who will be left on her own if the Apaches capture the stagecoach.

The symbolic weight of the scene, however, is heavier than the melodramatic. Pure white women—and here Lucy's baby underlines her role as a madonna figure—signify the arrival of civilization in the wilderness. Yakima, the Apache horse thief, is a relic of the wilderness, and Dallas the prostitute fits into the ambiguities of the frontier. Lucy Mallory represents the Western expansion of civilization into the wilderness. Snob though she is, she is what the men and the institutions of government are fighting for.

Dallas functions as the feminine half of the uncharacteristic (for Ford) au pair hero. Again the experience of World War II seems influential in the all-male world that Ford created in his later films. At this point he is more willing to accept a female role in frontier heroism. Like a Hawks woman, Dallas shares many of the characteristic traits of the traditional male Western hero, and she is successful in keeping her femininity as she breaks into the tight circle of men. Lucy, by contrast, keeps aloof; she is able to contribute nothing, and her sole function is to be protected. Dallas' life of prostitution marks her as an outsider from civilized society as much as Ringo's jail term marks him. She is a survivor after the Indian massacre of her family, as he is after the Plummers murdered his father and brother. Although she is tough, she is gentle and appears as a madonna figure herself when she first holds Lucy's baby. As a creature of the frontier, she has made the wilderness safe for Lucy and her baby, but, having done that, she can have no place of honor in the civilization she has helped create. When her role is completed, she has no alternative but to regress into the wilderness by taking a job in a bordello in Lordsburg or move on to some other frontier world. Her homelessless is tragic, but as a Western hero(ine) she is able to ride off with Ringo in the hope of starting a new world elsewhere.

Lucy and Dallas represent the traditional good/bad dichotomy that generally separates women in Western films. In *Stagecoach* the contrast is more complicated than the customary distinction between the young innocent from the East and the tough dance-hall girl who compete for the affection of the hero. In most Western films this competition is an erotic analogue of the competition between civilization and the wilderness for the heart of the Western hero. Ford, with the mixed feelings he has about civilization in this film, shatters the customary categories. Lucy is not only an ambiguous figure, but she is quite obnoxious. Dark haired and dressed in black, she repudiates the image of white normally associated with the refined girl from back East. Dallas, by contrast blonde and wearing light, figured clothes, appears almost girlish and innocent. The clothes reflect the inner state of soul rather than external status. Lucy's arrogance broods darkly over her character. She is capable of great malice in the cause of respectability, just like the ladies of the Law and Order League. Dallas, despite her dark career, radiates kindness, especially toward Lucy. But Lucy, for all her cruel Eastern ways, brings life into the wilderness. Delivering her baby at Apache Wells makes Lucy a matriarch of the new Western nation, and since the baby is called Little Coyote, she will represent the wilderness as well as her mother's abrasive Eastern ways. Not only has Ford recreated the commonplace "good bad girl" in Dallas, but he has presented in Lucy an extraordinary "bad good girl."

In Hatfield, Ford has abandoned any form of ambiguity. He is the epitome of everything that is suspect about the East. As a former officer in the Confederate army, he gave himself to a noble cause and then betrayed his status by changing his name and becoming a gambler. The Confederacy is a rich concept with many meanings for Ford. It represents the tragedy of a lost cause, the nobility of joining in a doomed quest, and, here, the burned-out quality of Eastern, civilized ways. If Doc Boone's suggestion is correct, he is a murderer as well, having shot a man in the back. John Carradine creates a character of artifice, with perfect diction and dress, but no substance and no real name. The Easterner is a fraud, living in the frontier as an amoral exploiter. He treats the others with overbearing superiority, using Lucy as a pretext for his own arrogance. In the final moments of the Indian attack upon the stagecoach the old nobility reasserts itself, and he becomes a fine soldier and heroic figure in his concern for Lucy.

Doc Boone is an especially complex tragic figure. He bears the name of Daniel Boone, yet because of his education he could be considered the most civilized man in that part of the territory. He has a medical practice, but no family and no roots in town. When he peels his name plate from the wall of his office as he is being evicted, the last shred of identity is taken away from him. The tension of his frontier existence is unbearable for him, and he takes refuge in drink. Having been driven out of Tonto, he seeks the only escape he knows: he attacks Peacock's sample case as a prelude to oblivion.

Alcoholic professional men, doctors (*My Darling Clementine*) and reporters (*The Man Who Shot Liberty Valance*), often express Ford's understanding of the tensions experienced by educated men caught in a frontier society in transition. Despite Doc's lapses into the wilderness of alcohol, both Ringo and Dallas come to him for advice, as though he were a wise father figure of the frontier whose experience can guide them to happiness, and even to a future world of civilization. It is perfectly fitting then that he and Curly, who speaks kindly of Ringo's father, form a paternal conspiracy to send Ringo and Dallas off to a new life in Mexico.

While Hatfield lives under an assumed name and Boone obliterates his own, Peacock is a man whose name and identity are continually garbled. At various times he is referred to as Hancock and Paycock. Doc Boone fixes upon his clerical suit and calls him simply "Reverend."[33] Peacock tries to clarify his name and status, but without much success. He is one of the thousands of nameless people, scarcely cut from heroic cloth, who ventured into the frontier for reasons that vary from selling whiskey to spreading the Gospel. Their names or functions make little difference; they are simply little people opening the frontier. They do, however, play a crucial role within the stagecoach nation, reminding the more flamboyant characters of fundamental American virtues like "a little Christian charity." Peacock lives with his family at the Eastern edge of the Kansas territory, so keeps only a tiny foothold on the frontier. As a whiskey salesman he brings firewater with its disastrous consequences into the wilderness, but as a make-believe minister he brings the civilizing virtues of religion into the frontier as well.

Gatewood is Ford's image of the greed of the business community as he steals the payroll from working people. This is, after all, a Depression Western. Gatewood represents the worst of the institutions of civilization. He blusters about bank examiners and government regulation. A visit from his shrewish wife, a supporter of the Law and Order League, initially leads him to the decision to take the payroll, but he receives little sympathy. His marriage and his social connections suit him quite comfortably. His wife's shrill behavior is only a mirror image of his own pompous self-righteousness. He abuses Buck unfairly, when Buck has merely used his valise for a pillow. He disappears from the screen during the gun battle, and his arrest provokes laughter, as though his posturing were finally exposed for the sham it is. The likes of Gatewood have no place on the frontier.

Buck, with his famous Andy Devine voice and girth, is a clown who is never allowed to offer an opinion. Since everything has to be explained to Buck, his stupidity is a device to allow exposition of background. He has a Mexican wife and a huge extended family living near a way station, and this makes him a man of neither civilization nor the wilderness but of the frontier. He is afraid of the Indians and wants to turn back, but Curly and the majority will not allow him, since they must face the danger together. During the attack, however, he emerges in the heroic mold himself, holding on to the reins even after he has been wounded. It is Buck who bumbles into the bar to tell Luke that Ringo is on the way; thus he collaborates in the second conquest of the wilderness, the rite of purification in Lordsburg.

Sheriff Curly Wilcox, a colorless character, is a bit too old to be considered a heroic lawman in the mold of Wyatt Earp, but he assumes the leadership role for the group and keeps it together through its trials. He is a guardian of law and order, but he has the fighting skills of the wilderness, and he knows how to temper the letter of the law with the common sense of the frontier. In contrast, Lieutenant Blanchard follows his orders to the letter, even though his action endangers the stagecoach. Curly arrests Ringo, disarms him, and keeps him in handcuffs, but when the Indians attack he uses Ringo's skills. He and Doc Boone together represent an older generation on the frontier. As the film closes, they remain behind as Dallas and Ringo ride away. They have no place to go.

Curly, in his own way, stands for the democratic ideals that keep the passengers together. He calls for a vote to see if they can agree to go on to Lordsburg, gives everyone a chance to speak, and keeps a form of order during the deliberations. The parliamentary procedures, however, are more frontier than *Robert's Rules of Order*. Curly tells Buck how to vote, and casts Ringo's vote for him. Only Peacock casts a valid negative vote, but Curly's block of three votes makes the consensus overwhelming. These votes are the first halting steps of democracy on the frontier. By vesting responsibility for deciding the course of their lives in the hands of each of the passengers, the democratic process plays its own role in regenerating flawed individuals and making of them a new nation in the wilderness.

The genius of *Stagecoach* is its brilliant combination of epic and chamber theater. With its vast exteriors it describes the heroic origins of America, and in its cramped interiors it shows the abrasions of individuals trying to survive. Ford once told his interviewer, Peter Bogdanovich, that Dudley Nichols' script traces its literary antecedents through Ernest Haycox's two-page story from *Collier's*, "Stage to Lordsburg," to Guy de Maupassant's famous story *Boule de suif (A Ball of Wax)*.[34] The French story is a scathing indictment of hypocrisy. It is the story of a prostitute who offers her services to a border guard in exchange for the safety of her fellow passengers, who in turn treat her with contempt for her immoral behavior.

Aside from the inclusion of a generous prostitute among the passengers on a stagecoach, there is little resemblance to *Boule de suif.* While de Maupassant writes about the emptiness of a culture because of its own hypocrisy, Ford and Nichols show regeneration through the community's efforts to push back the wilderness. In the end Dallas earns a form of grudging acceptance, even from Lucy. The film ends with hope for a new frontier, somewhere further out in the wilderness. While de Maupassant condemns corruption of the respectable, Ford extols the redemptive virtues of democratic society.

Stagecoach is simply a masterpiece. Viewed at this point in time it appears stale, but only because dozens if not hundreds of other filmmakers have tried to recreate Ford's success. It has been called the film that created the clichés, but it is far more accurate to call it the film that defined the archetypes: Ringo's huge white hat and Luke Plummer's equally huge black one; the sound of the bugle and the charge of the cavalry at the last possible moment; the comic sidekick and the tinhorn gambler.[35] Before *Stagecoach* John Ford had not made a Western in thirteen years, not since *Three Bad Men* in 1926. This one was well worth waiting for.

NOTES

1. Recounted in Peter Bogdanovich, *John Ford* (Berkeley: University of California Press, 1968), pp. 18–19.

2. Andrew Sarris, *Interviews with Film Directors* (New York: Avon, 1967), p. 103.

3. André Bazin's *What Is Cinema?* II (Berkeley: University of California Press, 1971), pp. 140–148, a collection of Bazin's essays, includes one here entitled "The Western: Or the American Film Par Excellence," which originally appeared as the preface to J.-L. Rieupeyrout's *Le Western ou le cinéma américain par excellence* (Paris:

Editions du Cerf, 1953). Robert Warshow's groundbreaking essay, "Movie Chronicle: The Westerner," appeared in *Partisan Review*, March–April 1954, and has been reissued in Robert Warshow's *The Immediate Experience: Movies, Comics, Theatre and Other Aspects of Popular Culture* (New York: Doubleday-Anchor, 1964), pp. 89–108.

4. Tag Gallagher's exhaustive critical biography *John Ford: The Man and His Films* (Berkeley: University of California Press, 1986), pp. 1–6, tries to separate fact from fiction in Ford's Irish connections.

5. Gallagher, p. 4, includes this information in vague terms: "At age eleven or twelve his father took him to Ireland, and he went to school there for several months." Peter Stowell, *John Ford* (Boston: Twayne, 1986), p. xvii, maintains that Ford took his first trip to Ireland in 1921, after his marriage.

6. Gallagher, p. 26.

7. Gallagher, pp. 462–68.

8. Gallagher, p. 8.

9. Bogdanovich, p. 36.

10. Andrew Sarris, *John Ford, Movie Mystery* (Bloomington: University of Indiana Press, 1975), p. 15, gives the number of Ford films as one hundred and twenty-five, with sixty-six released before 1930 and thirty before 1920. Most of these early films are lost. The first one is generally believed to be *Straight Shooting* (1917) with Hoot Gibson, but Francis' younger brother may have done the actual directing on titles attributed to others.

11. Joseph McBride and Michael Wilmington, *John Ford* (New York: Da Capo, 1980), p. 24.

12. George Bluestone, *Novels into Film* (Berkeley: University of California Press, 1966), pp. 65–90, discusses the transformation of the novel into the film. The analysis is primarily literary and concentrates on the script adaptation by Dudley Nichols.

13. David A. Cook, *A History of the Narrative Film* (New York: Norton, 1981), p. 24.

14. André Bazin, "The Evolution of the Western," in *What Is Cinema?* II, p. 156.

15. Frederick Jackson Turner, "The Significance of the Frontier in American History," in *The Frontier in American History* (New York: Holt, 1953), pp. 1–38. Turner has been criticized in recent years for oversimplification and especially for his neglect of industrialization and urbanization during the nineteenth century. This revision is important for professional historians, but it in no way compromises the usefulness of this essay as the historical basis for the dramatic conflict central to all Western films.

16. John H. Lenihan, *Showdown: Confronting Modern America in the Western Film* (Urbana: University of Illinois Press, 1980), p. 12, lists the seven basic plots of all Westerns attributed originally to critic Frank Gruber and repeated so often that they have become a critical commonplace: (1) railroad building, (2) ranchers vs. rustlers or sheepherders, (3) empire building: the opening of a territory, (4) revenge, (5) cavalry and Indians, (6) the outlaw, and (7) the marshal. Each of these variants is an adaptation of the civilization/wilderness conflict. Jim Kitses, *Horizons West* (Bloomington: University of Indiana Press, 1969), p. 11, in an equally reprinted paradigm, lists the variants on the civilization/wilderness dichotomy that is at the core of conflicts in the Western film.

17. The most insightful analysis of the character of the typical Western hero remains Warshow's, pp. 89–93.

18. Henry Nash Smith, *Virgin Land: The American West as Symbol and Myth* (New York: Vintage, 1950), pp. 55–57, shows the popularity of the Daniel Boone stories in nineteenth century America, and on pp. 57–63 offers his significance as an American myth.

19. Smith, pp. 109–115.

20. Schatz, pp. 59–60.

21. André Bazin, *What Is Cinema?* II, p. 151

22. Quoted in Schatz, p. 54.

23. Don Graham "High Noon (1952)," in William Pilkington and Don Graham, eds., *Western Movies* (Albuquerque: University of New Mexico Press, 1979), pp. 53–54, presents the two allegorical interpretations most frequently associated with the film.

24. Lenihan, p. 5, offers titles that signify the beginnings of serious critical attention for the Western film.

25. Jon Tuska, *The American West in Film: Critical Approaches to the Western* (Westport: Greenwood, 1985), pp. 1–15, offers a critique of the various methods.

26. Philip French, *Westerns: Aspects of a Movie Genre* (New York: Oxford University Press, 1977), pp. 28–30. Variations on the Kennedy and Goldwater Westerns led to Lyndon Johnson Westerns and William F. Buckley Westerns.

27. Will Wright, *Sixguns and Society: A Structural Study of the Western* (Berkeley: University of California Press, 1977), pp. 210–212.

28. Les Brown, *The New York Times Encyclopedia of Television* (New York: Times Books, 1977), p. 468.

29. Pilkington, pp. 3–5, offers his analysis of the final days of the Western film.

30. Christopher Frayling, *Spaghetti Westerns: Cowboys and Europeans from Karl May to Sergio Leone* (London: Routledge and Kegan Paul, 1981), pp. 37–67, describes the origins of Sergio Leone's style.

31. Varied forms of these place names appear in different commentaries: Dry Fork becomes Dry Ford, and Lee's Ferry becomes East Ferry. Similarly, in listing casts of characters, Luke Plummer, the most significant of the brothers, often becomes Hank. The third brother is Ike.

32. Sarris, *Movie Mystery,* p. 82.

33. David Clandfield, "Stagecoach," in Pilkington, p. 33.

34. Gallagher, p. 146.

35. McBride, p. 53.

Chapter Eight

THE DETECTIVE STORY
THE MALTESE FALCON

The Auteur: John Huston

John Huston (1906–1987) and his critics agree about very little, except about their refusal to attach the word "auteur" to his name. That agreement should be renegotiated, especially after the old man closed out his career by directing his daughter Anjelica Huston to an Academy Award in his sardonic *Prizzi's Honor* (1985) and captured the spirit as well as the words of that most challenging of authors, James Joyce, with his magnificent *The Dead* (1987), which was released a few weeks after his death. During the filming of this last masterpiece, Huston directed from a wheelchair equipped with oxygen to help relieve his emphysema, but he frequently removed the device to enjoy one long black cigarette after another.

Living life full speed ahead, while damning the torpedoes, was a pattern that began in Huston's earliest days in Nevada, Missouri.[1] His youth was unsettled at best. It might better be described as chaotic. His father Walter (1884–1950), whom John also directed to an Academy Award in *The Treasure of the Sierra Madre* (1948), had failed on the New York stage and had become a civil engineer in charge of the town's water supply. His wife, Rhea Gore, a New York newspaperwoman, followed her actor-engineer husband to western Missouri, but their marriage did not last. By 1909 Walter had left his wife and returned to the stage with a new romance, the actress Bayonne Whipple, but it was not until 1913 that the divorce from Rhea Gore was finalized. Back on the stage, Walter Huston toured the vaudeville circuits with John in tow. When John joined his mother, the two followed the racing set from one track to the next, where she could indulge her family's passion for both the animals and the betting. The theater, the horses, and the thrill of the longshot on fate became parts of John Huston's baggage from boyhood. Formal education did not.

Travel and instability had an impact on the boy's health, or so it seemed. By 1912 John was sent to a sanitorium because of suspected heart and kidney problems. He refused to accept the life of an invalid, and at night crept down to an icy waterfall where he rode the waters over the rocks to the pool beneath.[2] The sport was dangerous, but the boy preferred death by accident to death by disease. Fascination with risk for its own sake haunted Huston, boy and man. In his autobiography he recounts with relish the story of his climbing into a bull ring in Madrid. His leg became caught between the front hooves of the bull, and any movement of the bull's head could have eviscerated him. The bull did not move, and the would-be matador escaped without a scratch, simply because the animal decided not to move, a decision based on bovine whimsy and fate. Huston comments, "It was one of the high moments of my life."[3]

The waterfall therapy worked miracles for the young John Huston. In 1920 he left school to become a boxer and became quite good at it. In interviews he reminisces that he won twenty-three of twenty-five fights and reigned for a time as the Amateur Lightweight Champion of California.[4] The rules for amateur athletics may have been more flexible in those days, since he also recalls getting fifty dollars a night for his efforts. Aside from the resculpted nose that added character to the face of Huston the actor, boxing brought rewards of another kind. His first short story, "Fool," the tale of a friendship between two small-time boxers, was forwarded with the recommendation of Ring Lardner to H.L. Mencken, who published it in *The American Mercury* (March 1929). Forty years later Huston reworked the material into *Fat City* (1972).

After his brief career in the ring, Huston went to New York to join his father who was beginning to gain some notoriety in the theater. John wanted to act, but parts were few, and he was free to indulge his passion for horses by frequenting the bridle paths in Central Park. Discouraged by the theater, he accepted a commission in the Mexican cavalry where he could ride for free. He wrote a play, *Frankie and Johnnie*, returned to New York to try to have it produced, and eventually became a reporter for the *New York Graphic*, with help from his mother's connections. He lost that job because of an inability to distinguish fact from fiction in his writing. Walter Huston had made the transition to Hollywood and got John a job writing dialogue for William Wyler, but the teamwork and discipline were not to his liking. He went to Europe, and when his money ran out, he supported himself by singing on street corners in London and sketching for tourists in Paris. He became quite serious in his study of art, another youthful interest that resurfaced in his later career with *Moulin Rouge* (1952), the life of the impressionist painter Toulouse-Lautrec.[5]

In 1933, at the age of twenty-seven, John Huston returned to the United States, a brilliant young man with a half-dozen aborted careers behind him and very little promise in his future. He was more recognized as an amusing drinking companion than as a significant talent. Reminiscing about John Huston in the mid-1930s, Henry Blanke, producer of *The Treasure of the Sierra Madre,* recalls that Huston was "just a drunken boy; hopelessly immature. You'd see him at every party, wearing bangs, with a monkey on his shoulder. Charming. Very talented, but without an ounce of discipline in his makeup."[6] Blanke attributed the sudden focusing of Huston's talents and ambitions, if not his style of living, to his marriage to Leslie Black in 1937.

Whether the responsibilities of the married state changed Huston, or whether he realized that at age thirty-one he was squandering his life, is a moot point. What is more pertinent is that at age thirty-one he settled into his role as a scriptwriter at Warner Bros. and created screenplays for the finest directorial talents in Hollywood. With Clements Ripley and Abem Finkel he wrote *Jezebel* (1938) for William Wyler, and its star, Bette Davis (1908–1989), won an Academy Award with her role. Huston followed with *The Amazing Dr. Clitterhouse* (1938) for Anatole Litvak, a film starring Edward G. Robinson and Claire Trevor, supported by a young actor whose disfigured mouth—due to a gunnery accident in World War I—seemed certain to keep him from success as a leading man. The actor was Humphrey Bogart, who made a bit of a splash as Duke Mantee in *The Petrified Forest* (Archie Mayo, 1936), a role he had created on Broadway, but then seemed condemned to play hoodlums in low-budget crime stories. The team of Bogart, Robinson, and Trevor would be reunited by Huston the director in *Key Largo* (1948).

Huston followed with two scripts for William Dieterle, *Juarez* (1939) and the cult classic *Dr. Ehrlich's Magic Bullet* (1940). The next year he provided the screenplay for Raoul Walsh's *High Sierra* (1941), which in turn provided the launching pad for Bogart's rise to superstardom. The film marked a turning point in Huston's career as well. Jack Warner held the rights to Dashiell Hammett's detective story *The Maltese Falcon*. The story was scarcely fresh, since it had been shot as *The Maltese Falcon* (Roy Del Ruth, 1931) and as *Satan*

Met a Lady (William Dieterle, 1936). Huston asked Warner for a chance to direct, and Warner told him if he could produce a fresh script for the property, he could direct it. Not surprisingly, Huston accepted the challenge.

Sam Spade, the tough, amoral, cynical detective, fit comfortably into the Huston universe. George Raft was cast as the anti-hero, but withdrew, leaving the role open for Humphrey Bogart, who became the embodiment of Sam Spade and the mirror reflection of John Huston's outlook on life.

Hammett's Spade, Bogart and Huston, three voices blended into one, arose from the murky world of the Depression as the world sank irreversibly into another world war. They find themselves surrounded by ruthless powers beyond their control and so they profess a moral code of self-interest. Success or failure depends as much on chance as on hard work, but the outcome of human activity has little value, so success or failure is scarcely important. Life is not really important either, not even worth "a hill of beans," as Bogart would explain in *Casablanca* (Michael Curtiz, 1942). Since life and death are unimportant, danger is irrelevant and risk has a value in itself: it proves that one is alive. A Huston/Bogart anti-hero faces up to an enemy not to vanquish evil but rather to keep from "being played for a sap." Huston and Ernest Hemingway were personal friends as well as artistic kinfolk, and in *The Maltese Falcon* Huston moved Hemingway's fatalistic vision from the bull rings and bistros of Europe to the gritty streets of San Francisco. The geography changed, but the moral landscape was identical.

As a veteran scriptwriter Huston had every reason to have confidence in his ability to write the hard-edged dialogue for the project, but the camera set-ups provided a challenge. For the first time he returned to his training as a painter and sketched each shot before the crew assembled on the lot. His dark lighting captured the somber mood of his characters and the bleak message of the script. The result was the creation of that shadowy world, called "film noir," which would dominate the style of American films for the next ten years. *The Maltese Falcon* was nominated for an Academy Award in three categories: best picture, John Huston for best screenplay, and Sydney Greenstreet (1879–1954) for best supporting actor.

In his directorial debut John Huston set out several of the themes that he would return to in his next forty-five years. The search for the jewels hidden in the porcelain figurine is a quest that consumes the lives of the band of criminals, Kasper Gutman (Sydney Greenstreet), Joel Cairo (Peter Lorre), and Brigid O'Shaughnessy (Mary Astor).

They doublecross one another to take possession of the prize, only to find it worthless. Spade does not desire the wealth of the falcon for himself, but he does fall in love with Brigid. When he discovers her part in the scheme, he realizes that he must turn her in. He loses her, and thus his quest has become as futile as theirs.

With such a fatalistic view of life, it was inevitable that Huston would one day make a film of Herman Melville's classic American novel *Moby Dick*, which he completed in 1956. Captain Ahab (Gregory Peck) is perhaps the greatest representative in American literature of the man who becomes obsessed with his quest for an unattainable goal, only to find that his quarry finally destroys him. Melville's Ahab is touched with the hubris of the Greek tragic hero, a man who dared to defy the gods by striving to challenge the universe. For Huston the theological notion becomes secularized into a kind of fatalism befitting Hemingway. Ahab was simply destined to fail, much as Hemingway's fisherman in *The Old Man and the Sea* was destined not to bring his fish back to port. A personal God has nothing to do with success or failure; for Hemingway and Huston, the universe is just a very tough and unforgiving adversary.

Futility as a preoccupation of Huston's flavored his great war documentary, *The Battle of San Pietro* (1945). Through military maps, and with an emotionless voice, Huston the director and narrator explains the tactical importance of an obscure mountain ridge in Italy. The fighting is endless and futile. Casualties are staggering. Finally the Germans decide that the prize is no longer worth the effort, and they simply, surprisingly, decide to withdraw. The town is liberated, and to the theme of Gabriel Fauré's "Requiem"—"Lamb of God, who takes away the sins of the world, grant them peace"—the children leave their bunkers and reappear on the streets, to play, to forget the horror, and perhaps one day to find themselves in another war. The Allies have won the victory, but Huston offers no assurance that the lessons of the war have been learned.

Huston's last documentary for the army, *Let There Be Light* (1945), was judged too controversial for release to the public. In it Huston explores the psychological problems experienced by many returning veterans. In victory, neither the army nor the American public wanted to be reminded of the terrible cost of their triumph. The more important quest in the film is the struggle for sanity in a world gone mad with greed. The patients eventually succeed, but their battle for self-possession is every bit as terrible as the battle of San Pietro. Some, of course, do not succeed. War, for Huston, is the ultimate expression of the futility of the human enterprise. Little

wonder then that immediately after the war, before he returned to
Hollywood, he produced John-Paul Sartre's *No Exit* on Broadway. In
Sartre's devastating view of humanity, individual persons are bricked
into a tiny room, where they finally realize that "hell is the other
people."

In many of his films, embarking on a futile and destructive quest
is the result of greed. In *The Maltese Falcon*, for example, the criminals are singleminded in their quest for instant wealth. Spade appears
to be as free from conventional morality values as they, but he is
scarcely greedy. His willingness to earn what he gets sets him apart
from the others. For Spade, pride is the more operative motive: he
will not allow himself to be bought off.

Greed in the quest for riches is the major theme in Huston's first
film after the war, *The Treasure of the Sierra Madre*. The three prospectors (Humphrey Bogart, Walter Huston and Tim Holt) risk everything to locate a gold mine, endure hardship to extract the ore, and
plan to bring it to town. As their wealth accumulates, they begin to
mistrust one another and concoct plans to keep all the gold for themselves. Their schemes are futile, since just as they are within sight of
success, the gold falls into the hands of a psychopathic bandit, who
believes it is only sand and scatters it to the wind. Since success is not
really important, the surviving miners burst into raucous laughter.
Life is a practical joke, played by fate on its hapless pawns. As the
wind blows the gold dust across the desert floor, Huston shows that
the earth eventually reclaims its wealth, and mere humans, despite
their greed, are powerless to stop it.

In *The Asphalt Jungle* (1950), a jewel thief recently released from
prison (Sam Jaffe) organizes a brilliant robbery that will enable him to
retire in wealth. His team includes Dix Handley (Sterling Hayden),
who joins the scheme to earn enough money to enable him to return
to his family's farm in Kentucky. Wounded by a competing gunman,
he dies just as he enters the gate of the farm. Neither criminal
achieves his goal.

The theme of the thwarted quest reappears in Huston's late films
as well. In *The Man Who Would Be King* (1975) Daniel Dravot (Sean
Connery) is a British sergeant sent off to pacify a distant region of
India. He is mistaken for a god and made king, which accomplishes his
mission quite nicely. When he tries to perpetuate his rule by founding
a dynasty, the tribe discovers that he is human and executes him. He
plunges into the canyon with the regal crown just beyond his grasp.
Prizzi's Honor (1985) is a tale of intrigue among the Mafia in Brooklyn. After an involved series of double crosses, the beautiful but

deadly murderer (Kathleen Turner) fails to eliminate her rival, Charlie Partanna (Jack Nicholson). She dies in her quest for wealth and power, while Charlie, who murders her, has lost a woman he truly loved. After her death he stands alone by their car, now destined to operate the family but finding his victory hollow. In this scene Huston repeats the double failure of Sam Spade and Brigid in *The Maltese Falcon*, made over forty years earlier.

The frustration of a failed quest need not always involve violence and death. In his last film, *The Dead* (1987), Gabriel Conroy (Donal McCann) craves more than anything else the love and esteem of his wife Gretta (Anjelica Huston). After a long dinner party, she weeps as she reveals for the first time the story of a boy who once loved her, waited in the rain to say goodbye to her, and then, shortly afterward, died of pneumonia. Gabriel is tormented by her memories of her first love, and he realizes that because of that boy, now dead many years, there is a part of Gretta he cannot possess. As he tries to sleep, Gabriel ponders the brute indifference of the universe that allows the snow to fall indifferently on the living and the dead.

A Huston quest need not be futile. A strenuous quest undertaken without greed can be quite successful. In *The African Queen* (1951), for example, Charlie Allnut (Humphrey Bogart) and Rosie Sayer (Katharine Hepburn) sail, drag and cajole his rickety boat through jungle and swamp, while enduring all manner of adversity, with the intention of sinking a German warship patrolling the lake. Even when they are captured and all appears lost, they remain faithful to their quest and to each other, and ultimately they are successful. In *The Misfits* (1961), Gay Langland (Clark Gable) seeks both his macho notion of freedom and wealth by capturing wild mustangs in the desert. He will then sell the animals to a dog food processor. Roslyn Tabor (Marilyn Monroe) functions as a traditional Western-film domesticator and shows him the value of compassion. In Arthur Miller's screenplay, Gay, the misfit, surrenders his greed and his desire for a way of life that is passing away, and wins the love of a woman, a goal that he could never before admit to himself.

Despite elaborate plans and heroic effort, the outcome of the Huston quest is more often than not a matter of chance, and the element of luck becomes more pronounced in the later films. In *The Maltese Falcon* the relationships shift through each scene. Spade happens to be a survivor who followed the right hunches at the right times. In *The Treasure of the Sierra Madre* the three prospectors meet by chance in a flophouse, and Dobbs (Bogart) just happens to stop at the watering hole where the bandits find him. In *Key Largo* a hurricane strikes just as Johnny Rocco (Edward G. Robinson) is about to sell his counterfeit bills.

In several of the later films, the coincidences are even more visible. The criminal scheme in *The Asphalt Jungle* begins to unravel when the explosive used for the safe sets off a number of unrelated burglar alarms in the neighborhood. The police naturally respond in force, even though they cannot discover where the robbery has occurred. This confusion allows the robbers to escape, but in the process a watchman drops his gun and it goes off, wounding one of the robbers. The mastermind Doc Riedenschneider (Sam Jaffe) delays his getaway for two or three minutes to watch a young girl dance to a jukebox in a roadside cafe. This is just enough time to allow the police to identify him. The financier of the operation, Alonzo Emmerich (Louis Calhern), kills himself when the plan goes sour, which prompts his bodyguard to try to get in on the action by shooting and fatally wounding Dix Handley (Sterling Hayden). In *The Misfits* the wife of Guido (Eli Wallach) dies because he has no spare tire for the truck. When she begins a difficult labor, he cannot get her to the hospital.

Luck is not always fatal. In *The African Queen* it accomplishes what Charlie and Rose cannot do by themselves. They are captured by the Germans and brought aboard the boat they were trying to destroy, but their own boat, the African Queen, lies half submerged in the lake, with Charlie's homemade torpedoes just below the surface. The German sailors do not notice the hull, and the ship strikes the detonators.

Good luck can change suddenly, too. In *The Man Who Would Be King* Dravot leads a cavalry charge with an arrow protruding from his chest. He is unmarked because the shaft lodged in his bandoleer. The villagers conclude that he must be a god and declare him king. Thanks to his good fortune, the mission is accomplished without further bloodshed. When he decides to take a bride to perpetuate his reign, the reluctant girl panics. She scratches and bites his face, the blood flows, and the myth of divinity is shattered. Outraged at his deception, the villagers execute him.

From the first day that Brigid O'Shaughnessy slithered into Sam Spade's office, John Huston treated women as decidedly bad luck in any man's life. Married five times himself, he describes his wives as "a mixed bag. A schoolgirl, a gentlewoman, a motion picture actress, a ballerina and a crocodile."[7] Like Howard Hawks, Huston was interested in action and adventure among a small male band; women with their emotions only disrupted the lives of the striving men. "Beware of Eve," a comment attributed to Brendan Gill's analysis of John Huston's women, has more than a fragment of truth to it.[8]

From Mary Astor in *The Maltese Falcon* to Kathleen Turner in *Prizzi's Honor*, women have meant trouble for the heroic male figures. Even when they are strong and loyal figures like Katharine Hepburn in *The African Queen* or fragile and sympathetic characters like Marilyn Monroe in *The Misfits*, they disrupt the comfortable male world and force a change in the hero's vision of reality. In *The Asphalt Jungle* Emmerich is driven to his crimes by the frustration of living with an invalid wife who lies in bed and wants to play cards and by a young mistress Angela Phinlay (Marilyn Monroe) who needs money to support her ambitions for luxury. In *The Misfits* Roslyn tears Gay from his way of life as a free-living cowboy in the Nevada desert. Finally, it is the reluctant princess who, with nail and fang, exposes Dravot's humanity in *The Man Who Would Be King*. Gretta, in *The Dead*, intends no malice, but her capacity for love, which Gabriel cannot satisfy, spiritually destroys her husband.

Despite these several recurring motifs in John Huston's films, he is a director who gained little respect among the auteur critics and the various critical establishments influenced by them. Although he was involved in the creation of his films during every phase of production, one criterion for earning a reputation as an auteur, he received poor grades for the other two: his inconsistent personal vision and his eclectic visual style. As a result, he generally ranks fairly low among the American prestige directors according to the critics.

James Agee was the exception. In his famous essay of 1950, Agee writes: "To put it conservatively, there is nobody under fifty at work in movies, here or abroad, who can excel Huston in talent, inventiveness, intransigence, achievement or promise."[9] Agee commends Huston for that same impatience with abstraction and love of action that the French critics were to find praiseworthy in the films of Howard Hawks. Agee admires the way Huston avoids "feminine" emotion and depends on the excitement of the action itself to produce its own emotion. He approves of Huston's "kind of romanticism about danger," which he finds close to Hemingway's. Finally, he praises Huston's consistency, a point that later critics will not concede—and with good reason.

Agee's essay appeared early in Huston's career, and in determining a critical reputation, timing is crucial. Huston's output in the 1940s was extraordinary, and James Agee based his opinion on these early works. In the next decade, however, as the French critics began their work, Huston reached a low period in his artistic output. The impact of his mediocre films compromised the reputation of his finer ones, and finally compromised the reputation of the director himself.

To be blunt, Huston's talent is not consistent. By his own admission he directed a number of eminently forgettable films through the years. *Moby Dick* (1956) did not meet with a kind reception. *Heaven Knows, Mr. Allison* (1957), *The Barbarian and the Geisha* (1958), *The Roots of Heaven* (1958) and *The Unforgiven* (1960) met with little reaction of any kind. Following these were *The List of Adrian Messenger* (1963), *The Night of the Iguana* (1964), *The Bible* (1966), *Casino Royale* (1967), *Reflections in a Golden Eye* (1967), *Sinful Davey* (1969), *A Walk with Love and Death* (1969), *The Kremlin Letter* (1970) and *The Mackintosh Man* (1973). None of these were destined to enhance Huston's reputation. Furthermore, they tended to overshadow the rather solid, if unspectacular, achievements of this period, like *Freud* (1962), *Fat City* (1972), *The Life and Times of Judge Roy Bean* (1972), *The Man Who Would Be King* (1975), and the quirky but interesting *Wise Blood* (1979).

To be consistent with their own methodology, the auteur critics had to consider the works of a director as a totality. As they were carrying on this massive task, John Huston was producing some less than magnificent films. According to the auteur method, as it was employed at the time of its introduction into the English-speaking critical world, it is impossible to sift out the triumphs from the duds. When the corpus was taken as a whole, Huston was categorized as an inferior artist. In *Cahiers*, Jacques Rivette said quite simply in 1957: "Huston is finished."[10] Unfortunately, Huston's output in the next several years did little to change that opinion. When Andrew Sarris categorized American directors in 1968, John Huston fit into the list entitled "Less Than Meets the Eye." Sarris complains: "Even in his palmier days, Huston displayed his material without projecting his personality."[11] By this statement Sarris undermined the one criterion by which Huston might have claimed the title of auteur. According to Sarris' assessment, Huston may have been a dominant voice in every phase of production, but he did not put the stamp of his own personality on the films as a whole. He had the opportunity, but muffed it.

The criticism is well taken, even by John Huston. He did not aspire to be an auteur. He said quite bluntly: "I don't seek to interpret, to put my own stamp on the material. I try to be as faithful to the original material as I can."[12] Since Huston varied his techniques to fit his material, he lacked that consistent personal vision and visual style that became crucial to the auteurist critics, and through them to the various critical establishments now evaluating films. In an earlier age Agee found this variety of approach refreshing: "Each of Huston's pictures has a visual tone and style of its own."[13] Huston himself acknowledged his own visual eclecticism: "I never try to duplicate myself. One must avoid personal clichés."[14] Huston's flexibility, a virtue to one generation of critics, would become a liability for the next.

John Huston was a man of considerable literary ability and little formal education, and in his case the combination worked well. As a skillful writer, he was sensitive to the written word and able to understand what greater talents were trying to achieve with their material. He had little compulsion to impose his own idiosyncratic or quirky interpretations on the original he was adapting for the screen. Whether he recast the stories of Dashiell Hammett (*The Maltese Falcon*), Rudyard Kipling (*The Man Who Would Be King*), Malcolm Lowry (*Under the Volcano*), Stephen Crane (*The Red Badge of Courage*), Arthur Miller (*The Misfits*), Tennessee Williams (*The Night of the Iguana*), Herman Melville (*Moby Dick*) or James Joyce (*The Dead*), he saw his role as one of interpreter. As a literary man he treated his authors with respect and allowed them to speak for themselves, and with his painter's fine sense of design he selected the visual style that offered the greatest clarity to their words. Huston once said: "If there's a pattern to my work, it's that I haven't made any two pictures alike. I get bored too quickly."[15] The premise is reasonable, but it runs counter to the premises of the most influential school of critics of this generation.

Strictly speaking, then, John Huston does not rank very high on the lists of auteurs, yet the range of his productivity over the half century he was involved in the industry as writer, director, producer and actor raises him to a position of eminence on his own terms. Several directors have made as many poor works as Huston, but few have created as many films of excellence. If he does not merit the title of auteur, then some other title should be awarded: technician, entertainer, humanist, director, writer, artist—or all of the above. Yes, all of the above.

The Genre: The Detective Story

The primal detective is God, and one of the earliest detective stories appears in the third chapter of Genesis. Adam and Eve have committed a crime, secretly. God, walking through the garden in the cool of the evening, notices something suspicious in their behavior. Adam and Eve have sewn fig leaves together to hide their nakedness (3:8). Alert to the fact that something is amiss, he begins to question them about their new clothes and soon makes the deduction that they have eaten the forbidden fruit (3:11). During his investigation, God forces them to confess their crimes, but the two culprits try to plea-bargain by betraying an accomplice. Adam: "She gave me the fruit, and I ate" (3:12). Eve: "The serpent beguiled me, and I ate" (3:13). The moral code that has been violated is more important than personal relationships. Even though God feels great affection for them, they have broken the law and must be punished for their crimes. Justice is swift and irrevocable for all three perpetrators (3:14–19).

The individual literary character representing God is a prototype of the classical detective, and his quarry are characters out of a hard-boiled detective story. Together they set the patterns of the two major types of detective stories, as they will appear in pulp fiction and movies two and a half millennia after the Deuteronomic historians of Josiah's reign were polishing their jots and tittles in the Genesis narrative.

The classic detective, the descendant of God, would appear in American literature in the tales of ratiocination of Edgar Allan Poe (1809–1849) in the 1840s. In stories such as "The Murders in the Rue Morgue" and "The Purloined Letter," the classic detective Dupin is an aristocrat who remains happily removed from the sordid material he is investigating.[16] He keeps a god-like distance from criminal and victim alike. He can retreat into his comfortable rooms to contemplate the evidence. He is a man of extraordinary intellectual gifts, whose power of deduction inevitably leads him to a solution of the crime. His literary and cinematic descendant is Sherlock Holmes, the ever popular creation of Arthur Conan Doyle (1859–1930).[17] Mr. Moto, Charlie Chan, the Thin Man and Philo Vance are other renditions of the classic detective who appeared in the films of the 1930s. As Holmes applied his powers of deduction to the case, he proclaimed: "Elementary, my dear Watson," as though all problems could be solved by the superior intellect. The other classic detectives had their own versions of "Aha!"

The world of the classic detective is a rational one; it yields its mysteries to science and logic. The moral horizon is clear. An unambiguous crime has been committed, and the morally and intellectually superior individual enters the scene from on high, methodically sifts through the evidence, finds the crucial clue, uncovers a motive through superior knowledge of human nature, and swiftly and surely brings the culprits to justice. Once the crime is solved, he withdraws to his comfortable lodgings, a haven, or heaven, safely removed from the criminal element, where he remains until the authorities are once more baffled by an unsolvable crime. He does not socialize with low life.

So, to continue the anthropomorphic portrait of God created by the authors of Genesis, after disposing of Adam, Eve, and the serpent, God withdraws to his heaven, only to repeat his unfailing technique of interrogation and deduction in the next chapter, when Abel suddenly disappears and Cain tries to bluff his way through the murder: "Am I my brother's keeper?" (4:9). In the age of Noah he will perceive that the entire world is corrupt and order a cleansing rainstorm (6:5–7). At each instance of detective work, God enters the case from the outside, after the crime has been committed by inferior mortals. When he has convicted the malefactors, he leaves. Under no circumstance do the Genesis authors imply that God has been morally compromised through his involvement in the case. Quite the opposite is true. He lives in a world apart from the evil generated by his human offspring. God's moral stature gives him the power to detect evil and punish it, without being involved or tainted. That is the point of the stories.

Although God is the morally superior classic detective, Adam, Eve, and the serpent could be the villains in a hard-boiled detective drama. The presence of the serpent brings evil incarnate into paradise. Eden is a world with a shifting moral horizon. Good and evil co-exist, and evil has the power to insinuate its presence everywhere, so much so that its influence seems inescapable. Greed for power and knowledge (wealth hadn't yet been invented) already gnaws at the vitals of the first humans. They need only the slightest prompting from the evil one to commit their crime. Adam and Eve do not commit a crime of violence or passion, nor one fired by desperation. Living in quite comfortable affluent circumstances, they reach a calm, cool decision based on a desire for more. They are simply greedy.

In such a murky moral atmosphere, the actual crime is far more complicated than a simple jewel theft or murder. The crime is not a single neat act, but rather it arises from the web of interactions among the three perpetrators. Who then is really guilty? The serpent does not actually eat the fruit himself; he merely plants the idea in the others. Logically he could plead not guilty, since he only discussed the possibility with Eve and had nothing to do with the actual crime. For her part, Eve could claim that she was merely deceived by the serpent, and Adam that he merely wanted to keep peace in the family

by performing the morally neutral act of eating the food his wife set
before him. Where is the guilt for any of them? The three acting
together, however, violated the one essential moral code in the He-
brew canon by challenging God's dominion over the earth. Even
worse, when the three are confronted with their crime, they are willing to sell the others out with plausible, if self-serving, explanations.
The fact that a crime has been committed is clear enough, but trying
to discover exactly what it is and who is responsible is much more
difficult. Loose ends may remain, and that is a key characteristic of
the crime confronted by the hard-boiled detective.

In clear distinction from the classic detective and God, the hard-
boiled detective wades through a world of Edenic, or even more of
Watergate, complexity, and his boots often appear muddy. He knows
only that someone is lying, someone else has committed a misde-
meanor, and a third person would profit by another's downfall, but
because of the convoluted human dynamics at work, logic and science
can never completely untangle the web. He is not above bending the
law to find the answers, but he discovers that some mysteries do not
yield to a neat resolution.

The hard-boiled detective cannot approach this kind of world
from a safe refuge of wealth and respectability. He lives cheek by fang
with the criminals he hunts. He knows the bookies and the fences by
name. He is usually socially inferior to his clients. His office is seedy,
not elegant, and he drinks bourbon from a water glass rather than
brandy warmed in a snifter. He eats alone at lunch counters and
neighborhood bars, and unless he is meeting a beautiful, wealthy
client, he never sees linen tablecloths and polished silver. His felt hat
is shapeless, his suit is rumpled, and the tabs of his collar often pop out
over his lapels. His face, with its shadow of a beard, shows experience
rather than beauty. He is middle-aged. He often loses shootouts and
fistfights, but when he wins, it is through guile rather than athletic
ability. He sleeps too little, and even by the standards of the 1940s he
smokes too much.

The grubby appearance of his office, shared with a faithful and
efficient secretary, is as dark and ominous as the sordid outside world.
It functions as his refuge, a place of moral calculation and tranquility,
in the midst of an ethical whirlpool that threatens to burst through the
door with its frosted glass panel and suck him into the vortex. Here,
with his feet on the desk and his bottle in the bottom drawer, he is at
rest, a warrior waiting for the next summons to battle. The hard-
boiled detective does not have access to the officers' quarters enjoyed by the classic detective, but he merely crawls into a muddy

foxhole on a quiet sector of the front. Since he lives alone, his apartment is little more than a furnished room. It lacks a woman's touch. Its decor is marked by dark furniture and overflowing ashtrays.

This shadowy universe, created from late-Depression cynicism and pre-war nihilism, gave rise to a style of film-making that would dominate Hollywood from the late 1930s to the mid-1950s: the film noir. The term is attributed to the critic Nino Frank, who in 1946 borrowed the concept from the "Série Noire" books authored by Marcel Duhamel.[18] The term is an umbrella used to describe a visual style and thematic consistency that is generally believed to have begun with *The Maltese Falcon* and to have ended with *Touch of Evil* (Welles, 1958).[19] The French were quick to observe a kind of cynicism that had crept into American films in the late 1930s after the pro-American cheerleading films of the early years of the New Deal. In these new "black films," the margins separating good and evil become blurred, and the institutions of society are no longer capable of protecting citizens from criminal syndicates. That task falls to the lone detective, who years earlier gave up in disgust a career with the police or the insurance company to go out on his own. He understands the corruption of the institutions and the malice of the criminal. He has one foot in each camp, and thus stands as mediator between them.

In this role as mediator, the hard-boiled detective is a cousin of the Western hero.[20] Both are loners who know the ways of the gunman and surpass the villain in the skills of survival. The Western hero opens up the frontier by extending the rule of law; the hard-boiled detective fights a delaying action. Law has been established and the city has been founded, but civilization has grown sour. It is no longer capable of providing order for its citizens. On the contrary, the very institutions that the Western hero fought to establish have been taken over by the criminal. The hard-boiled detective fights back. He has no hope of reestablishing a pristine rule of order through a neat confrontation, like, for example, a shootout on the main street. He can only hope to thwart one criminal for one client at a time. He is paid for his services, the individual criminal goes to jail, but the city remains as corrupt as ever. While the Western hero as a loner struggles to establish civilization, the hard-boiled detective strives to carve out a solitary niche of personal morality for himself in a society that has already been established but has grown corrupt through its own fatigue.

The cynical themes of film noir grew out of the cultural climate, which was dominated by pessimism of the late Depression and the European war. This combination of historical factors led to the belief that human efforts were inadequate in shaping human destiny. The visual style, however, evolved from the artistic community gathered in Hollywood. The immediate progenitor is German Expressionism, an evolution that should not be at all surprising because of the great influx of talent fleeing from Nazi Germany and seeking political and artistic refuge in Hollywood.

German Expressionism was one of the major artistic high points of film art in the 1920s. As early as *The Cabinet of Dr. Caligari* (Robert Wiene, 1919), German film-makers began to recreate the dark fantasies of the Expressionist painters and graphic artists.[21] The films feature bleak contrasts between black and white as opposed to gray tones, a preference for sharp, oblique angles, shadows, mirrors, uneven horizons and a great deal of smoke and fog. Since the films of this period made no pretense at reality, but were more directed at a reproduction of the interior world of dreams, the effect was produced through elaborately painted sets and multi-leveled stages, with platforms placed at odd angles from the horizon. Costumes and props were grotesque, to reflect the subjective state of mind of the characters rather than to represent reality. When, for example, Dr. Caligari visits a local bureaucrat to obtain a legal document, the clerk is perched on a towering stool from which he can glare down at the poor victim of his authority. The shot represents Caligari's subjective sense of intimidation rather than an objective re-creation of a town clerk's office.

Expressionism moved into Hollywood with the emigrés, but in its new homeland the surrealistic style of the Europeans blended with American realism, especially as it was represented in the gangster films.[22] The slanted angles and dark shadows were no longer abstractly painted sets, but naturalistic settings, carefully lighted to produce the proper lines. Instead of a canvas backdrop with black painted shadows, the Hollywood designers shot spotlights through fire escapes and alleys in such a way that the shadows fell alike upon the wall of a dingy bedroom and on the face of a detective and his suspect. While German Expressionism reduced the interior landscape of dreams and fears to a visual representation, the American Expressionists blended dreams and reality, endowing mundane realities with an air of the sinister. As the country hovered on the edge of another European war, the world was, in fact, a sinister place.

From its inchoate form in *The Maltese Falcon* to a more developed visual style in *Citizen Kane*, both films that were directorial debuts by two visually sensitive yet thoroughly inexperienced directors, the film noir style appears even in a screwball comedy like *His*

Girl Friday (Hawks, 1940). The style favors night-time scenes and darkened rooms, oblique shadows and smoke or fog. Thematically the characters have some mark upon them from the past and little hope for improving their lot in the future. They go through the motions of looking for a better life, but a better life is not to be had, and they know it. In their quest, the narration keeps folding back upon itself, moving from straight chronological order to flashback or reminiscence to fill in the gaps left from the past and show why possibilities for the future are limited.[23]

Through its short but productive lifetime, the film noir passed through three distinctive phases.[24] Beginning with *The Maltese Falcon* and continuing through the war, the early phase of the film noir provides a showcase for the gray age of the seedy detective facing sinister and greedy criminals. The criminals concoct schemes to get rich quick, and the detectives, working alone by night, thwart their ambitions. The detectives are not custodians of public morality, since often they have to work without or against the police, but rather their own personal code is threatened. Criminal greed offends them. Dialogue carries the story, and action is kept to a minimum. Car chases, fistfights and shootouts are rare. Conversations about clues and motivations are commonplace.

After the war, the film noir entered its second phase, in which the criminals run wild through the city streets, and the legal authorities are incapable of controlling them through orthodox methods. Occasionally the police and politicians are involved in the crime syndicate themselves. Crime is not confined to a few greedy operators, but is a part of the social fabric, and only the detective, preserving a code of personal morality from an earlier age, is able to stop them. A fascination with "location" shooting gave these films a documentary look, as though revealing the evil that actually exists in the city streets.

The third phase, which began in the 1950s and lasted through *Touch of Evil*, moved from the dark side of society into the twisted interior world of the individual criminal. The themes dealt with psychosis and suicide. Crime and evil are not regarded as systemic, but as aberrations in the warped mind of an individual. Sometimes a crime was not even necessary, as in *Sunset Boulevard* (Billy Wilder, 1950), in which madness is the subject of the film. The fantasies of an aging actress (Gloria Swanson) rather than a murder are enough to expose the dark side of life.

After a short lifespan, generously calculated at two decades, the film noir passed out of vogue. By the early 1950s Hollywood had already been stunned by television's inroads into its audience. To lure audiences away from their tiny black-and-white screens, the motion picture industry tried to deliver spectacle. Hollywood turned to color and the wide screen. Sam Spade's claustrophobic office could not produce the same effect in Vista Vision, nor would his wrinkled gray suits make much of an impression in lurid Technicolor.

During the same period the distribution system became streamlined to meet new audience patterns. People no longer went "to the movies" a couple of times a week just to get out of the house. Instead they stayed home and watched television. The neighborhood houses that specialized in continuous showings of double features, with a change in program twice a week, gradually disappeared. Interest in the low-budget, black-and-white detective film, intended to be shown as a second feature, waned rapidly. The unending quest for the one blockbuster that would put the studio in the black for the year began, and continues to haunt Hollywood to this day.

The changing social climate in the United States is another factor that is believed to have contributed to the demise of the hard-boiled detective and his film noir world.[25] The earliest hard-boiled detectives are direct descendants of the gangsters. They are individualists who survive in the dark world of the city by bringing to justice other individualists who happen to disregard the moral code. After the war evil is present everywhere: the memory of Nazi spies prowling the streets gave way to the Red Menace. Everyone, even police and politicians, could be suspect. In this middle phase the hard-boiled detective embodies traditional American values, like integrity and loyalty, and he has the courage to stand up as an individual to cut through the webs of conspiracy around him.

During the Eisenhower years the third era of the detective film showed criminals as simply deranged aberrations in the American way of life. As the fury of the McCarthy years abated, the nation settled into an era of good feeling, and it was unfashionable to explore any flaws in the American social fabric. Thus began the age of the sunny MGM musical comedy. The role of the solitary figure restoring order to a troubled world passed over to the Western hero, who could be photographed against a Technicolor sunset on a wide-screen desert, and whose historical distance from the present masked any suspicion that he, and his creators, were exploring contemporary American social and political questions. In the 1950s it was the detective who rode off into the twilight, while the Westerner took over the town.

The Western not only restored a classic notion of male hero, but it also reestablished the position of woman on her pedestal as domesticator. The women who populate hard-boiled detective films never saw a pedestal, or even a stepstool. They are dangerous. A frontier woman, unless she works in a saloon, represents all the domestic American virtues that a hero will fight to establish and maintain. She is home, family, decency, and stability—all virtues extolled in the America of President Eisenhower and Norman Rockwell. A city woman in a detective film, by contrast, threatens to undermine the last remaining shreds of morality left on the urban landscape. Her charms distract the hard-boiled detective from his mission to reestablish order in the chaos of city life. He may fall in love with her and be tempted, at least for an instant, to cover up her crimes when he discovers that she is involved in the crime herself. More often than not, she is not a passive spectator as the men of the mob execute the crime, but she is a principal agent. She hatches the plot and pulls the trigger.

The "femme noir," as these shady characters in film noir are often called, is a daughter of the gangsters' molls in an earlier generation of films.[26] As second generation, she has all the advantages of her mother's ill-gotten wealth. Her speech is refined, and she mingles easily with socialites and heiresses, as though they had all attended the same finishing school. The moll knew her place as an ornament of the gangster. The femme noir reflects the changing roles of women. She is independent, tough and threatening. Her status no doubt reflects America's uneasy feelings about women entering the workplace and assuming new roles, especially during the war. Rosie the Riveter was a revolutionary figure, and thus an aunt by marriage to the femme noir. Woman, outside her traditional role, is dangerous.

Even if the mysterious woman of suspicion is eventually cleared of wrongdoing, the detective cannot maintain a love interest, since she challenges his way of life. He cannot maintain a lasting relationship. He must return to his office and his bourbon bottle to share the story with his faithful secretary, whose platonic, even maternal, concern for her boss restores working women to their traditional nonthreatening role as helpmate. As such the secretary offers invaluable support, but her role in solving the crime is at best marginal.

In recent years the genre of the hard-boiled detective and the film noir style have faded from the screen, with a few exceptions. *Chinatown* (Roman Polanski, 1974) recaptured the spark of Raymond Chandler, and with Jack Nicholson, Faye Dunaway and John Huston in starring roles, its success was guaranteed. *Dead Men Don't Wear Plaid* (Carl Reiner, 1982) featured comedian Steve Martin as the private detective. The film was a splendid spoof of both the genre and the style, a sure sign that both could no longer be taken seriously by anyone other than critics and film historians.

Dirty Harry (Don Siegel, 1971) and its sequels represent another type of parody. Harry Callahan, the title character played by Clint Eastwood, remains a member of the San Francisco police department. He is a loner only inasmuch as he makes his own rules. In this he is not only a loner, but a borderline psychopath, not far removed in psychiatric profile from the murderers he tracks down. He has become infected with the evil of his environment to a degree that would be impossible for the hard-boiled detective. He enjoys the violence, while a hard-boiled detective would try to avoid it. Harry's .07 Magnum represents an extension of his character every bit as much as Scarface's tommy gun did for him. His tag line, "Make my day," shows that he enjoys his work in a way that would be impossible for a hard-boiled detective.

The present age holds much in common with the age of the hard-boiled detective. After Watergate, Vietnam and an endless series of revelations about corruption in Washington, on Wall Street, and even on athletic fields, Americans today have every reason to be as cynical as Americans of the Depression and post-war period. With the bomb in our arsenals and the massive destabilization brought on by the emergence of the third world, we live in a similar state of self-doubt. The insoluble problems brought on by drugs, AIDS and homelessness give credence to despair that the institutions of society can do anything to alleviate human misery, and the changing role of women, for all its undoubted benefits, has shaken many American social and moral assumptions. The age seems to call for a new generation of hard-boiled detectives to lead us through our new crises with a bit of the old time morality intact. None is in the wings. Instead we have created *Rambo, The Terminator* and *Dirty Harry*. For us this is the way the world of moral problems ends: not with a solution, but with a bang—a very loud bang.

The Plot: *The Maltese Falcon*

After the titles, a scroll appears: "In 1539, the Knights Templar of Malta paid a tribute to Charles V of Spain by sending him a golden falcon encrusted from beak to claw with the rarest jewels—pirates seized the galley carrying the priceless token, and the fate of the Maltese Falcon remains a mystery to this day."

The last printed title identifies the locale, "San Francisco," and it is followed by shots of the waterfront and the Bay Bridge, which is reprised through an office window, with the sign "Spade and Archer." The camera tilts down to Sam Spade (Humphrey Bogart) at his desk, rolling his own cigarette, cowboy-style. His secretary, Effie Perine (Lee Patrick), enters and tells him that a Miss Wonderly wants to see him, and he will want to see her, because "She's a knockout."

Miss Wonderly (Mary Astor) enters, wearing a fox stole, and says she is visiting from New York and got Spade's name from the hotel. He invites her to tell her story. She is looking for her sister Corinne, who may have come to San Francisco with a man named Floyd Thursby. She claims that their parents have been away, but when they return they will want to kill Thursby. She wants to find them first. She received a letter from Corinne, but it contained little information. She answered the letter, via general delivery, saying that she would come to San Francisco to meet her. She stayed in the St. Mark's Hotel for three days, but Corinne never came. She wrote another letter via general delivery, and waited at the post office for her to come to the letter box. Thursby came instead, and she arranged a meeting at her hotel, hoping that Corinne would come with him.

At this point in the story, Miles Archer (Jerome Cowan), Spade's partner, enters the office. Spade repeats the story for Archer, and they plan to intercept Thursby, with or without Corinne, and get her to return home. Miss Wonderly says she is afraid of what Thursby might do. Marriage is out of the question, since Thursby is married and has three children. With a flirtatious look, Archer says he will stake out the hotel lobby himself. She places a hundred dollar bill on the desk, and Spade looks at her. She puts down a second bill, and Spade picks them up and shows her to the door. Archer comments that he spoke first for her, and Spade compliments him for having brains. The scene closes as the camera picks up "Spade and Archer" reflected from the windows in oblique shadows across the floor.

Archer walks through the night, turns and faces a revolver. One shot is fired point blank into his chest, and he rolls down an embankment, quite dead.

A phone rings in Spade's apartment. The police tell him that Archer is dead. Spade calls Effie to tell her to break the news to Iva (Gladys George), Archer's wife. Spade visits the scene of the crime with Detective Sergeant Tom Polhaus (Ward Bond), who reviews the evidence with him. Polhaus asks about Archer's case, and Spade reveals the name Thursby, but refuses to divulge anything more. He doesn't want to check the body because he says he has to go to tell Iva about Archer's death.

Spade calls Miss Wonderly and learns that she has checked out of the hotel. He returns to his apartment, and Polhaus and Lieutenant Dundy (Barton MacLane) appear. They called Spade's office, and Effie told them that she, not Spade, had contacted Iva. The police reveal that Thursby has been killed at his hotel, and Spade, who has been caught in the lie about going to Iva and will not discuss the case with them, is considered a suspect. The police and Spade alike assume that Thursby killed Archer because Archer was following him and the point is underlined by a newspaper headline linking the killings. Now they have to find out who killed Thursby, and why.

The next morning, when Sam returns to his office, Iva is waiting for him. They embrace more in romance than in consolation, and Iva asks Spade if he killed her husband so that they could finally be married. Effie knows of their romantic involvement, and when Iva leaves, she tells Sam that Iva had returned to her apartment only a few minutes before Effie arrived at three in the morning with the news of Archer's death. She thinks Iva might have killed him. Spade dismisses the idea, and Effie tells him he is too slick for his own good. Their conversation is interrupted by a call from Miss Wonderly, who is now registered in another hotel under the name of Miss Le Blanc. As Spade leaves, he tells Effie to have Archer's desk moved out and his name removed from the signs on the doors and windows.

At her apartment, Miss Wonderly (a.k.a. Le Blanc) reveals that her real name is Brigid O'Shaughnessy and that her story was a lie. Spade says he knew she was lying because she willingly paid him too much. She wants to be protected from the police, and he insists on knowing the real story. She pleads for help, and he refuses until he knows what is happening. She tells him that she is convinced Thursby killed Archer with the extra revolver he carried in his coat pocket. She reveals that she met Thursby in Hong Kong and wanted to track him down in San Francisco. He is not satisfied and begins to walk out, and she says she'll take her chances alone. He relents, but insists on getting five hundred dollars from her; she gives four hundred dollars, and he demands the balance. When she agrees to pawn her furs to raise enough money to live on, he returns one hundred dollars to her.

Spade returns to his office as the painter is finishing the new sign for the door: "Samuel Spade" He calls to warn his lawyer that there may be trouble, and as he is rolling a cigarette, Effie enters to announce Joel Cairo (Peter Lorre), who introduces the Maltese falcon into the case. He explains its worth and offers Spade five thousand dollars, no questions asked, if he can help recover it. Cairo draws a gun and intends to search the office, but Spade disarms him and knocks him unconscious. Spade searches his pockets and discovers several passports and a theater ticket. Cairo wakes up and says he is surprised to find that the falcon is not in the office. He enlists Spade to help, offering a hundred dollars, but Spade demands two hundred. When Spade returns the gun, Cairo holds it on Spade and says he will resume his search. Spade laughs at him.

On the street, on the way to the theater performance noted on Cairo's ticket, Spade realizes that he is being followed by Wilmer (Elisha Cook Jr.), and he easily loses him. Spade returns to Brigid's apartment. He mentions Joel Cairo, and she appears nervous. Spade complains that she has still not given him enough information. She asks for trust, and he kisses her warmly. They arrange to meet Cairo at Spade's apartment after the performance. As they enter Spade's building together, Iva Archer sees them from her parked car, where she has been waiting for Spade. Iva is visibly upset.

Spade and Brigid enter the apartment, and he notices Wilmer watching outside. Cairo enters, and he and Brigid negotiate for the falcon. She does not have it, but can get it within the week, and she claims she is willing to let it go for five thousand dollars after what happened to Thursby. She blames "the Fat Man" for the murder, and Cairo wants to know his whereabouts. Brigid alludes to Cairo's adventure in Istanbul; they trade accusations and she slaps him. He pulls a gun and Spade disarms him, as Polhaus and Dundy ring the doorbell. Spade will not let them in. They confront Spade with his involvement with Iva, who has apparently gone to them with the information out of jealousy. This gives Spade a motive for killing Archer. They are about to leave when they hear a scuffle inside. Brigid and Cairo have traded blows, and Cairo's forehead is cut. They concoct various stories to confuse the police, and in exasperation Dundy punches Spade. Spade throws them out. Cairo leaves.

Alone together, Spade insists on getting the story from Brigid. She spins a yarn about being paid to help acquire the falcon and about learning that Cairo intended to betray her, so she and Thursby hatched a plot to cut out Cairo. Spade does not believe her, and she admits she is a liar. He is about to kiss her when he notices that Wilmer is still waiting outside. A fade suggests that they remain together in Spade's apartment for the night.

The next morning Spade goes to Cairo's hotel and confronts Wilmer in the lobby. Cairo returns to the hotel, claiming that he has

spent the night under interrogation by the police. Cairo is hostile to
Spade, but Spade tells him to play along so that they can locate the
falcon through Brigid.

Spade returns to his office. Effie tells him that "she"—meaning
Iva, as it turns out—has been calling all morning and a Mr. Gutman
has called as well. Brigid is waiting in the inner office. Brigid says that
her apartment has been searched. Spade arranges for her to spend a
few days at Effie's apartment. Iva enters and tells Spade that she
called the police, hoping to get some information about Archer's
murder. She does not mention that she saw Spade enter the apartment with Brigid. Relying on Effie's observations, Spade tells Iva he
knows she is lying about being home all night the day Archer was
killed. He sends her home. Gutman calls and arranges a meeting
with Spade.

Wilmer answers the door to Gutman's apartment and withdraws.
Kasper Gutman (Sydney Greenstreet) tries to exchange information
with Spade, who tells him Cairo has offered ten thousand dollars for
its recovery. Gutman laughs at the price. Neither man will yield,
thinking the other knows where it is. Spade leaves in a fury, and as he
boards one elevator, Cairo exits the other. Spade is called before the
district attorney, and argues that he will not cooperate because the
police have tried to involve him in two murders and the only chance
he has to clear his name is to solve the crimes on his own. He
storms out.

Wilmer intercepts Spade on the street and leads him to Gutman
at gunpoint. In the hallway of the building, Spade disarms Wilmer and
continues on to Gutman, handing him both of Wilmer's guns. Gutman
feigns amusement and tells Spade the history of the falcon, which was
designed as tribute to Charles V of Spain in 1539 for the island of
Malta. The ship bringing the gift to Spain was captured by pirates and
the falcon vanished. In 1713 the falcon appeared in Sicily, and in
1840 in Paris it acquired a coat of black enamel to disguise its value.
When a shrewd dealer rediscovered the falcon in Istanbul in 1923,
Gutman tried on several occasions to acquire it without revealing its
true value. He believes that his agents, led by the late Floyd Thursby
and Brigid O'Shaughnessy, have it now, but he cannot get it for himself. As he tells this story, he keeps refilling Spade's glass with brandy.
Both believe that Brigid still has access to the falcon. Gutman offers
Spade twenty-five thousand dollars upon delivery, or a quarter of a
million, a quarter of its probable value, if Spade will wait until it is
sold, probably for one million dollars. Spade comments noncommit-
tally that it is a lot of money, but then he becomes groggy and realizes

that he has been drugged. Spade collapses, and Cairo appears with Wilmer from the back room. Wilmer kicks Spade in the head, and Gutman, Cairo and Wilmer then exit the apartment together, leaving Spade unconscious on the floor.

When Spade awakens, he calls Effie's home to speak to Brigid, only to find she has disappeared. He searches Gutman's apartment and discovers a circled notice in the newspaper that the "La Paloma" is arriving in port from Hong Kong that day. He rushes to the dock and finds the ship in flames. No one was injured, Spade is told, and no one remains aboard.

Back in his office, Effie is cleaning Spade's head wound, while Spade tells her the story. A stranger appears at the door, wounded and carrying a package wrapped in newspapers. He collapses and drops the bundle, which contains the falcon. The phone rings. Brigid is calling, but her message is interrupted by a scream. Spade tells Effie to call the police to report the killing, but not to mention the arrival of the falcon, which he takes with him. He identifies the dead man as Captain Jacoby, master of the "La Paloma."

He puts the package in a baggage check in the train station and mails the claim slip to a postal deposit box. Outside the station he finds a cab to take him to Brigid. The address is a vacant lot. He calls Effie and learns that Brigid has not contacted her. At his apartment building he finds Brigid waiting for him on the street, and when then they enter his rooms, Wilmer, Gutman and Cairo are waiting for them. They negotiate. Gutman gives Spade ten thousand dollars for his share. Spade demands more, but Gutman replies that Spade has produced nothing yet. Spade takes it and hands the envelope to Brigid. Spade tries to convince them to turn in Wilmer for the murders of Thursby and Jacoby, since the district attorney would like to put a neat end to the series of crimes. Without a clean conviction, Spade says he fears that he will remain a suspect himself. If the police try to put all the pieces together, they would end up with a tangle and risk losing any conviction. Wilmer, he concludes, could take the fall for two murders, Thursby and Jacoby, and take police pressure off the rest of them. Wilmer is enraged and threatens to kill Spade right there. For a moment they discuss handing over Cairo, but when Wilmer threatens Spade, Spade disarms him again and knocks him unconscious, and they agree to have Wilmer take the blame for all of them.

Spade insists on an explanation. Gutman says they had Wilmer kill Thursby to intimidate Brigid into cooperation. They recognized Jacoby's name and ship when they saw the notice of arrival in the newspaper, and they went to the dock to meet him. Brigid was there with him, and they struck a deal for the falcon, but Brigid and Jacoby escaped with the prize. They tracked them down to Brigid's apartment, and as Jacoby was trying to flee down a fire escape, Wilmer shot him. They then "persuaded" Brigid to tell them Jacoby was headed to Spade's office, and further to call in the hope of getting Spade out of the office before Jacoby arrived. They were too late.

Apparently satisfied with the story, Spade agrees to cooperate. Gutman wants to hold the envelope with the ten thousand dollars until the falcon is delivered. He opens it and claims that Brigid has stolen one of the thousand dollar bills. Spade counters that Gutman himself has palmed the money, and Gutman is amused at Spade's shrewdness. He returns the full ten thousand dollars, which Spade pockets. Spade agrees to retrieve the falcon now that the post office is open. He calls Effie and tells her about the claim check. She brings the parcel to them and leaves.

They open the bundle, and Gutman tries to scrape off the enamel, only to discover that it is a lead replica of the original and is of no value whatever. They first turn to Brigid and accuse her of switching the statues; then Cairo accuses Gutman of bungling the job by tipping off the previous owner to the value of the authentic falcon by his eagerness to buy it. Cairo bursts into tears. Gutman recovers and plans to return to Istanbul to continue his quest. Cairo will join him, but Wilmer has escaped. Gutman draws his gun on Spade and demands his ten thousand dollars back, but Spade keeps a thousand dollars for time and expenses. Cairo and Gutman leave.

Spade turns to Brigid, and his questions force her to explain that she killed Archer herself in hopes of pinning the crime on Thursby. Spade tells her that he will turn her in. She claims she always loved him, but Spade is not persuaded. He explains his code of loyalty, even to a man he despised. He explains that it is good for his business to pretend to play along with swindlers. Spade maintains that since she has never told the truth to him, he cannot trust her. If he let her go, she would hold his complicity in her crime over him to manipulate him. Since he knows about her murder, she might kill him someday to eliminate him as a witness. They kiss. Polhaus and Dundy enter, and Spade turns her over, along with the evidence he has gathered. They plan to meet at City Hall. Spade picks up the falcon and explains to Polhaus: "It's the stuff that dreams are made of." As he leaves the office, the elevator door closes in front of Brigid's face, like the sliding bars of a prison door. Spade descends down a stairwell surrounded by his own bars fashioned by the banisters.

COMMENTARY

The Maltese Falcon is not an easy film to follow, and that is its charm and its fascination. The script is rigorous in following the story from Spade's perspective and never reveals more than he knows, which at times is very confusing. Spade is a shrewd judge of human nature, it is true, but his is not an overpowering intellect. He struggles to put the pieces together, and often they do not fit. Viewers share his sense of futility and frustration.

The first "crime" that brings Spade into the case is Thursby's adulterous elopement with Corinne, an event that never happened to a person who does not exist. Archer's murder raises the stakes quite a bit, but it is almost forgotten in the quest for the falcon, and it is the last crime solved. Floyd Thursby is a catalyst for the action, but he never appears in the film. He seems to hold the key to Archer's murder, Brigid's involvement, and the falcon, but like Spade we never learn anything about him. When his murder is solved, it is not through Spade's brilliant deduction, but through Gutman's off-hand remark that he had Wilmer shoot him to scare Brigid into cooperation. At the same time, Gutman explains the murder of Captain Jacoby, a character who appears near the climax of the film and has no lines, yet is the actual possessor of the falcon. Only after he has been told about Brigid's part in the plan does Spade conclude that Brigid actually murdered Archer herself in hopes of framing Thursby and thus becoming sole owner of the falcon.

Spade is not a classic detective, so his quite ordinary powers of deduction come as no surprise. But the intractability of the plot reflects more on Spade's world than on Spade himself. No one can be trusted, and everyone lies. Iva Archer is unfaithful to Miles, but Miles appears ready to return the favor to Iva once Miss Wonderly arrives in his office. Iva is having an affair with Spade and wants to divorce Miles to marry him, but she is willing to turn Spade over to the police as a suspect in her husband's murder when she finds him and Brigid entering his apartment together. For his part, Spade is capable of betraying his own partner by consorting with his wife, and then of quickly betraying her by transferring his affections to Brigid, simply because she is "a knockout," even though he knows she has been lying to him at every point in their relationship.

Neither the police nor any other institution of society is able to impose any order on this chaotic world. In fact, they pose as much a threat to Spade as to the criminals. They uncover none of the evidence themselves and believe Iva when she implicates Sam, even though she is obviously motivated by jealousy. Lieutenant Dundy strikes Spade, just as though he were conducting a "third degree" interrogation of a criminal. Spade is friendly with the slow-witted Polhaus, and seems to have collaborated with him in the past. He is so familiar with police procedures and the workings of the district attorney's office that he might have been on the force himself once upon a time. Again, he knows the detective in Cairo's hotel, and has no problem in getting him to throw out Wilmer. Possibly they were on the force together in the old days. Clearly, Spade and the police force have parted company, and in his present crisis he knows that he cannot trust them with the evidence he has gathered. Ever the loner in this convoluted world, he feels he must act alone to keep himself out of jail.

The minor characters who prowl through this world are equally mysterious. Joel Cairo, with gardenia scent on his calling card, acts out the role of the stereotypical homosexual. He whines when he is cornered and weeps openly in frustration when he discovers that the falcon is a fake. He speaks with an odd but unidentifiable European accent, even though his name suggests the mysterious Middle East. Kasper Gutman has a German name but an obvious English accent. His bloated body is as much a parody of humanity as Cairo's effeminate speech and gestures. Both have wandered through the world, from Istanbul, where the falcon was thought to be in the possession of a Russian general, to Hong Kong, where Brigid and Thursby seize control of it, to San Francisco, in the search of a statuette that traveled from Malta to Sicily to France, where it continued its mysterious journeys in disguise, under a coat of black enamel. Neither man reveals anything of his past. Spade, like the rest of us, has difficulty figuring out who these men are, where they come from and what they really want. Gutman has to explain this worldwide puzzle to him, bit by bit.

Wilmer, on the other hand, is more Spade's alter ego. He poses no threat and no mystery for Spade. They inhabit the same planet, even though they are currently working in opposite hemispheres. Wilmer is the tough guy that Spade might have been in his younger days. Spade always spots Wilmer when he is trying to follow him, and he has no difficulty eluding him. When Wilmer draws a gun, Spade disarms him as easily as he does Joel Cairo. When Spade strikes a bargain with Gutman and Cairo, he proposes offering Wilmer to the police to clear the rest of them. Wilmer can offer no response. He is a dull-witted uncomplicated character, as American as the movie gangsters he tries to imitate. Wilmer actually committed the murders

Spade accuses him of, for the simplest of motives: Gutman told him to do it. At the end, Spade has Wilmer arrested with a simple phone call to Tom Polhaus, an equally limited man, who happens to be a police detective rather than a thug.

The character of Sam Spade orbits this planet of international intrigue like an eccentric satellite. His treatment of Miles and Iva reveals an arrested moral development. Spade is obviously less concerned with being fair to them than with getting what he wants for himself. When Brigid walks in the front door, Spade pushes Iva out the back. Effie discovers through a bit of shrewd detective work, by feeling the warmth in Iva's clothes, that she had just returned to her home minutes before Effie arrived with the news of Miles' death. Where had she been? The answer is never given directly, but it is possible that she had been at Spade's apartment, since they both knew that Miles would be away following Miss Wonderly. Almost immediately after she left his apartment, word of Miles' death comes through to Spade, and Iva arrives home only minutes before the ever efficient Effie arrives with the news. The theory is supportable, but never substantiated in the script. Iva's mysterious whereabouts on the night of the murder remain a loose end to the tangled mystery, but her relationship with Spade can lead to speculation of a most unsavory sort.

In a macabre gesture of contempt for the dead, Spade has Archer's name removed from the office only one day after the partner was killed while working on a case for the firm. Spade enjoys being a loner. Furthermore, Spade exploits Effie, the only person who is devoted to him, and he is a fraud about it. He continually addresses her with names of endearment, like "Precious," while using her shamelessly. Without any concern for her safety, he tells her to take Brigid into her home when her life is threatened. He leaves her alone with the body of Jacoby while telling her to lie to the police, and finally he tells her to pick up the falcon at the depot and bring it alone to Gutman's apartment. With equally little concern for her feelings, he calls her in the middle of the night and instructs her to tell Iva about Archer's death. Effie is unfailingly loyal to him, but he sees no reason to return her devotion. After all, he pays her, doesn't he?

Spade's relationship to Effie is clear and neat, if distasteful, but his dealings with Brigid fit into the complex, murky patterns of the other characters in the film. Miss Wonderly does provide a source of income for a detective agency that appears none too prosperous. If Spade knows she is lying from the start, as he claims, then he might feel that his initial ability to wangle the extra hundred dollars from

her might be parlayed into bigger payoffs later on. As their partnership develops, however, the lying continues, and Spade remains with
her, even though he cannot find out what she wants from him. He
claims, near the end of the film, that he feels a sense of obligation to
find his partner's murderer, but his affair with Iva makes suspect his
expression of devotion to Miles. Finally, he claims that he doesn't
want to be "played for a sap," which again could justify his remaining
with the case, even though he realizes that Brigid has been lying
to him.

Overlying all these possible motivations rests Spade's romantic
attraction to Brigid. Effie introduces her as "a knockout," as though
realizing that she is now effectively knocked out of Spade's life, at
least for a while. Miss Wonderly is not only a knockout (a word from
Spade's world) she is literally a "wonder." With her delicate bones
and refined manners, she represents everything that Spade (and Effie, for that matter) is not. She is an object of desire, not only for her
money and her status, but also for her person. Miles Archer is much
more obvious in his flirtatious reaction to her, and when she leaves
their office, Archer admits that Spade saw her first, but he boasts that
he had the good sense to speak up first by offering to take personal
charge of her case. Spade remarks that Archer has brains, but the
comment simmers with irony, since it was Spade who had just gotten
the extra hundred dollar bill from her merely by looking into her
eyes. By being more direct in expressing an interest in Miss Wonderly, Archer dies at her hand.

Even after Spade realizes that he is being used by Miss Wonderly, he never fails to answer her call of distress. When she is afraid
to return to her apartment, Spade takes her to his, and after getting
rid of Cairo and the police, while Wilmer waits outside, they apparently spend the rest of the night together. At this point it seems that
Spade has come close to the fulfillment of his quest for love and
respectability. Or is he just using her to solve the murder and the
mystery of the falcon? His motivations are never clear, probably not
even to himself, but in such a complex, morally convoluted world,
motivations are always mixed.

Brigid O'Shaughnessy, a true femme noire, is a character who
changes her personality as frequently as her name. Like a chameleon
in a box of Crayolas, she is in turn Miss Wonderly, a Wasp vision of
loveliness; Miss Le Blanc, a mysterious French woman, who is really a
"blank" to Spade, or a contrast of her blanc/white to his Spade/black;
and, finally, Brigid O'Shaughnessy, the Irish American girl who defies
all the ethnic stereotypes by her sophistication and relish for interna-

tional intrigue. Spade has no reason to believe that this name is any more authentic than the others. She uses her charms to get what she wants. Thursby succumbs and is murdered. Spade succumbs, too, but only for an instant. In the end he proves just as seductive as she, and she loses. She admits to being a liar, but demands that Spade continue to trust her even though she will not tell him the truth about the case. He admires her talent and comments, "You're good." He knows she is lying, but he continues to work on the case for her. She plays the helpless female, even though she is a killer. Spade sees through her little games, but it only makes him more cautious in dealing with her. It does not drive him away from her.

Greed motivates the other characters more unambiguously than it does Spade. They want the falcon and the wealth it will bring them. The statue becomes an obsession, and they are quite willing to kill for it. As the price spirals from the two hundred dollars that Cairo initially offers to Spade, to five thousand and ten thousand and finally to twenty-five thousand or even two hundred and fifty thousand, Spade becomes interested. In the final moments of the film he states that it is good for business to pretend to play along, but no one, not even Spade himself, can be certain that he would not have made a deal if he could have avoided being implicated in the murders. As the price rises, so does the willingness of the plotters to sell one another out. The final doublecross is their pact to hand Wilmer over to the police so that the rest of them can avoid prosecution. Spade takes the initiative in proposing the idea.

In Huston's world, however, a quest motivated by greed is doomed to disaster from the outset. After the doublecrosses, the arson of the "La Paloma" (which may be another example of Wilmer's ineptitude rather than a deliberate act), and murder, Gutman and Cairo find themselves outwitted by the Russian general in Istanbul who sent them scurrying off after a worthless forgery. Once Cairo dries his tears and Gutman ends his bluster, the two schemers plan to continue their fruitless search on the other side of the world. Their whole reason for living has become their quest, which in turn seems fated to failure. As they rush off, it seems all but certain that they will be no more successful this time than they have been in the past seventeen years since Gutman first decided he must follow the quest of his unholy grail. With a trenchancy rivaling Qoheleth in Ecclesiastes, Huston is using Gutman to point out the futility of human desires: "Vanity of vanities—all is vanity."

Brigid's quest is more complex than that of Gutman and Cairo. She wants the falcon, and has been willing to lie, murder and love to get it, yet in the end, when her treachery has been uncovered, she chooses not to leave for Istanbul with the others. Is it possible that she has transferred her goal, and now is more interested in Spade than in the falcon? Her motivation is as murky as his. If Spade, who represents for her some shred of human integrity in a tapestry of avarice and mendacity, has become her quest, then she is willing to sacrifice everything, including the falcon, to get him. Her sins, however, have made her quest impossible. Spade has endured all her deceit up to a point, perhaps because he is romantically attracted to her, but at the moment it appears they will both achieve their respective goals, each other, Spade's inner moral voice speaks out, and he turns her over to the police. He admits that he may "lose a few nights' sleep" over her, but, in true hard-boiled tradition, he adds that he'll "soon get over it."

In the end, the crime has been solved, but the solution is really immaterial to Spade. He is content to live and let live, as long as no one plays him "for a sap." The significant outcome of the story is that failure is universal. Archer wanted Brigid and is dead. Iva lost both her husband and Spade. Cairo and Gutman killed to get the falcon and failed once again. Wilmer tried to be a gangster, but Spade continually humiliates him and eventually turns him over to the police with a simple phone call. Brigid first tried to steal the falcon, and, failing that, seeks redemption through Spade, but he rejects her. And, finally, Spade himself—what does he want? In the end, only Brigid, but because of her crimes he cannot have her either. The authentic falcon, the ever elusive glittering prize that introduces greed and death with it wherever it goes, is still at large, bringing destruction to anyone who seeks it.

Throughout this odd quest for the falcon, chance governs the lives of Spade and his antagonists. Miss Wonderly claims she merely got Spade's name from her hotel. That chance recommendation put Spade in line to become murdered by Thursby, and just by chance, too, Archer interrupted their conversation and took the role upon himself. By luck he died and Spade lived. By a stupid blunder, Cairo circles the arrival time of the "La Paloma" in the newspaper, a mistake that allows Spade to track down the arrival of the falcon in San Francisco. The play of fate has its comic side, too. Just as Spade leaves Gutman, after their first meeting, he steps onto one elevator just as the door opens on the second and Joel Cairo steps out. Had Cairo's elevator arrived seconds earlier, Spade would have known earlier that Cairo and Gutman were working together.

This odd universe of elusive morality and convoluted motivation demands its own visual style, and the style that Huston, the former art student and painter, devised with his photographer Arthur Edeson captures the mood elegantly. Edeson, incidentally, provided the eerie effects for *Frankenstein* (James Whale, 1931) and would go on to create the atmosphere for *Casablanca* (Michael Curtiz, 1942). Critics may argue, as Thomas Schatz does, whether *The Maltese Falcon* is a true example of the film noir visual style.[27] The question is of more theoretical importance than would serve present purposes. At least this much is true: whether or not it can be called film noir itself, it is certain that *The Maltese Falcon* has the visual style that evolved over the next several years into unchallenged examples of the film noir style.

The film lacks the pure black-and-white contrasts that mark later examples of the type, and although most of the outdoor action takes place at night, the streets are dry and there is little fog or smoke, except for cigarettes. The use of shadow is important, especially for close-ups of Bogart, who blends in with his background and emerges into light with a frequency that reinforces his shadowy moral stature. Characteristically, Huston shoots all his actors at an angle rather than straight on, an effect that adds to the atmosphere of distrust. Light passing through windows or falling from street lights forms the oblique shadows of the German Expressionist style. The distorted shadow of "Spade and Archer," cast by the sunlight passing through the windows of their dingy office, reveals the twisted relationship of the two detectives and presages even more dire events to follow.

The sets are tight and confined, expressing the claustrophobic atmosphere of Spade's world, in which he is hemmed in by circumstances he cannot understand, let alone control. Often the angles formed by the seams of walls and ceilings are photographed in such a way that they intersect at odd angles. The entire set creates an atmosphere that is unsettling, which is an image of the unnerving world that Huston is creating. The other characters, for the most part, receive flat lighting, despite their shady dealings, a technique that the pure film noir will alter. Despite the setting in San Francisco, near the open spaces of the harbor, the sun never shines in the film. The sound stage sets, built to resemble exteriors, are dreary and flat. If then *The Maltese Falcon* lacks some of the characteristics of the later film noir, or even of *Citizen Kane*, released the same year, it certainly has enough to give serious critics reason to include it among examples of the type.

At the end of the film, Spade explains to Polhaus that the leaden bird he is carrying to City Hall for evidence is nothing but "the stuff that dreams are made of." The same could be said about *The Maltese Falcon*. The dream is not a happy one. The American dream of instant wealth has soured through the Depression, and the futility of human enterprise was never more apparent than when the Great Powers drifted toward a suicidal war. Huston's dream, on the edge of nightmare, would mark a new horizon in American film. Its cynicism bordered on despair, and the characters and the visual style gave a generation an image of its own moral quandaries.

NOTES

1. Stuart Kaminsky, *John Huston: Maker of Magic* (Boston: Houghton Mifflin, 1978), pp. 1–4, recounts the story of Huston's earliest days and the influence of his parents.

2. James Agee, *Agee on Film: Reviews and Comments by James Agee* (Boston: Beacon, 1966), pp. 321–322, discusses the importance of this incident with John Huston. The article originally appeared in *Life*, September 18, 1950.

3. John Huston, *An Open Book* (New York: Knopf, 1980), in the caption to a photograph following page 184.

4. Kaminsky, p. 6.

5. Gerald Platley, *The Cinema of John Huston* (South Brunswick, N.J.: Barnes, 1977), p. 94.

6. Axel Madsen, *John Huston* (Garden City, N.Y.: Doubleday, 1978), p. 40.

7. Quoted in Peter Flint's obituary of John Huston, *The New York Times* (August 29, 1987), p. 1.

8. Louis Giannetti. *Masters of the American Cinema* (Englewood Cliffs, N.J.: Prentice-Hall, 1981), p. 258.

9. Agee, p. 321.

10. "Six Characters in Search of Auteurs: A Discussion About the French Cinema," in *Cahiers du Cinéma* 71 (May 1957), in Jim Hillier, ed., *Cahiers du Cinéma: The 1950's* (Cambridge, Mass.: Harvard, 1985), p. 41.

11. Andrew Sarris, *The American Cinema: Directors and Directions, 1929–1968* (New York: Dutton, 1968), p. 156.

12. Gideon Bachman's interview with John Huston, *Film Quarterly* XIX, 1 (Fall 1965), reprinted in Andrew Sarris, ed., *Interviews with Film Directors* (New York: Discus, 1969), p. 257.

13. Agee, p. 327.

14. Flint, *New York Times* obituary, p. 1.

15. Giannetti, p. 262.

16. Thomas Schatz, *Hollywood Genres: Formulas, Filmmaking and the Studio System* (New York: Random, 1981), pp. 124–125, presents an admirable description of the differences between the classic and the hard-boiled detective.

17. Jon Tuska, *The Detective in Hollywood* (Garden City, N.Y.: Doubleday, 1978), pp. 1–20, presents a summary of the twin lives of Sherlock Holmes in fiction and in film.

18. Tuska, p. 341.

19. Paul Schrader, "Notes on Film Noir," in Barry Keith Grant, ed., *Film Genre Reader* (Austin, Tex.: Univ. of Texas Press, 1981), p. 170. Thomas Schatz, *Hollywood Genres*, p. 116, places more emphasis on visual style than on content and finds *Citizen Kane* (Welles, 1941) a more appropriate starting point for the film noir than *The Maltese Falcon*, even though the detective work in *Citizen Kane* is that of a reporter trying to write an obituary rather than that of a detective trying to solve a crime. What is remarkable is that the style appeared in several types of films within a relatively short period.

20. John Cawelti, " 'Chinatown' and Generic Transformation in Recent American Films," in Grant, ed., p. 183, suggests but does not develop the comparison between the hardboiled detective and the Western hero.

21. Lotte N. Eisner, *The Haunted Screen: Expressionism in the German Cinema and the Influence of Max Reinhardt* (Berkeley, Cal.: Univ. of California Press, 1973), pp. 17–27.

22. Schatz, p. 123, calls American Expressionism "the height of Hollywood's narrative sophistication and visual expression."

23. Schrader, pp. 175–176, categorizes the characteristics of the film noir.

24. Schrader, pp. 177–178, provides the outline for the three phases of the film noir period.

25. Schatz, pp. 139–140.

26. Cawelti, in Grant, p. 188.

27. *Hollywood Genres*, p. 116.

Chapter Nine

THE HORROR FILM
FRANKENSTEIN

The Auteur: James Whale

James Whale (1889–1957) scarcely ranks with the great auteurs like Ford or Hawks.[1] In Andrew Sarris' rankings of American directors he rates only eight lines among the film-makers listed as "Lightly Likable . . . talented but uneven directors with the saving grace of unpretentiousness."[2] His brief comment quite accurately summarizes the tragedy of Whale's artistic life: "Whale's overall career reflects the stylistic ambitions and dramatic disappointments of an expressionist in the studio-controlled Hollywood of the thirties."[3] This list of "Lightly Likables" includes some famous names, like Busby Berkeley (unpretentious?) and Mervyn LeRoy, but most are unknown to the general public, like John Cromwell, Mitchell Leisen and Charles Walters. James Whale fits comfortably in this company of minor figures.

Such obscurity is a bit surprising for the director of *Frankenstein* (1931) and several other classic horror films, but it is quite understandable. When the *Cahiers* writers began their second look at the American cinema, Whale had already passed from the scene, and as a result his most famous works never received the serious attention that might have been expected from a school of critics so interested in personal signatures and visual styles. The critical disinterest of the French passed through the British Film Institute to Andrew Sarris and through him to the other American auteur critics, and it has continued to the present. To this day the bibliography on James Whale is quite thin, even though *Frankenstein* has come back to life for a new generation of American viewers through the home video market.

Critics today are willing to admit that the film holds more substance than the average Saturday matinee thriller, and the appreciation of the visual style of James Whale grows in the estimation of serious film viewers.

Another factor influencing the critics is the fact that Whale's output was small, and taken as a totality—as the auteur critics insist —it was not terribly distinguished. He made only twenty-one films in a career that lasted little more than a decade. The limited productivity alone does not disqualify him from a higher ranking; after all, Orson Welles, one of the pantheon directors on the highest level of critical acclaim, made even fewer films, and, of those, several are truly awful. The difference between the recognition gained by the two men is one of personality and political good fortune.

Welles came to RKO with a reputation as a brilliant young actor and director of stage and radio productions. This Wunderkind from the East received a blank check, empowered to write and direct his own films as he wanted, because according to the scenario he was going to save the studio singlehandedly. The success of *Citizen Kane* (1941) inflated the young director's already outsized ego, and he continued to demand total control over his projects. He was an artist of sublime self-confidence, and his unwillingness to compromise and play the studio games allowed him to create several masterpieces but in the long run ruined his career as a studio director in Hollywood, where "getting along with the front office" is often as important as talent.

Whale arrived on the scene much more quietly a decade earlier, and he had none of Welles' immense fanfare or ego. His relationship to Hollywood was woven of finer thread. James Whale was always a studio director who tried to do his job creditably, no matter how ill-conceived the project was. As a team player rather than an independent producer, he rarely exercised the kind of control over either the selection of properties or the execution of the project that would mark him as a true auteur, or even that would let his own unique talents be used to their fullest. Welles told others what he wanted; Whale wanted to do what others told him.

Whale's artistic personality, bordering on insecurity, has deep roots. Born into a working class family of ten children in Dudley, Worcestershire, in the Midlands of England, he was ever sensitive about his humble origins in a class-conscious society. Even after he had become established in his new homeland, he continually struggled to separate himself from his modest background. He was so successful in blotting out his past that even the date of his birth has become a matter of some confusion.[4] His father tended a blast furnace, and his mother, a nurse, saw that her son received a strict Methodist training in the fear of human sin and divine retribution.

After some formal schooling James worked at a cobbler's shop and in an embossing mill, en route to become a laboring man, just like his father. During this time he developed his talent for drawing and went to night school to study art, since his parents could never have afforded a formal education for him.[5] As a young man he practiced the diction and manners of the upper classes, and preferred sketching to an apprenticeship in the mills. As he passed through the middle years in Hollywood, he adopted the manner of a retiring English gentleman. For the rest of his life, even after wealth and recognition were his, he remained insecure as an outsider to his adopted country and his adopted social class. Compounding his sense of alienation was the fact that he was homosexual before being openly "gay" became acceptable in Hollywood.[6]

When war broke out he secured a commission in the British Army, but glory on the battlefield was not to be his. During one of his first engagements with the enemy, young Lieutenant Whale led his company into a German trap and spent the next fifteen months as a prisoner of war in a camp near Hanover. He spent the time drawing, designing sets, and directing the plays the prisoners put on to pass the time. Nearing thirty at war's end, he spent a short time as a cartoonist on *The Bystander* before enrolling at the Ryland Memorial School in Birmingham, where he became involved as a designer and sometime actor for the local repertory company. He would never work as a laboring man again.

During the 1920s Whale gained some modest stature in British theatre circles. He graduated from set designer and stage manager to actor and director. By 1925 he passed from the local repertory companies to London, and in 1928, at the age of thirty-seven, by default he was hired to direct Laurence Olivier in R. C. Sherriff's *Journey's End,* a play about trench warfare in World War I. Three more established stage directors were certain that the play was destined to fail because, in the age of postwar prosperity, theater-goers would not want to relive the memories of the war. Contrary to their expectations, the venture was a spectacular success. Olivier soon left the cast because of a conflicting commitment and was replaced by Colin Clive. Together Clive and Whale took the play in triumph from London to New York. From there it would be only one more step to bring the drama to Hollywood and transform it into a film.

The timing could not have been better. Sound hit the motion

picture industry in 1927 and set off a panic in Hollywood. The studios were frantic to bring talent in from the New York and London stage to handle writing, staging and acting for the brand new medium of the talking picture. With his success in London and New York still fresh in the minds of the moguls, James Whale became, if not a "hot property" like Orson Welles, at least a very useful commodity. James Whale was, after all, a man of modest achievement. In 1928 he was nearing middle age, and *Journey's End* had been his only noteworthy success. He did, however, bring a decade of theater experience with him to his new home. He arrived in California confident in his ability to transfer *Journey's End* from stage to film.

The transition of both the play and its director would not be made immediately, however. Whale knew that he had to learn how to handle this new medium, and investors were not about to back an untried director for a major film. The director and the industry arranged a trial marriage in 1929, when Paramount signed Whale as a "dialogue expert." He worked with actor Richard Dix on *The Love Doctor* (Melville Brown, 1929), which failed miserably, and thus ended Dix's career as a romantic lead at Paramount. Whale, however, gained a genuine film credit to add to his dossier.

Several months before work began on *The Love Doctor*, Howard Hughes had finished shooting *Hell's Angels*, the story of air combat during World War I. The action footage was remarkable, but unfortunately the story was conceived and shot as a silent film, and with the public demanding sound, it could not be released. Hughes hired writers to script a melodrama that could serve as a narrative frame for the air battles, and, impressed with Whale's theater credentials, borrowed him from Paramount to direct the new dialogue scenes. Jean Harlow got her first major role, replacing Greta Nissen, a Norwegian actress whose accent disqualified her from the role of an English vamp. Squeezing a creditable performance out of her established Whale's reputation for working with actors.[7] Although credited on the release print not as a director but only as "Production Staged by James Whale," he had in fact become a film director.

Tiffany Studios held the option for *Journey's End*, and thus James Whale had his first experience with script writing and casting for the screen and, more importantly, trying to keep to a shooting schedule and budget in one of the poorest studios in Hollywood. In those modest circumstances Whale proved himself quite competent as an administrator. The film starred Colin Clive and received fine reviews when it opened in New York in April 1930, four months before *Hell's Angels*, which didn't.[8] While *Journey's End* was still receiving favorable publicity, Whale planned to cash in on his success. On the advice of his new agent, S. George Ullman, he left Hollywood and returned to the legitimate stage, while Ullman tried to line up a position for him as director in a studio with greater promise than Tiffany. By the time 1930 ended, for all practical purposes so had Tiffany. As the shipwrecked company began to slide under the surface, Whale sued the studio to get out of his contract and signed on with Universal.

Universal Studios did not have the class of MGM, but it did have an uncanny president in Carl Laemmle. His pictures made money, and during the 1920s its hottest properties were horror films staring Lon Chaney, like *The Hunchback of Notre Dame* (Wallace Worsley, 1923) and *The Phantom of the Opera* (Rupert Julian, 1925). The company also tried an occasional prestige film to burnish its image. In 1930 the studio held the rights to Robert Sherwood's *Waterloo Bridge*, which was slated for the prestige treatment. Since it is the story of a British soldier on leave in London during the war, where he meets an American prostitute (Mae Clarke), the film needed a British touch, and James Whale, who was becoming typecast as a director of British war stories, was available. Once again, Whale's timing was perfect.

Waterloo Bridge was another success. Carl Laemmle Jr., then head of production at his father's studio, was eager to repeat the success of *Dracula* (Tod Browning, 1931), which he had produced earlier in the year. He held the rights to *Frankenstein*, a play by Peggy Webling, based on the early section of the novel of 1818 by Mary Wollstonecraft Shelley. Whale was chosen to give the melodrama the proper atmosphere. Eager to move away from British war stories, Whale accepted, and the film was such a spectacular success that, ever after, James Whale has been associated with horror films.

Through his four great horror films, *Frankenstein* (1931), *The Old Dark House* (1932), *The Invisible Man* (1933), and his masterpiece *The Bride of Frankenstein* (1935), Whale put his own personal touch on his materials. These were not the blood and gore slasher films so beloved by adolescent audiences of a later era. Starting with *Frankenstein*, Whale carefully constructs a two-tiered dramatic pattern. On the upstairs level is the aristocracy, with its proprieties and pretensions; downstairs lurks the world of the monstrous, which serves as a grotesque reflection of the artificial world of the bourgeoisie.

The conflict between the two worlds creates an extraordinary richness in Whale's work. The upper level provides comic relief. In *Frankenstein*, the Baron (Frederick Kerr) is as blustery as any Colonel

Blimp of the English stage. Elizabeth (Mae Clarke), the love interest
of Henry Frankenstein, is fragile and must be protected, but Dr.
Henry Frankenstein (Colin Clive) is so inept in dealing with the real
world that he locks her in a room where she cannot escape the Monster (Boris Karloff). The element of social satire is unmistakable. By
the time he reaches *The Bride of Frankenstein,* Whale has broadened
his comic vision from a comedy of manners to a true Screwball Comedy, with its emphasis on fast-paced verbal humor that operates on
both levels, descending from the drawing room down into the laboratory and back up again. Even the monsters have gag lines.[9]

Henry Frankenstein is torn between the two worlds. As played
by Colin Clive, he is a pompous young man who shows every indication that he will develop into another Baron Frankenstein. While he
remains obsessed with his work on the Monster, he cannot complete
his plans to marry Elizabeth. Rather than begin the work of procreation by reproducing himself through natural means, he creates a grotesque image of himself in his laboratory. The Monster is Frankenstein's only offspring, and it embodies all the nightmare violence that
lurks deep down in his subconscious but that is repressed by the
bourgeois conventions of the daylight world. By retreating into his
laboratory and trying to replicate his own human form, Frankenstein
is subjecting himself to psychoanalysis and uncovering the monster
within. Whale provides the same analysis of society: ridiculous, re-
pressive conventions above the surface and murderous monsters
beneath.

Whale's own social background sharpens his vision of the complex world that he created. As a working class boy, he saw the foibles
of the upper reaches of the British caste system as apt material for
satire. With this, he is in the mainstream of the English comic theatre.
Through his early years, however, Whale aspired to join precisely
these circles of society that he parodies so ruthlessly. Quite simply,
through his studied university diction he tried to recreate himself into
another incarnation of Baron Frankenstein. Instead, through his tampering with nature, he had created a Monster of himself, a being that
fits comfortably in no identifiable class. The first notion is comic, the
second is horrifying.

Whale's homosexuality adds yet another dimension to his view of
the world. On the surface, Henry Frankenstein's thwarted desire for
marriage is laughable and leads him from one comic frustration to
another. Deep below the surface, however, is the horror that Henry
has created in his insane efforts to transform death into life. It turns
the drive for generativity into a sinister, distorted, reverse-mirror

image of marriage, something that Frankenstein (as well as Whale) finds loathsome. The offspring is not a son to carry on the line of Frankenstein, but a monster. In baldest terms, Whale was able to place in one and the same film a sharp and very funny satire of conventional patterns of marriage, and at the same time to express a horror for the unconventional pattern that his own life held for him. Like Henry Frankenstein, Whale discovers that his only offspring is a monstrous product of his own creativity.

The Monster, however grotesque, is not evil from birth. Like Mary Shelley's original creation, the child of nature has its gentle side. It loves flowers and children; it marvels at the light. Society, however, as represented by Frankenstein's physically deformed assistant, Fritz (Dwight Frye), torments it with fire and turns it into an outcast. The evil that destroys the monster, then, is an acquired characteristic. In this, Whale may well be commenting on the irrational forces of society that could not accept him as a loving, gentle being, but have turned him into what it perceives as a hideous and dangerous monster.

In *Frankenstein* Whale is able to balance both worlds by distancing himself and his audience from the material. He creates an illusion of objectivity by having an announcer appear on screen, before the title cards appear, warning audiences that they may be horrified by what they are about to see. Through this prologue Whale sets a light tone, mocking both the content of the film and the audience that will react to it.[10] In *The Bride of Frankenstein*, Mary Shelley (Elsa Lanchester) provides the prologue by warning her companions that the point of her story may have been missed in the earlier installment (Whale's film), and the remainder of the tale, based on later segments of Shelley's novel, clarifies her theme that a mere human creator is punished for trying to usurp the role of God by creating life. Whale reminds his audience that it is watching a film by beginning *The Bride of Frankenstein* with a resume of shots taken from the final scenes of *Frankenstein.*

In *The Bride of Frankenstein* Whale recreates his vision of a two-tiered world. The longing of the Monster for a mate merely reflects the desire of Henry Frankenstein (Colin Clive) for Elizabeth (Valerie Hobson). The upper world becomes subject to a satirical comedy of manners in the prologue with the effete presentations of Percy Bysshe Shelley (Douglas Walton) and Lord Byron (Gavin Gordon). In the action of the main story, Frankenstein and Dr. Pretorius are equally but more subtly absurd. Minnie the chambermaid (Una

O'Connor) with her nervous bird-like shrieks parodies the audience's reaction to rumors of monsters on the prowl.

The sinister Dr. Pretorius (Ernest Thesiger) makes a mockery of Henry Frankenstein's science by creating miniature humans that fit into Mason jars. He proudly shows Frankenstein his queen and then a king resembling Henry VIII. His third creation is an archbishop and the fourth a devil, who Pretorius notes looks quite a bit like himself.

The tiny people underline the theme of the film. The randy king, finding the asexual confines of his jar a bit restrictive, climbs out and tries to break through the glass of his queen's jar. The archbishop disapproves of the union as unholy, and bangs on his own jar to urge Pretorius to stop their union. Acting with divine indifference, the scientist picks up the king with a pair of tongs and drops him back into his own jar, sealing the lid with a teacup and saucer. The archbishop, it seems clear, would like to act to repress this carnal union, but he is powerless without the scientist. The churchman cannot usurp the role of God by regulating procreation, but the scientist can, and by interfering with the role of God, he oversteps his own role. With the frustrated king back in his jar, Pretorius then introduces a ballerina, as an idealized form of female beauty, even though she is tiresome by dancing only to one piece of music, and a miniature mermaid, that he made when experimenting with seaweed, as though stumbling upon the evolution of the species from sea creatures. The scene is quite comical, but quite serious in the movement of the story.

The theme of Pretorius' blasphemy is repeated with another comic twist later in the film when the mad doctor has a lunch of bread and wine on the coffin of a young girl whose brain he is acquiring for the Monster's bride. The sarcophagus is decorated with linens and candles to resemble an altar. The priest-scientist in his vestment-like surgical smock is interrupted at his meal by the Monster. He calmly offers his visitor a cigar, quite confident that he can control the dark powers of his colleague's creation more effectively than the archbishop in the mason jar could control the miniature king or even more than God himself can control the world. The Monster is easily placated, but only for a while.

In *The Bride of Frankenstein* the comedy even reaches into the nightmare world of the monsters themselves, as though Whale has become more comfortable laughing at the dark side of his nature. The Monster is a dark parody of human nature. In addition to longing for a mate, he learns to enjoy music, smoke cigars and drink wine. When the intended Bride (Elsa Lanchester) emerges from her electric incubation amid the sparks and coils that Whale borrowed from the creation of the robot Maria (Brigitte Helm) in *Metropolis* (Fritz Lang, 1926), she takes one look at the Monster and gasps. She is fetching in her white bridal shroud and lightning streak hair, but she wants no part of the groom with a bolt in his throat. The scientist has played God by creating woman, but he has failed in understanding love, even among monsters.

The comedy, however, takes a serious turn when the Monster makes the decision to stay in the burning laboratory with this would-be bride, while ordering Henry and Elizabeth to leave. It realizes there is no place in the world for artificially created life, and that Henry Frankenstein, having finally seen the folly of his scheme, must leave the nightmare world to join Elizabeth in a natural union that will produce natural offspring. This second destruction of the Monster, this time with his would-be mate—the first took place at the end of *Frankenstein*, even though in *The Bride of Frankenstein* it turns out that he only appeared to die—put an end to Whale's career with the genre. Whale was beginning to grow restive as a master of monsters. He wanted to branch out into more serious dramatic works, films on a level with *Journey's End*, the project that brought him to Hollywood in the first place.

This was naturally a source of some controversy at Universal Studios. The Laemmles, Carl Sr. and Jr., president and production head respectively, saw horror films as the bread-and-butter product of the studio, and James Whale was its most successful horror director. Between the two versions of the Frankenstein story Whale had also directed *The Old Dark House* (1932), with a screenplay adapted from the novel *Benighted* by J.B. Priestley and starring Charles Laughton, Boris Karloff, Melvyn Douglas and Raymond Massey. The story involved the classic case of travelers taking refuge in a castle on a stormy night. Their bourgeois reactions provide the comedy of manners, while the residents of the manor provide a rich underworld of horror. Arson, rape and murder fill the nighttime hours, and although the film has its element of horror, it would more properly be classified as a black comedy.[11]

The Invisible Man (1933) was based on a novel by H.G. Wells and introduced Claude Rains to American film audiences. Like Henry Frankenstein, Jack Griffin (Claude Rains) has tampered with experiments that stretch beyond the competence of the human mind and has rendered himself invisible, a nonperson. Like Frankenstein, too, his experiments had ruined his prospects for marriage to Flora Cranely (Gloria Stuart). The techniques Whale and his cinematographer Arthur Edeson devised to photograph an invisible man were nothing less than brilliant and horrifying. Other scenes are quite comic. Griffin sits in his silk dressing gown describing how cold it is to wander through the countryside naked so that he can remain invisible and complaining that he must hide after eating because his food remains visible until it is properly digested. Once again, the innkeeper, Mrs. Hall (Una O'Connor), provides the shrieks that parody the audience's reaction to the mysterious invisible man in her guest room.

In addition to a unique combination of horror and comedy, Whale the artist and cartoonist devised a consistent visual style for his thrillers. Borrowing heavily from the German Expressionist artists and set designers of the previous decade, he created sets with little relationship to reality. Frankenstein's castle in both films features the inevitable stone stairway. Slivers of shadows fall across the set in jagged streaks, a technique no doubt spoofed through the white streak in the Bride's hair. The look of a James Whale set could be chilling before a single horror had taken place. The designs could be called derivative, but at the same time no one executed the generic style as well and as consistently as James Whale.

Whale got his wish and moved over to different genres, but never duplicated his success with the horror films. *Remember Last Night?* (1935) combined elements of murder mystery and Screwball Comedy after the manner of the Thin Man series. He tried a musical, *Show Boat* (1936), which was both a critical and a financial success, but unfortunately Universal had also released a series of less-than-successful features that year and the Laemmles were reluctant to bankroll many of Whale's more extravagant projects.

Whale's film career reached the beginning of its end in 1937 during the production of *The Road Back*, based on Erich Maria Remarque's sequel to his famous novel *All Quiet on the Western Front,* which had been made into an enormously successful film by Lewis Milestone in 1930. The Nazi government objected strongly to the pacifist and anti-German tone of the work, and the Laemmles, ever aware of income from the European market, ordered the film recut and parts reshot rather than jeopardize European rentals. Whale was understandably furious. The irony of the Jewish moguls' altering a film to please Hitler was compounded by the fact that the new version was still thought to be too controversial for wide release. No one wanted to think of war and its aftermath in 1937. The movie was a financial disaster, and Whale's reputation for commercial dependability suffered a serious blow.

The Laemmles found they could make money by lending Whale

out to other studios. As was the case at Universal, he carried out the contract jobs that the studios provided. Of his films, Warner Bros.' *The Great Garrick* (1937) received some critical acclaim, as did United Artists' *The Man in the Iron Mask* (1939). During this period, MGM's *Port of Seven Seas* (1938), Universal's *Sinners in Paradise* (1938) and *Green Hell* (1940), and Columbia's *They Dare Not Love* (1941) were less than well received.[12] Quality scripts simply were not coming his way, and with a string of unsuccessful releases consistently appearing under his name as the world slipped into another major war, it seemed unlikely that he would ever again have stories from the likes of Mary Shelley, H.G. Wells, Alexandre Dumas and J.B. Priestley to turn into James Whale films.

Despite this abrupt collapse of his reputation, James Whale was not desperate. At the height of his success he formed a real estate corporation under the direction of George Lovett, who had invested wisely for him.[13] He led a rather reserved life: he could not tolerate alcohol and rarely drank. His relationships were unconventional, but on the whole rather stable. He did not squander his modest wealth in an extravagant lifestyle. On the contrary, he cultivated the image of the reserved English gentleman rather than the flamboyant Hollywood celebrity. In 1941 he withdrew from the world of film production into his own home, entertained friends in the evenings, and spent his days painting and attending screenings of films. On occasion he returned to the stage for another directorial challenge, but for the most part he led a quiet retired life. Rumors of sordid circumstances surrounding his death circulated widely at the time, but, according to his suicide note, failing health rather than a failed relationship had led to depression and the decision to take his own life.

The story of James Whale has no happy ending. The happiness comes after his death, when new generations of film viewers have been able to enjoy his fine horror films and when new generations of critics are willing to offer him respect for his solid but modest achievement.

The Genre: The Horror Film

According to the often repeated story, Georges Méliès, one of the pioneer film-makers in France, was experimenting with his new camera one sunny autumn afternoon in 1896.[14] He was trying to get a picture of a horse-drawn bus as it emerged from a tunnel, but just as he was in the process of getting the shot he wanted, the film jammed in the camera. Méliès did not want to waste the valuable film, and so he left the tripod in place and worked to free the jammed reel. Just as he succeeded, a hearse appeared at the mouth of the tunnel. When he developed the reel, he saw a miracle: a bus filled with cheery living passengers had been transformed into a hearse. Although he did not realize it at the time, Georges Méliès had discovered the natural suitability of film for presenting the macabre. A short time later, however, he developed this accidental discovery into *A Voyage to the Moon* (1902), *The Kingdom of the Fairies* (1903) and *Twenty Thousand Leagues Under the Sea* (1907). These early attempts to use "trick" photography to simulate fantasy were closer to our notion of science fiction, but before long the true horror film would be invented. Méliès himself did a *Dr. Jekyll and Mr. Hyde* in 1908, and the Edison studios created the first known *Frankenstein* in 1910.

"Horror" inevitably and unfortunately suggests today's low budget/high profit "slasher" films, like the endless *Halloween*, *Amityville* and *Nightmare on Elm Street* series. Most of the samples of classic Horror films are indeed low-budget films, and few were released by major studios. After those accidental similarities, however, the popular misconception and the reality of the Horror film diverge abruptly. First of all, as was the case with the Hard-boiled Detective genre, low budget does not necessarily mean low quality. The Horror film emerges from an illustrious literary lineage, and its enduring popularity suggests that it still appeals to some inner need in an audience. Although definitions of film genres often lack the precision of the natural sciences, and are universally less satisfying, some attempt at uncovering the nature of horror should help to clarify the point that true Horror films are in a category quite distinct from the blood-and-scream thrillers so popular with teenagers. Most Horror films, in fact, contain very little graphic violence.

Despite its roots in "high culture," the Horror film has made such an important impact on popular culture that its literary ancestry is often forgotten. Only the Western has provided more widely used icons. For popular recognition, right behind the six-shooter and Stetson rank the extended teeth and black cape of Dracula. People still speak of a mercurial person as having "a Jekyll and Hyde personality," and when some project produces unexpected and unpleasant consequences, they complain about having created "a Frankenstein," happily unaware that Dr. Frankenstein is the creator, not the monster. Why does Horror exercise such a grip on the popular imagination? Where did it come from, and how does it work?

Witches, ghosts and conjurers appear in the Bible and in the

classical literature of Greece and Rome. Devils play a central role in
the medieval mystery plays and achieved the level of high literature
with Milton's "Paradise Lost." Shakespeare and his contemporaries
routinely put witches and ghosts to work on the stage. With the appearance of Horace Walpole's *The Castle of Otranto* (1764), however,
these commonplace supernatural elements begin to take on a somewhat different meaning. They are no longer external forces from another world with which the hero interacts, but are objectivized functions of his own personality.[15] Starting with *The Castle of Otranto*, the
monsters, ghosts and vampires become projections of the dark side of
the hero's ego, the drive for unsuitable power and illicit sex that
horrify him as well as those around him and threaten to destroy him.
In Freudian terms, the monsters are creatures of the id cut loose from
the restraints of the superego.

To approach the distinction another way, terror by contrast
arises from some identifiable, external cause which may be an actual
threat or may be something innocent that is distorted through the
imagination.[16] A man in a hockey mask, for example, is waiting in the
woodshed with a machete, and when darkness falls he will hack a
group of teenagers to pieces. The terror has a solution within a defi-
nite period of time. The would-be killer will be destroyed in some
way and the teenagers will be saved, or he will succeed in killing them
so that he can return to haunt another cabin during yet another sequel. Or, if the imagination is involved, the "killer" may be literally
unmasked as the school nerd who is simply trying to frighten his
classmates because they did not invite him to join in their outing. One
way or another, the terror has a solution.

Horror, by contrast, arises from dreams and fits no rational categories. The vampire, the monster, and the wolf man can be van-
quished, but always with the understanding that they can return to
hunt their quarry on another occasion. They represent the dark side
of the human ego, real or imagined, that remains with an individual to
the grave. The fear is irrational, but real. Terror, on the other hand,
stands up to intellectual scrutiny: a violent crime is about to be committed, or averted. The agent can be identified. Horror lacks the
rationality of the conscious world; it is intellectual nonsense. It is no
more coherent than last night's dreams or nightmares. For this reason
the horror story reaches its peak just after the hero or heroine retires,
thus leaving doubt whether the perceived threat is real or a dream
fantasy.

The object of Horror, then, is not the construction of a coherent
narrative with a beginning, a middle and an end. It is the creation of

an atmosphere that captures the deep insecurities dwelling in every human psyche. For Walpole, the neoclassical tradition with the certainties of the Age of Reason was beginning to show signs of collapse. Ironically, as thinkers like John Locke (1632–1704) began to understand more about the workings of the mind, their followers in the next generation began also to realize its limitations.[17]

To a man like Walpole, the darkness of uncertainty was truly horrifying. To describe this state of insecurity, Walpole constructed a symbolic universe. The Castle with its dark corridors and damp, dark rooms is a manifestation of Manfred, its owner and the hero of the novel.[18] It is an isolated place, containing not only his twisted dark side, but also his ideals, imaged through the beautiful young women who may be destroyed because of him. The irrational is a threat. A mysterious prophecy found in a secret book reveals that he will lose his castle, a form of annihilation, and he cannot prevent it. His life, no more than his death, cannot be explained in purely rational categories, and the more he tries to understand, the more destruction he causes.

Walpole was not alone in viewing his age with a sense of horror and helplessness. Before his famous book was published in 1764, the Germans had already begun this literary exploration of the nonrational world with Heinrich August Ossenfelder's *The Vampire* (1748), and *The Castle of Otranto* was soon followed in Germany by Gottfried August Bürger's *Leonore* (1773). Johann Wolfgang von Goethe himself wrote *The Bride of Corinth* in 1797, the same year Robert Southey, an avid reader of the Germans, published *Thabala the Destroyer*. Southey's commentary on his own work found an extraordinary readership that included Wordsworth and Coleridge. Both of these introduced Gothic elements into their works, as did Percy Bysshe Shelley and Byron. In American literature the Gothic style influenced Hawthorne and, of course, Edgar Allan Poe.[19]

Walpole's novel spawned several popular variations on similar themes, like Clara Reeve's *The Old English Baron* (1771), William Beckford's *Vathek* (1786), and Matthew Lewis' *The Monk* (1795). The next century would bring Mary Shelley's *Frankenstein, or, The Modern Prometheus* (1818) Charles Robert Maturin's *Melmoth the Wanderer* (1820), and later Robert Louis Stevenson's *Dr. Jekyll and Mr. Hyde* (1886) and Bram Stoker's *Dracula* (1897). As Walpole saw in the Gothic tale an image of the disintegration of the Newtonian world of rational categories, the Victorians read the stories as parables of the disintegration of the moral order.[20]

Throughout the nineteenth century, these novels and dozens like them filled a need for popular entertainment. As literacy increased among the middle classes, a market for mass entertainment had developed, and high speed printing became necessary to meet the demands of the market. On the level of narrative alone, these stories were easy enough to follow, despite their irrationality, and they could always provide a good thrill for their readers. Sadly, the thematic elements and the symbolic universe that these books contained were ignored, and until recently they have received scant serious critical attention.

The central characters in Gothic fiction are not necessarily evil figures in themselves but they become implicated in evil, often through no fault of their own. They are imprudent and fail to recognize their human limitations in the face of preternatural phenomena. Like Adam with the Tree of the Knowledge of Good and Evil, they are curious about things better left alone. Not content with their status as humans and creatures, they overreach themselves. They manifest human pride, and the horror that they create with their pride takes the form of a monster or werewolf, which becomes a doppelganger of the hero.

The women are virginal, frail and utterly passive embodiments of the hero's ideals that are endangered by his pride. She is both threatened by his lust and rescued by his love. She is victimized by his unholy yearning for knowledge and saved by his scientific skill. By being the passive victim, she helps him realize the destructive implications of his actions, and thus saves him from himself.[21] Often a marriage cannot be consummated, and the resulting frustrated love generates a tension that threatens to destroy both lovers.

Often, too, the love is of an unholy variety, and incest, threatened or actual, becomes a common theme in Gothic fiction.[22] Through motives that are not altogether clear to him, the hero is overly protective of his captive sister or daughter, and his protective love threatens to destroy them. The erotic implications of his actions, of course, surface during dreams when inhibitions vanish and the hero/dreamer can no longer repress and ignore his unholy and destructive longings. The result is pure horror at the realization of the desires he is truly capable of. Dreams becoming nightmares provide the ordinary, irrational narrative mode of the Gothic style. The recollection of fear remains, even though the narrative line is incoherent and hazy.

Science, the purely rational, and pseudoscience, tainted with the occult, come into conflict as the hero tries to understand and control the irrepressible powers he has discovered. And always the action takes place at night in an isolated spot, like a tower or a castle, filled with spider webs and dust. The trees are bare and rain has been falling. The sources of light are inconstant. A dog—or is it a wolf?—howls in the background. The door creaks, and the fire in the huge hearth casts grotesque shadows on the walls. The icons of horror are unmistakable, and as a result they are the easiest of all genres to parody. Any child going to a Halloween party or any undergraduate in an introductory film-making class knows exactly what images create the effects of horror. By 1948 Charles Barton's *Abbott and Costello Meet Frankenstein* had transformed the subtle black comedy of *The Bride of Frankenstein* (1935) into slapstick. With *Young Frankenstein* in 1974, Mel Brooks turned the material into a comic book.

As the nineteenth century turned into the twentieth, the Gothic novel went through a rebirth in film. The imagery that contributed to the total effect of the horror story made a smooth and productive transition into the new medium. Georges Méliès' *The Voyage to the Moon* in 1902 proved immensely successful and profitable. By 1908 a film version of *Dr. Jekyll and Mr. Hyde* was produced in Chicago, and the Edison studios turned out a *Frankenstein* by 1910.[23] The darkened movie theaters became a suitable locale for horror.

The genre of Horror films went through its formative phase immediately after World War I in Germany under the influence of Expressionism. At the close of the previous century German and Swiss painters had developed a style of graphic art that stressed the interior landscape of the human mind rather than the objects the mind perceives.[24] Through the influence of Max Reinhardt's stage designs, the twisted angles and distorted shadows easily made the transition to the new art form of the cinema. The style provided a perfect setting for the Gothic fantasy and would be used repeatedly by the German film-makers and their imitators around the world.

Stunned from its defeat and bewildered by the economic chaos of the Weimar Republic, German film artists were ready to explore the irrational and malevolent forces of the universe. The benchmark film was *The Cabinet of Dr. Caligari* (Robert Wiene, 1919), the story of a mad scientist who was able to order his monster to kill on command. In the release print the story was set in a framing narrative so that the events seemed but the paranoid fantasy of a madman. The impact of the message was undercut, but the visual style of the Gothic film and the machinery of the mad scientist and his magic formulas remained intact.[25]

Several other excellent examples of the Expressionist style and the Gothic concerns soon followed *The Cabinet of Dr. Caligari*. In

1920 Paul Wegener recycled the ancient story of *The Golem,* about a rabbi in Prague who creates a monster from clay to defend his people against a pogrom. The rabbi, of course, who has already imitated God by creating life from inanimate clay, abuses his knowledge, gained from occult literature, and uses the creature for his own profit only to find it rebelling against his authority. The make-up of the Golem, played by Wegener himself, strongly influenced the look of the American monster in *Frankenstein* a decade later, and the sets and lighting are borrowed heavily from the Expressionistic stage of Max Reinhardt. A conch-shaped spiral staircase dominates the center of the rabbi's home, and the walls of Prague soar and dip as though they had been designed by drunken seagulls.

In 1922 F.W. Murnau created one of the most chilling of all the Dracula stories in *Nosferatu.* The hero of the story does not abuse the powers of the intellect trying to acquire knowledge and power that is unsuited to the role of a mere mortal, but he is simply foolish. He fails to understand the consequences of wandering into the Count's castle or reading the Book of the Vampires before he retires. Since he enters the imaginative universe of vampires as he falls into a sound sleep, both in an inn on his journey and after drinking wine at the castle, the margin between dream and reality is suitably blurred. It is never clear how much of Dracula's activity occurs in the real world, and how much in the dark world of the unconscious.

Count Dracula, the Nosferatu, is a Christ-image in reverse. He does not give his blood and his life to others so that they may live, but he takes blood and life of others so that he may live. He creates not life, but dead beings in the power of the Evil One, and as such he is a parody of the life-giving creator. He is overcome, at least for a while, by the self-sacrifice of the heroine, who offers herself to the vampire and detains him until daybreak when, caught in the first rays of the sun, he expires. She represents the triumph of love and self-sacrifice in the heart of her husband.

With *Metropolis* (Fritz Lang, 1926) the horror of death in life includes a social dimension. Not only the individuals involved but society as a whole suffers from a collective nightmare of the industrial revolution gone mad. Individuality is lost, and human beings are reduced to the role of cogs or even fuel for the machines they serve. The monsters are not ghouls or vampires, but the machines of the industrial age, which are designed to look like pagan effigies and to which living sacrifices of workers must be offered.

A mad scientist, Dr. Rotwang (Rudolf Klein-Rogge), uses his elaborate scientific apparatus to create a robot woman, a parody of the source of life, and uses it to control the masses. The elaborate electrical devices will influence the design of the sets for the creation of life in both *Frankenstein* and *The Bride of Frankenstein*. As a result of his insane scheme, the mad doctor is destroyed by flood, following the tradition of Noah, while his unnatural creation, an anti-Eve, is burned at the stake, in a manner reminiscent of Joan of Arc. Human love, as embodied in the romantic couple, is triumphant, thus opening the way for natural procreation.

Metropolis featured the multiple level setting to image the different levels of the human mind, from its dark lower recesses of factories and mines to its lofty, sun-drenched idealization of itself in the pleasure gardens of the wealthy. Lang, however, added the additional horror of using masses of human beings as set decoration. The mob scenes, deployed in symmetrical fashion, and machines built to resemble demons, add to the Expressionistic nightmare. This dark, murky underworld then represents both the rigid class divisions of a society that cannot face the poverty of the masses and the individual human mind that cannot face the cruelty it harbors in its lower regions.

Ironically, the dark images that came out of Germany in the 1920s embodied not only the dark substrata of German society as a whole, but a particular unrest in the nationalized studio Ufa (Universum Film Aktien Gesellschaft), where the images were created. The state-run studios were in continual financial difficulty since their founding in 1917, and efforts to strengthen their position led to large borrowings from Paramount and MGM, the "Parufumet (Par-Ufa-Met) agreement" in 1925.[26] This financial connection would prove to be the beginnings of a gangplank for German talent to flee to America, especially after Hitler's rise to power.

During the 1920s Hollywood was at the peak of its prosperity and the moguls planned to establish a worldwide monopoly on film production. It must be recalled that in the age of silent film, such a plan would not have been far-fetched, since foreign-language title cards would simply be inserted into the foreign-language release print to replace the English-language ones in the American version. Today, of course, the costs of dubbing or subtitles can often limit foreign distribution. To further its imperial designs, Hollywood opened its purse strings, and German talent, nervous about the future of Ufa and apprehensive about the thickening atmosphere of anti-Semitism, created a second gold rush to California.

This exodus included not only famous directors like Lang, Murnau, and Preminger, but a near flood of lesser known artists, designers and technicians. Many of the moguls were German-speaking them-

selves and were eager to hire their countrymen, who were acknowledged as the most proficient in the industry. At Universal, for example, Carl Laemmle Sr. had brought so many of his relatives into the
studio that by the mid-1930s as Hitler was solidifying his policies
against the Jews, the production team was known as "the German
Army" and German was the language of the set.[27] The language
added a note of authenticity for Expressionist fantasies like *The Bride
of Frankenstein,* but proved somewhat incongruous for *Show Boat,*
made the following year, when James Whale, the director, had a daily
battle to keep the Mississippi River from turning into the Elbe and
Paul Robeson from being costumed like a Polish guest worker.

Universal had a long-established reputation for horror thrillers in
the silent era, and when sound film came along at the end of the 1920s
and early 1930s, the studio had all the pieces in place to leap to the
forefront in the production of a new kind of literate and disturbing
Horror film. Warner Bros. introduced sound in 1927, and a new age
of the motion picture dawned on a terrified industry. Many of the old
stars and old formulas, like Slapstick Comedy, would not survive, but
Tod Browning's *Dracula* (1931), starring Bela Lugosi, proved immensely popular with audiences who lived with the horror and insecurity of the Depression every day of their lives. The new cycle of
sound-era horror had begun.

The German silent and American sound Horror films had much
more in common than visual appearance and themes. Both forms of
the Horror film arose from a period of social upheaval. For the Germans the postwar period had been traumatic, and for the Americans
the Depression had shaken a national faith in the land of boundless
opportunity. The experience of widespread poverty made Americans
more conscious of social class than at any time in their history. The
villains of the Horror films, in both Germany and the United States,
were the people responsible for the hard times: the wealthy and educated. As a result of their privileged status, these men feel themselves
above any known moral order, and they dare to play God with the
lives of the common man. The ordinary people are horrified at their
powerlessness before the impersonal forces that the upper classes
have loosed against them.

For Depression movie audiences in the United States, as for the
Germans of the previous decade, Horror films provided a forum to
ventilate resentment against the monied classes, who presumably
were responsible for the plight of the unemployed. Both groups, too,
reveled in the traditional suspicion of the very well educated, who
search for worthless information rather than anything that would

solve the practical problems of the poor. In America, the old distrust of high culture and learning, so often pilloried in comedy by the stock figure of the absent-minded professor, found a new form of expression. The theme of the mad scientist, so popular in German films of the 1920s, made an easy transition to the American screen of the 1930s.

The workers, who make up the bulk of German and American film audiences, feel threatened by forces—social as well as psychological—that they cannot understand and certainly cannot control. Feeling trapped and powerless is at the emotional heart of the experience of horror.[28] Movie-going audiences in postwar Germany and in Depression America certainly could identify with the plight of the victims in the Horror film. The victims can cringe and shriek, but they cannot save themselves.

With Universal clearly dominating the genre, its actors became identified with their roles in the public imagination and found it difficult to find acceptance outside the genre.[29] As is the case with the Westerns, very few actors dominate the genre, and they appear in little else. Bela Lugosi is Dracula, just as Boris Karloff is Frankenstein's monster. Lon Chaney Jr. was an actor of narrow range, and the variety of roles he played generally fell within the Horror genre. Character actors like Dwight Frye and Edward Van Sloan gave the Universal Horror films continuity, as though they were a series being presented by a repertory company.

As the world slipped into yet another world war, horror on the battlefield soon overwhelmed horror on the screen. The film industry turned to ever broader forms of parody to help audiences laugh at their fears. After the dark night of war came the horrible sunrise of the atomic age, and film makers found the horror located not in the id, but in mysterious radioactive clouds, as in *The Incredible Shrinking Man* (Jack Arnold, 1957) and monsters loosed by the hydrogen bomb like *Godzilla* (Inoshiro Honda, 1954). As space travel moved from comic books to engineers' blueprints, the horror came from unwelcome visitors from remote galaxies, like *Invasion of the Body Snatchers* (Don Siegel, 1956) and *The Thing* (Christian Nyby and Howard Hawks, 1951).

The horror in these modern mutants of the Horror genre still comes from humanity's arrogance in trying to probe realms beyond its own proper territory. In this respect, at least, they remain very close to the traditional mad-scientist theme of the classic period. They veer away from the classic patterns, however, by introducing an external threat rather than a monster born in the scientist's own dark

psyche. For this reason, most of the newer forms of the genre would
not be properly called Horror films.

Some films did continue to look inward, but often psychiatry
replaced mystery and the evil appeared as having psychological and
thus comprehensible roots. In *Psycho* (Hitchcock, 1960) the madman
explains the horror, and in *The Innocents* (Jack Clayton, 1961), based
on Henry James' *The Turn of the Screw*, the ghosts may be real, or the
product of the imagination of a very nervous governess. Satan returned with *The Exorcist* (William Friedkin, 1973), but the devil is an
external, intruding force from without that must be driven away. The
possessed child is innocent in her captivity and is able to offer no act
of love or self-sacrifice to obtain her own liberation. As forces of good
and evil struggle for possession of her innocent soul, the film is closer
to medieval mystery plays than to the classic Horror films.

The most common descendants of the classic Horror films today
are the extremely violent and morbid slasher films, also known as
spatter films because of their tendency to squirt blood over every
conceivable surface. These are triumphs of special effects, but to
what purpose? The fascination with mutilation and death, especially
among young people, remains a puzzle and the evidence is contradic-
tory. Don Siegel, director of *Invasion of the Body Snatchers*, once
explained that the purpose of his film, which incidentally contains
almost no on-screen bloodshed and for that reason is doubly terrifying, was "to scare [us] out of grayness."[30] He may have a point. In an
industrial society, when life is perceived as gray, a jolt to the senses
and emotions, even one rooted in revulsion, may be welcome.

Motion picture audiences continue to welcome fear in its many
related guises, but true Horror films, those coming from Germany in
the 1920s and from Hollywood in the 1930s, fit into a distinct category from the other forms of thrillers that have been popular in recent
years. They offer a unique perspective on a world perceived to be in
chaos, and an interesting look at our perception of ourselves in such
a world.

For a Christian, the films are extremely interesting for their dealing with the problem of evil. The threat of evil abounds in the world
of the Horror film, but it has no power until the human agent appro-
priates it through pride or folly. Then the hero must try to cope with
the consequences of sin by offering atonement, often in the form of
surrendering his own life for the salvation of others. In traditional
theological terms, the genre takes the notion of Original Sin quite
seriously, but places the effects of sin in the world squarely on the
shoulders of the individual exercising his privilege of free will. To

choose evil is to choose its consequences as well, and the recognition of the human capacity to choose evil is indeed monstrous—in fact, horrifying.

The Plot: *Frankenstein*

The curtain opens on a theatrical stage. The actor Edward Van Sloan appears in formal attire and speaks:

> Mr. Carl Laemmle feels it would be a little unkind to present this picture without a word of friendly warning. We are about to unfold the story of Frankenstein, a man of science who sought to create a man after his own image without reckoning upon God. It is one of the strangest tales ever told. It deals with the two great mysteries of Creation: life and death. I think it will thrill you. It may shock you. It might even horrify you. So if any of you feel that you do not want to subject your nerves to such a strain, now is your chance to— well, we've warned you.

The opening titles begin to roll in front of a background consisting of a mask with rays beaming from the eyes. This background dissolves into a design of eyes rotating around a central axis. The notion of "vision" is thus introduced into the film even before the action begins.

The action opens in a graveyard. A grave digger is lifting a rope from a recently interred coffin, while the priest reads "Lux perpetua luceat eis" ("May perpetual light shine upon them"). A bell slowly tolls as the camera tracks across the gathered mourners. The statues and images, one of a skeleton, teeter at grotesque angles to the horizon. The camera settles on Dr. Henry Frankenstein (Colin Clive) and his deformed assistant Fritz (Dwight Frye). In his first words, addressed to Fritz but ironically to himself, he whispers: "Down, down, you fool." The camera follows the departing mourners across the dark, wintry landscape. The gravedigger begins filling in the grave, and after he pats the earth into place with his shovel, he lights his pipe and departs.

Frankenstein and Fritz move toward the grave to disinter the body, and Frankenstein encourages Fritz to hurry because the moon is rising. He strokes the coffin and observes: "He is just resting, waiting for a new life to come." They roll the coffin on a cart to a gallows, where Fritz cuts loose the hanging victim. Frankenstein holds the lantern. The doctor observes that the neck of the dead man is broken and the brain is useless: "We must find another brain."

Cut to Goldstadt Medical College, so identified by a plaque. Professors have finished a demonstration with a cadaver, which they are covering with a sheet as one of the team bumps into a life-sized skeleton, suspended on an elastic cord. The skeleton bounces in a macabre dance, and the class erupts in laughter. Fritz looks through the window as Dr. Waldman (Edward Van Sloan) explains to the class the physiological differences between the normal brain and the criminal brain, which he has in identical glass jars. He offers to leave the brains for the students to observe privately. He dismisses the class, and the cadaver is rolled away on a gurney. The skeleton continues to bob in the background.

When the room is empty, Fritz pries open the window to steal the brain. He backs into the skeleton and is frightened. When he hears a noise, he drops the normal brain and the jar shatters. He returns and picks up the criminal brain.

Cut to a portrait of Henry Frankenstein, illuminated by the bright flame of a candle. A maid announces the arrival of Victor Moritz (John Boles) to Elizabeth (Mae Clarke). The room is bathed in light, and Elizabeth is wearing a long, light-colored gown. She tells him that she has just received the first letter from Henry in four months, but the message is mysterious: "You must have faith in me, Elizabeth. Wait. My work must come first, even before you. At night the winds howl in the mountains. There is no one here. Prying eyes can't peer into my secret. I am living in an abandoned old watchtower, close to the town of Goldstadt. Only my assistant is here to help me with my experiments." She is worried because on the day of their engagement, he told her of the great experiment he was working on. It sounded very mysterious.

Elizabeth is worried that Henry may be ill. Victor tells her that he saw Henry in the woods near Goldstadt, and Henry said he would let no one near his laboratory. Victor promises Elizabeth that he will go to Henry's old professor, Dr. Waldman, to find out more about the strange experiments. It is clear that he is in love with Elizabeth, who regards him as a dear friend, even though she is engaged to Henry. She is embarrassed by his devotion and gently shows him to the door, where they shake hands as he departs. She follows him into the hall, and tells him that she must go with him to visit Dr. Waldman.

Cut to the office of Dr. Waldman. Elizabeth asks why Henry left the university when he was doing so well. Waldman says that his experiments were far in advance of the university. He says that Frankenstein's "insane ambition to create life" had changed him. He needed more human bodies than the university could supply. Frankenstein's "insane dream" was to destroy life and then recreate it. Waldman reluctantly agrees to accompany them to visit Frankenstein's laboratory.

Exterior shot of the old tower at night in the rain. Fritz is on the roof. Inside, Frankenstein tends his electric apparatus and calls Fritz down to the laboratory level to join him, again addressing him as "Fool." He is delighted at the approach of the electric storm, which is crucial to his experiment. Fritz is startled when the hand of the cadaver suddenly slips off the edge of the table. Frankenstein boasts about the creature, without blood or corruption, and he calls particular attention to the brain that Fritz stole, which is now implanted in the cadaver's skull. Frankenstein says the brain is waiting to return to life.

Frankenstein and Fritz test the equipment one last time before the storm is at its height, which is expected in fifteen minutes. They hear knocking at the door. Frankenstein sends Fritz down the long stairway with a lantern to send the visitors away. Fritz opens a panel behind a grill on the door, and Waldman identifies himself. Fritz denics entry and slams the panel shut. As he starts back up the stairs, he stops to pull up a sock that has fallen around his ankle. Elizabeth and the two men shout up at Frankenstein to let them in, and he descends himself to send them away. Elizabeth pleads with him to let them in out of the storm.

Frankenstein opens the door and lets them enter, but begs them to go away. Elizabeth pleads with him, and Victor says that Frankenstein is "inhuman" and "crazy." Bridling at the accusation that he is "crazy," Frankenstein leads them up the staircase into his laboratory and asks them to sit down as though they are watching a theatrical performance. Frankenstein keeps Waldman from examining the cadaver, and tells him that he has discovered a ray beyond the ultraviolet that will endow the cadaver with life. Waldman skeptically asks Frankenstein if he thinks he can bring the dead back to life, and Frankenstein responds that the body never had life. It is totally his creation. He invites Waldman to examine his creation.

As the thunder becomes louder, Frankenstein and Fritz raise the body on pulleys up into the tower, while lightning augments the effects of the electric apparatus. When he brings the body back to the level of the laboratory, the hand moves, and Frankenstein is ecstatic in announcing: "It's alive!"

Cut to the well lit parlor of Baron Frankenstein (Frederick Kerr), where Elizabeth and Victor try to reassure him about his son's well-being. Pompous in a comic mode, like a Colonel Blimp, he is skeptical and thinks another woman is involved. Before he can finish his bluster, the local burgomaster Vogel (Lionel Belmore) enters, presents a bouquet to Elizabeth, and asks when the wedding will take place. The Baron tells them that there will be no wedding at all unless Henry comes to his senses. The burgomaster is upset because the town is already prepared for the wedding and will be disappointed if it is canceled. The Baron dismisses him, and then prepares to leave himself with Victor and Elizabeth to go to his son's tower laboratory to find out if Henry is involved with another woman.

Cut to Frankenstein's study in the tower. Dr. Waldman argues that the creature should be kept under guard because it may be dangerous. Frankenstein, smoking with contented, almost smug, satisfaction, asks where we would be if we never did anything that was "dangerous." He extols the spirit of scientific inquiry, and Waldman reveals that the brain in the creature is a criminal brain. Waldman says that Frankenstein has created a monster and it will destroy him. Frankenstein is startled to learn of the criminal brain, but the information does not seem to cool his enthusiasm for his creation.

Frankenstein tells Waldman that the creature has been kept in the darkness since his creation, but will soon be brought into the light. Heavy footsteps outside the door announce the arrival of the Monster. Frankenstein turns out the light to receive his creation. The Monster appears in the doorway and turns to face Frankenstein, and in two cuts the camera moves in to an extreme close-up. Frankenstein gestures for him to sit down and opens a skylight. The Monster has his first experience of light and gestures longingly toward it. Frankenstein closes the window and tells the Monster to sit down, and this time he seems to understand the verbal command.

Fritz suddenly enters and brandishes a torch at the Monster, who reacts in panic. Again, Frankenstein addresses him as "you fool." Using a club, they subdue the terrified Monster and chain him to the floor in a dungeon cell in the basement of the tower. Fritz torments him with a whip, and Frankenstein intervenes, ordering him: "Leave it alone." Once Frankenstein leaves the cell, Fritz brandishes the torch in the Monster's face, realizing that it is terrified of fire. Back in his study, Frankenstein tells Waldman that Fritz hates the Monster. They hear a terrifying scream, rush to the basement, and discover that the Monster has murdered Fritz. They succeed in locking the

Monster into his cell, but decide that it has become a murderer that must be destroyed.

After Waldman and Frankenstein anesthetize the Monster with a hypodermic needle, Victor arrives and tells them that Elizabeth and the Baron are coming. They drag the Monster back into his cell. Victor lets them in. They reach the upper level, but when Frankenstein sees his visitors, he faints. The Baron and Elizabeth persuade Frankenstein to leave his tower, and Dr. Waldman offers to dispose of the Monster. In the laboratory he has the anesthetized Monster on an operating table, but as he prepares to kill it, the Monster recovers consciousness, strangles him and escapes.

Cut to a light-drenched garden, with Elizabeth and Frankenstein having tea together. He says it is "like heaven" being with her again. He says that he never knew heaven was so close because his work got in the way. They plan to have the wedding as soon as possible. Cut to the Baron as he uncovers the orange blossoms in a glass container that had been used for three generations of Frankenstein weddings. Henry wears the cutaway morning clothes of the groom. It is the wedding day. The Baron invites the wedding party to drink special wine bottled by his grandmother, but which she did not allow his grandfather to drink. The Baron thanks her for saving it for him. A toast to the son of the house of Frankenstein is followed by another to the health of young Frankenstein. The Baron offers champagne to the servants, since he believes that they could not appreciate the fine antique wine, and they, too, toast the house of Frankenstein. Outside the villagers are reveling, all of them happy on "a couple of bottles of beer," as the Baron says. He goes out to the balcony to greet them. He tells them there is more beer where that came from. They applaud and begin a folk dance.

The Monster wanders through a thicket, while a woodsman bids goodbye to his infant daughter Maria (Marilyn Harris). He must go to the village, and he leaves the child behind to play with her kitten. By the water's edge, she sees the Monster emerge from the brush. She offers him a flower, and he is moved by her kind gift. She invites him to join her in throwing flowers into the lake to see them float like boats. When they exhaust the number of flowers, he throws her into the water to see her float and panics when she sinks.

The townspeople continue their festivities. Elizabeth in her wedding gown brings Frankenstein into her dressing room and tells him she is afraid. She is apprehensive about Dr. Waldman's absence and has a premonition of something coming between them. Victor knocks at the door and tells Frankenstein about the death of Waldman. He says that the Monster has been seen terrorizing the countryside. They hear a grunt and fear that the Monster is in the castle. In his confusion Frankenstein locks Elizabeth into her bedroom and begins a frantic search of the house. As the men search the castle, the Monster enters the window of the bedroom. Elizabeth shrieks, and the Monster flees as the servants and men enter the room.

In a long tracking shot, the father brings the body of young Maria, with one stocking down around her ankle, through the revelers in the town square. The townspeople converge on the house of the burgomaster and demand justice for the murder of Maria. In the castle, Frankenstein, now dressed in a light riding costume, tells Victor that a wedding is impossible as long as the Monster is loose. He leaves Elizabeth in Victor's care and departs to search for the Monster. Outside, the burgomaster organizes the search. He orders: "Light your torches and go." The crowd of vigilantes begins the search, amid the baying of bloodhounds and the glare of torches. The burgomaster continues to give orders.

Frankenstein leads his contingent into the mountains, but becomes separated from his band. He stumbles into the Monster and finds that his torch no longer intimidates his quarry. The Monster drags him, unconscious, to the upper level of a windmill. The townspeople, with their torches, gather at the base of the structure. Frankenstein and the Monster, hunter and quarry, glare at each other as equals through the turning gears of the windmill. Frankenstein tries to escape, but the Monster grabs him. They struggle. Frankenstein falls from the ledge and is caught on one of the rotating blades of the windmill. He drops safely to the ground. The villagers torch the windmill, and the Monster screaming in terror perishes in the flames.

Cut back to the castle as the maids, with a tray of wine glasses, knock at the door of Frankenstein's bedroom. They want the recuperating Henry Frankenstein to have a taste of his grandmother's special wine. The Baron takes the wine himself and proposes a toast: "A son for the house of Frankenstein." The maids repeat the toast.

COMMENTARY

The word "Frankenstein" invariably conjures up the image of Boris Karloff in his spectacular make-up by Jack Pierce of Universal Studios. The film, however, like the novel it is based upon, is not the story of a monster. It is emphatically the story of the Monster's creator, Dr. Frankenstein. In the novel his first name is Victor, but as the story made its way from novel to screen, he became Henry. His best friend from the novel, Henry Clerval, becomes Victor Moritz in the film.

Mary Shelley underscored the importance of the central character to the theme when she added the subtitle, *The New Prometheus*, after the demigod from Greek mythology who dared to steal fire from the heavens to give it to humans after the gods had decided to keep it from them as a punishment for their pride. The gods were infuriated by the impertinence of Prometheus and condemned him to spend eternity chained to a rock. Each day vultures would devour his liver, but at night the organ would grow back. He would have remained the center of this unending avian banquet forever, had not Hercules rescued him during one of his adventures. In another, later set of legends, Prometheus became a master craftsman of such skill that he created a human being out of clay. This second story was recycled into the Golem stories of Yiddish folklore, which provided the basis of the film of that name by Paul Wegner in 1920, and the film in turn provided Whale, Jack Pierce and Boris Karloff with much of the inspiration for the Monster's appearance in 1931.

The book and the film alike build on the Promethean elements in the story of Dr. Frankenstein. As the traditional "mad scientist," he defied the gods—Nature, a personal God or even human propriety—by trying to bring an unsuitable form of knowledge to humanity. By his experiments he hoped to solve the mysteries of life. Even more pointedly, by creating life, however monstrous, from dead matter, he dared to usurp the role of creator, which is appropriate to God/Nature alone. Like the figures of classic Greek tragedy, his tragic flaw is an overwhelming pride, hubris, that blinds him to his proper role as a human being. In her own introduction to the edition of 1831, Mary Shelley writes: "Frightful must it be, for supremely frightful would be the effect of any human endeavor to mock the stupendous mechanism of the Creator of the world."[31] As the author understood her own work, then, the horror comes not from the menace of the Monster but from the blasphemous pride of the scientist who cannot understand the consequences of his actions.

Whale shared that understanding of the meaning of *Frankenstein*, the novel and the film. In the prologue to *The Bride of Frankenstein*, the fictional Mary Shelley (Elsa Lanchester) tells Byron and Shelley that her publishers failed to understand the meaning of her original work. She says its purpose was to present the "punishment that befell a mortal who dared to emulate God." Since Mary Shelley wrote only one book on Frankenstein, it seems fair to conclude that Whale is using her persona to refer to his earlier work on the subject. The second film is, in fact, adapted from later portions of Shelley's novel.

Whale and his scriptwriters (Robert Florey, Garrett Fort and Francis Edward Faragoh) set the Promethean theme ironically in the prologue spoken by Edward Van Sloan, who will appear as Dr. Waldman, the scientist who mediates the legitimate aspirations and competence of scientific inquiry with the fatal ambition of his former student and younger colleague, Henry Frankenstein. His lightly patronizing air reduces the audience of the forthcoming film to a class of students. Thus he fuses the audience with Frankenstein by telling them that they are about to plumb "the two great mysteries of creation: life and death." He has already mentioned quite explicitly that the audience will see the story of "a man of science who sought to create a man after his own image without reckoning on God." He warns the audience that this kind of an adventure may "thrill" them or "shock" them or "even horrify" them, and then invites them to leave if they "do not want to subject [their] nerves to such a strain." Dr. Frankenstein and the film tread on sacred terrain, scarcely suitable for mortal eyes, and if the audience joins them, it does so at its own risk. By not heeding the warning, the audience becomes voyeur to the crime and, even more, collaborators in Frankenstein's morbid curiosity about the mysteries of life and death.

The theme of vision reappears in the background of the opening titles. A horrifying mask features two eyes that shoot forth powerful rays that penetrate into things human eyes should not see. The features of the mask are twisted in horror of the sights it witnesses. The mask dissolves into a spinning collage of eyes as though the voyeurs, Frankenstein and the audience alike, have grown dizzy staring at things unfit for human vision. The scene is an homage to a shot in *Metropolis* when the young men at a banquet scene stare at a robot made in the image of a sensual dancing woman who is programmed to seduce and destroy the entire city at the bidding of the evil scientist, Dr. Rotwang. In *Frankenstein,* the image of the eyes suggests the staring eyes of the motion picture audience as well as the penetrating vision of Dr. Frankenstein. Both can be lured to their destruction by what they see, or strive to see.

The figure of Henry Frankenstein so dominates the film that virtually every male character embodies some facet of his highly complex personality. The complexity is entirely appropriate, since Frankenstein represents the entire human race with its varied tissue of godlike ambition and human limitation, divine spirit and earthbound flesh in one. It is a meditation on the sin of pride that is every bit as fundamental as the account of the first sin in Genesis.

Dr. Waldman, for example, represents the man of science that Frankenstein could have become. He is learned but prudent, and he respects the sacred nature of his investigations. He expresses his disappointment to Elizabeth and Victor over Frankenstein's "insane ambition to create life." He puts his scientific knowledge at the service of his visitors and goes with them to see Frankenstein. His knowledge exercises a moderating influence on the experiment. Later, when the Monster murders Fritz and threatens to kill them all, it is Dr. Waldman who injects it with the anesthetic. Later, he prepares to perform the operation that will destroy the Monster. In both cases, he acts after Frankenstein has gained some insight into the horrible consequences of his creation. Waldman is present to use science to correct the mistakes of his colleague and former student, and eventually he will lose his own life in the performance of this duty. By losing his own life in an attempt to correct the sin of Frankenstein, Waldman functions like a secular redeemer. His death finally convinces Frankenstein of the monstrosity of his work. As a character, Waldman dies, but as a function of Frankenstein's personality, he is resurrected as a triumph of wisdom and conscience. Ultimately, Frankenstein's better side is victorious.

If the dignified Waldman represents the idealized side of Frankenstein's personality, Fritz the hunchback shows his deformed side. The physical deformity is but the image of the moral deformity of Frankenstein. Fritz lacks any moral sense whatever. Expediency propels his actions, whether it demands robbing a grave, cutting down an executed criminal from the scaffold, or stealing a human brain, any brain. His indifference to the selection of the "criminal" brain reveals his undeveloped moral sense: it makes no difference to him. Fritz hates the Monster, even more deformed than he is, because he is a visual reminder of his own monstrosity. He torments it with whips and torches until it finally destroys him. In this sequence, Whale demonstrates that by destroying Fritz the Monster also has the power to destroy Frankenstein, morally as well as physically. In fact, the murder of Fritz symbolically destroys the dark side, since Frankenstein sees the error of his insane ambition and agrees to let Waldman destroy the Monster, scarcely imagining that his scientific imprudence would end with Waldman's murder as well.

Both extremes within Frankenstein, the man of science and the man of a deformed moral sense, die early in the film, and Henry becomes simply a limited human being who wants to remedy the consequences of his actions. Surviving to the end with Frankenstein is his best friend Victor Moritz. Victor competes with Frankenstein for the love of Elizabeth, but he is completely generous and self-sacrificing in his affection. He offers her the kind of friendship that Frankenstein cannot as long as he is held captive by his ambition. Frankenstein, playing his self-appropriated role of creator, wants to continue the dynasty of his family with Elizabeth as his wife, but he transfers his passion to the experiment. He returns to her after he realizes that his Monster is an unholy creation. Victor is constant in his love for Elizabeth. In fact, he is the most loving side of Frankenstein's disposition, representing what Frankenstein would have been before he was seized by his insane scheme.

Victor is kind and loving, but also dreadfully dull. In Victor, Shelley and Whale face a problem that has always plagued authors of moral fiction. Sinners and those who flirt with sin are generally more interesting and sympathetic characters than the righteous. In "Paradise Lost," for example, Milton was not altogether successful in making God a more sympathetic figure than Satan. In the film, it is an inescapable conclusion that through his experience of sin and repentance, Frankenstein becomes a better man than Victor and thus a more suitable husband for Elizabeth.

Baron Frankenstein provides the comic relief with his harmless pomposity, but he also represents all the bourgeois traits that Henry cannot endure. If he had not been touched by his love of science and had not fallen into sin, Henry Frankenstein would have become the same dull country gentleman as his father, and he could not tolerate that happening to himself. The Baron is a snob, dismissing servants and burgomaster alike as fools unworthy of his serious attention. A man of little vision, he asks few questions of life and seems content with his pipe and fine wines. Henry needs more. With his brilliance and natural curiosity, he stretches his horizons far beyond the baronial estate. He has been to the university at Goldstadt, and he locates his laboratory in a watchtower where he can have vision and perspective on the world. Without the fire of inquiry, Henry could develop into another Baron. Whale uses the character of the elder Frankenstein to lampoon the petty nobility, a social class he both resents and envies.

One final male character remains. As Waldman and Fritz are projections of the strength and weakness respectively of Frankenstein's scientific genius, and if Victor and the Baron represent what he might have been without his gifts, then the Monster surely presents an image of what Frankenstein has made of himself. It is a visualization of the consequences of his mad act of trying to imitate or even replace God in the role of creator. Its repulsive appearance awakens Frankenstein to the monstrosity of his pride, almost as though the Monster were a living embodiment of the conscience of its creator.

Creature and creator have much in common. Both reach pathetically for the sun. Frankenstein builds an enormous apparatus to hoist his creature up into the sky, where it will be touched by lightning. The Monster stretches his hands toward a skylight, fascinated by the light. When Frankenstein closes the cover of the skylight on the Monster, it echoes God's closing the scientist off from the light. According to the Genesis stories, all creation begins with light, but this kind of light belongs to God alone. Frankenstein, like his creature, reaches for the light through his unholy experiments, and the Monster with his pathetic gesture provides an image of the same thwarted striving.

Both need companionship. When Frankenstein turns away from Elizabeth, he creates a monstrosity. To save himself, and the village, he must return to her. The Monster has no such option. As the dark side of Frankenstein's personality, the Monster's need for companionship ends in the murder of the child Maria. It destroys everything it tries to love, much as Frankenstein would have destroyed Elizabeth had he not come to his senses.

Both become more sympathetic characters as the film progresses. Henry Frankenstein appears at first as a totally amoral, self-centered scientist, and the Monster with his horrifying appearance is a brute and little more. Gradually, however, Whale reveals more about each. Frankenstein really did not understand the consequences of his acts until it was too late. The criminal brain was not his fault, but Fritz's, his dark alter ego. Despite its appearance, the Monster appears harmless enough until Fritz pushes a lighted torch in its face to see its reaction. Both seem victims: Frankenstein of his own actions, which he tries desperately to disown, and the Monster of external forces, represented by Fritz's sadistic games. At the climax of the film, the two face each other as equals through the grinding gears of the windmill. Fate winds out the destiny for both antagonists. Frankenstein has to kill his creation to atone for his sins, but it seems terribly unfair to the Monster, who, after all, did not ask to be created and had little control over his life once he was. In effect, Frankenstein has to kill part of himself if he is to live.

That moment in the windmill is one of pure horror. Frankenstein comes face to face with the evil that he is capable of creating and realizes the extent of his own malice. It will destroy him, unless he can destroy it. The outcome lies in doubt even as he plunges from the top of the tower and is caught on the blade, which cuts the horizon like a redemptive cross. The movement of the blades reverses itself and Frankenstein safely reaches the ground, battered but alive. The purgatorial fires that envelop the windmill destroy the Monster, that part of Frankenstein's ego that had to be purged so that the atonement for his pride might be complete. The shrieks of the Monster, trapped in the flames, arouse pity, but they do not raise any doubt that such a purgation is necessary.

Fire is a primal image that reappears at several key moments in the film. It first appears in the dark shadows of the cemetery when the gravedigger lights his pipe. The light of his match explodes on the screen, but his gesture is perfectly natural. That is the genius of the image. His corporal work of mercy in burying the dead completes the life cycle as designed by the creator, and with his simple task of covering a coffin with earth and patting it into place, he shares the work of God. Fritz and Frankenstein remain hidden in exterior darkness at the edge of the cemetery.

Fire in the wrong hands, however, can be frightening and destructive. It is the creative power of light and the fire of apocalyptic purification that belongs to God alone. As Frankenstein prepares his grand experiment, the scene shifts to Elizabeth's drawing room. Even though the room is well lighted, a three-pronged candelabra burns in front of Frankenstein's picture, thus associating him with fire. During the experiment he reaches for the fire of heaven by raising his creation toward an opening in the roof. When the Monster reaches for the light, the scene is one of lovely tranquility. The gesture is tender, almost childlike. When Fritz, the dark side of Frankenstein, enters the scene, fire becomes a menace and starts the chain of events that will lead to death both for Fritz himself and for Dr. Waldman.

Fire again becomes a menace near the end of the film when the townspeople light their torches to search for the Monster. By this time sympathy has so shifted to the Monster that the crowd becomes a frenzied mob and the Monster an object of persecution. The crowds have taken justice into their own hands, another form of usurping the role of God, and the prospect of their vengeance is terrifying. Finally, when Frankenstein and his creation face each other alone in the windmill, the fire threatens to consume both of them. The flame is no longer under the control of Frankenstein, but it becomes rather an impersonal force that must destroy the Monster and, if necessary, its creator as well. When challenged about the necessity of this final scene of purgatorial fire, James Whale rejected alternate conclusions and answered: "It has to be like that: you see it's all part of the ritual."[32]

As Frankenstein wrestles with his ambition, he is photographed in darkness that is ruptured by streaks of light and flame. As he settles into his appropriate role as creature, he appears in clear light. After he has left his tower and joins Elizabeth for tea in the garden, the scene is washed with a flat, shadowless sunlight. During the climactic confrontation at the windmill, the nighttime scene erupts in flame, but when the action shifts back to the Frankenstein mansion, again a flat light bathes the interiors. The scenes of quiet light suggest the calm illuminated state of Frankenstein's soul.

Not all the scenes of terror, however, take place in a setting of darkness and flame. The child Maria is murdered in a calm outdoor setting, and her father brings the body back through the dancing townspeople in sunlight reflected on the street scenes. When the Monster enters the mansion to threaten Elizabeth, the interiors remain well lighted. The level of illumination is fitting, since neither of these scenes involves Frankenstein's wrestling in the darkness for his own moral identity. For the greater part of the film, his soul is a battleground between the forces of light and darkness, and the characteristic night and flame motif is appropriate. After the battle has been won, incidents of horror remain, but the conflict is quite different and the flame imagery is no longer suitable. In these scenes the light is appropriate, since it allows the audience to observe the horror while enjoying a clear view as objective spectators. When Frankenstein wrestles with his conscience, the audience and he both submerge into a world of darkness.

Elizabeth, usually wearing light clothes and appearing in tranquil lighting, does not conform to the usual pattern of heroines in Horror films. Her light clothing and well lit settings suggest a real world, devoid of horrible fantasy and under the control of reason. As fiancée she embodies the powers of natural procreation. Fire is distorted light and represents a flight from reason into nightmare and Frankenstein's mad ambition to bypass natural human procreation to create life from death, not from another life like Elizabeth's. For her final appearance in the film, she wears the white bridal gown and veil, but even at this late moment the wedding ceremony cannot continue as long as the Monster lives. Frankenstein believes that locking her in her bedroom will ensure her safety, but his strategy actually endangers her life. She cannot escape when the Monster enters through the

window. Frankenstein's mistake must be completely destroyed before he can once again return to plans of marriage and a natural
family.

Elizabeth provides a variation on the customary role of the heroine in Horror films. Generally these women balance the roles of
victim and vamp. Being weaker and thus physically or sexually vulnerable to their male adversaries, they are potential victims who must be
rescued by the hero. At the same time, in some ways they bring the
danger upon themselves. At times they are openly seductive and
scorn warnings to be more circumspect. This is the traditional role of
the heroine in the Dracula stories, and of course her meeting with the
vampire is clearly sexual in character. In other cases, however, the
heroine's foolhardy behavior is quite innocent: she is simply imprudent or curious.

Elizabeth is a victim, but she does not fill the traditional "vamp"
role in either sense of the term. She wants to go ahead with plans to
marry Henry Frankenstein, and she is more revolted than curious
about his creation. She remains coolly distant from the action and has
the prudence to bring Victor and Dr. Waldman with her to visit Frankenstein's tower. She pleads with Frankenstein not to lock her into
the bedroom, and in this case she has far more sense than he. She
stands simply as the ideal of normal life that Frankenstein desires but
cannot have until he is purified of his sin. As such she is the embodiment of his natural impulses toward marriage and family.

Much closer to the customary victim/vamp is the child Maria. She
is too naive and innocent to realize the danger of the Monster, and she
invites him to play with her. Tossing flowers into the water is a fore-
shadowing of the senseless destruction of her own tender and beautiful life through drowning. The Monster squanders her life as easily as
she squanders the lives of the flowers in her harmless but destructive
game. The sexual overtones of the flowers remain on the symbolic
level. Maria is "deflowered" in the sense that she tragically loses her
innocence by being too trusting of the stranger. As her father carries
her body back into the town through the reveling peasants, the camera observes that one stocking has fallen down around her ankle. This
image offers only the subtlest suggestion of sexual innuendo. Nothing
in the film offers any hint of sexual molestation. In fact the fallen
stocking echoes Fritz's fallen sock, as though the pure evil that Fritz
represents leaves its mark on evil effects in the world. One image of
his deformity has fallen upon her as his victim.

One minor character plays such a small role that it is often ignored, but it is of major significance. The crowd gives the film its

distinctive Depression message. Like the members of the house of Frankenstein, the townspeople are powerless in the face of the danger that has been turned loose among them. They are victims not only of the Monster, but of the capricious, irresponsible schemes of the empowered classes. They are the ordinary people who celebrate weddings with music and dance and need only a bottle of beer to complete their happiness. Their complacency is shattered when one of their own, Maria's father, carries the body of his slain daughter slowly through the dancing revelers. The long tracking shot builds in power as the townspeople finally realize the horror that has taken place and fall silent. A moment later they gather at the burgomaster's house to demand action. Nothing but blood will satisfy them.

In economic terms the crowds form an instant rapport with American audiences during the Depression.[33] The upper classes have scorned them and by their imprudent financial manipulations have brought misery upon the working classes. Since they have no power to confront the monsters in their midst, the only solution for them is to assume the form of a mob and run frantically through the night shouting for blood.

The parallels may seem to forecast and even encourage a native form of Bolshevik uprising, but that is far from the total story. Films, as popular art forms coming from studios owned by very conservative businessmen, generally support the values of the dominant culture, and *Frankenstein* is no exception. The mob racing about in the night accomplishes nothing, nor does the inflammatory burgomaster provide effective leadership. The town is saved because Henry Frankenstein, who has become separated from his band, confronts the Monster alone. He has recognized his sin in tampering with nature—or, to keep the Depression analogy, the economy. But he has shown that he is now able to provide them with the natural heir that they need to maintain social and political stability in their tiny duchy. While the national leaders may have gotten the country into the Depression, they are the only ones who can remedy the situation. The old order is thus vindicated and reinstalled more securely than before, and the film ends with the Baron and the maids toasting "A son for the house of Frankenstein."

Whale's ambivalence toward the ruling classes is never more apparent than in this final scene. Henry remains isolated in his bedroom recovering from his fall from the windmill. The dithering old Baron carefully closes the door behind him and joins the maids alone. They have brought the special family wine for Henry, but the Baron takes it himself without offering them any. He proposes the toast, and the maids, without having any wine themselves, join in celebrating the continuation of the Baron's lineage by repeating the words of the toast as the Baron drinks alone.

Whale presents the Baron as a buffoon and thus the object of his comedy of manners. At the same time, he and the maids acknowledge that he is their best hope for security, and thus he becomes an object of their unrealistic respect. The Baron keeps them in a state of infantile dependence on him and his successors, but he and Whale believe that they are really capable of nothing else. Ever the working-class Englishman, Whale regards the petty aristocracy with an odd combination of admiration and contempt.

Whale's *Frankenstein* bristles with unresolved paradoxes, and surely that factor underlies its unending popularity. In his introduction Edward Van Sloan warned audiences that the film would be about life and death. He told the truth, but not the whole truth. The film is about much more: about ambition and contentment, about imagination and realism, about class struggles and social order, about sin and redemption. Most of all, it is about the human condition, and that is what makes it a classic.

NOTES

1. The date of James Whale's birth remains a mystery, for reasons that will soon become apparent. The standard reference works disagree by ten years: Leslie Halliwell, in *Filmgoer's Companion*, 8th ed. (New York: Scribners, 1984), p. 1067, lists the date as 1886. Ephraim Katz, *The Film Encyclopedia* (New York: Perigee, 1979), p. 1226, assures the reader that the date is 1896. Philip Kemp, in *World Film Directors: Volume One*, ed. John Wakeman (New York: Wilson, 1987), p. 1197, picks 1889. Thomas Milne, in "One Man Crazy: James Whale," in *Sight and Sound* 42 (Summer 1973), p. 166, notes the confusion and states that he has information that leads him to select 1889. James Curtis, in *James Whale* (Metuchen, N.J.: Scarecrow, 1982), p. 1, agrees with Milne, but then cites the memorial plaque at the niche in the columbarium where Whale's ashes are interred which cites 1893 (p. 204). The bulk of current opinion seems to rest on 1889, despite the memorial plaque.

2. Andrew Sarris, *The American Cinema: Directors and Directions 1929–1968* (New York: Dutton, 1968), p. 171.

3. Sarris, p. 187.

4. Cf. note 1, above.

5. Curtis, p. 2.

6. Kemp, p. 1197.

7. Curtis, p. 43.

8. Curtis, pp. 52–53.

9. Thomas Schatz, *The Genius of the System: Hollywood Film-making in the Studio Era* (New York: Pantheon, 1988), p. 229.

10. John Baxter, *Hollywood in the Thirties* (London: Zwemmer, 1968), p. 71.

11. Curtis, p. 97.

12. Milne, pp. 169–171 argues on artistic grounds against the commonly held belief that Whale went into a decline after *The Bride of Frankenstein*. He finds many virtues in the later films. As a critic heavily influenced by the auteur movement, he weights visual style quite heavily, and Whale's mastery of mise-en-scène is undeniable. Since Milne's reassessment, few critics have tried to rehabilitate Whale's reputation by analyzing these later films.

13. Curtis, pp. 142 and 181–184.

14. David A. Cook, *A History of the Narrative Film* (New York: Norton, 1981), p. 14.

15. Elizabeth MacAndrew, *The Gothic Tradition in Fiction* (New York: Columbia University Press, 1979), pp. 7–9.

16. The distinction between terror and horror is described in some length in James B. Twitchell, *Dreadful Pleasures, An Anatomy of Modern Horror* (New York: Oxford, 1985), pp. 16–19.

17. *Dreadful Pleasures*, p. 22.

18. MacAndrew, p. 13.

19. *Dreadful Pleasures*, pp. 112–113.

20. *Dreadful Pleasures*, p. 50.

21. William Patrick Day, *In the Circles of Fear and Desire: A Study of Gothic Fantasy* (Chicago: University of Chicago Press, 1985), pp. 17–19, discusses the relationship between the heroes and heroines in Gothic fiction.

22. James B. Twitchell, *Forbidden Partners, The Incest Taboo in Modern Culture* (New York: Columbia University Press, 1987), pp. 147–148.

23. R.H.W. Dillard, *Horror Films* (New York: Simon and Schuster, 1976), p. 1.

24. Lotte H. Eisner, *The Haunted Screen: Expressionism in the German Cinema and the Influence of Max Reinhardt* (Berkeley: Univ. of California Press, 1977), p. 10.

25. Siegfried Kracauer, *From Caligari to Hitler: A Psychological*

278   THE HORROR FILM

History of the German Film (Princeton: Princeton University Press, 1966), pp. 66–68.

26. Kracauer, p. 133.

27. Curtis, pp. 133–134.

28. D.L. White, "The Poetics of Horror: More Than Meets the Eye," in *Film Genre: Theory and Criticism*, ed. Barry K. Grant (Metuchen, N.J.: Scarecrow, 1977), pp. 124–127.

29. *Dreadful Pleasures*, p. 57.

30. S.S. Prawer, *Caligari's Children: The Film as a Tale of Terror* (New York: DaCapo, 1980), p. 272.

31. Mary Shelley, *Frankenstein, Or, The Modern Prometheus* (New York: Signet, 1983), p. xi.

32. Prawer, p. 22.

33. Gehring, p. 213.

PART III

Chapter Ten

A PERSONAL POSTSCRIPT

Priest professors in Catholic colleges have long ago entered the folklore of our tradition in America. Most educated Catholics of a certain age remember with fondness a particular priest or brother or sister who taught them Latin grammar, chemistry or English poetry way back when. Often these memories have been refracted through a prism of nostalgia and filtered through regret that fewer priests and religious are involved with education anymore. For a recently immigrant church, which saw itself as threatened by a dominant Protestant culture, Catholic education became both a stepping stone out of poverty and the key to the preservation of the faith. Having priests and religious in the classroom, teaching secular subjects, is a venerable part of the American Catholic tradition.

A priest teaching movies, however, does not quite fit the pattern. Students both at Georgetown and now at LeMoyne, who do not give a second thought to priest faculty members in the more traditional disciplines, show no mercy in raising questions about my involvement with films for the last twenty-five years. How did I become interested? What do I hope to accomplish?

The question fascinates me, not so much because of the vanity of an invitation to autobiography, but because in many ways my own experience offers a fairly good picture of the church's developing concern with film throughout the years. Although I still consider myself at mid-career, my interest in film has gone through several transitions that roughly parallel the involvement of the church in the movie business, as I tried to describe in the first part of this book. Although I have been professionally involved in films for twenty-five years, I feel as though I was present at the creation and an eyewitness to several stages of evolution. Let me reduce the development I described in the early chapters of this book to a personal reflection.

By way of parenthesis, what I find particularly intriguing in this story is the ease with which my religious superiors gave the necessary permissions for my beginning a long program of studies to gain a degree that offered limited attractiveness to the Jesuit schools of the day. (Not many Jesuit schools in the early 1960s had film or even communications departments. Continuing studies in English literature, my first love, would certainly have made me a more versatile player on the Jesuit team apostolate in the schools.)

The men who made these decisions may have been puzzled by my choice of an area of studies, but they were unfailing in their support during the long years of study. Many of them never went to the movies themselves, and of those who did, most, I am sure, went for pure escapist entertainment. They were administrators and churchmen, not visionaries, and I doubt that any of them could have put down on an index card the reasons for investing in my specialized education with the generosity that they did. I wonder if they had some dumb, vague intuition that this was an important area for the church to look into and know something about. Whatever their motives and insights, my roadway was dotted with green lights.

Nor do I claim visionary status for myself. In fact, I did not argue and cajole my way into film study through a battery of persuasive, pleading letters to superiors, simply because I did not have to. Film was merely at the top of the list of several subjects I could have pursued with enthusiasm. Perhaps like the men who controlled my future at the time, I had little more than a feeling that this is something important to look into as part of my future work as a priest.

Movies were a natural direction for my interests to follow in the postgraduate phase of my education. My father used to tour the theaters of several chains in New York. The work consisted mainly in buying tickets on an hourly basis and checking the numbers printed on the roll tickets against the size of the audience. Counting the house was an important skill for the work. A common scam in those days involved the doorman, who would retain the untorn ticket of an entering patron, and then slip it back to the cashier, who would resell the ticket "loose," that is, not from the roll. The sale would not be recorded on the ticket dispensing machine, and the two would then pocket the extracurricular receipts. As a fairly young child, I was dragged along in tow as an excuse to check children's ticket sales. By the time I reached high school, I was regularly spending Friday or Saturday at the movies. Not only did I see a tremendous number of films, all maddenly interrupted by the hourly "buys," but the work was the answer to a teenager's pocketbook. Since tickets were always bought in pairs, I could bring a friend, generally of the opposite persuasion, and through the high school years I must have saved a fortune in dating. Along with most other American adolescents of the 1950s, the movies were part of my world, perhaps even a larger part than for many. Who knows what ideas, attitudes and values I picked up during that time and what effect their lingering influence has had on my adult thinking? In any case, the movies formed an important part of my intellectual and emotional horizon.

Early involvement with "the industry" brought another benefit. Like most Catholics of the era, I never thought to doubt the value of the annual oath of allegiance to the Legion of Decency, and I knew with certitude that seeing a movie on the "C" list would be sufficient to imperil my eternal salvation. Movies were fun, but in my more scrupulous childhood moments they were also a threat. As a movie brat, however, I was able to join my father each year at the annual communion breakfast of the Holy Name Society of the Motion Picture Industry. After Mass at St. Patrick's Cathedral, two thousand or more people, many of them non-Catholic, gathered for breakfast at the Waldorf-Astoria Hotel to hear personalities in the entertainment in dustry describe their experiences in influencing the moral quality of films. Thus, while I was still struggling with the third declension in Latin, I took for granted the fact that the church is involved with motion pictures, not only to protect its own members from "the near occasions of sin," but to help bring a heightened sense of moral values to the screen.

Oddly enough, my own thinking in those years may be a fairly close approximation of the church's sense of its own mission in the world of the motion picture. This is not to imply that these concerns are those of a childhood phase, but rather they are interests that were generally acknowledged as valid as early as the 1950s. In fact the work continues to this day. The Legion of Decency has passed through its various incarnations as the National Catholic Office of Motion Pictures and the Department of Communications of the U.S. Catholic Conference. The office still provides a valuable service in providing ratings as guides, especially for parents, about the suitability of current films. Its second major function is to continue dialogue with the industry on questions of taste. Although most of the work of the department is now the responsibility of lay people, few would have any doubt about the propriety of a priest's contribution to the staff.

Similarly, the religious communities have become quite sophisticated in producing film and video to further the message of the gospel. Few could doubt the professional quality of materials provided, for example, by the Rev. John Catoir of the Christophers in New York, by the Rev. Ellwood Keiser, C.S.P., of Paulist Productions in Los Angeles, or the Rev. Michael Tueth, S.J., of the Sacred Heart Program in St. Louis. These and others, surely, have been effectively using film and videotape to improve the media atmosphere of the day. Again, even as early as the 1950s, few would challenge these roles of the church in the media.

During the 1950s, film work was the concern of the moral theologian and the catechist. By the middle of the next decade, the dogmatic theologian joined the cast. By this time, the writing of William Lynch, S.J., and Harold Gardiner, S.J., had made it possible for the movies to be taken as a serious art form by students of theology. During my seminary years I remember long discussions about the religious message of *La Strada* (Fellini, 1954) and *The Seventh Seal* (Bergman, 1956). Surely the serious films coming out of Europe in the postwar period would provide a new forum for dialogue between believers of different traditions and between believers and nonbelievers. The conversation could take place in either a university setting with students or at a cinema club for workers like those in Belgium and French-speaking Canada. As audiences discovered the theological content of the symbols and images, they could appreciate anew the relevance of religion to the concerns of contemporary people. My own doctoral dissertation, "The Lutheran Milieu of Ingmar Bergman's Films," is fairly typical of the kind of topics attracting eager young Jesuits at the time.

Although one can trace a continuity from this theological approach back to the earlier catechetical interests of the churches, a serious change had taken place. The main site of this type of work moved into the universities. Professional credentials in film work, as opposed to theology, became respectable. Church people like myself had the privilege of marching off to secular universities to learn what scholars with no particular religious objectives had discovered about film. We might keep theological concerns in our writing and teaching, but they would have to be academically acceptable to our peers. From this period on, we had the twin benefits of learning from professionals and from subjecting our own research to the test of open dialogue with those of no religious belief. Critical literature began to pour out of Paris and the British Film Institute in London. As the center of gravity slid toward the academy, the immediate catechetical bias of the work became less obvious.

Now film study came to resemble the other, more traditional academic disciplines, but with a difference. It was not a high priority item for the Catholic schools. In the notion of having priest teachers in the colleges to provide some contact with the church for young people as they enter adulthood, movies did not seem to warrant that position. Most schools were not eager to hire a movie professor just to offer an apostolic "contact," since many people in the academic community still doubted the scholarly respectability of studies of the popular arts. Could anyone imagine giving three credits to a student for a semester of sitting around watching cowboy movies?

As the 1960s collapsed in exhaustion into the 1970s, I took my brand new doctorate in film not to a classroom, but to *America*, where I began a temporary assignment as associate editor in 1971. The temporary assignment lasted for fourteen years. The move out of academics was initially a disappointment, but it turned out to be a prolonged postgraduate period. After a few years I became the regular reviewer of films, writing one page critiques of the American films released during the past few days. Since foreign films of an "intellectual" variety rarely gain distribution outside a few major cities, I was forced to write about the popular American films that would eventually reach most of the readership of the magazine. Often I was startled to discover that many of the analytical tools I had acquired in my study of the serious European films could be applied to popular American films. I was not writing down to an audience or to a subject matter, but on the contrary I was discovering for myself a mine of riches in current Hollywood production.

No one could doubt the technical excellence of the American film. Some could object that it is merely "slick," but the fact is that Hollywood to this day continues to attract the finest talent from around the world. Many American films each year are significant artistic statements. Furthermore, since movies today come not from the studios but from independent producers who risk their financial survival on a marketable product, the films by necessity must appeal to the concerns of the broadest possible audience. The best producers and directors have their fingers on the pulse of the American people. They know by instinct as much as by market analysis the kinds of themes that appeal to them. By contrast, television, another splendid barometer of the American psyche, is a disposable commodity. The networks fire shotgun blasts at the public, knowing that more projected series will miss the target than will win an audience and make a profit. They hope some new programs become hits, but they have replacements in line before the season begins. If a series makes it, the producers will offer a new episode each week; some will succeed, some will flop. From week to week they can tinker with the characters and situations. Films on the other hand force a producer to fire a rifle shot. If it misses with its one multimillion dollar bullet, the company will go bankrupt. They have to be extremely careful in gauging what the public wants and will accept.

Since I am sensitive to these market forces, many of my reviews in *America* read like social criticism. Of course. Many of the films provide an insight into American society, telling us what we think, really think, about war and peace, about marriage and family, about wealth and the American dream, about race, religion, sex, death and violence.

At this point the dialogue between the church and the film industry becomes more intangible, but ever more important. Reviewers and critics cannot do much to change the industry or the viewing public, as was hoped in the early Legion of Decency days, nor can they continue to draw religious messages from secular films, as was hoped in the sophisticated catechetical age of the 1950s. We can, however, act as mediators, helping the church understand the world as it exists today. We can point out the concerns of men and women in the real world by looking at the films they see, that is, the films that very shrewd producers and directors believe will appeal to the public.

The idea is maddeningly vague, but my presumption is that the gospel is never preached in a vacuum. Films give us a sense of the American people as we are and as we believe we are. For example, if we preach Christ as a hero restoring order to a fallen world, it helps to realize that heroes today are psychopathic killers who use violence indiscriminately, like Rambo, Dirty Harry and the Charles Bronson avenger characters. It should make us more careful in our Christology as well as our catechetics. This is not a question of substance, but of our rhetoric. Again, the widespread acceptance of profanity, nudity, recreational sex and gratuitous violence in films should show us that these are poor examples to cite if we want to fan the moral consciousness into a sense of outrage. Oppression, greed and abusive behavior seem far more repellent to people today.

The consciousness raising, I hope, would work in two directions at once. Not only can criticism in a religious context make the church more aware of the world it strives to evangelize, but it might, in ideal circumstances, help readers to reflect on their own attitudes and values. Films touch current experience with extraordinary immediacy. In fact, a good film should draw its audience into the lives of the characters and make it relive the events of the story. An effective critical essay should move, without inflicting violence on the artist or the work, from the text on the screen to the ideas and emotions it touches in the lives of the audience.

A critic with theological concerns strides across a perilous middle ground. At times, as I reread some of my reviews in *America*, I find an annoying homiletic or even moralistic tone. In such cases I have abandoned the text too easily and leapt into my own concerns. At other times I ask myself how a particular essay of mine would differ from one written by an atheist in a secular journal. This second instance is much less disturbing, since at least I have let the film speak for itself, which is the primary responsibility of any critic. I would like to go further with the material, but frequently enough the content does not support a particularly religious interpretation. Through the years since graduate school, I have become more respectful of the secular. I do not have to uncover a deep moral message, a Messiah figure or eucharistic imagery at meals to appreciate the excellence of the work. Why not simply enjoy the mayhem of the Marx Brothers for its own sake?

In 1985, it was time to retire my editor's blue pencil, end my fourteen year sabbatical and return to the classroom, first at Georgetown and two years later at LeMoyne. By this time in both institutions, film study had become an acceptable discipline—at least neither school suggested that I work part-time in the cafeteria to justify my salary.

Teaching film is a far different enterprise from writing reviews in a weekly magazine. First of all, it demands working day by day on a give-and-take basis with my younger fellow critics. Not only do they bring challenging, fresh perspectives to each film we view, but they refuse to be satisfied with conventional responses and the glib rejoinder. They want to know, and as a result I have had to rethink many of the ideas I took from the standard, approved books years ago. Second, and more to the point, in designing courses, I have had the luxury of selecting a series of films on particular topics or from a certain era and going into them at some length, pointing out their relationships to one another and to their social contexts. Journalist-reviewers never have the freedom to select the contents of their columns with the intention of developing some idea at length. They are at the mercy of last week's releases.

During the last five years of teaching—here, finally, I get to the point—I became more aware of the importance of film history as a service not only to the work of criticism and to my students, but to the service of the church. This puts the last piece of the puzzle into place. As thoughtful essays about contemporary films offer an avenue of access into contemporary American culture, then the study of past productions and the critical literature that accompanies them can help to provide a sense of our national identity as it has developed in the twentieth century. In this, it can be compared to any other form of historical scholarship.

My presumption here is that American society remains in process. To understand where it is at present and how it may develop in the future, it is enormously important to understand where it has been in the past. Films offer a time capsule of popular culture that can be as revealing of a people as the most insightful essays by political and economic historians. The movies tell us what the people saw and enjoyed, how Hollywood responded to the tastes that several extremely ingenious producers perceived in their new-found country. They show us how America's sense of itself changed in response to war and depression, Vietnam and Watergate, religion, communism and the Reagan revolution.

The religious communities have, by the nature of their particular interests, too often been ruled by the tyranny of the immediate. Few people in the church or the secular realm pay much attention to reviewers in the religious press until some "controversial" film is released, and then the interest is inevitably in some moral question. Teachers and preachers interested in tailoring their message to the sensibilities of their people may try to keep up on the television, movies and music they are exposed to in their nonchurch world. These efforts can be a tyranny of the trendy.

Thus, at the risk of being dismissed as a hopeless antiquarian, I have selected five classic films of the pre-World War II era for my five "Lessons From Hollywood." This does not mean that I reject contemporary films, many of which may one day be regarded as classics in their own right. Some day scholars may write learned books on the *Star Wars*, the *Rocky* or the *Godfather* films as cultural phenomena, but the films and the times are still too close to us. They need time to settle. Likewise, someday critics may put George Lucas, Steven Spielberg, Martin Scorsese and Francis Ford Coppola next to Ford and Hawks in the pantheon of American directors, but these contemporary directors are still unfinished symphonies. Perhaps, like John Huston, they will save the best wine for last.

Each of the five films I chose may be subjected to further analysis and revaluation, but their position in the canon of classics is not likely to be challenged seriously in the near future. The five directors have all finished their life's work, and their positions will almost certainly be maintained for several years to come. By this time social historians have provided a fairly good picture of the impact of the Depression, the New Deal and the preludes to world war. Quite simply, critics and students within the universities as well as in the religious communities now have a solid body of materials to reflect upon.

By way of comparison, when my students complain about having a steady diet of "old movies" in my classes, I ask if they react the same way to reading old poems when they study Keats or Donne or Milton. Contemporary poets, now writing in the small but prestigious literary journals, may one day be considered the equals of the masters, but not yet. In studying literature, it is important to learn about the preoccupations of the greatest artists in their own eras, how they used the language and what they say about the timeless workings of the human heart as well as about the times they lived in. When students read the great poets of the past, and the generations of critical evaluation and revaluation that followed their works, then they might be able to understand what contemporary poets are saying about our concerns and our times.

What I am suggesting to the religious communities, then, is what the secular, academic world has known for the last thirty years. Film is a young art form, scarcely a century old, but it has already produced a significant collection of artifacts and a substantial amount of critical literature. It has an autonomy, like the natural sciences or literature, that must not and cannot be baptized and then coerced into ecclesial servitude. Yet like the older disciplines, it has a great deal to tell us about the world in which we scratch out our own salvation while trying to share the good news with anyone who will listen.

Almost all the film history and criticism I teach these days could slide easily into the curriculum of a state university, and no one would complain about proselytism or violation of the separation of church and state. Likewise, most of my reviews could appear in secular journals, and I have the hope that this present study will reach readers of little or no faith as well as my own co-religionists. It would be an unparalleled delight if it were ever used as a text in non-Catholic schools. I tried to make it stand on its own as a work of secular film scholarship, allowing myself personal indulgence as a priest only in the last few pages. As a priest, however, I am compelled to search for the relationship between my work and the service of the church. This book has been a mid-career attempt to spell out that relationship.

INDEX

French religious perspective of, 71–72; genres of, 6; German, 15–16; Hollywood, 13–14, 15, 59, 60; as a homilist, 97; Italian, 61–62; knowledge of work of, 101; in 1960s, 43–44; production, 81; theology and, 47–48; verbal attacks on, 19

Film: A Democratic Art (Jowett), 17

Film artist, 39–40, 41

Film audience, 40–41, 82

Film criticism (*See also* French film criticism; specific schools): analysis and, 3; classic methods of, 2; feminist, 86; film review and, 2–3, 4; ideology and, 4; knowledge of how film works and, 101; for non-specialists, 2; objectivity of, 4; religious communities and, 4–5, 16; Sarris' view of, 77–78; sex-and-violence issues and, 5; studios and, 5–6; study of, 2, 4–8; styles of, 85–86; versus film education, 287

Film Culture, 74–75, 77

Film education, 99, 281–282, 287

Film Form (Eisenstein), 37

Film history, 76

Film industry: alliance of, with Smith, 18–19; American culture and, 12–13; celebrities and, 56–57; closing of movie houses and, in 1908, 18; commercial, 17; commercialness of, 56; federal censorship and, 23; in Germany, 15–16; monitoring of, 17; religion as big seller in, 20; religious communities and, 16, 17, 33, 286; rise of, 17; self-censorship and, 18, 23; tainted image of, in 1920s, 21–23

Film noir, 219–222

Film review, 2–3, 4

Film scholarship, 1–2

Film society, 45, 46

Film study, 97, 98–99, 285

The Filmviewer's Handbook (McAnany and Williams), 45

Finkel, Abem, 207

First Amendment, 23

Fleming, 71

Fleming, Victor, 6

For the Love of Mike (1927), 104

Ford, John (*See also Stagecoach;* specific films): academy awards of, 163; alcoholic professionals in films of, 199; army, image of, 171–172; Cheyenne nation and, 186; cynicism of, 172–175; early years of, 163–165; film societies and, in 1960s, 46; heroic figures of, 166–167, 172–174; homecoming theme of, 167–169; human quest and, 169–170; marriage of, 165; name change of, 165–166; recognition of, 163; romantic concept of America's Westward expansion of, 67; Sarris on, 162; self-introduction of, 162–163; silent films of, 166; vision of universe of, 175; Western film and, 178; Western genre and, 163; Western hero of, 170; Western theme of, 170–171

Miracle and, 72; moral impact of, 43

Lenore (Burger), 253

"Leopards and History: The Problem of Film Genre" (McConnell), 85

LeRoy, Mervyn, 131

Let There Be Light (1945), 209–210

Lewis, Jerry, 75

The Lights of New York (1928), 131

Literacy, 99

Little Big Man (1970), 186

Little Caesar (1930), 131, 139

Locke, John, 253

Logan, Joshua, 42

The Long Voyage Home (1940), 167–168

Lourdes miracle, 95

The Love Doctor (1929), 243

Lugosi, Bela, 258, 259

Lynch, William F., S.J.: approach of, 36; *The Diary of Anne Frank* and, 37–38; editing and, 37; Eisenstein and, 36–37; fantasy and, 38–39; film artist and, 39–40; film audience and, 40–41; *Film Form* and, 37; freedom of imagination and, 34–35; Hitchcock and, 38–39; *The Image Industries* and, 34–36; influence of, 284; manipulation of imagination and, 37–38; Maritain and, 35–36; on morality, 35–36; primary interest of, 98

MacArthur, Douglas, 169

Magnani, Anna, 58

Malamud, Bernard, 100

The Maltese Falcon (1931), 207

The Maltese Falcon (1941) (*See also* Huston): Academy Awards for, 208; American dream and, 238; auteur of, 205–215; chance in, 236; commentary on, 231–238; criminals in, 210; difficulty in following, 231; end of, 237–238; failure in, 236; femme noir in, 234–235; genre of, 215–224; greed in, 235; guests in, 235–236; minor characters in, 232–233; other films of, 207–208; plot of, 224–230; police in, 231–232; rights to, 207; romance in, 233–234; selection of, for study, 6; sets in, 237; Spade's character in, 231, 233; visual style in, 236–237

The Man in the Iron Mask (1939), 250

The Man Who Shot Liberty Valance (1962), 173–174, 186

The Man Who Would Be King (1975), 210, 212, 213

Mangano, Silvana, 58

Maritain, Jacques, 35–36, 85

Marital conflict, 107

Martin, Steve, 224

Marvin, Lee, 130

Marx Brothers, 46

Mason, Jackie, 100

Mass migration, 179–180

Massey, Raymond, 248

Mast, Gerald, 20, 147–148

Maverick, 184

Mayo, Archie, 207

McAnany, Emile G., S.J., 45

McCarey, Leo, 42, 73